REASONS *for* FAITH

MAKING A CASE *for the* CHRISTIAN FAITH

Essays in Honor of Bob Passantino and Gretchen Passantino Coburn

NORMAN L. GEISLER & CHAD V. MEISTER
EDITORS

CROSSWAY BOOKS
WHEATON, ILLINOIS

Library of Congress Cataloging-in-Publication Data
Reasons for faith : making a case for the Christian faith : essays in honor
of Bob Passantino and Gretchen Passantino Coburn / edited by Norman
L. Geisler and Chad V. Meister.
   p. cm.
  ISBN 978-1-58134-787-6 (tpb)
  1. Apologetics. I. Passantino, Robert. II. Coburn, Gretchen Passantino.
III. Geisler, Norman L. IV. Meister, Chad V., 1965–   . VI. Title
BT1103.R43   2007
239—dc22   2007019226

BP		17	16	15	14	13	12	11	10	09	08	07
15	14	13	12	11	10	9	8	7	6	5	4	3	2	1

"Norman Geisler and Chad Meister have gathered together many of today's top apologists in *Reasons for Faith,* a fresh, new book that serves as an excellent resource for anyone seeking answers regarding matters of faith. Well-documented, yet accessible for the everyday reader, the authors have set a new standard for collaborative writing in the area of apologetics. I highly recommend it!"

> —JOHN ANKERBERG, host of the award-winning apologetics
> TV program *The John Ankerberg Show* and coauthor of the
> bestselling Facts On series

"Throughout my years of ministry Bob and Gretchen have been two of my greatest teachers as well as two of my most faithful friends. I know of no Christian apologists more worthy of honor and emulation. This Festschrift is an apt tribute to their legacy as it provides just the formidable, relevant, wide-ranging, and winsome defense of the faith necessary to equip any believer to participate effectively in today's marketplace of ideas."

> —HANK HANEGRAAFF, president, Christian Research Institute and
> host of *The Bible Answer Man* radio broadcast

"The church today faces a bewildering array of issues that challenge the truth or plausibility of Christian claims. *Reasons for Faith* provides an informative and helpful response to many of these issues. Even those who may not agree with every argument or conclusion will benefit from careful reading of this significant work in Christian apologetics."

> —HAROLD J. NETLAND, Professor of Philosophy of Religion and
> Intercultural Studies and the Naomi A. Fausch Chair of Missions,
> Trinity Evangelical Divinity School

"Chad Meister and Norm Geisler have delivered a *tour de force* for apologetics in their work *Reasons for Faith: Making a Case for the Christian Faith.* Here is a treasure trove of rich apologetical information addressing a myriad of relevant subjects. This collection will fortify the believer in the faith, but it will also serve as an effective evangelistic tool for nonbelievers who are struggling with questions about the Christian faith. For saints and seekers alike *Reasons for Faith* is a must read and an apologetics classic in the making."

> —R. PHILIP (PHIL) ROBERTS, president, Midwestern Baptist
> Theological Seminary

"*Reasons for Faith,* edited by Norm Geisler and Chad Meister, is a handbook for defending the biblical worldview that every pastor should have on his desk and every thoughtful layperson could study with benefit. This is a timely and timeless book."

> —CHUCK COLSON, founder, Prison Fellowship

Contents

PART THREE
DEFENDING CHRISTIAN THEISM

PART FOUR
WORLD RELIGIOUS MOVEMENTS

Editors and Contributors

Francis J. Beckwith is Associate Professor of Philosophy and Church-State Studies, Baylor University. A graduate of Fordham University (Ph.D., philosophy), he holds the Master of Juridical Studies degree from the Washington University School of Law, St. Louis. Among his over a dozen books is *Defending Life: A Moral and Legal Case Against Abortion Choice* (Cambridge University Press, 2007).

E. Calvin Beisner is Associate Professor of Historical Theology and Social Ethics at Knox Theological Seminary in Ft. Lauderdale, Florida, where he teaches apologetics. He is also national spokesman for the Cornwall Alliance for the Stewardship of Creation. He is the author of *Answers for Atheists, Agnostics, and Other Thoughtful Skeptics* and has written many other books and articles.

Sean Choi is a Ph.D. candidate in philosophy at the University of California, Santa Barbara, where his main research interest lies in metaphysics and philosophy of religion. He also holds graduate degrees from Talbot School of Theology and Westminster Theological Seminary. Sean currently resides in Goleta, California, with his wife Sunny and daughter Charlotte.

Winfried Corduan is Professor of Philosophy and Religion at Taylor University, Upland, Indiana. He is the author of several books, including *No Doubt About It* (B&H) and *Neighboring Faiths* and *Pocket Guide to World Religions* (both InterVarsity Press). He is former president of the Evangelical Philosophical Society and is currently editor of the International Society of Christian Apologetics.

Miguel Angel Endara is Profesor Residencial for the Seminario Sud Americano (SEMISUD) in Quito, Ecuador. He also works as an adjunct online philosophy instructor for Azusa Pacific University. He earned his Ph.D. in philosophy from St. Louis University.

Norman L. Geisler is author or coauthor of over sixty books and hundreds of articles. Dr. Geisler holds a B.A. and M.A. from Wheaton College, a Th.B. from William Tyndale College, and a Ph.D. from Loyola

University in Chicago. He has taught at the college and graduate level for over forty-eight years.

R. Douglas Geivett is Professor of Philosophy in the Talbot Department of Philosophy, Biola University, where he was also director of the M.A. program in philosophy for ten years. He is the author of *Evil and the Evidence for God* and coeditor of *Contemporary Perspectives on Religious Epistemology* and *Faith, Film, and Philosophy: Big Ideas on the Big Screen.*

Alan W. Gomes is Professor of Historical Theology at Talbot School of Theology in La Mirada, California. Gomes edited the fifteen-volume *Zondervan Guide to Cults and Religious Movements*, has written numerous articles for academic and popular journals, and has recently produced an updated edition of W.G.T. Shedd's *Dogmatic Theology.*

Douglas Groothuis is Professor of Philosophy at Denver Seminary and the author of ten books, including *Truth Decay* (InterVarsity), *On Jesus* (Wadsworth), and *On Pascal* (Wadsworth).

Gary Habermas is Distinguished Research Professor and Chair of the Department of Philosophy and Theology at Liberty University. Fifteen of his thirty books are on the subject of the resurrection of Jesus, including *The Risen Jesus and Future Hope* (Rowman and Littlefield) and, with Michael Licona, *The Case for the Resurrection of Jesus* (Kregel).

David J. Hesselgrave is Professor Emeritus of Mission at Trinity Evangelical Divinity School where he also served as Department Chair and director of the School of World Mission and Evangelism. He is also co-founder (with Donald A. McGavran) of the Evangelical Missiological Society. His many writings include *Paradigms in Conflict: 10 Key Questions in Christian Missions Today* (Kregel).

H. Wayne House is Distinguished Research Professor of Biblical and Theological Studies at Faith Evangelical Seminary, Tacoma, Washington. He is past president of the Evangelical Theological Society and has authored, coauthored, or edited over thirty books.

Richard G. Howe has a B.A. in Bible from Mississippi College, an M.A. in philosophy from the University of Mississippi, and a Ph.D. in philosophy from the University of Arkansas. He teaches philosophy at Luther Rice University in Lithonia, Georgia.

Scott Klusendorf is President of Life Training Institute, where he trains pro-life advocates to persuasively defend their views in the public square. A passionate and engaging platform speaker, he has appeared on nationally syndicated programs such as *Focus on the Family*, *The Bible Answer Man*, and *Faith Under Fire*. Nationally, he has participated in numerous debates at the collegiate and university levels.

Louis Markos is a Professor in English at Houston Baptist University. He is the author of *From Achilles to Christ: Why Christians Should Read the Pagan Classics* (InterVarsity Press), *Pressing Forward: Alfred, Lord Tennyson and the Victorian Age* (Sapientia), and *Lewis Agonistes: How C. S. Lewis Can Train Us to Wrestle with the Modern and Postmodern World* (B&H).

Josh McDowell is an internationally known speaker, author, and traveling representative of Campus Crusade for Christ. He has authored or coauthored more than sixty books, including *More Than a Carpenter* and *New Evidence That Demands a Verdict*. Josh and his wife Dottie have four children.

Chad V. Meister is Director of Philosophy at Bethel College (Indiana) and Vice President of the Evangelical Philosophical Society. He has written or edited a number of books including *Building Belief: Constructing Faith from the Ground Up* (Baker) and *The Routledge Companion to Philosophy of Religion*, coedited with Paul Copan.

Mark Mittelberg is a best-selling author, international speaker, and a leading strategist and consultant in evangelism and apologetics. He is the author of *Becoming a Contagious Church*, the primary author of the recently updated *Becoming a Contagious Christian* training course, and contributing editor of *The Journey: A Bible for the Spiritually Curious*.

John Warwick Montgomery is Professor Emeritus of Law and Humanities at the University of Bedfordshire (U.K.) and Distinguished Professor of Apologetics and the History of Christian Thought at Trinity College and Theological Seminary (U.S.A.). He is also a member of the Bar of the U.S. Supreme Court and author/editor of more than fifty books in Christian apologetics and human rights.

J. P. Moreland is Distinguished Professor of Philosophy at Biola University and director of Eidos Christian Center. He has published over sixty journal articles and has written or contributed to over thirty-five books, including *Kingdom Triangle* (Zondervan) and *Consciousness and the Existence of God* (forthcoming, Routledge, 2008).

Eric Pement was formerly Executive Editor of *Cornerstone* magazine, where he regularly wrote on new religious movements. He is a board member with Evangelical Ministries to New Religions (EMNR) and is a staff member with The Centers for Apologetics Research. Eric is currently completing an M.Div. degree at North Park Theological Seminary.

Ron Rhodes earned his Master's and Doctoral degrees from Dallas Theological Seminary. He has written over forty books, many dealing with apologetic issues. He is the founder and president of Reasoning from the Scriptures Ministries, an apologetics organization. He also teaches cult apologetics at Southern Evangelical Seminary.

Jon Trott has been a member of Jesus People USA (JPUSA) since 1977. He was writer, editor, and editor-in-chief of *Cornerstone* magazine, and he is coauthor of *Selling Satan*. Currently he teaches and writes in various venues. Jon is married to Carol and has four adult children.

Jim Valentine has been involved in counter-cult apologetics and evangelism since the 1970s. He worked closely with Bob and Gretchen Passantino during their CARIS period. He currently ministers through the CARIS office in Milwaukee, Wisconsin.

Kurt Van Gorden is a former Utah pastor who directs two apologetic missions, Jude 3 Missions and the Utah Gospel Mission (established in 1898). He is a contributor and editor for more than a dozen books on apologetics in addition to writing *Mormonism* for the Zondervan Series on Cults (1995).

Foreword

Lee Strobel

As an atheist, I thought it was the worst news I could possibly get: my wife announced that after a season of spiritual investigation, she had decided to become a follower of Jesus. My immediate thought was that divorce was inevitable.

Yet in the ensuing months, I became intrigued by the surprisingly positive changes I observed in Leslie's character and values. Her transformation was so winsome and attractive that when she finally invited me to go to church with her, I decided to comply—at least *once*. And that's where I heard the message of Jesus articulated in a way I could understand for the first time in my life.

Still, I didn't believe it. As a skeptical journalist who had been trained in law, I harbored too many objections. I needed evidence that the Bible is trustworthy, and not a book full of myths and contradictions as I believed at the time. I needed facts to back up the supposed resurrection of Jesus, which I thought was the biggest fable of all. I needed a faith that was internally coherent and consistent with reality. I wasn't a good candidate for emotionalism or wishful thinking. Opinions weren't good enough; I required solid substantiation. I clearly needed "reasons for faith" before I'd embrace any system of spiritual beliefs.

So I launched what turned out to be a nearly two-year investigation of the facts undergirding the Christian faith. I studied cosmology and physics for clues about a Creator. I used historical analysis to check out the New Testament's reliability and claims concerning the resurrection of Jesus. I looked into other world religions to see if they could withstand similar barrages of critical scrutiny. I pondered whether evil and suffering disproved the existence of a loving God.

These are the kinds of issues you'll find explored in this terrific new volume on Christian apologetics. In the pages that follow, some of the most accomplished and thoughtful experts of our day spell out why Christianity makes so much sense. They back up their conclusions with clarity and logic, writing persuasively and compellingly about the reason for the hope that they have (1 Pet. 3:15).

The writers have much in common. Many of them were influenced by Gretchen and the late Bob Passantino, largely unheralded apologists who have quietly encouraged so many contemporary defenders of the faith. Like the Passantinos, these contributors also share something else: an abiding commitment to pursuing truth, wherever it leads them.

My own investigation led me to an unexpected conclusion on November 8, 1981. Assessing the evidence with as much objectivity as I could muster, I came to believe that Jesus really is the unique Son of God who authenticated his identity by rising from the dead. Nobody else, I realized, could open the door of heaven for me.

I didn't feel a rush of emotion at that instant. Instead, I experienced something even more profound: the rush of reason.

I trust that your own intellect will be expanded by what you'll encounter as you delve deeply into this book. If you're a Christian, it's my hope that you'll finish the last page with an even deeper appreciation for the factual foundation of your faith—and that you'll be freshly equipped to define and defend Christianity as you interact with others.

And if you're an open-minded spiritual seeker . . . well, get ready for a fascinating intellectual and spiritual journey. Perhaps you will find yourself swept up, as I was, in the power of the evidence that points toward a grace-bestowing God. In fact, here's my prayer: that as you honestly consider the contents of this book, you too will experience the rush of reason.

Lee Strobel, author, *The Case for Christ*
and *The Case for the Real Jesus*.

Preface

OUR GOAL FOR THIS BOOK is twofold: first, we wish it to be an effective tool for bolstering the faith of Christians and building the faith of seekers; second, we desire that it honor Bob Passantino and Gretchen Passantino Coburn. They have truly lived out the qualities of a Christian apologist, and it is to them that we dedicate this work.

The Bible makes it clear that as Christians we are to "always be prepared to give an answer" for our faith (1 Pet. 3:15, NIV). Such an answer may take a variety of forms and styles, and it may involve a host of different issues. Nevertheless, the ability to give reasons for faith—solid, rational, and powerful reasons—should be part and parcel of the follower of Jesus Christ. In this book we have included leading Christian apologists, philosophers, and theologians and have covered some of the most important and pressing issues of our day related to giving answers for the Christian faith.

We begin in Part One by examining two questions: "What is apologetics and why do we need it?" These chapters explore the nature of apologetics, its role in contemporary culture, and what it should look like—both in theory and in practice.

Part Two explores cultural and theological issues relevant to defending the faith today. From a careful examination of the essentials of faith, to an analysis of postmodern thinking, to the role of historical theology in apologetics, seven chapters are devoted to these relevant and cutting-edge topics.

Part Three hones in specifically on the defense of Christian theism. Three chapters are dedicated to arguments for the existence of God, one focuses on the enduring problem of evil, another examines recent criticisms of the Bible and Jesus' deity, and the final chapter takes a fresh look at the resurrection of Jesus.

Part Four explores religious movements such as Mormonism, Jehovah's Witnesses, Oneness Pentecostals, witchcraft, and Satanism. The last chapter sketches the need for apologetics in world missions, in particular where

Hindu-type religious thought (such as Hinduism, Buddhism, and the New Age) is involved.

Finally, a Postscript is included that presents a clear and concise manifesto for Christian apologists. Through nineteen theses, it clarifies the role of apologetics and inspires and challenges Christians to reflect, pray, and act effectively and biblically in our culture.

Providing reasons and evidences for faith, however, is only one aspect of Christian apologetics. The *manner* in which these reasons are presented is just as important as their content, for the same passage that instructs us to be prepared to give reasons for our hope concludes by admonishing us to do this "with gentleness and respect." In other words, the gospel of Christ should always be presented and defended in a spirit of love. It is this model of apologetics that Bob and Gretchen continually exemplified, combined with their expansive knowledge and inexorable zeal, which set them apart as paragons of apologetics.

Before Bob's death in 2003, he and Gretchen ministered together for close to thirty years. Through their Answers in Action ministry, they equipped Christians to share and defend their faith and helped countless seekers find faith. They have been widely respected in a variety of fields, including evangelism, apologetics, philosophy, and theology. They have advanced the gospel of Jesus Christ through many means—personal discussions, public lectures, research, radio and television interviews, and a wide variety of publications. Amazingly, they have personally influenced an overwhelming number of the leading Christian apologists of our day, and Gretchen's ministry is still going strong (see the Answers in Action web site—www.answers.org—for more information).

This book is a labor of love and gratitude for the Passantinos, who have worked tirelessly to shine as beacons of light and hope to Christians and seekers of all persuasions. We are thankful to the contributors of this volume for their outstanding work and their passion for evangelism and apologetics. We also wish to thank Eric Pement for his editorial work on several of the chapters and Lanny Wilson for his editorial support throughout the development of this project.

Our hope is that this work advances the gospel of Jesus Christ and inspires more apologists like the Passantinos to carry his torch and influence the world for his kingdom.

Chad V. Meister
Norman L. Geisler

PART ONE

What Is Apologetics and Why Do We Need It?

CHAPTER ONE

An Apologetic for Apologetics

Mark Mittelberg

I'D *LIKE* TO BECOME A CHRISTIAN, but I still have a few questions that
are hanging me up," said John Swift, a fast-talking, hard-hitting commer-
cial banker who worked in downtown Chicago.

"Let's talk about whatever is holding you back," I replied to John,
whom I had just sat down to meet with for the first time at the request of
Ernie, a seeker small group leader from our church who had been dealing with John's list of spiritual doubts and objections for some time. "But
you know you don't need to have an answer to every question in order to
become a Christian."

"I realize that," John replied, "but if I'm reading you guys right, my
main question deals with something you all think is a pretty big deal."

"Well, maybe. What is it?" I responded.

Emphatically, John shot back, "I don't believe in the resurrection of
Christ!"

At this point I had to concede that, yes, that issue is a pretty big deal to
us in the church. "I'll admit, John, that when I went to seminary, the resurrection of Christ was under the heading labeled BIGGIES. That's because
the Bible clearly teaches that this is one of the truths that is essential for
someone to believe in order to become a true follower of Christ. But I'm
curious, why don't you believe that Jesus rose from the dead?"

"It just doesn't make sense to me that a dead person could come back
to life. Everything I've ever seen supports the fact that dead people just stay
in the grave, and their bodies rot there—or get eaten by wild dogs! Why
should I believe it was any different for Jesus?"

It was a great question. As a friend of mine likes to say, "The last time I
checked, the death rate was still hovering at right around 100 percent!" So why

should we put our faith in a claim that contradicts everything we've ever seen or experienced related to people dying and then staying in their graves?

What would you say to a friend who challenged you with this kind of a question? Many Christians would simply reply, "Well, you have to take it on faith!" Or "The Bible says it's true, and that settles it. You just have to take God at his word!" Or some would just walk away and assume that the person was destined for judgment, unable to see the truth that God has revealed to his true followers. So why even try?

But the Bible tells us we should do whatever it takes to be ready to give a clear and thoughtful response. First Peter 3:15 says, "Always be prepared to give an answer to everyone who asks you to give the reason for the hope that you have. But do this with gentleness and respect."[1] The original Greek word that is translated "answer" in that verse is *apologia,* which means "a speech of defense." It's from this that we get our term *apologetics,* which is a reasoned defense of our faith.

So here's the deal: *all* of us who are followers of Christ are told in this verse to be ready to give good answers to back up our faith. This is not just for professional pastors, theologians, or seminary professors. But let's be honest: none of us ever feels completely up to the task! That's why it's so important to read and study books like this one, which is designed to help us do what the verse commands: "be prepared . . ."

Please don't misunderstand. I don't think evidence or reason alone leads people into God's family. I agree with the age-old cliché that says, "You can't argue people into heaven." But I *do* believe, based on both Scripture and experience, that good arguments, logic, and evidence are used by God's Spirit to help clear the path of intellectual roadblocks so guys like John Swift and countless others can take the message seriously and eventually decide to follow the one who died to pay for our sins and rose to give us new life. As it's often stated, apologetics is the handmaiden to evangelism. It serves, when appropriately applied, the greater purposes of the gospel and of the Christian mission to "go into all the world and make disciples."

So you might wonder, what ended up happening in my conversation with John? Well, rather than initially presenting him with evidence and reasons for the resurrection of Christ, I decided to first ask him what he'd been doing to study this matter for himself.

"Mostly," he replied, "I've just read and listened to the scholars who are

---

[1]Unless otherwise indicated, all Bible quotations in this chapter are taken from the New International Version.

part of something called The Jesus Seminar—and those guys have all kinds of negative things to say about the idea of Jesus rising from the dead!"

"I'm very aware of that," I said with more of an impatient tone than I'd intended, "but have you read any of the great books that present the actual historical evidence for the resurrection—like the writings of Norman Geisler, Josh McDowell, or Gary Habermas?"

"Honestly, Mark, I don't know about any of those books, and I've never heard anything that sounded like real evidence for Jesus' resurrection. Maybe you can fill me in a bit?"

"I'd love to," I replied as we began an hour-plus discussion about some of the key points of evidence. The more we talked, the more encouraged I was by John's receptivity, while being amazed and frustrated that such vitally important information—which has been around for some two thousand years—was so completely unknown to this inquisitive spiritual seeker.

The minutes flew by as we talked, and soon we were just about out of time. "Before you go," I said to John, "I'd like to loan you a book I recently picked up that I think will help deepen your understanding of the overwhelming amount of evidence that supports the resurrection of Christ." As I handed him my brand-new copy of *Jesus Under Fire*, edited by apologists Michael Wilkins and J. P. Moreland, I added, "I'm sure the whole book would be helpful to you, but I'd especially like to encourage you to read through the chapter titled 'Did Jesus Rise from the Dead?' by William Lane Craig—I think it will be particularly helpful to you."

Then I said one more thing that surprised even me. "John, I know you're a businessman who relates to goals and challenges. So let me urge you to read that chapter right away and to look further at some of the books I've been telling you about so you can see that the historical evidence strongly supports the resurrection of Jesus. Then, assuming you find this to be true, I want to challenge you to become a Christian before Easter, which is only a month away. That way you can finally celebrate the holiday for its real meaning!"

The look of intensity in John's eyes told me he was taking my words seriously. It wasn't more than a couple weeks later that he sent my book back with a note informing me that he'd already combed through the chapter by Bill Craig several times, then read the entire book, and had already purchased copies for himself and a few friends with similar questions! And it was only about two weeks after that, while I was on a speaking trip to Australia, that I phoned in one night to get my voice mails and heard a message from Ernie, John's seeker small group leader, telling me with great excitement that John had trusted in Christ just a few days before Easter!

When I got back home I called John to congratulate and encourage him—and only a few months later I had the privilege of baptizing him in the pond by our church. What a joy that was, and what a thrill it has been to see him grow in his faith ever since that time, even to this day!

So why is it so important that you and I be able to give an *apologia*—an answer or reason for our faith? Let's discuss two simple responses to that question: the love of people and the love of God.

THE LOVE OF PEOPLE

The story of John Swift is just one of many I could tell to illustrate the importance and potential impact of our being ready to engage in effective apologetics. Countless other people have been helped in similar ways, including my close friend and ministry partner, Lee Strobel, who himself had been an atheist who needed to see evidence that Christianity made sense and was based on facts before he was ready to put his trust in Christ. Today he's helping many others discover what he learned—that truth really is on the side of our faith.

Lee tells the story of another skeptic, a Harvard-educated lawyer from the Los Angeles area who had resisted Jesus and his teachings for his entire life. The man's brother was a Christian who prayed for him daily and did his best to reach out to him with the gospel for more than forty-eight years. His brother tried everything he could think of, including finally giving him a copy of Strobel's classic book *The Case for Christ*. He ignored the book for some time, until he was diagnosed with cancer and realized he didn't have long to live. He read it on his deathbed and, having finally seen and understood the evidence that backs up the faith, prayed and received the forgiveness and leadership of Christ.

Another example came one time when Lee and I did an outreach event like we've done together in ministry for years—a free-for-all Q & A in which we invite Christians to bring all of their friends who have questions, doubts, and objections about our faith. We usually promote these events as Firing Lines, and we're the ones under fire!

The format is simple: after a brief introduction from one of us, we open up the house microphones for anyone who would like to throw a spiritual question or challenge at us, no holds barred. We've found that if we do this while treating them with respect—including those we don't agree with—they tend to respect us as well, and we have some great interactions!

That particular evening we were almost ready to end the meeting when

I decided to take one more question. A man near the front of the room spoke up and said he'd heard that early Christian teachings were actually based on ancient pagan mystery religions and wondered what we thought. I sensed that the man was asking this question not just out of mild curiosity but with a deep concern to know what was true.

Now, the story behind the story was that I knew that in the days prior to this Lee had felt compelled to do some extra study on that very question, just in case it might come up—and here it was, the last one of the evening! So, trying to sound casual, I turned and said, "Lee, would you like to take a shot at that one?" Well, Lee, loaded for bear, pulled both triggers of the intellectual shotgun and gave an answer that was so clear, so powerful, and so thorough that there was not a shred of confusion or ambiguity left when he was finished. Christianity, he made abundantly clear, did *not* borrow from any mystery religions, though sometimes the reverse may have been true!

We found out later that this was the last question holding this man up in his spiritual journey and that afterward he prayed to give his life to Christ!

Another time I met with a man who had been visiting our church and had a lot of spiritual questions. After responding to his issues and objections for a couple of hours he finally leaned back in his chair, looked me in the eye, and said, "I guess you've answered all of my questions . . . so *now* what do I do?" I said, "Well, you talk to God, acknowledge that you now know these things are true, and ask him to forgive your sins and to begin to lead your life. Are you ready to do that?" He was, so we prayed together right then and there, and today he's a brother in Christ.

I tell these multiple stories to encourage and inspire us to remember that apologetics—the study of reasons for our faith—is not for the mere accumulation of knowledge. It's to give us the information we need to lovingly serve and help people for whom Jesus died and whom he sent us to reach.

The most famous verse in the Bible, John 3:16, says, "For God so loved the world that he gave his one and only Son . . ." So we should be ready to explain who that Son of God is and be able to articulate and defend the truth of his unique claims, mission, and work on our behalf, so that the much-loved people of this world will be able to "believe in him [and] not perish but have eternal life." This is, again, what the apostle Peter admonished us to do when he said to "always be prepared to give an answer to everyone who asks," and it's what the apostle Paul echoed when he challenged us in Colossians 4:5 to "Be wise in the way you act toward outsiders; make the most of every opportunity."

So the Bible says over and over that the motivation for and the focus of our apologetic efforts should be *people*—men, women, and children who matter deeply to the Father.

Let me pass on some helpful advice I received years ago from two of my spiritual mentors (to whom this book is dedicated), the late Bob Passantino and his wife, Gretchen. It was this: if you want to become a well-rounded and effective Christian apologist, then don't just read books and spend all of your time hanging out with like-minded believers. Get out there and actually *talk with real human beings* who have questions and objections. Try out the truths you've been learning in dialogue with them. Put your answers into play with some folks who will actually benefit from them!

Bob and Gretchen modeled this value together for decades, and I'll never forget the stories we heard at Bob's funeral from people who told of how he had been willing to interact with them for hours on end—sometimes even talking all night long—as he listened to their questions and gently but persistently challenged them with the claims of the Christian faith. As a result, many of them had entrusted their lives and eternities to Christ based on what they had learned and were therefore able to stand and speak that day as members of God's family.

When I was in graduate school I knew two fellow philosophy of religion students who loved God but who debated me and others constantly about whether apologetic arguments really do any good for nonbelievers. They said that because non-Christians start with non-Christian presuppositions, they could never rationally "get to God from non-God." I could never understand why guys who really believed that would spend so much time studying apologetics anyway, but I spent hours talking to them in the effort to try to understand their point of view—and them!

Finally, in exasperation, I asked these friends individually to tell me candidly whether their theories about what those outside of the Christian faith could and could not understand were based on their books and study alone or on actual conversations with people who really didn't seem able to access the information they were trying to communicate to them. Both of these guys, at separate times and locations, hung their heads and acknowledged what I'd suspected—that, no, they had never really talked to any non-Christians to try out their answers on them. They'd been so convinced by certain professors and books that it wouldn't do any good, they hadn't even tried! As I heard this I couldn't help thinking about how many people they could have helped but didn't—people like John Swift and Lee Strobel.

A couple years later, after one of these friends had gone into a program to get his doctorate in philosophy, I had the chance to get together with him to catch up a bit. When I asked him how his classes at the university were going, he said his studies were progressing pretty well. But then he somewhat sheepishly admitted that when his faith was challenged by his atheistic professors, "it seems to make a lot of sense to actually give them reasons and answers for what we believe."

Somehow being around people with genuine spiritual doubts and confusion helps us regain our bearings and reminds us of our mission: to bring the truths of the gospel to bear so that real people—people in our families and in our neighborhoods, people we know at work or at school, people who are like us as well as those who are very different from us, people on the other side of the town, the county, the country, and the world—will believe and receive Christ.

Before I move past the topic of what apologetics does for people, let me encourage you with a few thoughts on what studying and telling others about the evidence and logic behind our faith does for *us* as believers:

• It helps us grow in understanding our own beliefs as we learn about the evidence, the Bible, and other belief systems in the effort to help our friends move toward Christ.

• It give us clarity on what we believe, much as a final test in school helps us pull together all that we've learned—or should have learned—during the semester.

• It gives us confidence concerning why we believe what we believe as our faith stands up to scrutiny and challenges.

• It gives us spiritual stability, preventing us from being "tossed back and forth by the waves, and blown here and there by every wind of teaching . . ." (Eph. 4:14).

• It matures us in our faith and helps shape us for leadership in the church as ones who can "encourage others by sound doctrine and refute those who oppose it" (Titus 1:9).

• It expands our capacity to "love . . . God . . . with all [our] mind . . ." (Matt. 22:37).

So you see that apologetics is good for people in general—both for the recipients of the information as well as for us, the ones who study the evidence and share what we learn.

THE LOVE OF GOD

While it's clear that giving reasons for our faith serves and blesses people, it's also true that it serves and honors God. Think about this passage from Psalm 19:1:

The heavens declare the glory of God;
the skies proclaim the work of his hands.

If God went to all of the effort of creating a universe spectacular enough that it would declare his glory and then went through the process of revealing this fact to David and then saw to it that David wrote it down accurately and finally made sure that the biblical record was preserved for thousands of years so we would still have his message today, then don't you think we should at least *declare* that "the heavens declare the glory of God" to everyone who will listen? If so, then you're dangerously close to utilizing a couple of theistic and scientific arguments as apologetic tools for evangelism! Congratulations! We honor God by declaring what he declares and letting his truth impact people as it will.

If God is the God of truth, as we know he is, then we honor him whenever we defend his truth, not just to the already convinced, but also to people in "all nations," as Jesus said it in Matthew 28. And Jesus modeled this for us in many ways. He pointed to fulfilled prophecies as evidence for his divine identity; he did miracles in full view of his followers and detractors alike, later holding out those miracles as evidence to help people believe his claims; and he ultimately pointed to his greatest miracle, his own resurrection, as the supreme proof that he was indeed the Son of God. Surely we, likewise, honor him and the Father by pointing people to his fulfillment of the prophecies, his divine miracles, and his resurrection from the dead as we seek to move them toward him as their forgiver and leader!

The apostle Paul also honored God by living this value out in a powerful way. He tells us in 2 Corinthians 10:4–5: "The weapons we fight with are not the weapons of the world. On the contrary, they have divine power to demolish strongholds. We demolish arguments and every pretension that sets itself up against the knowledge of God, and we take captive every thought to make it obedient to Christ." Bold and powerful words from a first-rate, first-century, master apologist!

Further, Paul said in Philippians 1:7 that he was active in "defending and confirming the gospel." He didn't just proclaim the message—he also presented reasons why people should believe it. And it was Paul who told Titus that leaders in the church should be able, as the norm, to "refute those who oppose" the message (Titus 1:9). He also said in 2 Corinthians 5:11 that he was trying to persuade people to follow Christ because, as he says a few verses later, "Christ's love compels us." And he was described in Acts 28:23 as spending the last days of his life in Rome working from morning until evening as he "tried to convince them about Jesus from the Law of Moses and from the Prophets." And the very next verse reports that "some were convinced by what he said."

Throughout church history, starting with the apostles, then the early church fathers, and all the way through the centuries to today, courageous believers have been willing to take risks for the sake of the gospel as they not only declared the Christian message but also defined and defended it. Ignatius, for example, was a bishop of the church in Antioch around the turn of the first century. He was persecuted for his faith and ended up being martyred for Christ. But on the way to his execution he wrote letters that emphasized that Jesus "really and truly" was crucified for our sins, that he rose again on the third day, and that this proved conclusively that he was the Son of God as he claimed. This was not just the stuff of catechism or Sunday school classes for those who already believed; it was true truth that was available for everyone who was willing to listen. Ignatius didn't care whether it was the "pre-Christian" or the "post-Christian" era, or whether he was living in premodern, modern, or postmodern times—he simply knew that what he believed was true and that everyone needed to hear it because it represented *reality*.

We must have the same bold and tenacious attitude. Yes, the latter part of 1 Peter 3:15 tells us we must communicate with "gentleness and respect," and that's important. But it doesn't detract from the urgency we need as we do our best to proclaim the truth of Christ clearly and compellingly to a lost and dying generation.

Jesus said that the greatest commandment is to "'Love the Lord your God with all your heart and with all your soul and with all your mind.' . . . And the second is like it: 'Love your neighbor as yourself'" (Matt. 22:37–39). There are, I'm sure, many ways we can express this. But let me urge you to show your love to God and to the people he created and whom he "wants . . . to be saved and to come to a knowledge of the truth" (1 Tim. 2:4) by presenting them with the message of our Christian faith and then by being ready to compellingly and winsomely give them reasons to believe.

People like Don Hart will thank you. Like John Swift, he came to me with questions. He had attended an event at our church where a Jewish businessman described his investigation of the evidence that Jesus is the Messiah. That businessman not only ended up becoming a believer but also a Christian author and pastor, and now Don was confused. Could these messianic prophecies really point toward Jesus of Nazareth? Could he himself, a Jewish man, really become a follower of Jesus too?

I began to meet with Don to talk about his questions and concerns, and we had some great conversations over the months that followed. Along the way he challenged pretty much everything and hit me with some tough objections to the faith. But he also listened intently and did his homework when I asked him to read something for further study. And over time I saw him begin to open up, ever so slowly, until one day he was finally ready. Then, with great joy and anticipation, he prayed to receive Jesus as his Messiah and Savior.

Since that day Don has been living an adventure. Though already in his fifties at the time, he enrolled in a Master's program at Trinity Evangelical Divinity School, where he grew rapidly in his knowledge of theology and the Bible. A couple years later he graduated, and today he works as a biblical counselor at a counseling center where he encourages people every day in their spiritual development. And just today I called Don, whom I had not spoken to for years. After catching up a bit I asked him a simple question: "How important would you say apologetics is in our world today?"

"Absolutely critical" were the first words that shot out of Don's mouth. Then, apparently wanting to make sure I really got it, he said it again before going on in rapid-fire, staccato speech: "Absolutely critical! I mean, if you don't have a means of being able to answer questions—like the Ethiopian eunuch who said to Philip, 'How will I understand without someone teaching me?' . . . How would I support my beliefs? How would I know with conviction that something is true? And how would I help someone decide—"

And Don went on faster than I could write! I'd uncorked a veritable volcano! Here he was, a man who had been reached through an apologetics outreach event I had hosted, helped by apologetic answers I had given him, and taught through apologetics books I had loaned to him, and now he was getting all carried away on the phone giving *me* a passion-filled apologetic for apologetics! *I loved it!* And I hope you are encouraged by it too.

It's people like Don Hart who motivate me. And John Swift and Lee Strobel and many others. How about you? God wants to use *you* to reach people in your circles who are spiritually confused like those guys were. So take it seriously and get ready. Read on through the following chapters, written by some of the greatest apologists of our time, and let God fan the flames of your desire to help your friends find and follow Christ.

CHAPTER TWO

A Relevant Apologetic

Josh McDowell

SCHOOL SHOOTINGS. TERRORIST ATTACKS. Dangerous "designer" drugs. Teen suicide pacts. Sometimes it seems there's no end to the reasons to fear for our kids' safety and well-being.

But there are other fears, additional daily worries, and more imminent reasons for most of us to be frightened. If you're like me, what strikes fear into your heart is the daily possibility that your kids will fall prey to the wrong crowd, succumb to cultural pressures, and make wrong choices that will bring pain and suffering to their lives. That fear is real. And it never quite goes away.

In today's world, our kids quite possibly encounter more ethical and moral temptations, greater spiritual battles, and more emotional and relational struggles than any other generation in history. And our young people's exposure to sexual temptations, school violence, alcohol, illegal drugs, and a variety of other dangerous influences threatens to undo all we may try to teach them. Yet while we need to fear what our kids could be tempted to *do*, we need to be more concerned with what our kids are led to *believe*.

You see, the way our kids behave comes *from* something. Their attitudes and actions spring from their value system, and their value system is based on what they believe. My friend and Christian educator Glen Schultz puts it this way: "At the foundation of a person's life, we find his beliefs. These beliefs shape his values, and his values drive his actions."[1]

In his book *Kingdom Education,* Glen uses the diagram on the next page to illustrate this:

---

[1]Glen Schultz, *Kingdom Education* (Nashville: LifeWay Press, 1998), 39.

The Making of an Individual[2]

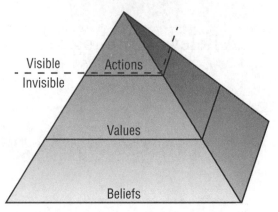

As you can see from the illustration, a young person's actions are just the tip of the iceberg, so to speak. Thus, if you're concerned that your young people might make wrong choices that will bring them pain, it's shortsighted to simply try to mold or control what they *do*. It is obviously better to instill right values within them, values that are based on solid biblical beliefs. Unless their actions are built on a solid foundation of biblical beliefs, you can expect their lives to reflect the pain and consequences of wrong choices.

WHAT DO THEY BELIEVE?

If your young people would say that religious beliefs are important to them and that the Bible is accurate, they are typical of today's churched youth. Eighty percent[3] of kids involved in evangelical churches agree that religious beliefs are important to them, and 61 percent[4] say the Bible is accurate. That's the good news. After all, this generation seems far more open and vocal about their faith—even to the point of wearing their Christian witness on T-shirts and worshiping with passion—than past generations. Research conducted by the Barna Research Group indicates that among Christian kids in evangelical churches, the vast majority (80 percent) believe that God created the universe and that God is personally involved in people's lives (84 percent).

That's as far as most of us see. Most parents, pastors, youth leaders, and Christian educators recognize a fervor and faith in our kids that largely encourages us. Sure, they have their problems. But they're okay. They

---

[2]Ibid., 40.
[3]Barna Research Group, "Third Millennium Teens" (Ventura, CA: The Barna Research Group, 1999), 47.
[4]Ibid., 52.

believe in God. They're following Jesus Christ. They hold pretty much the same beliefs their parents cherish. Right?

Not so fast. Dig a little deeper, and you'll probably discover that their views about God probably don't differ much from those reported by Rob Rienow, a youth minister at Wheaton Bible Church:

> Their answers were as individual as the kids themselves. One thought God was like his grandfather: "He's there, but I never see him." Another took a harder view, describing "an evil being who wants to punish me all the time." Two more opinions followed. Finally, the last teen weighed in: "I think you're *all* right, because that's what you really believe." In other words, as Rienow relates it, God is whatever works for you. On this, all of the youth agreed.[5]

"As individual as the kids themselves." That's the general story line. Thus, though most of our teens today say they believe in the God of the Bible, most also believe that Muslims, Buddhists, Christians, Jews, and all other people pray to the same god, even though they use different names for their god.[6]

Do all religions pray to the same god? An alarming 63 percent[7] of our kids think so, and 70 percent[8] of them say there is no absolute moral truth! So how do they determine what's right or wrong? Seventy-two percent[9] say they can tell when something is right by whether or not it "works" in their lives.

And do our kids believe Jesus rose from the grave? Do they think the devil and the Holy Spirit are real? Fifty-one percent of our kids don't believe in the resurrection of Christ, 65 percent don't think the devil is real, and 68 percent don't believe the Holy Spirit is a living entity.[10]

Though 87 percent of our kids believe Jesus was a real person who came to earth, and 78 percent believe he was born to a virgin, nearly half (46 percent) believe he committed sins, and over half (51 percent) say he died but did not rise from the dead.[11]

WHY BELIEFS MATTER

But so what? Does it really make a difference what our kids believe? We may prefer for them to have biblical beliefs, but what harm will come if

---

[5]John Leland, "Searching for a Holy Spirit," *Newsweek*, May 8, 2000, 61.
[6]Barna Research Group, "Third Millennium Teens," 48.
[7]Ibid.
[8]Ibid., 44.
[9]Ibid.
[10]Ibid., 51.
[11]Ibid., 48.

they don't? Will it really change the way our kids think and act in the real world? Actually, yes. And to an astounding degree.

Research consistently shows that what a person believes translates into behavior. A major survey of over 3,700 kids (all of whom were involved in an evangelical church) reveals that, compared to kids who possess a solid, biblical belief system, young people who lack such basic biblical beliefs are:

- 225 percent more likely to be angry with life;
- 216 percent more likely to be resentful;
- 210 percent more likely to lack purpose in life; and
- 200 percent more likely to be disappointed in life.[12]

These are just some of the findings that reflect what we said earlier: beliefs create values, and those values result in certain attitudes. But, of course, as the pyramid illustration showed, beliefs shape values, and values drive actions. In other words, the things our kids believe will result in specific behaviors.

That's why research has shown that kids—otherwise good kids from good families—who don't possess a biblical belief system are:

- 36 percent more likely to lie to a friend;
- 48 percent more likely to cheat on an exam;
- 200 percent more likely to steal;
- 200 percent more likely to physically hurt someone;
- 300 percent more likely to use illegal drugs; and
- 600 percent more likely to attempt suicide.[13]

While this may be disturbing, it should not surprise us. Beliefs matter because they form the values that determine our actions. But what may surprise you is the route we will need to take in order to correct the distorted beliefs our kids have about God and the truth of his Word.

BELIEVING ISN'T ENOUGH

Now, you may be among the few who could say, "But, Josh, I'm teaching my kids right. We have family devotions. I take them to a solid church, and I even send them to a great Christian school. Certainly my kids believe the right things. They'll be able to stand strong against temptation and evil influences—right?"

Now, my answer to that will sound like I'm contradicting myself.

---

[12]Ibid., 65.
[13]Ibid., 43.

Because I'm going to tell you that simply teaching your kids to believe in the right things isn't going to be enough to enable them to stand strong and make right choices in today's culture.

I know that sounds contradictory. I've been saying that beliefs matter and that if our kids don't have solid biblical beliefs they are 200 to 600 percent more likely to exhibit dangerous or destructive behaviors. So why isn't the solution simply teaching our kids the *right* things to believe? How can I say that believing the right things won't be enough to hold our kids steady when life's trials and tests come their way?

I can say that because your concept of what it means to believe in something is probably different—radically different—from that of your kids. Influenced by the rise of postmodernism, many kids today find it hard to swallow concepts such as the inerrancy of the Bible, and they're not at all convinced that the Jesus of the Bible is the way, the truth, and the life for "all the children of the world." Nearly half (48 percent) believe that it doesn't matter what religious faith you associate with "because they all believe the same principles and truth"; and 58 percent believe that all religious faiths teach equally valid truth.[14] And the vast majority (65 percent) either believe or suspect that there is "no way to tell which religion is true."[15]

It is not that our kids are rejecting Christianity as they know it—they have simply been influenced to redefine it according to their cultural setting. They are putting together their own religious canon in a smorgasbord style. They are led to believe it is better to pick and choose from various ideas and concepts of God and religion around them until they construct a tailor-made "faith," one that's just right for them. They are being encouraged to piece their faith together themselves; that way it will be theirs personally, and it will offend no one.

As *Newsweek* magazine reporter John Leland discovered, "Even more than their baby-boomer parents, teenagers often pick and choose what works for them. . . . As they sample from various faiths, students have become more accepting of each other's beliefs, even when those beliefs are stringent. Clayton, a high-school junior, says he is known among his classmates as 'the religious guy,' but this does not make him the odd man out. Clayton, 17, an evangelical Christian, is one of a growing minority of teenagers who are vowing to defer sex until marriage. 'There really is an

---

[14]Ibid., 51.
[15]Josh McDowell and Bob Hostetler, *Right from Wrong* (Nashville: Word, 1994), 263.

atmosphere of whatever you think is OK,' he says. 'Just don't tell me what to think. I'll figure it out myself.'"[16]

Clayton's stand for abstinence is encouraging. But his comments are less than reassuring, because they reflect the culture's encouragement to our youth to "figure it out" themselves. And what most are "figuring out" is a little truth here and a little error there—until they end up with erroneous beliefs.

Thus we have an entire generation of young people today who believe that truth is not true for them *until they choose to believe it*. They believe that *the act of believing makes things true*. And then, once they believe, those things will be true for them *only until they choose to believe something else*. As soon as something more "appealing" comes along, they are likely to begin believing *that*, whether it's biblical or not.

Some time ago I was speaking at a denominational youth conference. These kids were not just any kids. The denomination had assembled their top young people at this conference. They were the cream of the crop—solid Christian kids. Because I was planning to talk the next day about the truth of the Bible, I went from one young person to another in the course of my address and asked, "Why do you believe the Bible to be true?" The kids didn't have an answer.

The next day, before the morning session, a young man came running up to me and shouted, "I know the answer!"

He caught me off-guard. I wasn't sure what he was referring to, so I asked, "The answer to what?"

"To your question about why I believe the Bible is true."

"Okay," I said, "let's hear it."

"Because I believe," he answered with assurance. "Because I have faith."

"You're saying it's true because you believe it?" I asked.

"Yes!" He couldn't have sounded more convinced.

I looked around at the kids who had gathered to listen. Many of them were smiling and nodding their heads in agreement, as though this young man had solved a great riddle, and now it all seemed so obvious.

I then asked him, "Does this mean that the Bible would also be true for your neighbor or the kid down the street?"

"It would be if he believed it," the boy responded.

I gazed at him for a few seconds. His answers saddened me deeply, but

---

I knew he was all too typical of our kids today. Finally I said, "You know the basic difference between you and me?"

"What?" he asked, still smiling.

"To you," I said, "the Bible is true because you believe it. I believe it because it is true."

THE NEED FOR CONVICTIONS

Alarming as it may be, the fact is, the majority of our young people today—even the brightest and best of them—are in agreement with that young man. They believe that *the act of believing makes things true*. They have accepted a way of thinking that I call "subjective believism," a philosophy that states, "if you believe something is true for you, then believing makes it so." Thus, getting our kids to believe the right things isn't enough—because believing is a thoroughly subjective exercise to them.

To *believe* in something is to "accept it as true, genuine, or real."[17] But as we've pointed out, our kids are conditioned by today's culture to believe that nothing is objectively true, universally genuine, or actually real in an absolute sense. They think that something is true, genuine, or real only when *they accept it*, subjectively, for themselves.

That is why, if we are going to help our kids stand strong in the face of today's culture, we must help them develop beliefs that are not only correct but that are also so deeply rooted that no tempest can shake them, no storm can uproot them. They need more than personal opinions or lightly held suspicions. If our kids are going to withstand all the pressures and temptations in today's dangerous world, we have to help them move beyond "subjective believism" to firm convictions. They need to be so thoroughly convinced of what they believe that they will take a stand for it regardless of the consequences.

JUST THE FACTS?

But it's not enough to simply have convictions. The actions of terrorists and suicide bombers demonstrate that it's possible to have deep, abiding convictions . . . and still be tragically wrong.

That is why evidence is crucial to Christian convictions. Christianity is a uniquely verifiable faith because it is based on historical facts that are clearly recognizable by and accessible to everyone. To move our kids beyond belief to conviction, therefore, we must guide them through an

---

[17]*Merriam-Webster's Collegiate Dictionary*, tenth edition, s.v. "believe."

examination of the evidences for what they believe. Only then will they be equipped with true convictions that what they believe is objectively true. But even that's not enough.

Deep convictions are built not only on what the mind believes; they are formed also around what the heart has experienced. Christian faith is intended to be a personal experience; it should have a profound and *relational* meaning to each of our lives.

Most of our young people, however, don't understand what their faith actually means to their everyday lives. Yes, they may have been told that faith in Christ results in eternal life and involves a call to right living. But the vast majority sees little correlation between the things they believe (about God, truth, or the Bible) and their relationships with friends and family or their future in life. But that offers us a golden opportunity.

In the environment our kids today inhabit (and identify with), we must rethink and retool how we do apologetics. In the modern era, it was effective to persuade people with the preponderance of evidence. That mode of persuasion may still be effective for some, particularly those who retain a modernist mind-set. But for the vast majority of this generation, a new approach to apologetics is needed. We must develop and refine a more relational apologetic.

EVIDENCE AND EXPERIENCE

Our kids today need far more than a strictly modernist approach, which appeals to the intellect. They need far more than the postmodern viewpoint, which rejects truth and exalts personal experience.[18] They need to be helped to see how the truth—revealed in Jesus Christ himself and in the pages of the Bible—brings relational meaning to their lives that can be found nowhere else.

Therefore, our task is to present the Christian faith to our young people in ways that demonstrate that believing is an intelligent exercise of knowing what is objectively true and experiencing it relationally. When we do that, our kids will begin to develop the kind of deep convictions that will make them strong, even in the face of today's challenges.

It has always been the case that the deepest convictions are a result of not only convincing the mind, but also touching the heart. That's one reason Christianity has won the hearts and minds of so many through the last two millennia: it is intellectually credible *and* relationally compelling. Not only

---

[18]For more on the postmodern view of truth, see chapter 7 by J. P. Moreland in this book entitled "Postmodernism and Truth."

is the gospel *true*—it is also *meaningful* to our lives. Every truth Scripture teaches contains one common thread—an intimate, real relationship with God. And the true Word of God also happens to answer the fundamental questions of life: Who am I? Why am I here? Where am I going?

WHO AM I?

The Incarnation is an important doctrine of the Christian church. It is objectively true, regardless of whether we believe it. But it is far more than something we should agree with intellectually. It is also something we must know emotionally and experientially. The fact that God became human, dwelt among us, and then died for us is the means God has used to reconnect us with his loving heart and restore our broken relationship with him.

And that relationship, in turn, results in something else. It solves one of our kids' deepest dilemmas. It answers one of the most pressing questions of life: Who am I?

To a large extent we understand ourselves—our identity—in terms of our relationships. We perceive ourselves—and others around us—as this person's son or daughter, that person's husband or wife, and someone else's mother or father. We also distinguish ourselves as "the Rileys' neighbor," "Josie's friend," or "Richard's pastor."

Our relationships provide insight to our identity. But earthly relationships are limited. They cannot completely or exhaustively answer the question, Who am I? Each of us longs for a better answer to that question than "Carol's friend" or "John's son."

That is why it's so important, so crucial, for our children, students, youth group members, and church members to understand what the Incarnation means to their lives. The Incarnation sheds light on our true identity. Now that "God has sent the Spirit of his Son into our hearts," we can call God "Father" (Gal. 4:6, ESV). As the apostle John said, "See what kind of love the Father has given to us, that we should be called children of God; and so we are" (1 John 3:1, ESV). Jesus, through the Holy Spirit, "bears witness with our spirit that we are children of God" (Rom. 8:16, ESV).

Because Jesus Christ entered our world to redeem us and make us God's children, we are connected and bonded to God's family. The means God used to reconnect with you is the means by which he defines your identity. Because of the Incarnation, you, your children, students, youth group

members, or church members are now in God's family. You can realize your
true identity as a son or daughter of your Father God who relationally:

- accepts you unconditionally,
- loves you sacrificially,
- understands you intimately,
- relates to you continuously.

And that is all possible because "God so loved the world, that he gave
his only Son" (John 3:16, ESV) to be born supernaturally into the human
family to relationally connect us to God's family. Thanks to the Incarnation,
we can know who we are because we have experienced the connection of
knowing God personally. And that is precisely what a disconnected generation needs. We are no longer adrift and alone; we become rooted and
secure in a new relationship, for we now belong to God. We can say with
confidence," I know who I am: I'm a child of the King of the Universe!"
And while that identifies who you and I—and our children—are in this
world, that identity goes even deeper.

WHY AM I HERE?

I have spent decades defending the reliability of the Bible. It is God's truth.
It is the inspired Word of God. It is a road map to heaven. It is God's
instruction manual for living. But a relational apologetic must help our
youth by going further than all these things. We must not only help them
understand the Bible's truth and its message of salvation; we must also help
our youth experience the relational significance of God's Word.

The Bible is God's revelation of himself to us. It reveals a personal God,
the God who would "speak to Moses face to face, as a man speaks to his
friend" (Ex. 33:11, ESV). It is the revelation of a God who is passionate
about his relationship with us (cf. Ex. 34:14). And it is a revelation that,
from the first words Moses penned in the book of Genesis to the last word
John wrote in Revelation, reflects the loving heart of a God who wants us
to be in right relationship with him so that we can enjoy all the benefits
that relationship offers.

Scripture is the means by which God has chosen to introduce and
reveal himself to you so that he can enjoy a relationship with you. Moses
understood this, of course; he begged God, "If you are pleased with me,
teach me your ways *so I may know you*" (Ex. 33:13, NIV, emphasis mine).
God's Word—the record of all his ways—is given to us for a very relational
purpose: so we may know him and enjoy all the blessings of a relationship

with our loving Creator. When we approach the Scriptures in order to know God and have a relationship with him, that not only brings a temporal blessing but also results in eternal life. Jesus prayed to his Father, "And this is eternal life, that they know you the only true God, and Jesus Christ whom you have sent" (John 17:3, ESV).

That is what people need, of course. They need to see God's Word as the revelation of the one true God who desires to have a relationship with them, a relationship that brings blessing now and for eternity. They must also be helped to experience how God's Word meets their need to know, Why am I here?

We were created to live happy, fulfilled lives. We were made to know the gratifying joy of being accepted, approved of, appreciated, with the ability to freely love and be loved. We were designed to experience a fulfillment and satisfaction beyond measure, a contentment and peace beyond understanding, and an abundant life beyond belief. And that kind of meaningful life comes only from living in fellowship with God and conforming to his likeness. The Bible, in providing us with an accurate revelation of God, allows for us to know him for who he is and thus fulfill our potential and purpose of becoming like him. That is the significance of the Bible to each one of us and to our everyday lives. God's Word is the perfect lens to see—and then reflect—the divine nature of God.

WHERE AM I GOING?

As I have spent a lifetime demonstrating the reliability of the Bible, I have also devoted myself to the overwhelming evidence for the resurrection of Jesus Christ from the dead. But our kids today are not greatly impressed by evidences for the resurrection because they are not convinced of its relevance in their lives. They may have some appreciation for the resurrection's importance in securing their salvation, but they generally don't give its truth another thought.

But that is because they have not been helped to see that the resurrection of Jesus from the dead answers the third great question of life: Where am I going? The fact of the resurrection is intensely relevant to our kids because it provides the answer to where we are going in life and in death. For we—every one of us—are destined to have our struggles, suffering, and death transformed into blessings, joy, and eternal life.

In Romans 8 the apostle Paul says, "Even we Christians, although we have the Holy Spirit within us as a foretaste of future glory, also groan to be released from pain and suffering" (v. 23, NLT). So it's clear here that optimism doesn't come from denying our present pain. He then goes on to say that "the Holy Spirit helps us in our distress. . . . And we know that God causes everything to work together for the good of those who love God and are called according to his purpose for them" (Rom. 8:26–28, NLT). Paul had the answer: The Holy Spirit, who lives inside each individual Christian, is there to help us as our trust is placed in a sovereign God who knows what he is doing, for he will cause everything to work together for the good.

This is not a belief that says everything that happens on this death-cursed world is somehow good. Death is not good. Pain is not good. Sorrow, sadness, and suffering are not good. But by trusting in God not only as our Savior but also as our sovereign, risen Lord we can be confident that he will cause all things to work together for our good and his glory. Our confidence and conviction in a God who loves us beyond words and causes all things, even tragedies, to work together for the good can produce within us a spirit of gratitude, courage, and optimism in the face of life—and even death.

Faith in a sovereign God moves us beyond a human perspective on life to an eternal perspective. The apostle Paul was a living example of this eternal mind-set. Listen to his heart of gratitude as he shares his God-inspired letter to the church of Corinth. Read the words carefully. Note how the hope of the resurrection provided him with a sense of courage and optimism, even in the most difficult times:

> We are pressed on every side by troubles, but we are not crushed and broken. We are perplexed, but we don't give up and quit. We are hunted down, but God never abandons us. We get knocked down, but we get up again and keep going. . . . We know that the same God who raised our Lord Jesus will also raise us with Jesus and present us to himself along with you. All of these things are for your benefit. . . . That is why we never give up. Though our bodies are dying, our spirits are being renewed every day. For our present troubles are quite small and won't last very long. Yet they produce for us an immeasurably great glory that will last forever! So we don't look at the troubles we can see right now; rather, we look forward to what we have not seen. For the troubles we see will soon be over, but the joys to come will last forever. (2 Cor. 4:8–9, 14–15, 16–18, NLT)

What an amazing approach to life's problems! Paul didn't run from difficulties or try to deny they existed to avoid the pain. He acknowledged his suffering and viewed the trials of life from an eternal perspective, knowing that the God of all comfort was there to ease his pain (see 2 Cor. 1:3–4). He trusted in a sovereign God who would cause everything to work together for the good. Paul's faith in a God who had everything under control enabled him to see the difficulties of this life as producing "an immeasurably great glory that will last forever."

And how could Paul say that the glory and joy will last forever? Because the ultimate good is our eternal inheritance, a guarantee of living in God's presence forever. "Now we live with a wonderful expectation," Peter said, "because Christ rose again from the dead. For God has reserved a priceless inheritance for his children" (1 Pet. 1:3–4, NLT). Though we may endure pain, grief, and suffering here on earth, because Christ's death was followed by his resurrection, we can know that such things are temporary and that much greater things await us.

The significance of the resurrection is that through it Jesus Christ is saying to us, "Trust me. I'm alive and in control of every situation. I will take your struggles and change them into blessings. I will take your suffering and turn it into joy. I will even take your physical death and transform it into eternal life. And how can I do that? I'm the sovereign, almighty Lord of the universe who can do all things and who causes everything to work together for the good of those who love God and are called according to his purpose for them. So trust in me, no matter what."

THE ROAD TO CONVICTION

We can demonstrate to our kids not only what is *objectively true* about the Christian faith but also how that is *relationally meaningful* to their lives. In fact, we not only can—we *must*. That is why I have dedicated my efforts to a broad new campaign entitled True Foundations (www.truefoundations.com), which provides a fresh framework and innovative means of introducing and teaching Christianity to kids in a way that combines truth and relationship. We must do all we can to effectively ground the next generation of kids (and ourselves) in the truth—and in the relevance of the truth—and so enable them to live as "children of God without fault in a crooked and depraved generation, in which [they] shine like stars in the universe" (Phil. 2:15, NIV).

CHAPTER THREE

Apologetics for the
Twenty-first Century

John Warwick Montgomery

I. WHERE WE ARE AND WHY THIS IS IMPORTANT[1]

We Christian believers concerned with defending the faith once delivered to the saints need to recognize the unique cultural situation in which we find ourselves shortly after the turn of the new millennium. This uniqueness stems from a combination of factors by no means limited to increased secularism and secular self-satisfaction. The major factors are: (1) An enlargement of what Canadian sociologist Marshall McLuhan termed "the Global Village"—the exponential increase in world communications, resulting in continual, unavoidable contact between believers and unbelievers. (2) Pluralism, to an extent unknown in past ages, even during the Hellenistic period; its consequence being a multiplying of sects, religious and philosophical viewpoints, and the interpenetration of worldviews (e.g., Eastern religions transmogrified into Western "New Age" orientations). (3) Increased sophistication on the part of religionists. Examples, among many, include Scientology's use of legal intimidation to stifle criticism of the movement, paralleling the employment of legal teams by multinational corporations to protect their public image;[2] also,

---

[1]This is a modified version of an essay that was offered as an invitational lecture at the Hope for Europe conference of the Evangelical Alliance, held in Budapest, Hungary, April 27–May 1, 2002. A version of the essay was also published in German as "Die Verteidigung der Hoffnung in uns—Apologetik fuer das 21. Jahrhundert," in Thomas Mayer and Thomas Schirrmacher, eds., *Europa Hoffnung Geben* (Hamburg, Germany: VTR, 2004), 48–61.

[2]As an English barrister, I was consulted on the *Bonny Woods* v. *Church of Scientology* matter a few years ago. Woods and her husband were converted from Scientology to evangelical Christianity and began a counter-cult ministry to help others leave Scientology. Thereupon they were sued for defamation by the Church of Scientology. With its vast financial resources, the Church could easily have bankrupted the Woodses, even though the latter were in the right legally. Our strategy was to apply to the Court for discovery of all the foundational records of the Church on the ground that the only way to know if the Church had in fact been defamed was to find out what it really believed and practiced vis-à-vis its

al-Qaeda's use of highly sophisticated computer technology to further their interests and terrorist agendas could be added.[3] (4) A growing realization, stemming in large part from the events of September 11, 2001, that all religions are *not* in fact "saying the same thing" in spite of what we were told by generations of liberal clergy and comparative religion teachers.

Why are these considerations so important? Recognition of the current situation is vital because only by knowing it, will we direct our apologetic to the real needs of the unbeliever. The bedrock principle here is: 1: **Apologetics is not dogmatics**.

By this we mean that whereas dogmatics begins with God's special revelation of himself in Holy Scripture and expounds its content, apologetics begins where the unbeliever is: "becoming all things to all people, that we might save some . . . a Jew to the Jew and a Greek to the Greeks."[4] This does not mean, to be sure, that in apologetics we alter the eternal message to fit the unbeliever's situation or needs. That message is the same yesterday, today, and forever. Our methods of communicating the everlasting gospel will be developed, however, according to the personal, social, and cultural context, which never remains constant. If this fundamental distinction is not understood, *either* dogmatics will be absorbed into apologetics (to the loss of the gospel) *or* apologetics will be swallowed up in dogmatics (so that the defense of the gospel will make sense only to those who already believe it). The first of these errors is that of the religious liberal; the second is endemic among religious conservatives.[5]

II. AVOIDING TWENTIETH-CENTURY MISTAKES

We have just observed that there are mistakes characteristic of the two chief theological polar opposites. Let us now observe a few of the other particularly unfortunate errors of doctrinaire religious liberals and conservatives

---

members and how it proselytized. As we expected, the Church dropped the action rather than revealing what it was up to.
[3]Cf. Reuel Marc Gerecht, "The Gospel According to Osama bin Laden," *Atlantic Monthly,* January 2002, 46–48.
[4]Classically, to be sure, dogmatics and apologetics were treated as two of the three branches of Systematic Theology (the third being ethics). Today in theological faculties apologetic instruction has virtually disappeared. At best, it sometimes appears in compromised form in courses in philosophy of religion.
[5]See my book *Faith Founded on Fact* (available, along with most of my apologetics writings, from the Canadian Institute for Law, Theology, and Public Policy, Edmonton, Alberta, Canada; www.ciltpp.com). Sadly, the great Calvinist dogmatician Cornelius Van Til believed that his great apologetic accomplishment, over against B. B. Warfield, was to make the God who reveals himself in Scripture the starting-point for apologetics as well as for dogmatics. Warfield, however, knew what he was doing: an apologetic that insists that the non-Christian start where the Christian starts is really no apologetic at all. At best it is preaching; at worst it is simply counterproductive.

as background to a discussion of how to move forward on a much more solid apologetic basis.

The Conservatives

The "Bible Christian" often sees no distinction between preaching and revivalism, on the one hand, and evangelism and apologetics on the other. He or she will use tracts that do little more than quote Bible passages. One thinks of R. A. Torrey's little booklet consisting of non-Christian questions, accompanied with Bible texts supplying the answers. The difficulty (should it not be obvious?) is that today one can hardly assume that the non-Christian is really a lapsed Christian who knows that the Bible is true but has fallen into a life inconsistent with it. With a plethora of alternative "holy books" (Qur'an, Bhagavad-Gita, Book of Mormon, etc.), we presume at our peril that the unbeliever will simply accept whatever we quote from the Bible. The very term *revival* used so frequently in evangelical circles as equivalent to *evangelism* shows how unrealistically we view the condition of the average non-Christian today. In point of fact, we must demonstrate the revelational character of the Holy Scriptures over against competing claims to inscripturated truth. And our personal "holiness" is hardly a proof of biblical revelation any more than our failings remove from its veracity. As Luther nicely put it, the entire gospel is *extra nos* (outside of us).

Some learned conservatives make the deadly mistake of confusing *apologetics* with *philosophy*. How do they do this? They spend their energies discussing questions that have little or no bearing on the truth of the faith or relevance to the acceptance of it. For example, the relationship of time to creation: could God have logically functioned before the creation of temporality? (At a meeting of the Evangelical Philosophical Society in the U.S.A. several years ago, I made myself unpopular by citing St. Augustine, who when confronted with the question "What was God doing before he created the world?" replied, "Preparing hell for people who ask questions like that.") We are thus brought to our next axiomatic truth: 2. **Apologetics is not philosophy.**

This is true not merely because, as apologist Edward John Carnell was wont to say, there are as many apologetics as there are facts in the world. That is to say, apologetics employs every true fact and every true discipline in its behalf: history, science, jurisprudence, literature, art. The particular reason why apologetics must not be reduced to philosophy is that the abstract questions of traditional philosophy are either purely *formal*, dealing with issues of logic and not with issues of fact, or are so arcane that they do not touch the central elements of the gospel (acceptance of the death of our Lord for our sins and his resurrection for our justification). The gospel is a matter of *fact*, and its acceptance will necessarily depend on whether the documentary records of Jesus' ministry are sound, whether the testimonies to his life and work are accurate, and whether one can accept his claims and his resurrection from the dead. Important philosophical issues do indeed bear on this case (issues such as the legitimacy of miracle evidence), but the case is, in the last analysis, a *factual* one. Metaphysical problems can be discussed from now until just after the Last Judgment and the crucial question of the facticity of the gospel still remain untouched. And it is the gospel's factual truth that constitutes, and has always constituted, the heart of the Christian proclamation and the heart of the Christian apologetic.

Related to the error just discussed is the conservative tendency to think that the best apologetic strategy consists of showing that Christian affirmations are indeed philosophically "meaningful," i.e., not irrational or technically nonsensical. One of the most influential and important Christian philosophers of our time has succeeded in showing, for example, that the existence of evil is not logically incompatible with the existence of an omnipotent, omniscient Deity. Fine! But logical possibility is hardly the same as de facto existence! There is nothing *logically* absurd in a claim that the Big Bang was the product of a Divine Burp, but that hardly means that such occurred.

There is no substitute for evidence in our defense of the faith. Life is bigger than logic; and again and again things apparently irrational have turned out to be true on the basis of the factual evidence in their behalf. Thus, the physical characteristics of light (particulate and undulatory) are mutually inconsistent, since waves are not particles and particles are not waves. But the evidence is incontrovertible, and so the photon. The parallel issue of the Trinity will be assisted only peripherally by philosophical discussions of the meaningfulness of the concept. Our apologetic thrust must be the historical evidence that Jesus, in rising from the dead, validated his claim to deity, and thus his affirmations that he and the Father are one,[6] that the Holy Spirit is "another" (Greek, *allos*, "of the same kind qualitatively") as himself,[7] and that the church is to baptize in the name (*one* name) of the Father and of the Son and of the Holy Spirit. If these facts are genuine,

---

[6]John 14:8–11.
[7]John 14:16.

we have answered the question. We do not understand the mechanism any more than we do in the case of the nature of light, but that does not alter the factual character of things in the least.

The Liberals

We have already noted that the religious liberal's overwhelming tendency is that of accommodation to the secular climate, thus losing the message which he is endeavoring to communicate. Here is a sad example: In 1950 Rev. Leslie Badham published a solid volume of Christian apologetics titled *Verdict on Jesus: A New Statement of Evidence*. Badham was a distinguished conservative churchman and a fine communicator. For some thirteen years he was Vicar of Windsor and Chaplain to Her Majesty the Queen (who has never been happy with broad-church liberalism). During his ministry he was equally at home in the pulpit and on the airwaves as a radio broadcaster. *Verdict on Jesus* was expanded in a second edition in 1971. After Badham's death, his son, presently Dean of Theology in the University of Wales at Lampeter, took over the book. There followed third (1983) and fourth (1995) editions, the text of which remained substantially that of the original author. However, Badham's son supplied new introductions to these editions, purportedly to update the book. The point of the original volume was to argue for the de facto reliability of the biblical accounts of the life of Christ and the consequent veracity of his claims. Badham's son, however, having accepted the so-called "historical criticism" of the biblical narratives, supports John Hick's position in his work, *The Myth of God Incarnate*—namely, that the Incarnation is but metaphorical in character. "Hence," the reader is told, "it is possible to make a total faith commitment to Jesus as God Incarnate while believing that the language is true in a metaphorical rather than an ontological sense."[8] This, of course, not only constitutes heresy by the standards of the Ecumenical Creeds of the Universal Church but also entirely evacuates of meaning his father's powerful original argument for Christian faith. As I have maintained elsewhere in my critique of Hick's position, once one accommodates to the poor scholarship of higher criticism, the loss of fundamental Christian teaching is logically inevitable and an effective apologetic rendered impossible.[9]

---

[8]Paul Badham, Introduction to Leslie Badham, *Verdict on Jesus* (fourth edition; Wantage, UK: Ikon Productions, 1995), xv.

[9]John Warwick Montgomery, "Why Has God Incarnate Suddenly Become Mythical?" in *Perspectives on Evangelical Theology*, ed. Kenneth S. Kantzer and Stanley N. Gundry (Grand Rapids, MI: Baker, 1979), 57–65; reprinted in C. E. B. Cranfield, David Kilgour, and J. W. Montgomery, *Christians in the Public*

A second gross error of the religious liberal is to capitulate to postmodern thinking in its refusal to take seriously the objective character of external reality. It is the position of contemporary thinkers such as Jacques Derrida that to try to find a core of objective meaning in the world or in literary materials such as the Bible is a chimerical quest. There are necessarily as many valid interpretations as there are interpreters, we are told, and interpreters always approach objects of study from their own personal, cultural, and presuppositional viewpoints. Moreover, in the case of literary works, meanings are always multilayered and can never be fully understood by efforts to get at an author's original intention or purpose.[10]

Such a perspective is, of course, very hospitable to the religious liberal, who has never had a serious view of the unity of the Scriptures, has always regarded the Bible as a product of diverse human cultural experiences, and has had a powerful tendency to substitute for the doctrine that God created us in his image a humanistic theology of *our* creating God (and theology) in *our* image.

Religious liberals have never seemed to see the fundamental illogic in the view that reality outside of us—including biblical narrative—has no objective meaning and that each person can never go beyond the limits of his or her own "personal story" in understanding the world, the Bible, or religious truth. In fact, this approach falls into an infinite regress of solipsism if carried to its logical conclusion.[11] If the Bible (or anything else) has no objective meaning, neither do the writings and assertions of the postmodernists! To communicate at all, we must assume that at least our own oral and written statements can be understood in the sense in which we have intended them. But if so, we can hardly claim that this is not the case for the communications of others, including those of our Lord, who said, "He who has ears to hear, let him hear" and condemned those who perverted the clear word spoken by his Father through Moses and the prophets.[12] A sound Christian apologetic requires a serious view of objective reality and of a Bible that does not speak with forked tongue.

Additionally, religious liberals (especially in England) readily succumb

---

Square (Edmonton, Alberta, Canada: Canadian Institute for Law, Theology, and Public Policy, 1996), 307–316.

[10] See, *inter alia*, Stuart Sim, ed., *The Icon Critical Dictionary of Postmodern Thought* (Cambridge, UK: Icon Books, 1998).

[11] Two excellent counteractives to such thinking are: Noretta Koertge, ed., *A House Built on Sand: Exposing Postmodernist Myths about Science* (New York: Oxford University Press, 1998); and Kevin J. Vanhoozer, *Is There a Meaning in This Text? The Bible, the Reader and the Morality of Literary Knowledge* (Leicester, UK: Apollos/Inter-Varsity Press, 1998).

[12] Cf. Luke 16:29–31.

to a "via media" style of thinking. By this we mean the ability not to come down too hard on any side of any disputed question for fear of offending someone, particularly the popular or lionized secularist. Here again the byword is accommodation—the utterly false assumption that Christianity can gain friends and converts by modifying its teachings to make them more palatable to the secular mind-set.

Unhappily, this tendency is by no means limited to the religious liberal. In evangelical circles, especially in the United Kingdom and the European continent, it is becoming harder and harder to find those who will unqualifiedly affirm biblical inerrancy. "After all," we are told, "the word isn't mentioned in the Bible; and the gospel and Christian experience cannot be hurt by minor historical errors or contradictions in the Scriptures." To which we reply, neither does the word *Trinity* appear in the Bible, but we dismiss it at our theological peril. And if the biblical writers cannot accurately describe the Temple in Jerusalem, for example, what makes anyone think that they are correct when they talk about the Heavenly Jerusalem? One would think that the former would be far less demanding than the latter! Did not our Lord say, "If I have told you earthly things and you believe not, how shall you believe if I tell you of heavenly things?"[13]

We also have the sad, mediating concessions recently made by some evangelical thinkers to the so-called "Openness of God" theology, whereby, in the supposed interest of preserving human freedom, God's omniscience is jettisoned. Certain charismatics, in particular, have thought that this provides a more human face for God and a more attractive Deity in the eyes of potential converts. Hardly! One ends up with a God who cannot promise anything on which poor sinners can depend since he, no less than his creatures, is limited to statistical prediction of the future. One of the greatest genuine apologetic appeals continues to be that which, according to the Venerable Bede, converted the Northumbrians in the seventh century: the argument that our life, like that of a sparrow flying briefly into a lighted hall and quickly disappearing again into darkness, is one of utter uncertainty and that "if this new teaching has brought any greater certainty, it seems fitting that it should be followed."[14]

---

[13] John 3:12. All Scripture quotations in this chapter are author's translation.
[14] Venerable Bede, *Ecclesiastical History*, ii. 13. Cf. John Warwick Montgomery, *The Suicide of Christian Theology* (Newburgh, IN: Trinity Press, 1998), especially 42–43. The great contemporary English Christian jurist Lord Hailsham of St Marylebone titled his second autobiography, *The Sparrow's Flight*; at his Memorial Service a poem of his composition was read at his request in which he referred to himself as just such a sparrow.

III. THE WAY FORWARD

To avoid the errors—both liberal and conservative—just delineated, what must we do? How can we achieve a vigorous, sound apologetic for the twenty-first century? Consider five minimal requisites.

First, there must be *a vigorous attack on the utterly fallacious notion that one does not need Jesus Christ for a fulfilled life.* It has often been observed that those who cannot be convinced that they are sick will not go to a doctor. We need to employ the writings of the existentialists (Sartre, and especially Camus[15]) and of the depth psychologists and psychoanalysts to point out the misery of the human condition apart from a relationship with Christ. This should not be in the least difficult, since these thinkers have proclaimed the meaninglessness of life and the void at the center of the human heart. Carl Gustav Jung, to take one example, has analogized the human condition to that of the nursery character Humpty Dumpty—broken and unable to put himself back together again.[16] And, what is even worse, as Jacques Lacan points out, "The analysand's basic position is one of a refusal of knowledge, a will not to know (a *ne rien vouloir savoir*)." The analysand (that is, the one who is undergoing psychoanalysis) wants to know nothing about his or her neurotic mechanisms, nothing about the why and wherefore of his or her symptoms. Lacan even goes so far as to classify ignorance as a passion greater than love or hate: "a passion not to know."[17] "How," the jocular question is put, "does a psychiatrist differ from a coal miner?" Answer: "The psychiatrist goes down farther, stays down longer, and comes up dirtier." One of the very few positive results of the September 11, 2001 horror was that it drove many Americans back to church (at least for a time!). Why? Because they were reminded of the fragility of life, the inevitability of death, and their inability to control their own destinies. The twenty-first-century apologist needs to drive these truths home, based upon universal human experience.

In the second place, the effective apologist *must be willing to engage in an uncompromising, frontal attack on prevailing non-Christian worldviews.* Liberal accommodationism has to be rejected out of hand. Any gains from compromise are trivial when compared to the losses—losses in integrity and in the power of the gospel message.

---

[15]Though Camus is universally regarded as a secular existentialist, at the time he was killed in a car accident he was seriously considering Christian baptism from one of my students, then guest preacher at the American Church in Paris: see Howard Mumma, *Albert Camus and the Minister* (Brewster, MA: Paraclete Press, 2000).

[16]Cf. John Warwick Montgomery, *Myth, Allegory and Gospel* (Minneapolis: Bethany House, 1974).

[17]Bruce Fink, *A Clinical Introduction to Lacanian Psychoanalysis: Theory and Technique* (Cambridge, MA: Harvard University Press, 1997), 7.

How do we attack secular viewpoints? Not on peripheral issues (their failure to live up to their own principles, for example), but *at the presuppositional heart of their beliefs.* The efficient way to destroy a condemned building is not to start on the roof, removing the tiles one by one; it is to blow up the foundations, after which the entire building will fall. Take the case of Marxism: its fundamental error is to assume that modifications in the means of production in society will produce "new men," a proletariat capable of creating a perfect, classless society.[18] But throughout human history, modifications of the environment external to man have *never* changed man's selfish nature. The precise same fallacy lies at the heart of liberal western, utopian social planning. Tear down slums, replace them with clean, new buildings, put the same people into the new buildings, and the buildings soon become slums again. As Jesus summed it up (and human experience entirely confirms this): "That which comes out of the man, that defiles the man. For from within, out of the heart of men, proceed evil thoughts, adulteries, fornications, murders, thefts, covetousness, wickedness, deceit, lasciviousness. . . . All these evil things come from within, and defile the man."[19] Only a personal, living relationship with Jesus the Savior can transform the heart: "If any man be in Christ he is a new creature: old things are passed away; behold, all things are become new."[20]

Moreover, we must not be afraid to *attack the fallacious logic of non-Christian positions.* Even though, as pointed out earlier, the refutation of unsound viewpoints does not establish the truth of one's own, it is vital to remove the false hopes that often keep non-Christians from even considering the case for Christianity. Take, as an obvious example, the Qur'anic picture of Jesus, contradicting the very essence of the New Testament description of him as the unique Son of God, come to earth to die for the sins of the world. Since the New Testament testimony comes from eyewitnesses or close associates of eyewitnesses, whereas Mohammed's material appears on the scene six hundred years later, no one with any historical sense would prefer the latter to the former.[21]

Another classic piece of non-Christian illogic is the oft-heard argument that belief in a Creator God solves nothing, since one is still left with the question, "Who created God?" However, since an infinite regress solves nothing, one must stop the reasoning process either with the universe or

---

[18]See John Warwick Montgomery, "The Marxist Approach to Human Rights: Analysis and Critique," *Simon Greenleaf Law Review,* 3 (1983–1984), *passim.*
[19]Mark 7:20–23.
[20]Second Cor. 5:17.
[21]See John Warwick Montgomery, "How Muslims Do Apologetics," *Muslim World,* 51 (April and July 1961), reprinted in his *Faith Founded on Fact* (Nashville and New York: Thomas Nelson, 1978).

with a Creator of the universe; and since the universe is patently contingent (nothing in it can explain itself), it is far more sensible to appeal beyond it to a non-contingent, absolute, Creator God than to deify the universe by pretending, mythologically, that it really *isn't* contingent at all! Those who do the latter show that it is the unbeliever who is the myth-maker, not the theist (demonstrating, not so incidentally, that Freud had it exactly reversed when he asserted that believers in God mythologically create an illusion of divine existence). In point of fact, it is the theist who is the realist, and the atheist who creates the illusion that the world is self-sufficient, self-explanatory, and therefore absolute.[22]

In the third place, besides being willing and prepared to press home the hopelessness and illogic of non-Christian worldviews, the twenty-first-century apologist *must offer positive, compelling evidence in support of the Christian claim.* Note carefully the apostle's language: "Be ready always to give an answer [Greek, *apologia*] to every person who asks you a reason for the hope that is in you."[23] Merely preaching the good news or announcing the hope is *never* enough! One must *always* give a *reason* for the hope. This can be stated axiomatically: 3. **Apologetics is not preaching.**

What kind of positive evidence is to be presented? The focus must be a demonstration of the soundness of our Lord's claim to be "the way, the truth, and the life," so that the seeker can appreciate why he declared that "no man comes to the Father but by me." We are not in the business of persuading people to become deists, theists, or members of particular religious organizations. We are in the business of persuading people to accept Jesus as personal Savior—as the only One who can "save them from their sins." To make this case, there is no way to avoid arguing for the soundness of the New Testament documents, the reliability of the testimony to Jesus contained therein, and the facticity of his resurrection from the dead as the final proof of his claims.[24]

Such argumentation can benefit greatly from, for example, Theodor Zahn's great commentary on the Gospel of John, establishing the apostolic authorship of the book, and Adolf Harnack's reasoning to support the dating of the Synoptic Gospels within the generation of Jesus' crucifixion

---

[22]John Warwick Montgomery, *Christianity for the Toughminded* (Minneapolis: Bethany House, 1973), 21–34.

[23]First Peter 3:15.

[24]See John Warwick Montgomery, *History, Law and Christianity* (Edmonton, Alberta: Canadian Institute for Law, Theology, and Public Policy, 2002); *Where Is History Going? Essays in Support of the Historical Truth of the Christian Revelation* (Minneapolis: Bethany House, 1969). *Where Is History Going?* has been published in German under the title, *Weltgeschichte Wohin?* (Stuttgart-Neuhausen: Haenssler Verlag, 1977).

(the Acts of the Apostles must have been written before A.D. 64–65 since it does not record the death of Paul, its central personage. Luke's Gospel, by the same author, had to have been written before Acts; and Luke employed Mark as one of his sources, driving the date of composition of Mark back even farther). In general, the pretensions and the subjective, bad scholarship of the form and redaction critics must be fought on every front. Higher criticism is the single most deadly foe that the twenty-first-century apologist must defeat.[25] To retreat into pietism or an Averroes-like doctrine of "twofold truth" ("yes, the Gospels are historically unreliable, but no, our faith experience of Jesus remains firm") is to destroy all the credibility of the Christian message and eliminate any meaningful apologetic for its truth.

A fourth essential requisite for an effective contemporary apologetic is the *willingness to address the most difficult issues troubling the unbeliever.* So often Christians offer pat answers to minor difficulties (reconciliations of the king lists in the books of Kings and Chronicles; explanations for the apparent tension between "faith" in Paul and "good works" in James; etc.) while ignoring or bypassing that which really keeps the non-Christian from becoming a Christian. We must be prepared to face such issues as the perceived irrationality and lack of justice in the world (the Holocaust; September 11, 2001). The unbeliever will balance these against our case for Jesus' claims and may think that the horrors entirely outweigh any argument for "God in Christ, reconciling the world to himself." Here we will need to break new ground. For example, we can point out that the critical consideration is not the number of horrific events in history weighed against the single event of Jesus Christ (a matter of quantity), but the *qualitative* issue of whether even if only one instance of evil and irrationality existed in human history, that would be consistent with the existence of a loving God coming to earth to die for a fallen race. Since love entails free will, and since the God of the Bible reveals himself as perfectly good, irrationality and evil (on whatever scale) will be the creature's fault, not the Creator's; and God's willingness to suffer undeservingly for us should fill us with gratitude rather than eliciting criticism of his morality. Such argumentation may not exhaust the question, but it at least does not sidestep the non-Christian's genuine concerns.

Finally, the twenty-first-century apologist needs to take apologetics far more seriously. He needs to *incorporate apologetics into* every *aspect of*

---

[25]The German works of Gerhard Maier are particularly to be commended in this regard; in English, see his *The End of the Historical-Critical Method*, trans. E. W. Leverenz and R. F. Norden (Eugene, OR: Wipf and Stock, 2001).

his or her ministry—*every* sermon, *every* class, *every* evangelistic activity. We have woefully neglected our responsibility to train our young people in the solid case for Christianity, and then we wonder why they depart from the faith under the influence of secular university instruction. We give our parishioners and our missionaries no foundation in the defense of the faith and then wonder why our evangelistic efforts show so little fruit in a world where people have long moved beyond accepting something just because someone else believes it.

In a word, we need to return to our biblical and theological foundations to find the place that apologetics should have in Christian ministry. That place is absolutely clear. We are to do as the apostle did: "While Paul waited for them at Athens, his spirit was stirred in him when he saw the city wholly given to idolatry. Therefore disputed he in the synagogue with the Jews . . . [and] in the market daily with them that met with him, [and with] certain philosophers of the Epicureans and of the Stoics. . . ."[26] We are to become "all things to all people, that some might be saved, a Jew to the Jew and a Greek to the Greeks," which necessarily entails giving reasons for the faith, since that is what so many of our contemporaries, Jews and Gentiles, require before they will commit themselves to a faith-position. We must not reduce the faith once delivered to the saints to a cultic matter of inner experience and personal testimony. There are enough irrational religions and sects in our twenty-first-century world without giving the unbeliever the impression that Christianity is just another one of them. And so, a final (and, this time, positive) axiom: 4. **Apologetics is always giving a reason for the hope.**

---

[26]Acts 17:16ff.

CHAPTER FOUR

A Biblical Argument for
Balanced Apologetics:
How the Apostle Paul Practiced
Apologetics in the Acts

Acts 14:8–18; 17:16–34

H. Wayne House

I. INTRODUCTION TO APOLOGETICS METHODOLOGY

Defense of the Christian faith is central to the ongoing viability of Christianity in its struggle with false religions and ideologies, and with assisting persons to embrace the gospel of Christ. Those who would desire to share the good news of Jesus immediately encounter individuals who do not share the same view of the world, their own need of salvation, the credibility and value of the Scriptures, or knowledge of Jesus as he is presented in the Bible.[1] The religions of the world make belief claims that are at considerable variance with what is set forth in Christianity,[2] including cults of Christianity,[3] and even in the West where Christianity was once held to be the accepted religion, a majority now have little knowledge of the biblical claims regarding Jesus the Messiah or of the need of salvation through him.[4] A common

---

[1]See Terry C. Muck for a discussion of how world religions and ideologies differ from Christian claims and Muck's suggestions on how to establish common ground with them. Terry C. Muck, "Is There Common Ground Among Religions?" *Journal of the Evangelical Theological Society*, 40:1 (March 1997): 99–112; also see Harold A. Netland, "Apologetics, Worldviews, and the Problems of Neutral Criteria," *Trinity Journal*, 12:1 (Spring 1991): 39–58.

[2]See H. Wayne House, *Charts of World Religions* (Grand Rapids, MI: Zondervan, 2006).

[3]See H. Wayne House, *Charts of Cults, Sects, and Religious Movements* (Grand Rapids, MI: Zondervan, 2000).

[4]Beliefs in God, Jesus, the Bible, and other Christian claims have continued to drop in the United States but are still much higher than in Europe. See the following polls on the Worldwide Web: "Poll: Christian Beliefs," Blue Meme, http://bluememe.blogspot.com/2004/12/poll-christian-beliefs.html (last visited

division of faith and fact, the religious and the secular, and even the viability of objective truth claims pervades our culture.

In view of this ignorance, rejection, or repudiation of Christian truth claims by potential converts, the evangelist must decide how to bridge this resistance to Christian truth. Does the Christian apologist and evangelist share with the potential convert any common ground that may serve as a basis for answering the unregenerate person's questions that are at variance with Christian claims, or is the unregenerate "evangelee" totally incapable of understanding rational and evidentiary arguments without special revelation? This is determined by one's methodology, as well as perspectives on God, creation, man, and sin.

A. The Problem in Deciding Methodology

Most recognize that divine revelation is divided into two general areas— namely, general revelation that is found in the broader creation and in human conscience, and propositional revelation from God that is in Holy Scripture. Apologists differ as to whether God intends to use the former to assist men and women in receiving salvation through what is known as natural theology, or whether Scripture alone is empowered to lead an unregenerate person to salvation in Christ. That general revelation may be a tool in evangelism or pre-evangelism finds support in Roman Catholic theology and the majority of Protestants, while those who support only Scripture being used by God are largely within Reformed theology, though even here they are a minority. Additionally, the extent to which an unregenerate person is capable of responding in saving faith to either natural or special revelation is debated among theologians and apologists. Some believe that the Spirit of God may aid reason in accepting evidence of God's existence and even truth regarding the redemptive work of Christ, while others believe that only the efficacious work of the Spirit of God in bringing the unregenerate to a salvation knowledge of God as it is revealed in Scripture is able to save. In the midst of all of this debate is the matter of common ground. What may be a basis of discussion with a person still unconvinced of the truth of the gospel? Do believers and unbelievers share a common ground philosophically that provides a bridge over which the believer may lead the unbeliever to faith in Christ?

February 25, 2007); "Beliefs about Jesus' Resurrection among Christian Laity and Clergy," Religious Tolerance, http://www.religioustolerance.org/resurrec8.htm (last visited February 25, 2007); "Comparing U.S. Religious Beliefs with Other 'Christian' Countries," Religious Tolerance, http://www.religioustolerance.org/rel_comp.htm (last visited February 25, 2007); "The Religious and Other Beliefs of Americans 2003," The Harris Poll, http://www.harrisinteractive.com/harris_poll/index.asp?PID=359 (last visited February 25, 2007).

What presuppositions of unregenerate persons hinder or help them to come to the truth of the gospel?

Figure 1: Classical Apologetics (Natural Theology)

Step One: Arguments for undeniable first principles (laws of logic, self-existence, existence of truth, reality, meaning, morality)

Step Two: Traditional theistic arguments for existence of God (cosmological, teleological, ontological, and moral)

Step Three: Empirical and historical evidences for Christian truth claims (miracles; the life, death, and resurrection of Jesus Christ; truthfulness of Scripture)

B. Methods of Apologetics

Based on their view of these issues addressed in the preceding paragraph (see Figure 1), apologists have largely divided themselves into three broad schools of apologetics[5]—classical apologetics, evidential apologetics, and presuppositional apologetics.[6] The *Classical Method*[7] is generally practiced in three steps (i.e., philosophical, theistic, and evidential). First, the apologist approaches the person being addressed from first principles, such as the laws of logic or the fact of one's own existence. With this established, then, the various theistic arguments for God's existence are given. The third step, building on the first two, is to demonstrate that certain empirical or historical evidences may be proved regarding matters such as the truthfulness of Scripture, miracles, or the resurrection of Christ. The Classical apologist believes that the unconverted, though separated spiritually and ethically from the true God, nonetheless has rational capacity to understand argument and draw truthful conclusions when false assumptions are set aside. The use of first principles and theistic proofs is often known by the name Natural Theology.[8]

---

[5]One may also include fideism, the view that Christian truths are beyond reason and should only be accepted by faith. This view was held by Søren Kierkegaard, Karl Barth, and to some extent Martin Luther. For the latter, see, H. Wayne House, "The Value of Reason in Luther's View of Apologetics," *Concordia Journal*, 7:2 (March 1981): 40–53. For a brief overview of these four views, with their strengths and weakness discussed, see H. Wayne House, *Charts of Apologetics and Christian Evidences* (Grand Rapids, MI: Zondervan, 2006).

[6]A recent book adds two other methods of apologetics to the three above: the Reformed Epistemology Method and the Cumulative Case Method. Many others could be included for a thorough treatment. My purpose in this article, however, is not to discuss in detail the various methodologies; so I will restrict myself to the three in the text. For more information see Steven B. Cowan, ed., *Five Views on Apologetics* (Grand Rapids, MI: Zondervan, 2000), 15–20 and the review at "Five Views on Apologetics, Apologetics Index," http://www.apologeticsindex.org/a108.html (last visited January 25, 2007).

[7]The term *classical* is used because this method was used by the first apologists of the second and third century of the Christian era.

[8]For further description of Classical Apologetics, see Norman L. Geisler, "Classical Apologetics," *Baker Encyclopedia of Christian Apologetics*, Baker Reference Library (Grand Rapids, MI: Baker, 1999), 154–156; for a critique of some classical apologists, see George J. Zemek Jr., "Classical Apologetics: A Rational Defense," *Grace Theological Journal*, 7:1 (Spring 1986): 111–123.

Norman Geisler, a Classical apologist, provides a helpful example of how this argument may be made:

The Steps. The overall argument in defense of the Christian Faith can be put in twelve basic propositions. They flow logically one from another:

1. Truth about reality is knowable.
2. Opposites cannot both be true.
3. The theistic God exists.
4. Miracles are possible.
5. Miracles performed in connection with a truth claim are acts of God to confirm the truth of God through a messenger of God.
6. The New Testament documents are reliable.
7. As witnessed in the New Testament, Jesus claimed to be God.
8. Jesus' claim to divinity was proven by an unique convergence of miracles.
9. Therefore, Jesus was God in human flesh.
10. Whatever Jesus (who is God) affirmed as true, is true.
11. Jesus affirmed that the Bible is the Word of God.
12. Therefore, it is true that the Bible is the Word of God and whatever is opposed to any biblical truth is false.

The Application. If a theistic God exists and miracles are possible and Jesus is the Son of God and the Bible is the Word of God, then it follows that orthodox Christianity is true. All other essential orthodox doctrines, such as the Trinity, Christ's atonement for sin, the physical resurrection, and Christ's second coming, are taught in the Bible. Since all these conditions are supported by good evidence, it follows that there is good evidence for concluding that orthodox Christianity is true.

And since mutually exclusive propositions cannot both be true, then all opposing world religions are false religions. That is, Buddhism, Hinduism, Islam, and other religions are false insofar as they oppose the teachings of Christianity. Therefore, only Christianity is the true religion.[9]

Figure 2: Evidentialist Apologetics

Step One:	Use evidences to demonstrate God's existence and the truth claims of Christianity.
Nature of evidence:	Historical, archaeological, rational, scientific, and experiential

The second view is the *Evidential Method of Apologetics*, conspicuously named for its emphasis on evidences. This method shares with the Classical Method belief that the unregenerated has the capacity to hear

---

[9]Norman Geisler, "Argument of Apologetics," *Baker Encyclopedia of Christian Apologetics*, 36. References in the original quote had cross-referencing to internal articles in the *Encyclopedia* and have been deleted from the quote given in the text.

rational argument and to be convinced of certain truths, though there is the recognition in both views (see Figure 2) that sin does distort the way in which information is received. The evidentialists do not argue that truth claims made in Christianity may be demonstrated in an absolute way, but rather that they can be shown to be most likely true. Rather than using the two- or three-step deductive method of Classical apologists, the evidentialist seeks to demonstrate God's existence and other Christian claims inductively and not in any particular order or rational relationship.[10] What is argued largely depends on what the concern or question of the potential convert might be, so that matters relating to biblical veracity, the existence of God, the possibility of miracles, or even experiential issues may be discussed one after another.

Advocates of the last method, the Presuppositional Method of apologetics, have a considerably different perspective regarding the possibility of common ground between the believer and unbeliever than the other two methods presented.[11] Sin keeps the unregenerate sinner from sharing conceptions of truth or morality with the regenerate who has been released from the bondage of sin and is now able to understand the wisdom of God. The presuppositionalist assumes the biblical revelation in all matters relating to conceptions of reality and logic. His task is to demonstrate to the unregenerate, who is using irrational methods and distorted truth (see Figure 3), that only biblical presuppositions provide the necessary means to make sense of the world and of life.[12] Consequently, the apologist must presuppose the special revelation of God in presenting a defense of Christian truth; all knowledge must be understood presupposing the existence of the God of the Bible.

Figure 3: Presuppositionalist Apologetics

Assumption:	Assumes truth claims about God and Christ as revealed in Scripture.
Procedure:	Demonstrate that only biblical presuppositions make sense of reality and attempt to show unbeliever that his presuppositions are irrational. Last of all reveal that only Christianity provides proper foundation for life and thought.

---

[10]For further description of Evidential Apologetics, see Geisler, *Baker Encyclopedia of Christian Evidences*, 42; for a spirited defense of Evidential Apologetics against the view that the proclamation of Scripture, apart from arguments regarding the truthfulness of Scripture, is sufficient, see John Warwick Montgomery, "The Holy Spirit and the Defense of the Faith," *Bibliotheca Sacra*, 154:616 (October 1997): 387–395; see for a presuppositional response to the value of evidences, John C. Whitcomb Jr., "Contemporary Apologetics and the Christian Faith, Part IV: The Limitations and Values of Christian Evidences," *Bibliotheca Sacra* 135: 537 (January 1978): 25–33.

[11]The chart (Figure 4) contrasting Evidentialism and Presuppositionalism may prove helpful to the reader. This will largely serve as a contrast also with Classical Apologetics in those areas in which it also differs with Presuppositionalism in the same questions of evidence, the nature and purpose of revelation, and the nature of man and sin as does Evidentialism.

[12]For further description of Presuppositional Apologetics, see Norman L. Geisler, "Presuppositional Apologetics," *Baker Encyclopedia of Christian Evidences*, 607–608.

In reading apologists with these varying perspectives one sometimes gets the feeling that they are like ships passing in the night. It often appears to be a question of emphasis and definition of terms. Neither Classical apologetics nor Evidential apologetics, in general, believe that arguments for the existence of God or proof of biblical historicity will cause a person to embrace Christ,[13] but that the reception of the gospel through the work of the Holy Spirit is necessary.[14] Also, few presuppositionalists would believe that the unfallen person is incapable of acknowledging God's existence (in fact, this is presupposed) or that certain facts of history or science are true, even miracles, but only that none of this will cause the fallen person to embrace Christ. Fallen man needs the gospel and the work of the Spirit of God. In reality, apologists representing these two schools reveal in their writings much that they hold in common: that there is the *sensus divinitatus* spoken of by Calvin in which humans have innate knowledge of the existence of a divine being, that there is objective truth to be known, that humans are fallen creatures, that they are incapable of embracing the truth of Christ apart from the divine work of the Holy Spirit, that presenting rational arguments for God's existence, proof of the authenticity of the Scripture, and evidence for the resurrection is never a substitute for the proclamation of the good news of Jesus' death, burial, and resurrection.

If, then, these competing methodologies have so much in common, when all of the innuendos and misrepresentations are brought into check, may it be that they both have something to offer to the apologist who desires to present the gospel of Christ to fallen humanity? I believe so. Let us briefly see what one apologist suggests may offer an impasse to warring apologetic forces.

---

[13]Classical apologist William Lane Craig comments: ". . . what about the role of the Holy Spirit in the life of the unbeliever? Since the Holy Spirit does not indwell him does this mean he must rely only upon arguments to convince him that Christianity is true? No, not at all. According to the Scripture, God has a different ministry of the Holy Spirit especially geared to the needs of the unbeliever." William Lane Craig, *Apologetics: An Introduction* (Chicago: Moody Press, 1984), 19. See additional discussion on the Holy Spirit at 20. "Warfield agreed with Calvin that proofs cannot bring people to Christ or even convince them of the divine authority of Scripture. Nonetheless, Warfield believed that the Holy Spirit exercises his convincing power through them." Norman L. Geisler, "Warfield, B.B.," *Baker Encyclopedia of Christian Evidences*, 769. Bernard Ramm, an evidentialist, says, ". . . no well-grounded apologist will state that the philosophic demonstration of Christianity saves a man, but it is, to the contrary, quite evident that no man will give the necessary credence to the Word if he has certain mistaken notions and biased opinions about the facts and nature of the Christian religion." Bernard Ramm, *Protestant Christian Evidences* (Chicago: Moody Press, 1953), 15.

[14]Montgomery says, "Ultimately a non-Christian must make a moral choice as to what he will do with the objectively sound case for Christianity. If he exercises his will to accept the Christ of the Scriptures, that act must be attributed to the Spirit alone as a pure gift of grace. But the monergistic event of conversion no more denigrates or renders superfluous the work of the apologist than it does the work of the preacher or evangelist who presented the saving message to the individual in the first place. The Holy Spirit does not create the gospel or the evidence for it; He applies what is preached and defended to produce salvation." John Warwick Montgomery, "The Holy Spirit and the Defense of the Faith," *Bibliotheca Sacra*, 154: 616 (October 1997): 392.

Ronald Mayers points out that this division one finds between Classical/ Evidential apologetics and Presuppositional apologetics is not something new. The ideas of these systems date back to the Greeks between Plato and Aristotle and later between Descartes and Locke.[15] The contrast is akin to the debate between deduction and induction, between the perspective of innate principles from which we must deductively construct our worldview and whether we must instead construct our view of reality inductively a little bit at a time.[16] Similarly, presuppositionalists believe that we must presuppose God innately whereas evidentialists (and I would add Classical apologists except they also accept deduction from first principles that both saved and unsaved share by virtue of the *imago Dei*) aver that a case should be built from the pieces of historical and scientific evidence that demonstrates the truthfulness of Christian truth claims.[17] After positing the ways in which these approaches to apologetics are different from their historical precursors, Mayers asks, "Must these two approaches to knowledge remain mutually exclusive, or nearly so, in Christian apologetics?"[18] He follows his question with a surprising but encouraging conclusion:

> It is the contention of a Both/And apologetic that both evidentialism and presuppositionalism are correct. God most definitely is the self-existent Creator, but He is also the One who not only makes our history possible, but has frequently joined us. As Creator, God is certainly the presupposition of everything. Presuppositionalism is correct: there is nothing if there is not God. Evidentialism is correct also, however, because this Creator God does invade our history, and we trace His historical path not only via the more abstract archeological trails that inductively support the truth of the Old Testament, but likewise establish the historical reliability of the Gospels that leave us an incarnate God/Man and not simply a fine ethical teacher, as C.S. Lewis showed in his *Mere Christianity*.
>
> In one sense, presuppositionalism begins with God while evidentialism begins with man. They are both right! As Creator, God is primary and logically prior to all our thoughts. There is a difference, however, between logical priority and existential beginning. We are not God and thus must begin "where we are." John Calvin, I believe, knew this well and begins his *magnum opus* with these words:

---

[15]Ronald B. Mayers, "Both/And: A Biblical Alternative to the Presuppositional/Evidential Debate," *Evangelical Apologetics*, in Michael Bauman, David W. Hall, and Robert C. Newman, eds. (Camp Hill, PA: Christian Publications, 1996), 35. See also an entire book by Mayers on balanced apologetics: Ronald B. Mayers, *Balanced Apologetics: Using Evidences and Presuppositions in Defense of the Faith* (Grand Rapids, MI: Kregel, 1984).
[16]Mayers, *Evangelical Apologetics*, 35.
[17]Ibid., 35.
[18]Ibid., 36.

> Our wisdom, in so far as it ought to be deemed true and solid wisdom,
> consists almost entirely of two parts: the knowledge of God and the
> knowledge of ourselves. But as these are connected together by many ties,
> it is not easy to determine which of the two precedes, and gives birth to
> the other.[19]

I believe that Mayers is correct in his assessment. There is a common
ground between non-presuppositional (Classical and Evidential) and presuppositional apologetics, as stated earlier. All evangelical apologetics agree
that human depravity is total and that sin has permeated the entirety of
each human. This separates men and women from the necessary association with God required for eternal life, and it also causes people to reason
wrongly. It is to be acknowledged that unregenerate persons deny the true
God and live in ways contrary to him. But does this mean that the unregenerate cannot do anything on the human plain?[20] Surely not! The fact is
that no one can deny that unregenerate people carry on life in ways not dis-
similar to the regenerate. In the spiritual realm they can believe in a divine
being and worship this being, though ignorantly. In the sphere of the intellect, the unregenerate can reason and research in the same manner as the
regenerate, recognize at least some things that are true, understand passages
of Scripture. Moreover, they have affective actions not any less than the
saved, for they may excel in the arts and sciences. In the ethical and social
realm they can act with magnanimity toward family and friends, showing
genuine love and concern and even great sacrifice. These are all examples
of what theologians have recognized since Calvin[21] as the common grace of
God, though aspects of this doctrine may even be seen in Augustine.[22]

Dennis Johnson presents a good case for common grace being used
on the unregenerate. They are able to use the *imago Dei* in various positive pursuits as those stated in the previous paragraph and to understand

---

[19]Ibid., 36–37, quoting John Calvin, *The Institutes of the Christian Religion*, J. T. McNeill, ed.
(Philadelphia: Westminster Press, 1960), 1.1.1.

[20]This appears to be acknowledged by Van Til, when he says, "The actual situation is therefore always
a mixture of truth with error. Being 'without God in the world' the natural man yet knows God, and, in
spite of himself, to some extent recognizes God. By virtue of their creation in God's image, by virtue of the
ineradicable sense of deity within them and by virtue of God's restraining general grace, those who hate
God, yet in a restricted sense know God, and do good." Cornelius Van Til, Introduction, *Introduction
to Systematic Theology* (Phillipsburg, NJ: P&R, 1974), 27, quoted from Dennis E. Johnson, "Spiritual
Antithesis: Common Grace, and Practical Theology," *Westminster Theological Journal*, 64:1 (Spring
2002): 87.

[21]Summarizing Calvin's perspective, Berkhof says, "This is a grace which is communal, does not pardon
nor purify human nature, and does not effect the salvation of sinners. It curbs the destructive power of sin,
maintains in a measure the moral order of the universe, thus making an orderly life possible, distributes
in varying degrees gifts and talents among men, promotes the development of science and art, and show-
ers untold blessings upon the children of men." Louis Berkhof, *Systematic Theology* (Grand Rapids, MI:
Eerdmans, 1939, 1941; revised and enlarged), 434.

[22]Ibid., 433.

truth about the world and God.[23] He quotes Calvin when he speaks of the advances of pagan culture:

> Whenever we come upon these matters in secular writers, let that admirable light of truth shining in them teach us that the mind of man, though fallen and perverted from its wholeness, is nevertheless clothed and ornamented with God's excellent gifts. If we regard the Spirit of God as the sole fountain of truth, we shall neither reject the truth itself, nor despise it wherever it shall appear, unless we wish to dishonor the Spirit of God. . . . Shall we deny that the truth shone upon the ancient jurists who established civic order and discipline with such great equity? Shall we say that the philosophers were blind in their fine observation and artful description of nature? Shall we say that those men were devoid of understanding who conceived the art of disputation and taught us to speak reasonably? Shall we say that they are insane who developed medicine, devoting their labor to our benefit? What shall we say of all the mathematical sciences? Shall we consider them the ravings of madmen? No, we cannot read the writings of the ancients on these subjects without great admiration. We marvel at them because we are compelled to recognize how preeminent they are.[24]

Johnson continues with important insight. He says that there is a great division within humanity of those born anew and those who are still dead in their sin, but common grace is a unifying element between these two extremes. Believers and unbelievers err in maintaining consistency when it comes to truth, though the unbeliever has a fundamental inclination to "suppress the truth" (Rom. 1:18).[25] But common grace keeps the unbeliever from doing this at every instant. In contrast the efficacious grace of God saves Christians and gives them a fundamental disposition to embrace God, though at times they fail in this commitment to God.

We may put together these two components of common grace and the innate properties of the *imago Dei*. These enable an unregenerate person who has no spiritual life from God and has total inability in himself to appropriate the spiritual things of God. Neither of these can save a person, but they in concert may help a person to be sensitive to events, words, and gospel proclamation that the Holy Spirit may choose to use to bring a person to Christ through the gospel (2 Thess. 2:13–14).

---

[23]Dennis E. Johnson, "Spiritual Antithesis: Common Grace, and Practical Theology," 74.
[24]Ibid., 75, quoting John Calvin, *Institutes of the Christian Religion*, ed. J. T. McNeill, trans. F. L. Battles, 2 vols.; LCC (Philadelphia: Westminster Press, 1960), 1:273–274.
[25]There is divided opinion on the meaning of "suppress" in Romans 1:18. See S. Lewis Johnson Jr., "Paul and the Knowledge of God," *Bibliotheca Sacra*, 129:513 (January 1972): 67.

Here then we must emphasize that there is a tremendous difference between stating a fact that is true and embracing that fact in some form of commitment. The unbeliever is capable of stating a fact. He or she may believe *that* something is true, but this is only half the battle in regard to becoming a person born from above. For example, Jewish, non-Christian Pinchas Lapide acknowledges that Jesus came back from the dead, that this is the only reasonable explanation for the evidence. Even acknowledging this, he does not consider Jesus to be the Messiah.[26] Others, even in Jesus' day, knew that Jesus died on the cross or that he did marvelous miracles. So what! They may know as true the same things that a regenerate person knows as true. But this is not enough. We must remember that though the man without the Spirit may know the things of God (Rom. 1:18ff.), he is incapable of receiving or appropriating the things of God that relate to one's position before God and in God (1 Cor. 2:14). There is a marked distinction between knowing truth and having the proper interpretation of the truth.[27] The latter is from the Holy Spirit as the believer observes and meditates on the special revelation of God. (see Figure 4).

Mayers identifies three forms of knowledge—namely, logical, empirical, and intuitive.[28] Paul, in Romans 1, seems to assert these three forms. According to Paul, God created a world that is intended to be discovered[29] and even though humanity has fallen into sin, the apostle indicates that they should be able to deduce the existence of God from that creation. Moreover, this knowledge of God is found within man. The problem in the passage, then, is not that man cannot know God and not that the way to this knowledge is inadequate. The encumbrance is that human response is to suppress, to be without gratitude, to become futile and foolish, and to distort the knowledge of God. Nonetheless, unsaved humans can come to know God, the true God, without trusting this God. This is proved by the fact that Pharaoh and the Egyptians were able to know Yahweh in a non-salvific way because of the proofs he gave to them of his existence, his power, and his identity (Exod. 7:3–5; 10:1–2).[30]

---

[26]Pinchas Lapide, *The Resurrection of Jesus: A Jewish Perspective* (Philadelphia: Augsburg, 1983).

[27]Alister McGrath explains the importance of connecting facts to significance. See Alister McGrath, "Apologetics to the Jews," *Bibliotheca Sacra*, 155:618 (April 1998): 136–138. McGrath says, "Christians need to do more than simply prove that Jesus died on a cross and rose again. They need to convey the significance of those facts for the fallen, lost world," 137.

[28]Ronald B. Mayers, *Balanced Apologetics*, 36–57.

[29]"Something about human nature seems to prompt it to ask questions about the world. And something about the world seems to allow answers to be given to those questions." Alister E. McGrath, "Apologetics to the Greeks," 263. For a discussion of the uniqueness of Planet Earth for the possibility of scientific discovery, see Guillermo Gonzalez and Jay W. Richards, *The Privileged Planet: How Our Place in the Cosmos Is Designed for Discovery* (Washington, D.C.: Regnery, 2004).

[30]See discussion at Ronald B. Mayers, *Balanced Apologetics*, 49–52.

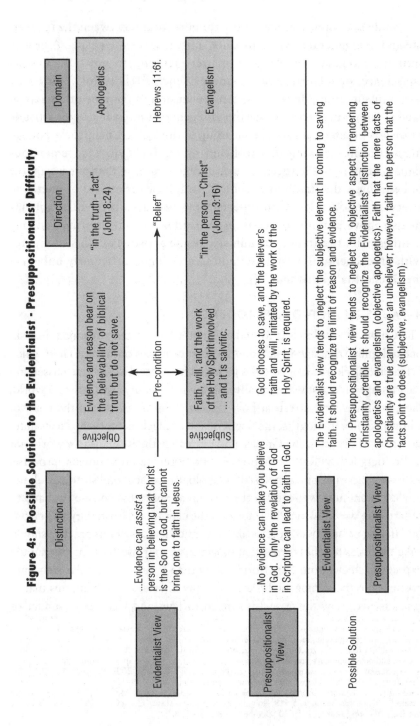

Figure 4: A Possible Solution to the Evidentialist - Presuppositionalist Difficulty

| Distinction | Direction | Domain |

Objective

"in the truth - fact" (John 8:24)

Apologetics

Evidence and reason bear on the believability of biblical truth but do not save.

←— Pre-condition —→ "Belief" Hebrews 11:6f.

Subjective

"in the person – Christ" (John 3:16)

Evangelism

Faith, will, and the work of the Holy Spirit involved ... and it is salvific.

Evidentialist View

...Evidence can *assist* a person in believing that Christ is the Son of God, but cannot bring one to faith in Jesus.

Presuppositionalist View

...No evidence can make you believe in God. Only the revelation of God in Scripture can lead to faith in God.

God chooses to save, and the believer's faith and will, initiated by the work of the Holy Spirit, is required.

Evidentialist View

Presuppositionalist View

Possible Solution

The Evidentialist view tends to neglect the subjective element in coming to saving faith. It should recognize the limit of reason and evidence.

The Presuppositionalist view tends to neglect the objective aspect in rendering Christianity credible. It should recognize the Evidentialists' distinction between apologetics and evangelism (objective apologetics). Faith that the mere facts of Christianity are true cannot save an unbeliever; however, faith in the person that the facts point to does (subjective, evangelism).

So then, common grace is the common ground between the regenerate and unregenerate, but it does not substitute for the gospel. A person cannot be regenerated only by matters relating to creation, nature, conscience, or historical events and evidences.[31] The Holy Spirit may use events in one's life to bring comprehension of truth or other acts of God in common grace to place the unregenerate into the proper attitude or disposition to embrace the meaning within the gospel proclamation, moving from believing *that* to believing *in*. Truly sin has tremendous impact upon both the regenerate or unregenerate, so that one is capable of believing either truth or falsehood, to follow the ethical or unethical course of conduct. It is God's special work of grace that enables humans to rise above the impact of sin in one's life. We may see this dynamic manifested in the apologetic ministry of the apostle Paul, his encounter with unregenerate Jews in Asia and Greece, and particularly unbelieving intellectuals in Athens.

II. PAUL'S METHOD OF APOLOGETICS

The Christian who desires to make Christ known faces a formidable task, one not unlike that encountered by the first centuries of the church in which vying philosophies and ideologies jockeyed for acceptance by the masses and the message of Christ was virtually unknown.[32] In our post-Christian world, then, we must look afresh at how the early church presented the truth of Christ and how apologists, theologians, and evangelists proceeded to counter the views of the Jews, the Greeks, and ultimately the Romans in a world not unlike ours today. Rather than enter into a debate on various approaches to apologetics that might be used by apologists to accomplish this goal, my modest intent now is to look at the proclamations of the apostle Paul and to observe the way in which he presented the claims of Christianity to persons of differing perspectives, specifically Jews and Gentiles.[33] His practice should enlighten us as to what forms of apologetics we may use and what we should expect to achieve from our efforts, rather than taking a particular trenchant posturing in the apologetic task. Part of my interest in studying this matter is to discover how the gospel is offered to Jews and Gentiles in similar or

---

[31]Though I believe that common grace may enable the fallen creature to exercise his innate abilities founded in the *imago Dei*, common grace cannot save, and apart from the regenerative work of the Holy Spirit a person will not receive the grace of God in salvation. As Shedd has said, "Regeneration rests upon God's election and not upon man's preparative acts, upon special grace and not upon common grace." W. G. T. Shedd and Alan W. Gomes, *Dogmatic Theology* (Phillipsburg, NJ: P & R, 2003; third edition), 781.

[32]See Terry C. Muck, "Is There Common Ground Among Religions?," 99–112.

[33]See Alister E. McGrath, "Apologetics to the Jews," 131–138; Alister E. McGrath, "Apologetics to the Greeks," *Bibliotheca Sacra*, 155:619 (July 1998): 259–265; Alister E. McGrath, "Apologetics to the Greeks," *Bibliotheca Sacra*, 155:620 (October 1998): 387–398.

different terms and with similar or different expectations, and whether these presentations assume a certain level of biblical and philosophical sophistication on the part of the hearer.

A. The Theology Underlying Pauline Apologetics in Romans 1

Underlying Paul's preaching was his theology of God and human depravity. He argues that God has revealed himself in creation and in human conscience so clearly that human rejection of that true knowledge of God and lack of gratitude for the goodness of God leaves all humanity without excuse. Numerous studies have been done on this passage, but generally most commentators and theologians would agree on the above assessment. Note his words that "what may be known of God is manifest in them, for God has shown it to them. For since the creation of the world His invisible attributes are clearly seen, being understood by the things that are made, even His eternal power and Godhead, so that they are without excuse, because, although they knew God, they did not glorify Him as God . . ." (Rom. 1:19–21, NKJV). Thus, the text is plain: "they knew God." Moreover the divine nature is "understood," and "what may be known" is manifest in them. There can be little doubt that humans, as fallen creatures, have revelation that can be understood by them. However, even with this, we are speaking of knowing a fact, not about knowing or receiving God personally.

The pagan world did not know God as Savior, but there was little dissension in the recognition of a divine being or power, giving Paul ample ability to connect with his audiences in Asia and Greece. For example, Xenophon (444–360 B.C.) says, "The supreme God holds himself invisible, and it is only in his works that we are capable of admiring him."[34] Plato (429–347 B.C.) says, "God the eternal, the chief ruler of the universe and its creator, the mind alone beholds; but that which is produced we behold by sight."[35] Cicero (106–43 B.C.) speaks of the undeniability of a divine power: "I am convinced entirely that that which could effect so many and such great things must be a divine power"[36] and "Though you see not the Deity, yet by the contemplation of his works, you are led to acknowledge a God."[37] Maximus (A.D. 200) says, "The Barbarians, all

---

[34]Xen. *Mem.* 1.iv.c.3. [Xenophon, *Memorabilia*], cited from Thomas S. Millington, *The Testimony of the Heathen to the Truths of Holy Writ* (London: Seeley, Jackson, and Halliday, 1863), 557.

[35]Plat. *Tim. Loc.* c.5. [Plato, *Timaeus*], cited from Millington, *Testimony of the Heathen*, 557.

[36]Cic. *Disp. Tusc.* 1.I.c.26. [M. Tullius Cicero, *Tusculanae Disputationes*], cited from Millington, *Testimony of the Heathen*, 557.

[37]Cic. *Disp. Tusc.* 1.I.c.28. [M. Tullius Cicero, *Tusculanae Disputationes*], cited from Millington, *Testimony of the Heathen.*, 557.

of them, acknowledge the existence of a deity."[38] Aelian (A.D. 200) says, "No one of the barbarians ever was an Atheist," and "Not one of them ever fell into contempt of the gods, or ever called in question whether they existed or not, or whether they took care of human affairs or not."[39] And again Cicero says, "There never was any nation so barbarous nor any people in the world so savage as to be without some notion of gods. Many have wrong notions, for that is the nature and ordinary consequence of bad customs; yet all allow that there is a certain divine nature and energy."[40]

In spite of this knowledge of God, the knowledge, due to human depravity, has caused mankind to exchange "the truth of God for the lie" (Rom. 1:25, NKJV). The lie, in the context, seems to be that the true God is material and a creature, the very problem that the unregenerate developed in their worship of deity, in which they "changed the glory of the incorruptible God into an image made like corruptible man—and birds and four-footed animals and creeping things" (Rom. 1:23, NKJV). This view of God stands in stark contrast to the understanding of God among the Jews.

B. Paul's Proclamation to the Jews

The Jews were knowledgeable of biblical religion from the Hebrew Scriptures and the LXX[41] in the Diaspora;[42] so one who desired to present Jesus to them had a point of common ground. They already worshiped the God of Abraham, and many anticipated the coming of the Messiah. Thus one could do as Apollo did in the synagogues of Alexandria or as Paul did in the synagogues of Israel, Asia Minor, and Greece, arguing from the Scriptures that Jesus is indeed the Messiah and Savior. These Jews and God-

---

[38]Max. Tyr. *Diss.* 38. [Maximus Tyrius, *Dissertations*], cited from Millington, *Testimony of the Heathen,* 557.

[39]Ael, *Var. Hist.* 1.II.c.31. [Claudius Aelian, *Varia Historia*], cited from Millington, *Testimony of the Heathen,* 557. Bromiley is correct that "Speculative atheism was hardly known in the ancient world; the atheism referred to in the OT (Jer. 5:2; Ps. 10:4; 14:1) is a so-called practical atheism." G. W. Bromiley, "Apologetics, Biblical," *The International Standard Bible Encyclopedia* (Grand Rapids, MI: Eerdmans, 1988; 2002, revised edition), 1:189. "With the words 'There are not atheists, least of all in the hereafter,' Van Til expresses his conviction that all men know God in the utmost depths of their being. Paradoxically, though, men do not want to know God, and may claim to be atheists. Thus, the same person is in a sense both a theist and an atheist. Only the grace of God in Christ can create in such a person a true saving knowledge of the Godhead." Cornelius Van Til, *The Defense of the Faith*, third edition (Philadelphia: P & R, 1967), 153, quoted in David L. Turner, "Cornelius Van Til and Romans 1:18–21: A Study in the Epistemology of Presuppositional Apologetics," *Grace Theological Journal*, 2:1 (Spring 1981).

[40]Cic. *Disp. Tusc.* 1.I.c.13. [M. Tullius Cicero, *Tusculanae Disputationes*], cited from Millington, *Testimony of the Heathen,* 557.

[41]LXX is the Latin Roman numeral for the number 70, after the supposedly seventy translators of the Greek Old Testament, called the Septuagint.

[42]The Diaspora (Greek for scattering of seeds), in our discussion, refers to dispersion of Jews throughout the Greco-Roman world after the exile of the Jews after the fall of Jerusalem in 586 B.C. The Septuagintal word may be in reference to the word "dispersion" in Deuteronomy 28:25.

fearers believed the Scripture, and if they could be shown that Jesus fulfilled the prophecies regarding the Messiah, then the move to belief in him was a logical step, notwithstanding the sinful human nature.

What about the Greeks and Romans, however, who had virtually no knowledge, if any, about the biblical revelation, no point of connection or acceptance of biblical authority?[43] Would quoting a biblical passage be persuasive in bringing them to an acceptance of their Savior? They shared in common with the Jews the fallen nature of humanity and all that entails regarding the capacity of accepting the truth of God, but they shared little in the understanding of biblical revelation and authority that supplies the information that faith must embrace.

C. Paul's Proclamation to the Gentiles

We find in the Acts of the Apostles the only two instances of addresses by Paul before Gentile audiences, to the Lyconians in Asia Minor (Acts 14:15–17) and to the Greeks in Athens (Acts 17:22–31). Both of these are familiar to most of us, particularly the address in Athens. These sermons share some important common features that are helpful to us in understanding how the apostle Paul dealt with potential converts to the Christian faith who had not already been exposed at length to special revelation in the Old Testament. This should provide for us an example that we may use in approaching individuals in our progressively pagan society that is biblically illiterate and often ignorant or even hostile to the truth of God.

1. His Preaching in Acts 14

Paul and Barnabas came to Lystra, a city of Lyconia, after a successful, though troublesome, ministry in Iconium among the Jews and apparently God-fearers in the synagogue.[44] Upon arriving in Lystra, he came to a city that appar-

---

[43]"To Jews, who already know that God is one, and that He is the living and true God, the gospel proclaims that Jesus is the Christ, but pagans must first be taught what Jews already confess regarding the unity and character of God." F. F. Bruce, "The Book of Acts," *The New International Commentary on the New Testament* (Grand Rapids, MI: Eerdmans, 1954), 293.

[44]Polhill comments, "There was evidently no Jewish synagogue in Lystra. There was at least one family of Jewish extraction there, since Lystra was the home of Timothy and his Jewish mother (16:1). By and large, however, Lystra seems to have consisted primarily of Gentile pagans; and their reaction to the lame man's healing reflects that background." J. B. Polhill, "Acts," *New American Commentary* (Nashville: Broadman & Holman, 1992), 312. Carnu comments regarding the lack of a Jewish presence in Lystra: "Luke's notation 'the Jews who were in those parts (τοὺς Ἰουδαίους τοὺς ὄντας ἐν τοῖς τόποις ἐκείνοις)' (16:3)—together with his admission that 'Jews came from Antioch and Iconium (Ἐπῆλθαν δὲ ἀπὸ Ἀντιοχείας καὶ Ἰκονίου Ἰουδαῖοι) (verse 19) and the fact that he mentions no synagogue in the city—may otherwise imply that no established Jewish community existed in Lystra itself. . . . (Timothy's mother would then presumably have assimilated into the Greek community, a fact perhaps confirmed by her failure to circumcise her son [see 16:1f.])." Hilary LeCornu, with Joseph Shulam, *A Commentary on the Jewish Roots of Acts, I: Acts 1–15* (Jerusalem: Netivyah Bible Instruction Ministry, 2003), 774.

ently had no synagogue; so Paul was preaching the gospel to the Gentiles, apparently in the streets.[45] After he healed a man who was crippled, he and Barnabas were wrongly perceived to be the gods Hermes and Zeus.[46]

The confusion of these people regarding the identity of these men of miracles (in healing the man at the gate, Acts 14:8–10) was not that unlikely, since ancient thought, as seen in the *Odyssey*, said:

> *The gods, inspecting mortal actions, deign,*
> *In forms like these to round the earth and main;*
> *Just and unjust recording in their mind*
> *And with sure eyes observing all mankind.*[47]

The identity of Zeus and Hermes as gods is also expected since they more often moved among men.[48] It is also to be expected that humans who recognized their identity would sacrifice to them.[49] There is a legend in the vicinity of Lyconia that helps explain why the people so quickly and expressively began to worship Barnabas and Paul (Acts 14:13, 18). New Testament scholar Craig Keener gives this legend:

> Local Phrygian legend told of an ancient visitation by Zeus and Hermes to Phrygia. In the story only one couple, Baucis and Philemon, received them graciously; the rest of the population was destroyed in a flood. Knowing some form of the story in their own language, the Lycaonians are not about to make the same mistake ancient Phrygia had made; they want to honor Paul and Barnabas, whom they mistake for gods. People sometimes considered miracle workers as gods.[50]

Once Paul and Barnabas were able to quiet down the crowd attempting to sacrifice to them, Paul addressed them with three major points.

---

[45]"Although some philosophers lectured in halls or served wealthy patrons, most preached their philosophical wares on street corners or in marketplaces; powerful speakers like Dio Chrysostom criticized philosophers like Epictetus who reserved their lectures for the classroom. Like an ancient philosopher, Paul here preaches on the street rather than in a synagogue." Craig S. Keener, *The IVP Bible Background Commentary, New Testament* (Downers Grove, IL: InterVarsity Press, 1993), 361–362.

[46]It is likely that Barnabas is considered to be Zeus because of his more mature and stately presence, as well as the fact that Paul was the speaker and so was viewed to be Hermes.

[47]Hom. *Odyss.* 1.XVII.v.484. [Homer, *Odyssey*], cited from Millington, *Testimony of the Heathen*, 539.

[48]For example, "Disguised in human shape, I, Jove, descend from high Olympus, and travel round the world." Ov. Met. 1.I.v.212.; "I, Mercury, the messenger of Jove, greatest of the gods am come to this land." Eurip. *Ion*. V4; [Euripides, *Ion*], cited from Millington, *Testimony of the Heathen*, 539.

[49]For example, "Jupiter and his brother, who rules over the wide ocean, together with Mercury, were on their travels. Hyrieus caught sight of them. As soon as he could recover self-possession, he sacrifices the ox, the tiller of his farm, and roasts him on a large fire." Ov. *Fast.*, 1.V. v495–514. [Ovid, *Fasti*], cited from Millington, *Testimony of the Heathen*, 540.

[50]Keener, *IVP Bible Background Commentary*, 362.

First, he announced that he represented the true and living God[51] who created all things, unlike their lifeless idols who could do nothing. Second, this true God had previously allowed pagans to be in their ignorance, and third, he provided for their needs, giving witness of his existence. We should expect that the apostle Paul surely said more than Luke records, but it is very obvious that Paul spoke in terms that could be understood by the crowds, and that underpinning this address was the richness of Paul's understanding of the theology of the Old Testament.[52] What is surprising is that there is no statement of the gospel in his speech to the multitude, but it may be that the tumultuous situation hindered him in his attempt.[53] This is markedly different from the calmer atmosphere among the intellectuals at Athens where he developed his two-part approach of creation and redemption.

Does Paul's message at Lystra show inconsistency with his teaching in Romans 1:18–25? They certainly are not addressing the exact same themes, but they are in no way contradictory. In both texts Paul argues that God reveals himself to humanity through his works in creation. Creation is open for all to see; so it is a point of common familiarity with Paul's hearers. They may not know of the God of which he speaks, but they have seen him in his works of nature and providential care. Because of this they are now account-able since the days of the nations' walking in their own ways has passed.[54] There is little evidence of anyone becoming a Christian at Lystra, but a similar sermon in Athens bears fruit.

2. His Preaching in Acts 17

Luke provides for us a brief rendition[55] of what must have been a much longer speech that Paul gave in Athens. In this defense before the learned council

---

[51]See LeCornu's analysis of "living God": "While to the people of Israel and to godfearers the proclamation of the gospel can begin with Jesus—who is the 'Messiah, the son of the living God (ὁ χριστὸς ὁ υἱὸς τοῦ θεοῦ τοῦ ζῶντος)' (Mt. 16:16)—for the Gentiles God must first be established as the one true and living God (cf. Dt. 6:4) (see 17:22–31)." LeCornu, with Shulam, *A Commentary on the Jewish Roots of Acts, I*, 782; also see the discussion by Page: "T.R. has τὸν θ τὸν ζῶντα, probably as seeming more precise and emphatic. Paul however very frequently has θεὸς ζῶν, e.g., 2 Cor. 6:16; Rom. 9:26, where he is quoting from Hos. 1:10 κληθήσονται υἱοὶ θεοῦ ζῶντος; and so regularly in LXX. With no article. Cf. too in illustration of the phrase the well-known Hebrew method of confirming an oath, 'Jehovah liveth', e.g. Hos. 4:15 μὴ ὀμνύετε ζῶντα κύριον; Jer. 4:2 ὀμόσῃ ζῇ κύριος." T. E. Page, *The Acts of the Apostles* (London: Macmillan), 171.

[52]LeCarnu provides much detail on the Old Testament passages that Paul probably relied on for the thoughts he developed in his sermon. LeCornu, with Shulam, *Commentary on the Jewish Roots of Acts*, 780–785.

[53]Robertson thinks that "Paul does not here mention Christ because he had the single definite purpose to dissuade them from worshipping Barnabas and himself." A. T. Robertson, *Word Pictures in the New Testament, III: The Acts of the Apostles* (Nashville: Broadman Press, 1930), 213.

[54]Polhill, "Acts," *New American Commentary*, 312.

[55]Less than two minutes to deliver orally.

of Athens, the Areopagus,[56] the apostle provides a similar, but more complete, model of how he ministered to those who had no acquaintance with the Scripture or the life and death of Jesus and its meaning for salvation.

Figure 5

Paul gives every indication that he is comfortable in the situation he finds himself in Athens.[57] He had already been addressing the crowds that frequented the marketplace, the Agora (Acts 17:17), and were always willing to listen to (see Figure 5) some new idea (Acts 17:21).[58] Paul's appearance before the Areopagus was probably inevitable since this group of learned scholars was responsible for evaluating new philosophies that

---

[56]Though the term may refer to the hill, called today Mars Hill, it is more likely that Luke is speaking of the council, or at least an informal forum of the council. There are a number of references to the Areopagus in Greek authors. For example, "There is a hill opposite the citadel at Athens, which the Athenians call the hill of Mars, or Areopagus." Hdt. *Hist.* 1.VIII. c.52 (Herodotus [484–ca. 425 B.C.], *Histories*), cited from Millington, *Testimony of the Heathen*, 544; "There is at Athens, a certain hill of Mars, where the gods first sat in judgment concerning blood, where savage Mars, in wrath for the impious nuptials of his daughter, slew Halirrothius, the son of the ruler of the ocean, where from that time there is a most pious and firm judgment for the gods." Eurip. *Electr.* V.1258 (Euripides [ca 480–406 B.C.], *Electra*), cited from Millington, *Testimony of the Heathen*, 544; "Some of the philosophers held resolutely that there were not gods, and Euripides the tragedian signified as much in his writings, though he dared not openly proclaim his opinion for fear of the court of Areopagus." Plut. *De Placit. Philos.* 1.I.c.7 (Plutarch [ca A.D. 46–127], *De Placita Philosophorum*), cited from Millington, *Testimony of the Heathen*, 544; "Are you not afraid lest he shall commence a suit against you in Areopagus." Lucian. *Vit. Auct.* c.7 (Lucian [A.D. 120–180], *Vitarum Auctio*), cited from Millington, *Testimony of the Heathen*, 544; "Dolabella referred the cause to the Areopagites at Athens, as to judges more grave and experienced than ordinary." Aul Gell. 1.XII. c.7 (Aulus Gellius [ca. A.D. 125-180]), cited from Millington, *Testimony of the Heathen*, 544.
[57]J. Daryl Charles, "Engaging the (Neo)Pagan Mind: Paul's Encounter with Athenian Culture as a Model for Cultural Apologetics (Acts 17:16–34)," *Trinity Journal*, 16:1 (Spring 1995): 49.
[58]"Theophrastus describes among the characters of Athens the lover of the marvelous who greets his acquaintance with 'Whence came you? What say you? Have you any fresh news?' and adds 'Truly theirs seems to be a most wearisome mode of life, passing entire days, as they do, in running from shop to shop, from the portico to the forum, with no other business than to promulgate idle tales, by which to afflict the ears of all they meet.'" Theophr. *Charact.* XXIV (Theophrastus [370–ca. 285 B.C.], *Characters*).

might be influencing the Athenian people. It is this council before whom Socrates also appeared and was sentenced to death for introducing to the youth of Athens strange deities (*daimwn*),[59] similar to those here (*xenwn daimoniwn*), Acts 17:18). Luke may even be attempting to draw some parallel between Socrates and Paul.

Unlike Lystra, Paul had less hurry at Athens in giving his proclamation about God, his works, his judgment, and finally his Redeemer. In this defense before the court the apostle attempts to build a bridge of classical literature and beliefs to the theological disclosure of God about whom the Athenians have no knowledge—the unknown God whom they worshiped in ignorance (Acts 17:23).

The address of Paul was well-organized and well-reasoned. First, he treated his audience with respect, even using the same phrase of Socrates in the *Apology*, "Men of Athens,"[60] though we should not understand him to be patronizing them since such was forbidden before the Areopagus.[61] Second, he started with an idea and sources that they could understand and largely agree with, though he invested their terms with fuller meaning from another worldview. Moses, in the creation account of Genesis 1, did much the same by using contemporary Canaanite terminology but investing them with correct theological perspective.[62] Charles rightly understands Paul's method here: "it wraps universal truth in the language and idiom of the day, culminating in a uniquely Christian expression of biblical revelation, and inviting the listeners to a higher metaphysical ground."[63]

What we need to understand about the Pauline strategy and methodology is that he took them from the known to the unknown, from the partly correct thinking they possessed to thinking that was enlightened by the Scripture, even though he never quoted it. He never belittled the Athenians, though verse 16 tells us he was deeply troubled[64] by the town full of idols,[65] saying that he recognized that they were very religious (*not* superstitious).[66]

---

[59]Plato, *Apology*, 24.11.1.

[60]Ὁ τι μεν ὑμεῖς, ὦ ἄνδρες Ἀθῆαῖοι. Plato, Apology, I.1.

[61]Keener, *IVP Bible Background Commentary*, 373: "It was customary to begin a speech by complimenting the hearers in the opening *exordium*, designed to secure their favor. This practice seems to have been forbidden at the Areopagus, but this would not prevent Paul from starting on a respectful note."

[62]For examples of this practice in the Old Testament, see Gerhard Hasel, "The Polemic Nature of the Genesis Cosmology," *Evangelical Quarterly*, 46:2 (April–June 1974): 89–90.

[63]Charles, "Engaging the (Neo)Pagan Mind," 55.

[64]Vincent translates the term as "provoked," which has similar meaning and is better than "stirred," as in NKJV.

[65]Jamieson says, "meaning the city, not the inhabitants. Petronius, a contemporary writer at Nero's court, says satirically that it was easier to find a god at Athens than a man." R. Jamieson, A. R. Fausset, and D. Brown, *A Commentary, Critical and Explanatory, on the Old and New Testaments* (Oak Harbor, WA: Logos Research Systems, 1997).

[66]"Josephus says, 'All men say that the Athenians are the most pious of all the Grecians.' Pausanias bears similar testimony, 'All the Athenians exceed all in their diligence about the gods.' This character is con-

Paul was very much in line with Peter's admonition to give a defense for the hope within him with gentleness and fear (1 Pet. 3:15).

The two dominant themes Paul sought to convey were creation and redemption.[67] As Charles has said, "Paul verifies the claims of divine revelation by introducing the notion of *creatio ex nihilo* and bodily resurrection, the core of the Christian *kerygma*. Both concepts, inextricably related, are untenable to the Hellenistic mindset, due to contemporary views of the universe, the body, and the soul."[68] Moreover, though he spoke in Greek philosophical terms, he was weaving together Old Testament theology.[69]

Figure 6

In this talk presuppositionalists, evidentialists, and classical apologists all have material to consider, learn, and emulate. Charles says, "To the extent that the Athenians—and the men of the Areopagus—have no

---

firmed also by many other historians." Millington, *Testimony of the Heathen*, 542; "This city [Athens] goes beyond all in worshipping and reverencing the gods." Soph. *Oepid. Colon.* V.1006 (Sophocles [495–406 B.C.], *Oedipus Coloneus*).
[67]Alister E. McGrath, "Apologetics to the Greeks," 260–261.
[68]Charles, "Engaging the (Neo)Pagan Mind," 54.
[69]See Hilary LeCornu, with Joseph Shulam, *A Commentary on the Jewish Roots of Acts, II: Acts 16–28* (Jerusalem: Netivyah Bible Instruction Ministry, 2003), 962–973; see the chart at Clinton E. Arnold, gen. ed., *Zondervan Illustrated Bible Backgrounds Commentary, John–Acts* (Grand Rapids, MI: Zondervan, 2002), 391. Polhill gives sources that support both an Old Testament and Greek philosophy basis for Paul's speech. Polhill, "Acts," 369.

Christological understanding, Paul's discourse on creation and the cosmos serves as a necessary 'pedagogical-missionary preamble,'"[70] using the words of Veilhauer.[71] In agreement with presuppositionalists, Paul accepts the innate knowledge of God the Creator and human moral accountability. The Greeks did not know the identity of the one who had truly created everything and who held them responsible, but Paul was giving this information to them in connecting the unknown god[72] that they worshiped (see Figure 6) with the true God of whom they had distorted knowledge and thus worshiped in ignorance.[73] The examples that Paul used to develop his theology of God (namely, that God does not need temples or service,[74] vv. 24–25, his immanence, v. 28, and his immateriality, v. 29[75]) were shared

---

[70]Charles, "Engaging the (Neo)Pagan Mind," 56.

[71]P. Vielhauer, "Zum 'Paulinismus' der Apostelgeschichte," in *Aufsätze zum Neuen Testament* (Munich: Kaiser, 1956), 13, quoted in ibid.

[72]There is both literary and archaeological evidence for "unknown gods" in the ancient world, but as of yet no statute to "an unknown god." Paul may have altered the inscriptions for his purposes, or there may have been an altar with just the singular. No one is quite sure how to understand the text here in light of the scanty evidence. See the literature that mentions these sources: "Let us adore the Unknown at Athens, stretching forth our hands towards heaven." Lucian, *Philop*. c. 29 (Lucian [A.D. 120–180], *Philopseudes*). The reason for these statutes is recounted from a story about a plague in Athens that gave rise to the altars: "Various are the opinions as to the origin of this inscription. Diogenes Laertius gives the following account of it.

> When the Athenians were afflicted by a plague, and the priestesses at Delphi enjoined them to purify their city, Epimenides took some black sheep and some white ones and led them to the Areopagus, and from thence he let them go wherever they chose, having ordered the attendants to follow them, and wherever any one of them lay down, they were to sacrifice them to the god who was the patron of the spot, and so the evil was stayed. Owing to this one may even now find in the different boroughs of the Athenians altars without names, which are a sort of memorial of the propitiation of the gods that took place.

Diog. Laert. *Epimen. Vit.* (Diogenes Laetius [third century B.C.], *Epimenides Vitae*, from *De Vita Moribus Philosophorum* (*Lives and Opinions of Eminent Philosophers*)." For Greek Text, see ΕΠΙΜΕΝΙΔΗΣ at http://www.mikrosapoplous.gr/dl/d101.html#epimenides.

[73]Paul's use of "ignorance" twice in the passage (vv. 23, 30) may be a statement of irony that the intellectually famed Athens was ignorant of God.

[74]"The Deity, if he be truly deity, lacks nothing." Eurip. *Herc.fur.* v.1345. "After the Magus who directs the sacrifice has divided the flesh, each goes away with his share, without setting apart any portion for the gods; for the god they say, requires the soul of the victim and nothing more." Strab. 1.XV.c.3. "God is absolutely exempt from wants; and the virtuous man, in proportion as he reduces his wants, approaches nearer to the divine perfection." Plut. *Comp.Arist. c. Caton.* c.4.

[75]Ancient poems are relevant here:
> "*Let us begin from Jove. Let every mortal raise*
> *His grateful voice to tune Jove's endless praise.*
> *Jove fills the heaven—the earth—the sea—the air:*
> *We feel his spirit moving here, and everywhere.*
> *And we his offspring are.*" Arat. Phaen. *v. 1.*

> "*Most glorious of immortals, Thou many-named,*
> *Always almighty, prime ruler of Nature,*
> *Governing all by law, Jove, hail!*
> *For mortals all, Thee to address is meet;*
> *For we are thy offspring.*" Cleanth. Hymn. in Jov.

"The first generations of men were of a noble spirit; and, if I may so speak, the immediate offspring of the gods." Senec. *Epist.* 90; "You carry a god about with you, wretch, and know nothing of it. Do you suppose I mean some god without you, of gold or silver? It is within yourself you carry him." Epict. 1.II. c.8; "From any obscure corner of the world you may rise to heaven. Rise then, and show yourself worthy of the Deity; a god not made of gold or silver; for of such materials it is indeed impossible to form a likeness of God." Senec. *Epist.* 31.

beliefs with the Stoics listening to him,[76] though sharing little with the Epicureans (this may be a similar strategy to that employed by Paul later before the Sadducees and Pharisees in Acts 23:6–9).

Note the words of McGrath: "This episode illustrates the manner in which Paul was able to exploit the situation of his audience, without compromising his integrity."[77] Evidentialists and Classical apologists also can take heart in the passage, for Paul clearly seeks common ground with his hearers and uses logic and evidence to move them toward his major theological point, that since God is Creator and sustainer of all, he then also is the judge of all and has the right to decide who will sit as judge for him. In this case it is Jesus, whom he has raised from the dead.

Now it is true that many scoffed at the mention of the resurrection of Christ,[78] but apart from the grace of God through a special revelation (see Matthew 16:17; John 6:37, 65), all of them would have rejected Paul's message on that day in Athens. Instead, several believed Paul's words (Acts 17:34).

CONCLUSION

One may observe from the example of Paul, and from his theology in Romans 1, that humans are capable of understanding the truth of God because they are created in the image of God. Because of this, humans innately recognize the existence of the true God, but sin within them suppresses and distorts that knowledge. Nonetheless, the common or special grace of God is at work through the proclamation of truth (in creation and redemption) to begin the clarifying work of who God is and what he has done. God has left many and varied witnesses of himself in general revelation and does so in order that humans have no excuse when they reject him. And reject the true God they will, but this is not the end of the story. Both Jesus and the apostle Paul used rational argument and evidences to help overcome the impact of sin on the intellectual, emotional, and volitional aspects of man's nature. To believe that Paul in Acts 14

---

[76]"The mention of these schools is not incidental. Paul would take up some of their thought in his Areopagus speech, particularly that of the Stoics, and thoroughly redirect it in line with the Creator God of the Old Testament." J. B. Polhill, "Acts," 367.

[77]Alister E. McGrath, "Apologetics to the Greeks," 261.

[78]The god Apollo is said to have spoken against the idea of physical resurrection. Bruce says, "The idea of a resurrection of dead men was uncongenial to the minds of most of Paul's hearers. All of them but the Epicureans would no doubt have agreed with him had he spoken of the immortality of the individual soul; but as for resurrection, most of them would endorse the sentiments of the god Apollo, expressed on the occasion when that very court of the Areopagus was founded by the city's patron goddess Athene: 'Once a man dies and the earth drinks up his blood, there is no resurrection.'" Bruce, "The Book of Acts," 363–364.

and 17 was merely preaching empty words that he considered void of any effect would be incredulous, and his sermon in Acts 17 bore spiritual fruit.

In spite of this, no one can actually be born from above unless the heart is opened through the Holy Spirit to reception of the gospel. Unbelievers can understand truth, even quite accurately, about God and Scripture. This, however, concerns only the issue of facts. The interpretation of these facts so that a person will receive Christ comes only to persons as the Spirit of God helps the person properly understand how the facts relate to him (meaning). Apologetics cannot bring a person into the kingdom of God, but such a defense serves to assist a potential convert to receive the God of revelation when the Spirit works. Classical, evidential, and presuppositional apologetics all agree on this point, and they all have validity dependent on whether one is speaking about the use of common grace by the Spirit or special grace by the Spirit. But the main point is that it is God who, through various methods, must clear the mind and change the heart for men and women to be saved.

CHAPTER FIVE

The Character of the Good Apologist: An Appreciation for the Life and Labors of Bob Passantino

E. Calvin Beisner

FASTEN YOUR SEATBELT AND catch your breath. You're embarking on a whirlwind tour of a man who was himself a whirlwind—a man of whom one person wrote after his death at age fifty-four, "Bob's 'processor' ran at twice the clock speed as the rest of ours, and so he accomplished more for the Lord in his time than most of us will if we should make it past 100!"

Bob Passantino was a remarkable apologist. Most people would automatically assume this meant primarily that he was tremendously learned, particularly in philosophical, scientific, historical, and other arguments for the truth of the Christian faith. He was that. I don't remember ever having called Bob with a question about any apologetic issues, no matter how arcane, on which he wasn't already well informed and able to point me to half a dozen good sources. But many other apologists are remarkably learned, too. What distinguished Bob—and I must use his first name, not only because he was my brother-in-law but also because that's how he wanted anyone to refer to him—was that his brilliant intellect, vast learning, strong logic, and uncommon common sense came along with a bundle of other virtues that enabled him to practice apologetics more winsomely than anyone I have ever known.

This is why one person commented shortly after his death, "I have heard influential apologists of our day refer to Bob in passing, as an example to be followed." As another put it, "His life embodied the principle of 1 Peter 3:15–16":

*[S]anctify Christ as Lord in your hearts, always being ready to make a
defense to everyone who asks you to give an account for the hope that is
in you, yet with gentleness and reverence; and keep a good conscience so
that in the thing in which you are slandered, those who revile your good
behavior in Christ will be put to shame.*[1]

Another passage to which Bob and his wife and ministry partner,
Gretchen (my sister, whom I taught everything she knows!), appealed
frequently to describe how apologetic ministry should be done was
2 Timothy 2:24-26:

*The Lord's bond-servant must not be quarrelsome, but be kind to all,
able to teach, patient when wronged, with gentleness correcting those
who are in opposition, if perhaps God may grant them repentance leading to the knowledge of the truth, and they may come to their senses and
escape from the snare of the devil, having been held captive by him to do
his will.*

Bob embodied—and Gretchen embodies—that passage.

The aim of this essay is to sketch, through his personal example as seen
by many who knew him, eleven virtues that made Bob an extraordinary
apologist: intellect, courage, humility, passion, humor, patience, generosity, energy, teamwork, friendship, and love. These are the virtues most
frequently mentioned by those who commented about him on a memorial
page at the Answers in Action web site after his death. I shall draw heavily
from their comments, usually without identifying the authors. I will alert
you from the outset that many times the comments address three or four
or even more of these virtues simultaneously. That is because they were
all tied together in Bob. They were *integrated* because Bob was a man of
integrity.

Come along then and see Bob through the eyes of those who knew
him.

INTELLECT

Bob Passantino was a man of "vast knowledge," "clear thinking," an
"amazing mind," and "tenacity in studying." "His mind was always
active, and every conversation was a wonderful, breathtaking adventure,"
said one. "I was always amazed at Bob's genius," remarked another, "the

---

[1]Unless otherwise indicated, Scripture quotations in this chapter are taken from *The New American
Standard Bible*, copyright © 1960, 1962, 1963, 1968, 1971, 1972, 1973, 1975, 1977, and 1995 by The
Lockman Foundation and are used by permission.

rapidity with which he absorbed information, picked apart arguments, and subjected everything to the critiques of Scripture and logic." "No one came close to his knowledge and clarity," and "He gave me, and countless others, the desire not only to know the truth, but to know how to study and think better," said two others.

No doubt the vast breadth and depth of Bob's knowledge were effects of, in part, something he did a few years after I first met him. My parents, when they gave their permission for Bob to marry Gretchen, worried, "Will Bob" (who had little formal education) "be able to give Gretchen" (who was in graduate school) "the intellectual stimulation she'll need?" Not long after that, Bob, who worked at a blueprint company running a copier, a job that really demanded only about an hour or two of his attention each day, read through the twenty-four volumes of the 1969 edition of *Encyclopedia Britannica* in a summer! Even more amazing, he comprehended and retained what he read.

That was, of course, just the beginning of his reading odyssey. He went on to read thousands of books and articles. "It was Thanksgiving 1982, if my memory serves me correctly," wrote one person. "Bob walked into the kitchen with a handful of books. He said that these books were his reading for the day." He wasn't the only one to observe Bob's appetite for reading. Another wrote, "Bob had stayed up the whole night before, reading ten books to prepare for [a] seminar."

Encounters with Bob in a bookstore were legendary. "Bob would do book reviews for customers walking the aisles. Sometimes he would tell you so much about a book you really didn't need to buy it." I remember many such times firsthand. Bob and Gretchen also made a ministry of taking Christians to good bookstores and giving them tours to acquaint them with the resources available for their growth. There is no telling the great fruit this bore in hundreds of lives.

Bob was, as one writer put it, "someone that I could always go to for help with theological and philosophical problems," but his learning was much broader. He could speak learnedly on astrophysics and subatomic physics, on archaeology and zoology, on economics and criminology and the Marx Brothers. During conversations, "trails led off the beaten path and opened my eyes to aspects I never would have imagined," said one, and when another asked his help on almost any issue, "He would tell me the latest research on the issue, recommend a couple of books, and give me three or more ways of solving the problem." Consequently, another wrote that he never spent "a moment" with Bob in which he "did not learn something."

No wonder one eulogist said Bob wore "the mantle of C. S. Lewis," and another remarked, "He was C. S. Lewis incarnate—only smarter."

Bob in an argument was a spectacle worthy of the Colosseum. "It was never a good idea to get on the other side of an argument from Bob — he was *right*!" "I gave up trying to argue with him," one person wrote; "not only was he a better debater than I, he was right!" One man who later became a professional apologist himself wrote, "I know a lot of apologists. Each one has his own area of expertise and set of strengths. When confronted by a particularly difficult opponent, the practical thing to do is to seek assistance from the appropriate expert. But, like so many others, I quickly learned it was easiest to just call Bob. Bob was the whole package. Not only could he track any opponent to the Christian faith, he was always five steps ahead of them." Another wrote:

> I almost felt sorry for the hapless people who found themselves on the receiving end of Bob's razor-sharp intelligence as he turned their hackneyed arguments to ruins, their protestations to sighs. Nobody got the better of Bob! (He could talk faster than most people could even think!) Many people came to know the truth of God from him, though.

But Bob wasn't just in it for the sake of winning arguments. He was in it because he loved truth and he loved people—and for him those two loves were inextricably tied together since people need truth, especially the Truth that sets them free. "His passion for the simple truth of the gospel and his innate ability to dissect philosophical arguments was absolutely remarkable, and his enthusiasm was contagious." Truly, as one memorializer put it, Bob "taught us not only how to think, but how to live."

COURAGE

Bob and I go back almost as far as he and Gretchen do. When he appeared in a bookstore asking for help in witnessing to Jehovah's Witnesses, she referred him to me. We became a team, studying JW materials, figuring out refutations, going to Kingdom Halls and Watchtower study nights and asking embarrassing questions—loudly!—until the overseers finally took us into side rooms for conversations that would last till the wee hours of the morning. One night an elder got frustrated and stormed out of the room. An hour or so later, the remaining elders and we had moved our conversation to the front porch when we heard the screech of tires on pavement. Around the corner came a Chevy El Camino, and it screeched to a halt in front of us. The angry elder jumped out, leveled a rifle or shotgun at us, and shouted, "Now you get out of here!" We went. We didn't shake the dust off our feet till we'd rounded the corner, where he couldn't see us. We were brave, but not stupid!

"I never heard Bob talk down to anyone, and I never heard him back down either," said a eulogist. Another called him "positively fearless," and still another described him as "a bulldog, but in a friendly, disarming, almost naive way"—a wonderful, not quite oxymoronic description that should challenge any apologist. One friend wrote:

> Experiencing Bob sharing his faith with cultists was amazing. You could tell after about fifteen minutes that they would probably rather be having a root canal than having Bob systematically dismantle their worldview and then share the real Jesus with them. I know they walked away thinking, "Who was that guy?"

HUMILITY

No doubt Bob's courage stemmed partly from his vast knowledge. He knew he wouldn't often encounter an argument against Christianity for which he wasn't ready—and that if he did, he could find answers later through study. But that wasn't all. "He wasn't afraid to look stupid," wrote one friend, because he was also humble. Truth was far more important to him than winning an argument, and if by losing an argument he could learn more truth, he was delighted.

Bob's humility was palpable, and many who wrote about him after his death testified to it. His "breadth and depth of knowledge was truly staggering, surpassed only by the humility and graciousness by which he approached both people and ideas," said one person, and another, "Bob was evidence that knowledge does not necessarily puff up, as love was unmistakably present in his life." Bob "taught me the value of living as a humble servant of God," and he "used his mind and determination to extend the Kingdom of God without having to have a bunch of letters behind his name." He had "a mind like a steel trap, yet he never made those around him feel inferior." "His love for truth and his concern for friends meant that he would not pull any punches. But he would do so in a way that made you feel better about yourself. He was a teacher, and you were the pupil, and yet he would not hesitate to ask your advice, to be your pupil." One person remarked with particularly keen insight and appreciation:

> Of all the great teachers and apologists out there, Bob mirrored Christ the best in exhibiting humility with brains, I believe one of the hardest virtues to achieve. I have been awestruck in the way he truly did treat everyone equally. I know of no one who lived that more than he.

Bob exhibited "tolerance and fairness." He was "a good friend who was not only loyal, honest, and generous in spirit, but an intellectual sparring partner who was so serious about philosophy and theology that he never took himself too seriously." This humility led someone to write as if addressing him:

> I imagine most men of your intellectual prowess learn early that they have the advantage over others and can use that advantage to rise to the top of the socioeconomic food chain. But with all that intellectual power, you at the same time possess the most humble of spirits. You could have used your gifts to make your life luxurious and comfortable, but you chose, along with your soul mate, to be rich toward God instead, laying up treasure in heaven.

"Few people will ever know the true impact Bob had on worldwide apologetics," said one apologist after his death, "since he humbly and freely gave his knowledge away."

PASSION

Humility didn't make Bob a shy, reserved, retreating wallflower—far from it. He exhibited "unrelenting enthusiasm for the gospel and the Christian life."

"I enjoyed his enthusiasm and his good humor, but most of all I was impressed by his passion for the Truth," one person wrote. That passion often meant going in unexpected directions, unpopular even with fellow evangelicals. With his "sincerity and guilelessness, and with his passion for truth," and being "open and more Christlike than many dogmatic types," he applied the same criteria to Christian thinkers that he did to non-Christians. "He had the courage to criticize bad and harmful ideas popular among his own group," a courage shown in *Witch Hunt* (1990), which laid bare the faulty logic and harmful impacts of some sloppy cult and occult apologists' work.

His passion wasn't just for the abstract, though. He was passionate also for persons, first and foremost for Christ. His "enthusiasm for the Lord is contagious," said one, and another wrote, "Every interaction and conversation I had with Bob pointed to the cross." His love for Christ bore fruit in love for others. He "specialized in people and the encouragement of spiritual growth. His only goal in life was to bring each person he had contact with to a realization of the logical truth of Christ." He "infected" others; he "cheered our hearts and made us feel special." He was "not interested in material things. He only wanted to help people find God!"

HUMOR

Passion for ideas makes some people humorless, perhaps for fear that their cherished ideas might be found wanting, or perhaps for fear that their own dignity might be challenged if they were ever proven wrong. Neither was the case for Bob. Everyone who knew him well experienced his humor—usually within minutes of meeting him. People remembered "his smile, his wit, his mind, and his care"—a sign that his humor wasn't at others' expense. There was a "playfulness, and curiosity, about Bob's mind that was downright contagious." He was "so funny, so kind, so humble," one could never feel cowed by him. One friend called him "personable, funny, informed, and loving," and another said, "I always got a kick out of him. I thought he was a humorous person; he made me laugh a lot when around him."

Indeed, as one friend observed, "It was practically a requirement to laugh when Bob was around." Another wrote, "I'll miss his wisdom, his encouragement, his partnership, and especially his humor. There's no one else quite like him." When I read one person's comment that "if reincarnation was true, Bob was a reincarnated Socrates," what first leapt to my mind was not Socrates's brilliance but his keen wit. Bob certainly had that.

Except when grieving over another's pain or loss, Bob radiated almost incessant joy, and this was the deep root of his humor. It was also crucial to his apologetic effectiveness, as Craig Hazen, director of the Christian Apologetics Program at Biola University, noted: "Bob was a brilliant man and a first-rank apologist. To me, though, it was his deep and infectious joy in serving the Lord with his amazing intellectual gifts that will be remembered most. His ministry will have ripple effects for many generations."

PATIENCE

His passion for truth and people coupled with his good humor gave Bob another great apologetic virtue—patience.

> If there was any question, any tough issue, I knew I could send anyone to him, and he would talk with them, would like them, wouldn't burn any bridge, but would be a great example of Jesus Christ. He was always patient when working through any biblical issues. No matter how many times I didn't grasp something, rather than get frustrated or mad or shun me because I wasn't an intellectual equal, he'd just view it as a challenge and try to figure out a way to help me understand through another avenue. There are very few Christian professors or pastors who want to spend the time of day with their audiences, who care, and that's what made Bob special.

Many made such remarks. "One never felt rushed, like you had anything else to do than 'be there' for whatever need was before you." As in the apostle Paul's description of love as "patient and kind" (1 Cor. 13:4), Bob's patience bore fruit in kindness. "Bob's approach to me was with kindness that gave comfort. He was inclusive, which meant I (as a non-scholar in the midst of scholars) wasn't left out."

His patience also led him to do what many teachers and apologists find difficult: *listen* carefully to others. One person said Bob was "a man who could both listen and understand," and another wrote, "Not only did he give brilliant answers, he asked brilliant questions and listened brilliantly." The result was receptivity in others: "He wanted to know what I thought. This stimulated me to think and learn."

GENEROSITY

Passion for truth, passion for people, and patience together make high demands on an apologist. No selfish man can live them out. It takes far too much time, effort, and money to learn and communicate on so many different issues to so many different people in so many different ways. It is not surprising, then, that one of the most frequently recurring themes in comments about Bob after his death is that of his generosity, especially with his time. "Bob had a great passion for getting to know Jesus and sharing it generously with anyone who had honest questions. He gave the most precious things to others that he had—his time, himself, and his beloved Lord Jesus."

Through their years in apologetic ministry, supported primarily by donations, Bob rarely told people of their monetary need—to the extent that if anyone did, it was mainly Gretchen. (*Somebody* had to do it!) Bob was simply too busy ministering to think about it. He was "truly unaffected by money."

"With his intelligence and ability to learn he could have easily gone into a secular career and made a lot of money, but he chose to forsake all worldly wealth for a much higher calling that has now yielded him a much greater reward."

Despite their almost always tight finances, "Bob and Gretchen's house was always open for people to stop by and stay as long as they liked. If it got to be around dinnertime they didn't hesitate asking you to stay and eat with them. You were just part of their family for the evening."

The one thing more people seem to have noticed about Bob than anything else was his willingness to give of that most precious of all commodities—the one with which very few busy scholars seem very generous: *time*. He was "generous with his time and gentle with his tongue." He "always made time for me, even if it was inconvenient." "Bob was seldom too busy to talk to me. We had many long conversations. Whether the subject was apologetics, theology, philosophy, politics, heresy, current events, or child-rearing, Bob was always enthusiastic and insightful as he helped me think through the issues." "One of Bob's crowning characteristics was the time that he so freely gave to people." Bob "would spend all the time needed to reach a soul."

A phrase that recurred often in the comments after Bob's death was "wee hours." It is as if no one could know Bob long without coming to think of him in terms of "wee hours." One writer remembered "talking into the wee hours of the morning. Nobody else on the planet could keep me awake at 3 in the afternoon, let alone until 3 in the morning, talking about purgatory. Bob could." Another person commented: "I recall him staying well past midnight to answer various theological, philosophical, biblical—you name it—questions . . . with such passion and zeal and with true love for the Lord." That writer wasn't the only one who remembered Bob that way. Another wrote, "I never went home from Bob and Gretchen's house before midnight (and even then, I had to tear myself away)," and still another, "Bob would stay up until 3 or 4 A.M. with me when everyone else had left, to talk about anything and everything."

His focus on people made Bob generous with his time. "As long as I had the time, Bob had the time." He recognized their needs and accommodated them. "Bob always made time for me to thoroughly answer my questions and to encourage me in my own ministry." He was "always willing to take the time to sit down one on one and answer any question (no matter how simple or foolish)."

For years, Bob and Gretchen hosted the Mars Hill Club for apologetic lectures and discussions. The schedule generally called for it to end about 8:30 or 9 P.M., but the end was really the beginning:

"Mars Hill was great, and the very best part was the fact that after the class was over you took the time and talked with me in the parking lot until 3 A.M., and the only reason we stopped was the fact that a neighbor called the police on us. That is the passion Bob gave to apologetics and to friendship."

"I once imposed on Bob to help me with a question on the phone. I will never forget the time he took with me and his brilliant answer"—a comment that no doubt thousands could have made through the years, like one who wrote, "I'm sure there are countless others like myself who had called Bob on the phone from time to time to have him so generously give of his time, his wisdom, and, of course, his humor." Indeed, Bob on the phone was a phenomenon:

> Armed with a mere back-of-an-envelope and a short-corded phone, I called him thinking I could get a couple of resources for a certain topic in a book I was writing. Needless to say, thirty seconds later I was motioning like crazy to my wife to bring me more to write on—anything—while [Bob] gushed golden suggestions. How generously he helped me, a total stranger to him!

His death left a particular void in the world of telephone apologetics. As one person commented, "I can't imagine not being able to call you or have you call us and have those strange, long, wonderful conversations about everything theological and otherwise." Said another, "I felt almost guilty at how helpful he was, even on the telephone, for I was sure he had a million other things to do that were probably more important. But he always made time to enthusiastically point me to the answer of my question, or where I could find it, as though he had nothing else to do."

ENERGY

This kind of personal ministry required enormous energy, another attribute that many noticed in Bob. One person called him "the most respectable middle-aged man with ADD I've ever met!" He "contained boundless energy, a zest for life, and a genuine love for people that I have never seen duplicated." "Talking a mile a minute, [Bob] shared his bounty of ideas with rapid-fire delivery and a twinkle in his eye." "The first time I met Bob, we talked and debated till the wee hours of the morning. I ended up falling asleep on his living room floor. Bob wore me out"—an observation others shared. One wrote of "his joking way of saying, 'If I can't convince you I'm right, I can at least wear you out!'" Another wrote, "I remember those philosophical conversations that would last all night long. You said, 'If I can't outthink you, I can outlast you.' Bob, you would do both with no problem." All this made Bob infectious: "He talked with me, a complete stranger, with such energy and conviction I thought, I wanna be like this guy."

One writer summed up Bob's energy in describing his first encounter with Bob in a bookstore:

> I heard a man running intellectual circles around another, so I whispered to the book store attendant, "Who is that?" He replied, "Bob Passantino. You should introduce yourself." So I did. An hour later I walked out to my car eyes wide-open! I scratched my head in awe that such a man existed. What shocked me even more was that Bob cared enough about our conversation that he continued calling. Always inquiring, probing, and leaving me with more mental food than I could chew on and digest, Bob was a pleasure to talk with, and I will remember him as the man who chased truth and combated lies!

TEAMWORK

No one could have done alone what Bob did. That is why so many people came to think of Bob and Gretchen as a package deal. The first name didn't roll off the tongue without the second as an automatic follow-up.

"What I admired so much was how Bob and Gretchen were such partners and friends," one wrote. "They had the ideal working relationship, complete with finishing each other's sentences (when Gretchen could get a word in edgewise) and joking around as well as working on their jointly written articles." Another wrote, "I don't think a moment passed when they both didn't laugh out loud, disagree with each other momentarily, or quickly answer a tough question."

Their energy, intensity, passion, and intellectual rigor could have resulted in their being obnoxious. Not Bob and Gretchen. "*Gracious* is a word that hangs in the air when speaking of them." "You and Gretchen were some of the few people I really trusted. You never laughed at my questions, unless I wanted you to, and you were always respectful of differing points of view of Scripture." "They would give their knowledge and wisdom to us without ever making us feel as if we had been talked down to. And that was not because of some false humility on their part. It was that they did not just impart knowledge, but would also lift up and encourage the seeker of it. They helped us discover the truth rather than simply dole it out." They naturally incorporated others into their team, an image some- one else described when he called Bob a "coach for our spiritual journey and also a coach to the other coaches—a mentor like none other."

The generosity many noticed in Bob was equally evident in Bob and Gretchen as a team, as shown by this comment addressed to him after he died:

> You and Gretchen have healed the damaged faith of thousands. You have allowed us to believe with both our minds and our hearts. You have taught us to rejoice in truth and not simply in good feelings. You have made a home with an open door and an open hearth. You have displayed the riches of the Kingdom by sacrificing your own time, energy, and money to causes far larger than yourselves. You have been patient with the young, the foolish, and the naive inside the faith. (We have been all these.) You have been eloquent and compelling with the jaded, the despairing, and the resistant outside the faith. You two have lived out an intimacy that could complete one another's sentences.

FRIENDSHIP

Good coaches, mentors, and teammates tend to build friendships, and many people remember Bob especially as a friend. He was a "wonder- ful human being with a smile as big as his heart." One said, "From the moment I met him it was as if he knew me," and another wrote, "He was so kind to me." "Bob always had a way of making you feel like you'd been friends forever." His friendliness was evident not just in personal encounters but everywhere: "He made a crowded class- room setting seem like an intimate, lively, cheerful chat among good friends." It wasn't just general, it was particular: "He always treated me as though I was the most important person in the room." And it was always spreading: "I referred to your care of my family and close friends when they had questions, and because of your deep compassion, brilliance, and integrity, they became your good friends."

Bob's friendliness displayed itself in respect for others. "After a par- ticularly energetic group discussion, Bob and I continued discussing ways in which a particular point could be made—well past 2 A.M. This brilliant man, knowledgeable to an extent that I will never be, nonetheless treated me as though my words had real value to him." As another put it:

> The breadth of his reading was astonishing, the depth of his understanding was remarkable, and his ability to physically outlast me in our discussions was just incredible! But as knowledgeable and bright as he was, that wasn't the reason I visited as often as I did. It's because *I always felt safe and welcome and cared about in his presence*, and I think most of the other people who spent time with him experienced and were blessed by that same Christian love and compassion.

LOVE

Friendship, as C. S. Lewis discussed it in *The Four Loves*, is a rare and particularly rich form of love, and such "love was the key to [Bob's] life." "He was always there giving people help, advice, humor, etc. But the most I admire about him is his love for people and the Lord." He was "a fun, intelligent, and most of all, loving guy, and an example to the body of Christ to boldly defend and proclaim the Word of God in the face of the world's opposition."

The first of the two "Great Commandments" is to love the Lord our God with all our heart, soul, strength, and mind; the second is to love our neighbors as ourselves. Bob did both. People remarked that he had "a great mind [and] a greater heart and love for the Lord whom he served." One said that he "literally bubbles with the love of the Father all over, through and through, to the hilt and beyond, never ceasing," and another said, "The love of God flowed through every discussion I ever had with him." "He loved and cared for me."

Even more commented on Bob's love for those whom he met from all walks of life. "Bob would fill you up with his love by teaching, by his embrace, by his broad smile, by the hospitality in his heart, by his undeniable commitment to loving Christ." "With Bob, everyone was welcomed. He valued each person, showing them that they were accepted and loved by him and by God. He would spend hours reasoning for truth, with gentleness and respect." From the time I saw Bob, a young father with his sick child in his arms, crying because his daughter Mary was in pain, it was always apparent that he had a special place in his heart for the suffering and the underdog. That is apparent in this comment:

> He spent countless hours on the phone answering questions I had about difficult things. He never thought any question was a bad question. He

never ignored anything I asked. He was so patient in answering every single one. He filled the need I had to be fostered in my intellect. He encouraged me in my mind. I was too young and insecure to think anything good about myself at the time, but Bob was the first person in my life who nurtured my mind. He was the first to cause me to even consider that I was bright during a time when I was suffering.

"He knew so much, yet every time I spoke with him he made me feel like I was the smart one," said another; "I still don't know how he did it." "He had an elite Oxford mind in a blue-collar body. His heart was soft as a lamb's, but his skin was tough as steel wool. No matter the topic, over time I have never heard him be offended by the question. Truth and love lived in Bob comfortably. How refreshing was his laughter!"

People recognized that Bob's generous gifts of time and knowledge were the fruit of his love. He "loved people deeply, and he certainly did share his time generously." "Bob treated people as if he had eternity to spend with them, because he did want to spend eternity with them."

Of particular importance to the apologist is how he thinks of and treats enemies of the faith. "The most important thing I learned [from Bob] was to love those who oppose you," said one person. Bob "always expressed the logic of Christ's message while projecting God's love." He "considered his friends who were not Christians to be at least as important as his Christian friends." He "cared about people who didn't know his Lord and used all his powers to persuade them of the truth of the gospel." To the amazement of those who knew of it, Bob and Gretchen were among the very few people Church of Satan founder Anton LaVey counted as friends—despite, perhaps even because of, the fact that they never concealed their faith in Christ. They saw in him a man deeply hurt by many experiences in his life, and they sought diligently and often through the years to minister to those hurts by the love of Christ.

CONCLUSION

One person wrote of Bob that he was "the most Christian person I ever knew." Such superlatives come easily when thinking of Bob. One called him "the most dynamic person I have ever met or probably will meet." I think I know why: because Bob so embodied the combination of intellect, courage, humility, passion, humor, patience, generosity, energy, teamwork, friendship, and love. Bob was "full of love, passion, and truth. In his search for wisdom, truth, or knowledge he was unrelenting. In his desire to speak to anyone interested in the exploration of the truth he was an instant friend and mentor. He exhibited a love, an openness and respect for others that fundamentally changed my life."

Bob's passing left a great void in today's Christian apologetics. One apologist wrote:

> Even twenty years ago, he had already become twice the apologist I've ever been; by the time of his death, he was a hundred times. But I also was always amazed at Bob's energy—unbounded, jovial, bursting energy that could keep him going fresh and strong right through the night when the rest of us would be gasping for air and pleading for some sleep—and his wonderful love, compassion, patience, and genuine friendliness toward all who came to him with questions, whether they were professors or street persons, Christians or atheists or New Agers or neopagan witches. He made everyone feel important, respected, welcomed. He never gave people reason to think he regretted the hours and hours he invested in them.

In 1980 Bob's path and mine turned different directions in our service for the Lord. But through the ensuing years of our geographic distance, I continued to admire his work, respect his genius, and be grateful for his integrity and devotion to truth—even when the truth meant bursting some popular Christian balloons. We disagreed on some things—I a Calvinist, he a Lutheran; I a classical (not Van Tilian!) presuppositionalist, he an evidentialist—but always I respected his understanding. Like many others, I cringed at the thought of having to argue against him—ever, about anything!

Bob's friend of thirty years and fellow apologist Elliot Miller, editor of the *Christian Research Journal*, expressed well the sense of loss so many of us felt on Bob's graduation:

> Who else gives of his time so freely to anyone and everyone who asks of it? Who else has demonstrated such a lifelong, unswerving dedication to truth and excelling at apologetics? Who else has mastered the fine points of philosophy and logic so well that the atheists who don't run when they see him coming learn a new respect for biblical theists? Who else so makes it his responsibility to understand and answer every new challenge to biblical truth that comes along, whether influential or obscure? To whom else will I go when I'm struggling with an intellectual problem that most do not understand or care to understand, let alone help me find an answer?

During the six months or so before Bob's death, 2 Corinthians 4:7–18 was often on my mind. All who knew Bob will recognize how well the passage fits him:

> But we have this treasure in jars of clay, to show that the surpassing power belongs to God and not to us. We are afflicted in every way, but not crushed; perplexed, but not driven to despair; persecuted, but not forsaken; struck down, but not destroyed; always carrying in the body the death of Jesus, so that the life of Jesus may also be manifested in our bodies. For we who live are always being given over to death for Jesus' sake, so that the life of Jesus also may be manifested in our mortal flesh. So death is at work in us, but life in you.

> Since we have the same spirit of faith according to what has been written, "I believed, and so I spoke," we also believe, and so we also speak, knowing that he who raised the Lord Jesus will raise us also with Jesus and bring us with you into his presence. For it is all for your sake, so that as grace extends to more and more people it may increase thanksgiving, to the glory of God.

> So we do not lose heart. Though our outer nature is wasting away, our inner nature is being renewed day by day. For this slight momentary affliction is preparing for us an eternal weight of glory beyond all comparison, as we look not to the things that are seen but to the things that are unseen. For the things that are seen are transient, but the things that are unseen are eternal. (ESV)

Bob Passantino believed; therefore he spoke. And he spoke, and he spoke, and he spoke. To all who, like me, learned so much from him, there comes now the challenge to follow his example. Believing, we, too, must speak.

PART TWO

Cultural and Theological Issues in Apologetics

CHAPTER SIX

The Essentials of the Christian Faith

Norman L. Geisler

INTRODUCTION

Almost everyone agrees with the ancient dictum, "In essentials unity; in non-essentials, liberty, and in all things, charity." Disagreements emerge when someone asks, what are the essentials? Since the essential doctrines are the basis for our unity, and since true unity is not possible without unity in the truth, it is crucial that we be able to identify the essential truths of the Christian faith. So it is important to historic orthodox Christianity to know precisely what these essential doctrines are.

TWO WAYS TO APPROACH THE QUESTION OF ESSENTIAL DOCTRINES

There have been other attempts to define the fundamentals of the faith. Fundamentalism of the early 1920s came up with similar but overlapping lists that included doctrines like the virgin birth, the deity of Christ, his atoning death, bodily resurrection, and second coming, and the inspiration of Scripture.[1] But clearly this list is incomplete since it does not mention the Trinity, the depravity of mankind, the sinlessness of Christ, his bodily ascension, and salvation by grace through faith—just to mention some other crucial doctrines. Others, looking at the doctrines of the early creeds of Christendom, take a historical approach. But is there any way to do it biblically?

A positive answer emerged several years ago while I was finishing Volume Three (*Sin and Salvation*) of my *Systematic Theology*. By looking at the core truths of the gospel and its doctrinal underpinnings, I was able

---

[1]See Ernest R. Sandeen, *The Roots of Fundamentalism: British and American Millenarianism, 1800–1930* (Grand Rapids, MI: Baker, 1978).

to identify fourteen soteriological doctrines that are necessary for our salvation to be possible.[2]

A THEOLOGICAL LIST OF ESSENTIAL DOCTRINES

The theological approach simply begins with the teachings of the New Testament on salvation and asks what the essential doctrines on salvation are without which salvation would not be possible. It takes the gospel, defined by Paul in 1 Corinthians 15:1–8—which is the power of God unto salvation (Rom. 1:16)—and asks: What biblical truths are necessary to make this possible? In Romans 1–8, Paul, speaking of the gospel (Rom. 1:16), spelled out three aspects of salvation "in it" (1:17).[3] After discussing condemnation (chapters 1–3a), he laid out the gospel in three stages: justification (3b–5), sanctification (6–7), and glorification (8). Justification is defined as salvation from the past penalty of sin; sanctification is salvation from the present power of sin; and glorification is salvation from the future presence of sin. It remains then to identify which doctrines are necessary to make these three stages of salvation possible. The following doctrines seem to fall under these three categories.

1. Justification: Salvation from the Past Penalty of Sin

Eleven doctrines appear to be necessary to make justification possible: 1) human depravity, 2) Christ's virgin birth, 3) Christ's sinlessness, 4) Christ's deity, 5) Christ's humanity, 6) God's unity, 7) God's triunity, 8) the necessity of God's grace, 9) the necessity of faith, 10) Christ's atoning death, and 11) Christ's bodily resurrection. Without all of these, no human being could attain a legal standing before God as righteous. For we are all sinful in and of ourselves (Rom. 1–3a) and can only be declared righteous before God if the Just (Christ) dies for the unjust (humans) so that the just Judge (God) can be just when he justifies the unjust. That is, God's wrath must be satisfied before he can release his mercy and save sinners by declaring them righteous in his eyes (Rom. 3b–5).

2. Sanctification: Salvation from the Present Power of Sin

Two more doctrines are necessary for this second stage of salvation: 12) Christ's bodily ascension and 13) Christ's present high-priestly intercession.

---

[2]A later study of the early Fathers and Creeds led to the same conclusion. See below and the articles we did for *The Christian Research Journal* in 2005 on this topic (Vol. 28, No. 5).

[3]Unless otherwise indicated, Scripture quotations in this chapter are taken from *The Holy Bible: English Standard Version*.

The second stage of salvation is called sanctification. Unlike justification, sanctification is not a positional matter before God; it is a practical matter on earth. It does not, like justification, save us merely from the penalty of sin, but it delivers us from the day-by-day power of sin. To put it in an Old Testament illustration, it took God only a single day to get Israel out of Egypt (justification), but it took him forty years to get Egypt out of Israel (sanctification). Likewise, it takes God only a single instant to justify us, but it takes a lifetime to sanctify us.

Why are these two facts necessary for sanctification? Because Jesus said of his ascension, "It is to your advantage that I go away, for if I do not go away, the Helper [the Holy Spirit] will not come to you; but if I go, I will send him to you" (John 16:7). His ascension to the Father was to present the official completion of his earthly mission of salvation. It also signaled the beginning of his priestly ministry on behalf of our sanctification, for there at the right hand of the Father he ever lives to make intercession for believers (Heb. 7:25). It was by virtue of his blood that he entered heaven on our behalf (Heb. 9:11–12). As the accuser of the brethren (Satan) charges us with our sins before God (Rev. 12:10), Christ our advocate (1 John 2:1) pleads the efficacy of his atoning blood before the Father.

3. Glorification: Salvation from the Future Presence of Sin

Christ's second coming (Doctrine 14) is necessary for the completion of our salvation. Even when Christ ascended, the angels foretold his return saying, "This same Jesus, who was taken up from you into heaven, will come in the same way as you saw him go into heaven" (Acts 1:11). Christ's second coming signals the final defeat of death and sin (1 Cor. 15:24–25). For by it we are delivered from death (Heb. 2:14), pain, and suffering (Rev. 21:4). Paul reminds us that presently "the whole creation [is] groaning . . . wait[ing] eagerly for adoption . . . the redemption of our bodies" (Rom. 8:22–23). Then we will be saved from the very presence of sin. "We shall be like him, because we shall see him as he is" (1 John 3:2). "For now we see in a mirror dimly, but then face to face" (1 Cor. 13:12).

From early times the creeds and confessions of the Christian faith made it clear, as Scripture does, that Christ's second coming and reign will include the separation of the saved from the lost (Matt. 25), the resurrection of the just and unjust (John 5:28–29; Rev. 20:4–6), and the eternal states of heaven (Rev. 21–22) and hell (Rev. 20). The Athanasian Creed, for example, reads: "At whose [Jesus'] coming all men shall rise again with their bodies;

and shall give account of their works. And they that have done good shall go into life everlasting: and they that have done evil, into everlasting fire." Thus, conscious everlasting bliss for the redeemed and conscious everlasting punishment of the unredeemed is part of this fourteenth fundamental of the Christian faith.

What Makes a Doctrine Essential?

There are many important teachings of Scripture (like the prohibitions against blasphemy, idolatry, adultery, and murder) that are not in the list of essential doctrines for salvation. So, what makes a fundamental doctrine fundamental? Judging by the doctrines pronounced essential by the historic Christian church, two basic characteristics emerge. *It must be a doctrine connected to our salvation*; that is, it must be soteriological or salvific in nature. *It must undergird the gospel*, which is essential to salvation (Rom. 1:16). That is to say, salvation as God has revealed it would not be possible without this being true.

This criterion is clearly revealed in most of the essential doctrines. Obviously, the Trinity, the deity of Christ, and his atoning death and bodily resurrection are all necessary for our salvation. Further, as shown above, his ascension, present advocacy, and second coming are necessary for salvation in the broad sense that includes not only justification but also sanctification and glorification. However, there are other doctrines that do not appear to be necessary for our salvation that have made the list.

What about the virgin birth? Was it essential for our salvation? Certainly the underlying doctrine to which the virgin birth points—the sinlessness of Christ—is essential to salvation, for another sinner cannot be the savior of sinners.[4] He would need a savior himself. A drowning person can't save another drowning person. But was the virgin birth necessary for Christ's being sinless? This much seems certain: anyone born the natural way would have been—short of divine intervention—a sinner like the rest of us (Rom. 3:23; 5:12). And the virgin birth was one

---

[4]Precisely how the virgin birth prevented Christ from inheriting Adam's sinful nature is debated among scholars. The exact mechanism remains a mystery—at least to me. Several possibilities have been suggested, but none have gained universal acceptance. Two things seem clear as parameters of a viable explanation. It must have been something that preserved the genetic connection of Christ with Adam (which a virgin birth does through Mary, Christ's natural mother), whose race Christ was representing and saving (cf. Luke 3:38; Rom. 5:12–21; 1 Cor. 15:45; Gal. 4:4). Also, it must be something that does not involve a natural generation of male and female, which is the way we inherit Adam's fallen nature. These parameters would appear to eliminate several explanations that have been offered, namely: 1) that the sin nature is passed on only through the father's genes. But the mother has fallen genes too; and 2) that God directly created a new sinless nature (not genetically connected to Adam) in Mary's womb as opposed to supernaturally fertilizing an ovum of Mary's.

way to circumvent this. Whether it was the only way or whether, say, an immaculate conception of Christ would have worked is both moot and irrelevant. The virgin birth was one way to do it, and it was the way God chose to do it. Anything but a virgin conception would have interrupted the sinless heavenly Father-Son relationship. And only a virgin conception would interrupt the earthly father-son relationship since Adam and prevent the inheritance of a corrupt human nature and eventual death. An immaculate conception of Christ would not have done this. In addition, it was important, if not crucial, to our salvation that God supernaturally signify which of all the persons born of women (Gen. 3:15; Gal. 4:4) was his Son, the Savior of the world.[5] An immaculate conception of Christ would not have been an outward "sign" that drew attention to the Savior's supernatural and sinless nature from the very beginning. Hence, both by the underlying doctrine of Christ's sinlessness and by its nature as a supernatural sign, the virgin birth was a divinely appointed necessity for our salvation.

An Important Distinction

A crucial distinction emerges from the above discussion. The fourteen critical doctrines are essential for *making salvation possible*. However, one does not have to express explicit belief in all of them *in order to be saved*. The complete list of essential Christian doctrines for making salvation possible include: 1) human depravity, 2) Christ's virgin birth, 3) Christ's sinlessness, 4) Christ's deity, 5) Christ's humanity, 6) God's unity, 7) God's triunity, 8) the necessity of God's grace, 9) the necessity of faith, 10) Christ's atoning death, 11) Christ's bodily resurrection, 12) Christ's bodily ascension, 13) Christ's present high-priestly intercession, and 14) Christ's second coming, final judgment (heaven and hell), and reign. All of these are necessary for salvation to be possible in the broad sense, which includes justification, sanctification, and glorification.

However, it is not necessary to *believe* all of these to be saved (justified). The minimum necessary to believe in order to be saved today is:[6] 1) human depravity, 4) Christ's deity, 5) Christ's humanity, 6) God's unity, 8) the necessity of God's grace, 9) the necessity of faith, 10) Christ's aton-

---

[5]See J. G. Machen, *The Virgin Birth of Christ* (New York: Harper & Brothers, 1930).

[6]It would appear that in the Old Testament the content necessary to believe (cf. Gen. 15:6; Heb. 11:6; Jon. 3) was less than in the New Testament (cf. Acts 4:12; 16:31; Rom. 10:9–10). For there is no evidence that every Old Testament believer knew that a person named Jesus who was God would die for his or her sins and rise again (see my *Systematic Theology*, Vol. 3, *Sin and Salvation* [Minneapolis: Bethany House, 2004], 414–416).

ing death, and 11) Christ's bodily resurrection. Of course, the sinlessness of Christ (3) is implied in his virgin birth (2) and at least two persons of the Trinity (7) are implied in God's unity (6) and Christ's deity (4). Some of the fourteen are not necessary to believe at all in order to be saved. For example, it is not necessary to believe in the virgin birth, the bodily ascension, Christ's present intercession, or his second coming and final judgment as a condition for obtaining a right standing with God (justification). Even some of those that are necessary may be more implicit than explicit beliefs (e.g., human depravity and God's triunity.[7]

As far as depravity is concerned, one must believe that he is a sinner in need of a Savior, but not all that the orthodox doctrine of depravity involves (like the inheritance of a sin nature). Likewise, while the deity of Christ is entailed by the view, and this involves two persons who are God, there is no reason to believe that one must understand and explicitly believe for salvation the orthodox doctrine of the personality and deity of the Holy Spirit who is united with the other two persons in one nature. Indeed, many people do not understand this clearly, even years after they are saved.

The entire list of essential doctrines is essential to make salvation possible, but not all are essential to believe in order for one to be saved. All are essential to believe to be a *consistent* Christian, but not all are necessary to believe to become an *authentic* Christian.

A HISTORICAL APPROACH TO ESSENTIAL DOCTRINES

What is of great interest is that these same fourteen essential salvation doctrines appear in the early confessions and creeds of the Christian church. Thus, there is a historical confirmation of theological process by which we have come to the same conclusions.[8]

The Apostles' Creed(s)

I believe [9] in God [6], the Father Almighty, the Creator of heaven and earth, and in Jesus Christ, His only Son, our Lord [4]: Who was conceived of the Holy Spirit [7], born of the Virgin Mary [2, 3], suffered [10] under Pontius Pilate, was crucified, died [5], and was buried. (He descended into hell.) The third day He arose again from the dead [11]. He ascended into heaven [12] and sits at the right hand of God the Father [13] Almighty,

---

[7]Of course, belief in Christ's deity, which is necessary, implies some kind of plurality in God's unity, but it does not in and of itself entail the full doctrine of the Trinity.
[8]F. L. Cross, ed. *The Oxford Dictionary of the Christian Church*, second edition (Oxford, UK: Oxford University Press, 1978), 1070.

whence He shall come to judge the living and the dead [14]. I believe in the Holy Spirit, the holy catholic [universal] church, the communion of saints, the forgiveness [8] of sins [1], the resurrection of the flesh,[9] and life everlasting [14]. Amen."

It is noteworthy that all fourteen salvation doctrines are in this Creed.

The Nicene Creed (A.D. 325)

Likewise, the Nicene Creed contains all fourteen essential salvation doctrines:

We believe [9] in one God [6], the Father, the Almighty, maker of heaven and earth, of all that is, seen and unseen. We believe in one Lord, Jesus Christ, the only Son of God [4], eternally begotten of the Father, God from God, light from light, true God from true God, begotten, not made [4], of one Being [6] with the Father; through him all things were made. For us and for our salvation [10] he came down from heaven, was incarnate of the Holy Spirit [7] and the Virgin Mary [2, 3] and became truly human [5]. For our sake he was crucified [10] under Pontius Pilate; he suffered death and was buried. On the third day he rose again [11] in accordance with the Scriptures [15]; he ascended into heaven [12] and is seated at the right hand of the Father [13]. He will come again in glory to judge the living and the dead, and his kingdom will have no end [14]. We believe in the Holy Spirit, the Lord, the giver of life, who proceeds from the Father [and the Son], who with the Father and the Son is worshiped and glorified [7], who has spoken through the prophets [15]. We believe in one holy catholic and apostolic Church. We acknowledge one baptism for the forgiveness [8] of sins [1]. We look for the resurrection of the dead, and the life of the world to come [14]. Amen.

In addition to the fourteen essential salvation doctrines, the Nicene Creed makes reference to the Scripture (an epistemological fundamental) as the basis for the Creeds.[10]

---

[9]Not until modern times was the word "flesh" gnosticized into "body," a softer word that can more easily be understood in less than a material sense. This is contrary to the whole history of the Creed up to and through the Reformation. More importantly, it is contrary to the New Testament (Luke 24:39; Acts 2:31; cf. 1 John 4:2; 2 John 7). See N. L. Geisler, *The Battle for the Resurrection* (Nashville: Thomas Nelson, 1989, Chap. 6). The neo-orthodox theologian Emil Brunner declared emphatically, "Resurrection of the body, yes: Resurrection of the flesh, no!" See *The Christian Doctrine of Creation and Redemption: Dogmatics*, Vol. 2 (Philadelphia: The Westminster Press, 1952), 372. Many neo-evangelicals followed suit (see George Ladd, *I Believe in the Resurrection of Jesus* [Grand Rapids, MI: Eerdmans, 1976], and Murray Harris, *From Grave to Glory* [Grand Rapids, MI: Zondervan, 1990]).

[10]Various updated translations of this have been adopted by different groups, but the general content remains the same.

The Athanasian Creed (c. A.D. 428)[11]

While most scholars no longer believe that Athanasius authored this Creed, it does reflect his strong emphasis on the deity of Christ. In addition, it is the earliest and strongest explicit creedal statement on the Trinity. It reads as follows:

> Whoever will be saved: before all things it is necessary that he hold the Catholic Faith: Which Faith except every one do keep whole and unde-filed;[12] And the Catholic Faith is this: That we worship one God in trinity, and Trinity in Unity: neither confounding the Persons: nor dividing the Substance [Essence]. For there is one Person of the Father: another of the Son: and another of the Holy Ghost. But the Godhead of the Father, of the Son, and of the Holy Ghost, is all one: the Glory equal, the Majesty coeternal. . . . The Father [is] uncreate[d]: the Son [is] uncreate[d]: and the Holy Ghost [is] uncreate[d]. . . . So the Father is God: the Son is God: and the Holy Spirit is God. . . . So are we forbidden by the Catholic Religion: to say, there be three Gods, or three Lords. The Father is made of none: neither created, nor begotten. The Son is of the Father alone: not made, nor created: but begotten. . . . And in the Trinity none is afore, or after another: none is greater, or less than another. But the whole three Persons are coeternal, and coequal. . . . He therefore that will be saved, must thus think of the Trinity. Furthermore it is necessary to everlasting salvation: that he also believe rightly the Incarnation of our Lord Jesus Christ. For the right Faith is, that we believe and confess: that our Lord Jesus Christ, the Son of God, is God and Man; God, of the Substance [Essence] of the Father; begotten before the worlds: and Man, of the Substance [Essence] of his Mother, born in the world. Perfect God: and perfect Man, of a reasonable soul and human flesh subsisting. Equal to the Father, as touching his Godhead: and inferior to the Father as touching his Manhood. Who although he be God and Man; yet he is not two, but one Christ. One; not by conversion of the Godhead into flesh: but by taking of the Manhood into God. One altogether; not confusion of Substance [Essence]: by unity of Person. . . . Who suffered for our salvation: descended into hell: rose again the third day from the dead. He ascended into heaven, he sitteth on the right hand of the Father God Almighty. From thence he shall come to judge the quick and the dead. At whose coming all men shall rise again with their bodies; And shall give account of their works. And they that have done good shall go into life everlasting: and they that have done evil, into everlasting fire.

---

[11]Philip Schaff claims it "is a clear and precise summary of the doctrinal decisions of the first four ecumenical Councils between 325 and 451 A.D." (See *The Creeds of Christendom*, 1.37). This would place it after A.D. 451.

[12]Anglicans and most Protestant bodies have adopted this Creed, though some have strong reservations about the condemnation to hell of all who reject the Creed in its entirety.

Several things are noteworthy about this Creed. First of all, in addition to affirming essential doctrines of the previous creeds, it emphasizes the Trinity and the incarnation of Christ. Second, it was directed against many heresies. Against Trithesim, it affirms "there are not three Gods: but one God." Against Monophysitism, it asserts that there is no "confusion" or commingling of the two natures. Against the Nestorians, it declares that there is a "unity" of the two natures in one Person. And as opposed to Arianism, the Son is declared "coequal" in "substance" with the Father and was not "made" but "uncreated" and "eternal." As to the alleged logical absurdity that the infinite God cannot become finite Man, it makes it clear that Deity did not become humanity but that the Second Person of the Godhead assumed a human nature in addition to his divine nature. Of course, this eliminates the heresy of Adoptionism that Jesus was merely a man who was adopted into the Godhead as Son. It was not the subtraction of Deity but the addition of humanity. Even Apollinarianism is excluded since it refers to the Son being fully human, a "perfect Man, of a reasonable soul and human flesh subsisting," not partially human.

Finally, this is the first of the creeds to explicitly address the nature of the final judgment after Christ's second coming as everlasting life (heaven) for the saved and everlasting fire (hell) for the lost. Since they are used in parallel and since "everlasting life" entails conscious existence, then so does everlasting fire. The phrase "perish everlastingly" also implies consciousness since in annihilation one would perish instantly, not everlastingly. Thus the creed also pronounces Annihilationism as heretical. And since it implies there will be some people in both places, Universalism is excluded from orthodoxy as well. In short, this is an incredible creed that explicitly anathamatizes more heresies than any other early creed.

The Creed of Chalcedon (A.D. 451)

This Creed was adopted in an ecumenical session. It embraces all the preceding creeds and adds to the unfolding theological essentials. It declares:

> Following, then, the holy fathers, we unite in teaching all men to confess [9] the one and only Son [4], our Lord Jesus Christ. This selfsame one is perfect [3] both in deity [4] and in humanness [5]; this selfsame one is also actually God [4, 6] and actually man [5], with a rational [human] soul and a body [5]. He is of the same reality as God [4] as far as his deity is concerned [7] and of the same reality as we ourselves as far as his humanness [5] is concerned; thus like us in all respects, sin [1] only excepted.

Before time began he was begotten of the Father, in respect of his deity [4], and now in these "last days," for us and on behalf of our salvation [10], this selfsame one was born of Mary the virgin [2], who is God-bearer in respect of his humanness [5]. We also teach that we apprehend this one and only Christ-Son, Lord, only-begotten—in two natures; and we do this without confusing the two natures [4, 5], without transmuting one nature into the other, without dividing them into two separate categories, without contrasting them according to area or function. The distinctiveness of each nature is not nullified by the union. Instead, the "properties" of each nature are conserved and both natures concur in one "person" [4, 5] and in one reality [hypostasis]. They are not divided or cut into two persons, but are together the one and only and only-begotten Word [Logos] of God, the Lord Jesus Christ. Thus have the prophets of old [15; we will examine this fifteenth crucial doctrine later] testified; thus the Lord Jesus Christ himself taught [15] us; thus the Symbol of Fathers [i.e., the Nicene Creed] has handed down to us.

In addition to the other essentials, The Chalcedonian Creed stresses the triune Godhead, the virgin birth of Christ, his humanity and deity, and the hypostatic unity of his two natures in one person, without separation or confusion. Also, the perfection and completion of both natures is emphasized, along with the eternality of the Son, before all time. Besides the accent on the union of the two natures, the creed goes so far as to call Mary the God-bearer (*theotokos*) because the person to whom she gave birth, with regard to his human nature, was also God, with regard to his divine nature.

DISCERNING CRITERIA FOR ORTHODOXY

The above numbering in the brackets in the creeds reveals that all fourteen of the essential salvation doctrines stated above are also found in these early creeds. While most sections of Christianity accept these first three creeds and four councils as a definitive definition of orthodoxy, all do not give the same weight to the creeds. Roman Catholics accept twenty-one church councils as authoritative. The Eastern Orthodox Church accepts only the first seven. Non-Catholics only accept four and point to numerous doctrines pronounced by later councils that are contrary to Scripture.[13] These include worshiping icons, venerating Mary, praying for the dead, purgatory, the necessity of works for salvation, the inspiration of the Apocrypha, the

---

[13]See Norman L. Geisler, "The Historical Development of Roman Catholicism," *The Christian Apologetics Journal*, 4 (Spring 2005): 21–62, published by Southern Evangelical Seminary, Charlotte, NC (www.ses.edu).

worship of the consecrated Communion elements, the bodily assumption of Mary, and the infallibility of the Pope.[14] The Reformed view (following Luther and Calvin) generally accepts only the first four church councils since, beginning with the fifth council, objectionable doctrines begin to emerge. The Anabaptist view, which was part of the radical Reformation, including most Baptist, Congregationalist, charismatic, Mennonite, Free Church, and Independent Churches, comes from this tradition. Early Anabaptists included Balthasar Hubmaier, Jacob Hutter, Hans Denck, and Menno Simons. While many in this tradition had great respect for the Apostles' Creed and were evangelical in their central doctrinal beliefs, they rejected any ecclesiastical authority, holding strongly that the Bible alone has divine authority.[15] This is not to say that they believe there is no value in confessions, nor that the early creeds did not contain essential orthodox doctrine. It is simply to say that only the Bible is infallible and divinely authoritative. To cite Thomas Aquinas, who summed up what many Fathers before him believed, "We believe the successors of the apostles only in so far as they tell us those things which the apostles and prophets have left in their writings" (Aquinas, *On Truth*, 14.10, ad 11).

The Difference between Explicit and Implicit

Not all the essential doctrines in the creeds are stated explicitly. The doctrine of Scripture is one example. While it is everywhere implied as the only infallible basis for Christian belief, it is nowhere treated explicitly. No creed or council ever treated it, but all of them implied it and cited it.

Likewise, the doctrine of human depravity is not explicitly treated in these early creeds, but it is implied in the statements about Christ dying for our "sins" and the need of "remission" of sins and "forgiveness."

It is this distinction between explicit and implicit belief that has led many theologians to speak of *fidei implicitus* (implicit faith). For example, a person who believes in the deity of Christ and the oneness of God is implicitly a Trinitarian, even though he may not believe (because he is yet untaught) in the formal doctrine of the Trinity. It would seem that such a person who believes the gospel (that the Lord Jesus Christ died for their sins and was raised from the dead) can be saved without yet being an explicit Trinitarian.

---

[14]See Norman L. Geisler and Ralph MacKenzie, *Roman Catholics and Evangelicals: Agreements and Differences* (Grand Rapids, MI: Baker, 1995).

[15]This view has been wrongly characterized as *solo Scriptura* by Keith Mathison in *The Shape of Sola Scriptura* (Moscow, ID: Canon Press, 2001). See my review in *The Christian Apologetics Journal* (Spring 2005): 117–129, www.ses.edu.

The Difference between Doctrines Necessary for Salvation and Doctrines Necessary to Believe to Be Saved

Not all soteriological essentials are necessary to explicitly believe in order to be saved. For example, the virgin birth is nowhere stated as part of what is necessary to believe in order to get into heaven. Nonetheless, if Jesus was not actually born of a virgin, then he would have been sinful like the rest of the natural-born sons of Adam (Rom. 5:12f.). And if he was not sinless, then he could not be our Savior from sin. So, as already noted, there is a distinct difference between what must be *true* in order for us to be saved and what must be *believed* in order to be saved.

Likewise, someone could not believe, could even disbelieve, in the second coming of Christ and still be saved. Of course, if there were no second coming, then he cannot be saved in the complete sense of being saved from the very presence of sin someday (glorification).

The Difference between Denial of and Not Believing a Doctrine

There are certain essential doctrines that one may not believe and still be saved. Someone may not believe in the virgin birth, inspiration of Scripture, ascension of Christ, his advocacy before the Father, and his second coming and still be saved. He may not believe them because he does not even know about them. Or he may know them and still not believe they are part of what is needed to believe in order to be saved.

However, there are certain things that one cannot deny today[16] and still be saved. One must believe the gospel—that Christ died for our sins and rose again (1 Cor. 15:1–6). He must believe "in [his] heart that God raised him [Jesus] from the dead" (Rom. 10:9). He must "believe on the *Lord* Jesus Christ" (Acts 16:31, NKJV, emphasis added). Since "Lord" (*kurios*), used of Christ in the New Testament, means deity,[17] then it would follow that one cannot deny the deity of Christ and be saved. Of course, if one was not instructed in the deity of Christ, then it is conceivable that he could not believe it and still be saved. Certainly not all Old Testament saints understood the deity of the Messiah and believed it as

---

[16]We say "today" because in the progress of revelation God has ordained that more content be explicitly believed today (e.g., the "name" of Jesus—Acts 4:12; John 3:18; 3:36; 8:21) than he did in Old Testament times (cf. Gen. 15:5–6; Jon. 3).

[17]That the word "Lord" as used of Jesus in the New Testament means deity is clear from the facts that: It is the common translation of the word *Yahweh* (Lord), which only means God in the Greek Old Testament (the Septuagint). It is the New Testament translation of Old Testament Scripture that refers to *Yahweh* (Matt. 3:3; 22:44). It is used in the context of worshiping Christ (John 20:28; Phil. 2:11), but God alone was worshiped.

a condition for being saved. But if someone knows about Christ's deity and yet denies it, there is no New Testament ground for affirming that he is saved. It is a normatively necessary condition for salvation today (Rom. 10:9; Acts 2:21, 36; 3:14–16; Acts 5:30–32; 10:36; 16:31; 1 Cor. 12:3). One must "believe on the *Lord* Jesus Christ" to be saved (Acts 16:31, NKJV, emphasis added). He must believe in his heart and confess with his mouth "the *Lord* Jesus" to be saved (Rom. 10:9–10, NKJV). This would mean that one who believes that Jesus is Michael, a created angel (as Jehovah's Witnesses do), cannot be saved. Likewise, no Mormon who believes that Jesus is the brother of Lucifer can be saved. This would also mean that any Arian (a follower of the fourth-century Arius) who denies the deity of Christ cannot be saved.[18]

The Difference between Heresy and Salvation

There is a difference between being heretical and being lost. One can be heretical on some doctrines and still be saved. Being saved (justified) is dependent only on believing certain saving truths like the deity, death, and resurrection of Christ for our sins. But one may disbelieve the virgin birth, inspiration of the Bible, the ascension, and the second coming and still be saved. In short, one can be heretical on a number of doctrines and still be saved. Such a person is, of course, unbiblical and inconsistent. But better to be inconsistently saved than consistently lost. Of course, it is better yet to be consistently saved, but that is not the question at hand.

The Difference between Being Heretical on One Doctrine and Heretical on All Doctrines

If a person denies one essential doctrine, does that make him a heretic? It makes him heretical on that particular doctrine he denies, not heretical on everything else. For example, if one denies the inerrancy of the Bible, he can still be saved. Inerrancy, as epistemologically important as it is, is simply not part of the plan of salvation necessary to believe in order to be saved. Likewise, one can deny the virgin birth and still be saved for the same reasons. Being unorthodox on one doctrine does not mean he is not orthodox on other doctrines. Of course, one must be orthodox on certain salvific doctrines mentioned above in order to be saved.

---

[18]Of course, it might be possible that some Arians are not properly informed about the deity of Christ, having only an implicit faith in it, but are still saved. But in this case the proof that they have this implicit faith in the deity of Christ would be that when properly taught from Scripture about it, they place their faith in Christ's deity explicitly (cf. Acts 19:1–6). Even Arius himself appears to have changed his view and accepted the conclusion of the Nicene Creed, which affirms the deity of Christ.

THREE DIFFERENT KINDS OF ESSENTIAL DOCTRINES

One important doctrine absent from the above list of fourteen doctrines necessary for salvation is (15) the inspiration of Scripture. The earliest creeds do not even mention it, and the later creeds do not elaborate on it. The basic reasons for this emerge from the nature of the situation. First, the doctrine was not questioned. It was an accepted fact in the early church that the Scriptures were the basis for the Creeds. Indeed, the early Fathers cited the New Testament over thirty-six thousand times—every verse except eleven![19] Further, the Creeds were formed in response to heretical teaching, and no early teachers in the church questioned the divine authority of the Scriptures.[20] In short, the Creeds were not about Scripture; they were based on Scripture. This becomes clear in later Creeds that do refer to Scripture as their basis.

There are other reasons why different lists of essentials or fundamental doctrines have been proposed. One reason is the failure to distinguish between three different kinds of fundamentals: soteriological, epistemological, and hermeneutical.

A Soteriological Fundamental

Soteriological fundamentals are those having to do with salvation. In short, if these doctrines are not true, then salvation is not possible. This is why these fourteen doctrines are essentials of the faith, as the foregoing discussion shows.

In addition, salvific (saving) fundamentals may be divided into those necessary for justification (e.g., Christ's death and resurrection), those necessary for sanctification (e.g., Christ's ascension, his present session as our advocate), and those necessary for glorification (e.g., his second coming and final judgment).

An Epistemological Fundamental

Conspicuous by its absence from the list of fundamentals is (15) the inspiration of Scripture, which was listed as one of the great fundamentals of the faith by modern conservatives like B. B. Warfield, Charles Hodge, and J. Gresham Machen. The reason for its absence is that we were speaking about soteriological (salvation) fundamentals. One can

---

[19]See Norman L. Geisler and William Nix, *A General Introduction to the Bible* (Chicago: Moody Press, 1968), 431.
[20]See Norman L. Geisler, *Systematic Theology*, Vol. 1, *Introduction and Bible* (Minneapolis: Bethany House, 2003), Chap. 17.

be saved without believing in the inspiration and (consequent) inerrancy of the Bible.[21] An inerrant Scripture is not necessary for salvation. People were saved before there was a Bible, and people are saved through reading errant copies of the Bible. Further, *belief* in inerrancy is not necessary in order to be saved. Inspiration and inerrancy are not a test for evangelical authenticity but for evangelical consistency. Belief in inspiration and inerrancy is not part of the plan of salvation one must believe to be saved. But they are part of the foundation that makes that plan of salvation knowable. In order for us to have a sure foundation for what we believe, God deemed it necessary to provide an inerrant Word as the basis of our beliefs. As Thomas Aquinas put it, "In order that salvation might the easier be brought to man and be more certain, it was necessary that men be instructed concerning divine matters through divine revelation."[22] John Calvin added, "Our faith in doctrine is not established until we have a perfect conviction that God is the author [of Scripture]. Hence, the highest proof of Scripture is uniformly taken from the character of him whose word it is."[23]

Therefore, inspiration is not a soteriological fundamental—it is an epistemological fundamental. Epistemology (Greek, *episteme*) deals with how we know. And without a completely true, divinely authoritative revelation from God, such as we have in the Scriptures, we could never be sure of the doctrines that are necessary for our salvation. Nonetheless, the great ecumenical creeds do mention "the Scriptures" as being the basis for what we believe (see above). So they do give recognition to this epistemological essential of the faith.

A Hermeneutical Fundamental

A third kind of fundamental is presupposed in this whole discussion: a hermeneutical fundamental. All the above fundamental doctrines relating to our salvation are based on (16) a literal, historical-grammatical interpretation of Scripture.[24] Without this there is no orthodoxy. Most cults specialize in denying this literal method in part or in whole. This is how they can so easily twist Scripture to their own heretical advantage.[25] The

---

[21]Inerrancy follows logically from divine inspiration. For if the Bible is the Word of God and God cannot err, then it follows logically that the Bible cannot err in anything it affirms (or denies). See Norman L. Geisler, ed., *Inerrancy* (Grand Rapids, MI: Zondervan, 1979).

[22]See Thomas Aquinas, *Summa Theologica*, 1.1.1.

[23]John Calvin, *Institutes of the Christian Religions*, trans. Henry Beveridge (London: James Clarke, 1953), 1.7.4.

[24]Geisler, *Systematic Theology*, Vol. 4, Chap. 13.

[25]Norman L. Geisler and Ron Rhodes, *Correcting the Cults* (Grand Rapids, MI: Baker, 2005).

whole Protestant doctrine of *sola Scriptura* (the Bible alone) is based on the precondition of a literal interpretation[26] of the Bible.[27] So the literal hermeneutic is the fundamental method that makes all the doctrinal fundamentals possible.

SUMMARY AND CONCLUSION

Knowing which doctrines are essential to the Christian faith is necessary for the preservation of orthodox Christianity, the delineation of heresy, and the identification of cults. It is also necessary for Christian unity, for there is no true unity without unity in the truth. And there is no essential unity without unity in the essentials. And there is no unity in the essentials without knowing what the essentials are.

Both theologically and historically, the essential doctrines of the Christian faith are the pillars that support the gospel. Soteriologically, we have shown there are fourteen of these. But in addition to these, there is one epistemological fundamental (15)—the inspiration and inerrancy of Scripture. This is the source and foundation of all the essential salvation doctrine. In this sense, it is the fundamental of the fundamentals. However, none of these doctrines would be possible were it not for (16) the literal historical-grammatical method of interpretation. This, then, is the hermeneutical fundamental of the faith. Thus, there are sixteen essential doctrines by which to know the orthodox Christian faith, the basis for true unity. It is within this context that the famous adage is applicable: "In essentials, unity; in non-essentials, liberty, and in all things, charity."

WORKS CITED

The Apostles' Creed

Aquinas, Thomas. *On Truth*, 14.10, ad 11.

_____. *Summa Theologica*, 1.1.1.

The Athanasian Creed, c. A.D. 428

Brunner, Emil. *The Christian Doctrine of Creation and Redemption: Dogmatics.* Vol. 2. Philadelphia: The Westminster Press, 1952.

Calvin, John. *Institutes of the Christian Religion.* Trans. Henry Beveridge. London: James Clarke, 1953.

---

[26]Of course, the "literal" method does not mean there can be no figures of speech. It means that the whole Bible is literally true, just as the author meant it, even though not everything in it is true literally. There are parables, metaphors, and many figures of speech in the Bible, all of which convey a literal truth.
[27]See the articles and reviews in the *Christian Apologetics Journal* (Spring 2005), www.ses.edu.

The Creed of Chalcedon, A.D. *451*

Cross, F. L., ed. *The Oxford Dictionary of the Christian Church*, second edition. Oxford, UK: Oxford University Press, 1978.

Geisler, Norman L. *The Battle for the Resurrection*. Nashville: Thomas Nelson, 1989.

_____. *Inerrancy*. Grand Rapids, MI: Zondervan, 1979.

_____. "The Historical Development of Roman Catholicism." *The Christian Apologetics Journal*, 4.1. (2005): 21–62.

_____. "A Critical Review of *The Shape of Sola Scriptura* by Keith Mathison." *Christian Apologetics Journal*, 4.1 (Spring 2005): 117–120.

_____. *Systematic Theology*. Vol. 1, *Introduction and Bible*. Minneapolis: Bethany House, 2002.

_____. *Systematic Theology*. Vol. 3, *Sin and Salvation*. Minneapolis: Bethany House, 2004.

Geisler, Norman L. and Ralph MacKenzie. *Roman Catholics and Evangelicals: Agreements and Differences*. Grand Rapids, MI: Baker, 1995.

Geisler, Norman L. and William Nix. *A General Introduction to the Bible*. Chicago: Moody Press, 1968.

Geisler, Norman L. and Ron Rhodes. *Correcting the Cults*. Grand Rapids, MI: Baker, 2005.

Harris, Murray. *From Grave to Glory*. Grand Rapids, MI: Zondervan, 1990.

Ladd, George. *I Believe in the Resurrection of Jesus*. Grand Rapids, MI: Eerdmans, 1976.

Machen, J. G. *The Virgin Birth of Christ*. New York: Harper & Brothers, 1930.

Mathison, Keith. *The Shape of Sola Scriptura*. Moscow, ID: Canon Press, 2001.

The Nicene Creed, A. D. *325.*

Sandeen, Ernest R. *The Roots of Fundamentalism: British and American Millenarianism, 1800–1930*. Chicago: University of Chicago Press, 1970. Reprint, Grand Rapids, MI: Baker, 1978.

Sandeen, Ernest R. *The Origins of Fundamentalism: Toward a Historical Interpretation*. Minneapolis: Fortress Press, 1968.

Schaff, Philip, ed. *The Creeds of Christendom*, Vol. 1. sixth revised edition. New York: Harper, 1919.

CHAPTER SEVEN

Postmodernism and Truth

J. P. Moreland

PERHAPS ONE OF THE MOST important topics in our day is truth. Indeed, the nature and knowledge of truth are foundational to the way people think about and live their lives. Historically, the classic correspondence theory of truth has been the prominent view, and it has outlived most of its critics. But, so we are often told, these are postmodern times; the classic model—once entrenched in the western mind-set—must now be replaced by some form of neo-pragmatism or some other anti-realist model of truth. That is, it must be replaced if one is concerned about the rampant victimization reflected all around us. Thus, the phrase "we hold these truths to be self-evident" now reads "our socially constructed selves arbitrarily agree that certain chunks of language are to be esteemed in our linguistic community." Something is radically amiss here!

From a careful read of the previous paragraph, it is no doubt obvious that I am an unrepentant advocate of the correspondence view of truth and have a certain disdain for the various anti-realist views. My aim in this essay is twofold: 1) to sketch out the correspondence theory and the postmodern rejection of it; and 2) to identify five confusions of which I believe postmodernists are guilty. I then conclude by warning that not only are postmodern views of truth and knowledge confused, but that postmodernism is an immoral position and that people who love truth and knowledge—especially disciples of the Lord Jesus—should do everything possible to stop the plague of postmodernism.

THE CORRESPONDENCE THEORY OF TRUTH

In its simplest form, the correspondence theory of truth is the view that a claim—technically, a proposition—is true just in case it corresponds to reality; that is, a proposition is true when what it asserts to be the case is the case. In order to get clearer on the meaning of the correspondence view of truth, some technical language is necessary. Put generally, *truth obtains when a truth-bearer stands in an appropriate correspondence relation to a truth-maker.*

Some clarifications are in order. First, what is a truth-bearer? A truth-bearer—the thing that is either true or false—is not a sentence, statement, or other piece of language but a *proposition.* A proposition is, minimally, the content of a sentence. For example, "Snow is white" and "*Schnee ist weiss*" are two different sentences that express the same proposition. A sentence, on the other hand, is a linguistic object consisting in a sense-perceptible string of markings formed according to a culturally arbitrary set of syntactical rules, a grammatically well-formed string of spoken or written scratchings/sounds. Sentences are true in case they express a true proposition or content. We will return to the topic of propositions later.

Second, what about truth-makers? What is it that makes a proposition true? The best answer to this question is *facts.* A fact is something (technically, it is a "state of affairs") that obtains in the world. For example, the grass's being green, an electron's having a negative charge, or God's being all-loving are all facts.[1] Consider, then, the proposition that *grass is green.* This proposition is true just in case a specific fact, namely, grass's being green, actually obtains in the real world. If Sally has the thought that *grass is green*, the specific state of affairs (grass actually being green) "makes" the propositional content of her thought true just in case the state of affairs actually is the way the proposition represents it to be. The grass's being green makes Sally's thought true even if Sally is blind and cannot tell whether or not it is true and even if Sally does not believe the thought. In other words, reality makes thoughts true or false. A thought is not made true by someone believing it or by someone being able to determine whether or not it is true. Put differently, evidence allows one to tell whether or not a thought is true, but the relevant fact is what makes it true. It goes without saying that "makes" in "a fact makes a proposition true" is not causal but rather is a substitution instance of "in virtue of"—the proposition is true in virtue of the fact.

Our study of truth-bearers has already taken us into the topic of the correspondence relation. Correspondence is a two-placed relation between

---

[1]For present purposes, this identification of the truth-maker will do, but the account would need to be filled out to incorporate future states of affairs that will obtain or counterfactual states of affairs that would have obtained given such and such.

a proposition and a relevant fact that is its intentional object. A two-placed relation, such as "larger than," is one that requires two things (say, a desk and a book) before it holds. Similarly, the truth relation of correspondence holds between two things—a relevant fact and a proposition—just in case the fact matches, conforms to, corresponds with the proposition.

Why Believe the Correspondence Theory?

Why should one accept the correspondence theory of truth? A number of reasons could be offered, but perhaps the simplest one is an argument called the descriptive argument. The descriptive argument places careful attention on the description and presentation of a specific example of one's coming to experience truth in order to see what can be learned about truth itself. As an example, consider the case of Judy and Al. While at home, Judy receives a call from a local car dealership that the vehicle she recently ordered—a Mazda MX-5 Miata—has arrived and is ready to go. At this point, a new mental state occurs in Judy's mind—the thought that her Mazda MX-5 Miata is in the dealership parking lot.

Judy, being aware of the content of the thought, becomes aware of two things that are closely related to it: the nature of the thought's intentional object (her Mazda MX-5 Miata being in the dealership parking lot) and certain ways of determining the truth of the thought. For example, she knows that it would not be relevant for verifying the thought to visit the local coffee shop and order a latte. Rather, she knows that she must take a series of steps that will get her to the appropriate dealership and look for a particular salesman in order to confirm the vehicle's arrival.

So Judy heads out for the dealership being guided by the proposition that *the Mazda MX-5 Miata is in the dealership parking lot.* On the way, suppose her friend Al joins her, though Judy does not tell Al where she is going or why. They arrive at the dealership, and they both see the Miata. At that moment Judy and Al simultaneously have a certain sensory experience of seeing the Mazda MX-5 Miata. But Judy has a second experience that Al does not: Judy experiences that her thought matches, or corresponds with, an actual state of affairs. She is able to compare her thought with its intentional object and "see," or be directly aware of, the truth of the thought. In this case Judy actually experiences the correspondence relation itself, and truth itself becomes an object of her awareness. In this case, "truth" is ostensively defined by this relation that Judy experiences.

POSTMODERNISM AND TRUTH

It is difficult to define or even characterize postmodernism, given its loose alliance of diverse thinkers from the various academic disciplines. Nonetheless, it is possible to provide a fairly accurate characterization of postmodernism in general since its friends and foes understand it well enough to offer debate on its strengths and weaknesses.[2]

As a philosophical position, postmodernism is primarily a reinterpretation of what knowledge is and what counts as knowledge. More broadly, it represents a form of cultural relativism about such things as reality, truth, reason, value, meaning, the self, and other notions. On a postmodernist view, there is no such thing as objective reality, truth, value, reason, and so on. All these are social constructions, creations of linguistic practices, and as such are relative not to individuals but to social groups that share a common narrative.

Postmodernism denies the correspondence theory, claiming that truth is simply a contingent creation of language that expresses customs, emotions, and values embedded in a community's linguistic practices. For the postmodernist, if one claims to have the truth in the correspondence sense, this assertion is a power move that victimizes those judged not to have the truth.

Five Confusions That Plague Postmodernism

According to Brian McLaren, making absolute truth claims becomes problematic in the postmodern context. Says McLaren, "I think that most Christians grossly misunderstand the philosophical baggage associated with terms like *absolute* or *objective* (linked to foundationalism and the myth of neutrality). . . . Similarly, arguments that pit absolutism versus relativism, and objectivism versus subjectivism, prove meaningless or absurd to postmodern people. . . ."[3] McLaren not only correctly identifies some central postmodern confusions, but his statement indicates he exhibits some of the confusions himself. Let's try to unpack some of the philosophical baggage to which McLaren refers and bring some clarity to the confusion.

---

[2]For a helpful introduction to postmodernism, see Joseph Natoli, *A Primer to Postmodernity* (Oxford, UK: Blackwell, 1997). See also, J. P. Moreland and William Lane Craig, *Philosophical Foundations for a Christian Worldview* (Downers Grove, IL: InterVarsity Press, 2003), Chap. 6; Garrett DeWeese and J. P. Moreland, "The Premature Report of Foundationalism's Demise," in *Reclaiming the Center: Evangelical Accommodation in a Post-Theological Era*, ed. Justin Taylor, Millard Erickson, and Paul Kjoss Helseth (Wheaton, IL: Crossway, Books, 2005), 81–105.

[3]Brian McLaren, "Emergent Evangelism," *Christianity Today* (November 2004), 42–43.

#1: Misunderstandings about the Nature of Absolute Truth

The first postmodern confusion involves misunderstandings about the nature of absolute truth. In a metaphysical (and correct) sense, absolute truth is the same thing as objective truth. On this view, people discover truth, they do not create it, and a claim is made true or false in some way or another by reality itself, totally independently of whether the claim is accepted by anyone. Moreover, an absolute truth conforms to the three fundamental laws of logic (i.e., identity, excluded middle, and noncontradiction), which are themselves absolute truths. Furthermore, a commitment to the absolute truth of some particular proposition entails no particular thesis about how one came to know that proposition.

By contrast with the metaphysical notion, postmodernists claim that a commitment to absolute truth is rooted in what's called "Cartesian anxiety" (from René Descartes's method of doubting everything in his search for undeniable or "indubitable" truth) and its need for absolute certainty. What this amounts to is the view that if one accepts the absolute truth of a certain claim, then it follows that one is also accepting the view that one can be undeniably certain about the claim. However, since there is very little that one can be *undeniably* certain about, this creates a kind of epistemological anxiety. Thus, one postmodernist recently opined that commitment to objective truth and the correspondence theory is merely "an epistemic project [that] is funded by 'Cartesian anxiety,' a product of methodological doubt. . . ."[4]

As I have already pointed out, this claim is entirely false philosophically. Advocates of a correspondence theory of objective truth take the view to be a realist metaphysical thesis, and they steadfastly reject all attempts to epistemologize the view. Moreover, historically it is incredible to assert that the great western thinkers from Aristotle to Descartes—correspondence advocates all—had any concern whatever about any sort of Cartesian anxiety. The great correspondence advocate Aristotle was hardly in a Cartesian quandary when he wisely pointed out that in the search for truth, one ought not expect a greater degree of epistemic strength than is appropriate to the subject matter, a degree of strength that varies from topic to topic. The correspondence theory was not born when Descartes got up from his armchair, and postmodernists lose credibility when they pretend otherwise.

---

[4] Philip Kennison, "There's No Such Thing As Objective Truth, and It's a Good Thing, Too," in *Christian Apologetics in the Postmodern World*, ed. Timothy Philips and Dennis Okholm (Downers Grove, IL: InterVarsity Press, 1995), 157.

#2: Two Confusions about Knowledge and Objectivity

Postmodernists also reject the notion that rationality is objective on the grounds that no one approaches life in a totally objective way without bias. Thus, objectivity is impossible, and observations, beliefs, and entire narratives are theory-laden. There is no neutral standpoint from which to approach the world. Therefore, observations, beliefs, and so forth are perspectival constructions that reflect the viewpoint implicit in one's own web of beliefs. For example, Stanley Grenz claims that postmodernism rejects the alleged modernist view of reason that ". . . entails a claim to dispassionate knowledge, a person's ability to view reality not as a conditioned participant but as an unconditioned observer—to peer at the world from a vantage point outside the flux of history."[5]

Regarding knowledge, postmodernists believe that there is no point of view from which one can define knowledge itself without begging the question in favor of one's own view. "Knowledge" is a construction of one's social, linguistic structures, not a justified, truthful representation of reality by one's mental states. For example, knowledge amounts to what is deemed to be appropriate according to the professional certification practices of various professional associations. As such, knowledge is a construction that expresses the social, linguistic structures of those associations, nothing more, nothing less.

These postmodernist claims represent some very deep confusions about the notion of objectivity. As a first step toward clearing away this confusion, we need to draw a distinction between psychological and rational objectivity. It is clear from the quote above that Grenz's confused understanding of objectivity is at least partly rooted in his mistaken conflation of these two senses. *Psychological objectivity* is detachment, the absence of bias, a lack of commitment either way on a topic.

Do people ever have psychological objectivity? Yes, they do, typically in areas in which they have no interest or about which they know little or nothing. Note carefully two things about psychological objectivity. For one thing, it is not necessarily a virtue. It is if one has not thought deeply about an issue and has no convictions regarding it. But as one develops thoughtful, intelligent convictions about a topic, it would be wrong to remain "unbiased"—that is, uncommitted regarding it. Otherwise, what role would study and evidence play in the development of one's approach to life? Should one remain "unbiased" that cancer is a disease, that rape is

---

[5]Stanley Grenz, *Revisioning Evangelical Theology* (Downers Grove, IL: InterVarsity Press, 1993), 15.

wrong, that the New Testament was written in the first century, that there is design in the universe, if one has discovered good reasons for each belief? No, one should not.

For another thing, while it is possible to be psychologically objective in some cases, most people are not psychologically objective regarding the vast majority of the things they believe. In these cases, it is crucial to observe that a lack of psychological objectivity does not matter, nor does it cut one off from knowing or seeing the world directly the way it is or from presenting and arguing for one's convictions. Why? *Because a lack of psychological objectivity does not imply a lack of rational objectivity, and it is the latter that matters most, not the former.*

To understand this, we need to get clear on the notion of rational objectivity. *Rational objectivity* is the state of having accurate epistemic access to the thing itself (e.g., having accurate knowledge of a thing). This entails that if one has rational objectivity regarding some topic, then one can discern the difference between genuinely good and bad reasons/evidence for a belief about that topic and one can hold the belief for genuinely good reasons/evidence. The important thing here is that bias does not stand between a knowing subject and an intentional object, nor does it eliminate a person's ability to assess the reasons for something. Bias may make it more difficult, but not impossible. If bias made rational objectivity impossible, then no teacher—including the postmodernist herself—could responsibly teach any view the teacher believed on any subject! Nor could she teach opposing viewpoints because she would be biased against them!

We will return below to the topic of cognitive access to the objects of consciousness, but for now I simply note that Grenz exhibits the twin confusions, so common among postmodernists, of failing to assess properly the nature and value of psychological objectivity and of failing to distinguish and properly assess the relationship between psychological and rational objectivity.

#3: Confusions between Classical Foundationalism and Foundationalism Per Se

To put it simply, foundationalism is the view in epistemology that knowledge and belief rest on the foundation of basic beliefs. Postmodernists reject foundationalism as a theory of epistemic justification. For example, as they assert "the demise of foundationalism," Stanley Grenz and John Franke observe with irony, "How infirm the foundation."[6] Rodney Clapp claims

---

[6]Stanley J. Grenz and John R. Franke, *Beyond Foundationalism: Shaping Theology in a Postmodern Context* (Louisville: Westminster John Knox Press, 2001), 38. Grenz and Franke use the phrase "the demise of foundationalism" ten times in the first fifty-four pages (Part I) of the book.

that foundationalism has been in "dire straits" for some time, avowing that "few if any careful thinkers actually rely on foundationalist thinking," even though they cling like addicted smokers to "foundationalist rhetoric." Says Clapp, evangelicals "should be nonfoundationalists exactly because we are evangelicals."[7] Nancey Murphy is concerned to justify a "postmodern" theological method in the face of "a general skeptical reaction to the demise of foundationalism in epistemology."[8]

A major reason for this rejection is the idea that foundationalism represents a quest for epistemic certainty, and it is this desire to have certainty that provides the intellectual impetus for foundationalism. This so-called Cartesian anxiety is alleged to be the root of foundationalist theories of epistemic justification. But, the argument continues, there is no such certainty, and the quest for it is an impossible one. Further, that quest is misguided because people do not need certainty to live their lives well. Sometimes Christian postmodernists support this claim by asserting that the quest for certainty is at odds with biblical teaching about faith, the sinfulness of our intellectual and sensory faculties, and the impossibility of grasping an infinite God.

Unfortunately, this depiction of the intellectual motives for foundationalism represents a confusion between foundationalism per se and an especially extreme Cartesian form of foundationalism, with the result that versions of modest foundationalism are simply not taken into consideration. To see this, note that *foundationalism* refers to a family of theories about what kinds of grounds constitute justification for belief, all of which hold the following theses:

(1) A proper noetic (i.e., mental or intellectual) structure is *foundational*, composed of properly basic beliefs and non-basic beliefs, where non-basic beliefs are based either directly or indirectly on properly basic beliefs, and properly basic beliefs are non-doxastically grounded, that is, not based entirely on other beliefs.

(2) The basing relation that confers justification is irreflexive and asymmetrical.

(3) A properly basic belief is a belief that meets some Condition C, where the choice of C marks different versions of foundationalism.

Classical foundationalism, of which the Cartesian project is the para-

---

[7]Rodney Clapp, "How Firm a Foundation: Can Evangelicals Be Nonfoundationalists?" in *Border Crossings: Christian Trespasses on Popular Culture and Public Affairs* (Grand Rapids, MI: Brazos, 2000), 19–32.
[8]Nancey Murphy, *Anglo-American Postmodernity: Philosophical Perspectives on Science, Religion, and Ethics* (Boulder, CO: Westview, 1997), 131–132.

digm example, holds that Condition C is indubitability (or some relevantly similar surrogate): the ground of the belief must guarantee the truth of the belief. It is recognized in nearly all quarters that classical foundationalism is too ambitious. Even granting, as I certainly would, that there are some indubitable beliefs, there simply aren't enough of them to ground our entire noetic structure. Further, it clearly seems that certain beliefs that are not indubitable may legitimately be held as properly basic—for example, beliefs grounded in perception, memory, or testimony. And more: classical foundationalism is motivated largely by the belief that certainty is a necessary condition of knowledge, or that one must know that one knows in order to have knowledge. But these analyses are either too strict or lead to an infinite regress, leading in either case to the skeptic's lair.

In point of fact, the past three decades have witnessed the development of various versions of foundationalism that avoid the criticisms leveled against the classical version. Among contemporary epistemologists, modest foundationalism of some form is, as one philosopher put it, the "dominant position."[9] Thus, it is intellectually irresponsible for Clapp, Murphy, and others to claim that foundationalism is losing favor among philosophers. As far as I can tell, apart from intellectual dishonesty, this false viewpoint can be sustained only by conflating classical foundationalism with foundationalism per se, but this is simply mistaken, as the widespread acceptance of modest foundationalism makes clear. Modest foundationalism holds that Condition C is something weaker than indubitability: the ground of the belief must be truth-conducive. Thus at least some properly basic beliefs in a modest foundationalism are defeasible (subject to being shown to be false by subsequent evidence).

#4: Confusions about the Identity of the Truth-Bearer

As we have already seen above, the informed correspondence theorist will say that propositions are truth-bearers. What is a proposition? Minimally, it is the content of declarative sentences/statements and thoughts/beliefs that are true or false. Beyond that philosophers are in disagreement, but most would agree that a proposition 1) is not located in space or time, 2) is not identical to the linguistic entities that may be used to express it, 3) is not sense-perceptible, 4) is such that the same proposition may be in more than one mind at once, 5) need not be grasped by any (at least finite) person to exist and be what it is, 6) may itself be an object of thought when, for

---

[9]Michael R. DePaul, "Preface," in *Resurrecting Old-Fashioned Foundationalism*, ed. Michael R. DePaul (Lanham, MD: Rowman and Littlefield, 2001), vii.

example, one is thinking about the content of one's own thought processes, and 7) is in no sense a physical entity.

By contrast, a sentence is a linguistic type or token consisting in a sense-perceptible string of markings formed according to a culturally arbitrary set of syntactical rules. A statement is a sequence of sounds or body movements employed by a speaker to assert a sentence on a specific occasion. So understood, neither sentences nor statements are good candidates for the basic truth-bearer.

It is easy to show that having or using a sentence (or any other piece of language) is neither necessary nor sufficient for thinking or having propositional content. First, it's not necessary. Children think prior to their acquisition of language—how else could they thoughtfully learn language—and, indeed, we all think without language regularly. Moreover, the same propositional content may be expressed by a potentially infinite number of pieces of language, and thus that content is not identical to any linguistic entity. This alone does not show that language is not necessary for having propositional content. But when one attends to the content that is being held constant as arbitrary linguistic expressions are selected to express it, that content may easily be seen to satisfy the non-linguistic traits of a proposition listed above.

Second, it's not sufficient. If erosion carved an authorless linguistic scribble in a hillside—for example, "I'm eroding"—then strictly speaking it would have no meaning or content, though it would be empirically equivalent to another token of this type that would express a proposition were it the result of authorial intent.

Postmodernists attack a straw man when they focus on the alleged inadequacies of linguistic objects to do the work required of them in a correspondence theory of truth. Speaking for himself and other postmodernists, Joseph Natoli claims that "No one representation, or narrative, can reliably represent the world because language/pictures/sounds (signifiers) are not permanent labels attached to the things of the world nor do the things of the world dwell inside such signifiers."[10] Unfortunately, even granting the fact that language (and certain sensations) is problematic if taken to represent things in the world (e.g., that the language/world hookup is arbitrary), it follows that human subjects cannot accurately represent the world only if we grant the further erroneous claim that representational entities are limited to language (and certain sensations). But this is precisely what the sophisticated correspondence theorist denies.

---

[10]Natoli, *A Primer to Postmodernity*, 18.

Again, Richard Rorty says, "To say that truth is not out there is simply to say that where there are no sentences there is not truth, that sentences are elements of human language, and that human languages are human creations. Truth cannot be out there—cannot exist independently of the human mind—because sentences cannot so exist, or be out there. . . . Only descriptions . . . can be true and false."[11] It should be obvious that Rorty attacks a straw man and that his argument goes through only if we grant that sentences are the fundamental truth-bearers.

#5: Confusions about Perception

Postmodernists adopt a highly contentious model of perception, often without argument. The result is that postmodernists are far too pessimistic about the prospects of human epistemic success.

Postmodernists adopt a linguistic version of Rene Descartes's idea theory of perception (and intentionality generally). To understand the idea theory, and the postmodern adaptation of it, a good place to start is with a commonsense, critical realist view of perception. According to critical realism, when a subject is looking at a red object such as an apple, the object itself is the direct object of the sensory state. What one sees directly is the apple itself. True, one must have a sensation of red to apprehend the apple, but on the critical realist view, the sensation of red is to be understood as a case of being-appeared-to-redly and analyzed as a *self-presenting property*. What is a self-presenting property? If property F is a self-presenting one, then it is by means of F that a relevant external object is presented directly to a person, and F presents itself directly to the person as well. Thus, F presents its object mediately though directly, and itself immediately.

This is not as hard to understand as it may first appear. Sensations, such as being-appeared-to-redly, are an important class of self-presenting properties. If Jones is having a sensation of red while looking at an apple, then having the property of being-appeared-to-redly as part of his consciousness modifies his substantial self. When Jones has this sensation, it is a tool that presents the red apple mediately to him, and the sensation also presents itself to Jones. What does it mean to say that the sensation presents the apple to him mediately? Simply this: it is in virtue of or by means of the sensation that Jones directly sees the apple itself.

Moreover, by having the sensation of red, Jones is directly aware both of the apple and of his own awareness of the apple. For the critical real-

---

[11]Richard Rorty, *Contingency, Irony, and Solidarity* (New York: Cambridge University Press, 1989), 4–5.

ist, the sensation of red may, indeed, be a tool or means that Jones uses to become aware of the apple, but he is thereby directly aware of the apple. His awareness of the apple is direct in that nothing stands between Jones and the apple, not even his sensation of the apple. Because that sensation presents the apple directly, though as a tool, Jones must have the sensation as a necessary condition for seeing the apple. On the critical realist view, a knowing subject is not trapped behind or within anything, including a viewpoint, a narrative, or a historical-linguistic perspective. To have an entity in the external world as an object of intentionality is to already be "out there"; there is no need to escape anything. One is not trapped behind one's eyeballs or anything else. It is a basic fallacy of logic to infer that one sees a point-of-viewed object from the fact that one sees an object from a point of view.

Before leaving the critical realist view, it is important to say that the theory does not limit self-presenting properties to those associated with the five senses and therefore does not limit the objects of direct awareness to ordinary sensory objects. The critical realist will say that a knowing subject is capable of direct acquaintance with a host of non-sense-perceptible objects—one's own ego and its mental states, various abstract objects like the laws of mathematics or logic, and spiritual beings, including God.

By contrast, for Descartes's idea theory, one's ideas—in this case, sensations—stand between the subject and the object of perception. Jones is directly aware of his own sensation of the apple and indirectly aware of the apple in the sense that it is what causes the sensation to happen. On the idea theory, a perceiving subject is trapped behind his own sensations and cannot get outside of them to the external world in order to compare his sensations to their objects to see if those sensations are accurate.

Now, in a certain sense postmodernists believe that people are trapped behind something in the attempt to get to the external world. However, for them, the wall between people and reality is not composed of sensations as it was for Descartes; rather, it is constituted by one's community and its linguistic categories and practices. One's language serves as a sort of distorting and, indeed, creative filter. One cannot get outside one's language to see if one's talk about the world is the way the world is. Thus, Grenz advocates a new outlook, allegedly representing some sort of consensus in the human sciences, that expresses "a more profound understanding of epistemology. Recent thinking has helped us see that the process of knowing, and to some extent even the process of experiencing the world, can occur only within a conceptual framework, a framework mediated by the social community in which we participate."[12]

It has been noted repeatedly that such assertions are self-refuting. For if we are all trapped behind a framework such that simple, direct seeing is impossible, then no amount of recent thinking can help us see anything; all it could do would be to invite us to see something *as* such and such from within a conceptual framework. Given the self-refuting nature of such claims, and given the fact that we all experience regularly the activity of comparing our conceptions of an entity with the entity itself as a way of adjusting those conceptions, it is hard to see why anyone, especially a Christian, would adopt the postmodern view. In any case, I have seldom seen the realist perspective seriously considered by postmodern thinkers, and until it is, statements like Grenz's will be taken as mere mantras by many of us.

FINAL REMARKS ABOUT THE IMMORAL NATURE OF POSTMODERNISM

For some time I have been convinced that postmodernism is rooted in pervasive confusions, and I have tried to point out in this essay what some of them are. I am also convinced that postmodernism is an irresponsible, cowardly abrogation of the duties that constitute a disciple's calling to be a Christian intellectual and teacher.

In her provocative book *Longing to Know*, Ester Meek asserts that humans as knowers exercise a profound responsibility to submit to the authoritative dictates of reality.[13] Thus, "It is not responsible to deny objective truth and reality in knowing; it is irresponsible. It is not responsible to make the human knower or community of knowers the arbiters of a private truth and reality; it is irresponsible."[14] Again, Meek claims that "Good, responsible knowing brings blessing, shalom; irresponsible knowing brings curse."[15] In another place Meek warns that . . . the kind of freedom implied by the thought that we humans completely determine our reality leaves us with a gnawing sense of the relative insignificance of our choices. I think it leads not to total responsibility but to careless irresponsibility, both with regard to ourselves and with regard to other humans, not to mention to the world. And, paradoxically, it leads not to

---

[12]Grenz, *Revisioning Evangelical Theology*, 73–74.
[13]Ester Lightcap Meek, *Longing to Know* (Grand Rapids, MI: Brazos Press, 2003), 146–147.
[14]Ibid., 148.
[15]Ibid., 179.

a deeper sense of [communal or individual] identity and dignity but to a disheartening lack of it."[16]

We Christians need to pay careful attention to Meek's claims. As humans, we live and ought to live our lives not merely by truth but by knowledge of truth. Knowledge of truth gives us confident trust and access to reality. Moreover, as those called to be teachers and scholars for the church and, indeed, for the unbelieving world, we are called not only to impart and defend truth, but to impart and defend knowledge of truth, and even more, to impart and defend knowledge of truth *as* knowledge of truth. This entails that we must impart and defend the notion that we do, in fact, have knowledge of important spiritual and ethical truths. Among other things, this gives confidence in truth and knowledge to those we serve. Thus, we are irresponsible not simply if we fail to achieve knowledge of reality; we are doubly irresponsible if we fail to impart to others knowledge *as knowledge*. The corrosive affects of postmodernism eat away at the fulfillment of these duties and responsibilities that constitute our calling from Almighty God.

Meek goes on to point out that the achieving of knowledge and the teaching of it as knowledge . . . calls for courageous resolve. And this courageous resolve, when proven true, merits the deep admiration of others."[17] The need for such courage is especially grave today as we labor in an intellectual milieu in which the worldviews of naturalism and postmodernism both entail that there is no non-empirical knowledge, especially no religious or ethical knowledge.

Faced with such opposition and the pressure it brings, postmodernism is a form of intellectual pacifism that, at the end of the day, recommends backgammon while the barbarians are at the gate. It is the easy, cowardly way out that removes the pressure to engage alternative conceptual schemes, to be different, to risk ridicule, to take a stand outside the gate. But it is precisely as disciples of Christ, even more, as officers in his army, that the pacifist way out is simply not an option. However comforting it may be, postmodernism is the cure that kills the patient, the military strategy that concedes defeat before the first shot is fired, the ideology that undermines its own claims to allegiance. And it is an immoral, coward's way out that is not worthy of a movement born out of the martyrs' blood.[18]

---

[16]Ibid., 182.
[17]Ibid., 167. For the best, most accessible treatment of postmodernism available, see Douglas Groothuis, *Truth Decay* (Downers Grove, IL: InterVarsity Press, 2000).
[18]I wish to thank Garry DeWeese for helpful comments on an earlier draft of this paper.

CHAPTER EIGHT

Politics, Faith, and the Separation of Church and State[1]

Francis J. Beckwith

THE UNITED STATES CONSTITUTION addresses religion in only two places. The first is in Article VI, in which a religious test for public office anywhere in the United States is prohibited. The other place is in the First Amendment of the Bill of Rights, which contains a sequence of words that many Americans can recite by memory: "Congress shall make no law respecting an establishment of religion, or prohibiting the free exercise thereof. . . ." The phrase "separation of church and state" has been employed by many as a shorthand way to describe the legal principles that they believe are the basis for the religion clauses of the First Amendment. But the religion clauses are notoriously vague, for they give us no direction as to the precise meaning of "free exercise," "establishment," or even "religion."

It is clear, however, from the text that the First Amendment was intended to limit the law-making power of *Congress* and not any other branch of the state or federal governments. But since the early twentieth century the Supreme Court has in a piecemeal fashion begun applying the First Amendment to all governments in the United States.[2] It was not until 1947, in the case of *Everson v. Board of Education*,[3] that the Supreme Court would apply the establishment clause to a non-federal govern-

---

[1]This chapter is adapted from the article "Gimme That Ol' Time Separation: A Review Essay," *Chapman Law Review*, 8.1 (2005): 309–327.
[2]The Court first incorporated the freedom of speech and press clauses, eventually incorporating the entire First Amendment. See *Gitlow v. New York*, 268 U.S. 652, 666 (1925); *Near v. Minnesota*, 283 U.S. 697, 707 (1931); *De Jorge v. Oregon*, 299 U.S. 353, 364 (1937); *Cantwell v. Connecticut*, 310 U.S. 296, 303-304 (1940); and *Everson v. Board of Education*, 330 U.S. 1 (1947).
[3]330 U.S. 1 (1947).

ment. It justified this move by a doctrine of constitutional interpretation known as *incorporation*: the fundamental rights of citizens protected by the Fourteenth Amendment (1868)—life, liberty, and property without due process—imply most of the rights in the Bill of Rights, including the rights that are found in the First Amendment. That is, these First Amendment rights (including both religion clauses) are incorporated through the Fourteenth Amendment. Whether such a move is justified is outside the scope of this chapter. Needless to say, even if it is not justified, Americans have grown so accustomed to thinking of their federal Constitutional rights as restraints on all governments—federal, state, and local—that even a logically sound argument against incorporation is not likely to get very far.

The notion of "separation of church and state" is a largely unquestioned dogma in American political and legal discourse, even though the phrase does not appear in the text of the Constitution, and a plain reading of the religion clauses is just as consistent with some forms of moderate separationism as it is with strong separationism.

Although it is difficult to precisely define the difference between moderate separationism and strong separationism, it seems to me that the following is a fair distinction. (1) Both affirm that the government should maximize religious liberty consistent with the public good as well as prohibit both ecclesiastical control of government powers and government control of ecclesiastical powers. (2) Moderate separationism does not attempt to marginalize religion in public life and thus would, for example, support public funding programs for similarly-situated religious and secular entities. On the other hand, strong separationism forbids any direct aid to religion even when similarly-situated secular entities are given aid. In addition, strong separationists seem willing to marginalize the political proposals of religious citizens if those proposals are religiously motivated, though similarly-situated non-religious citizens who offer proposals based on secular grounds are unlikely to suffer the same fate.[4]

I. STORY OF A SLOGAN

In his masterful work, *Separation of Church and State*,[5] Philip Hamburger shows that separationism has achieved its status in American politics and jurisprudence largely as the result of an ignoble pedigree that harnessed an

---

[4]See Carl H. Esbeck, "Myths, Miscues, and Misconceptions: No-Aid Separationism and the Establishment Clause," *Notre Dame Journal of Law, Ethics & Public Policy*, 13 (1999).
[5]Philip Hamburger, *Separation of Church and State* (Cambridge, MA: Harvard University Press, 2002).

ambiguously understood slogan—*separation of church and state*—to advance a particular view of religion, state, and liberty whose proponents consider it the "American way." Hamburger tells the story of this slogan, which was famously employed by Thomas Jefferson in his "Letter to the Danbury Baptists":

> Believing with you that religion is a matter which lies solely between man and his God, that he owes account to none other for his faith or his worship, that the legislative powers of government reach actions only, and not opinions, I contemplate the sovereign reverence that act of the whole American people which declared that *their* legislature should "make no law respecting an establishment of religion, or prohibiting the free exercise thereof," thus building a wall of separation between Church & State.[6]

Because Jefferson is one of America's Founding Fathers, this letter—which Jefferson wrote as President—has the status of a sacred text in separationist circles. Among some Christian church-state separationists, Jefferson's "Letter to the Danbury Baptists" carries with it an authority not unlike Paul's letter to the Galatians. And yet Jefferson's letter is, after all, a type of communication that Presidents produce at least several times a day to a wide range of constituencies. Given that, it seems somewhat dubious to base constitutional doctrine on what amounts to nothing more than a note to political allies seeking the President's support for their religious liberty. This note was not part of an executive order, proposed legislation, or even a directive offered by the President to the U.S. attorney general as a suggested way to interpret the Establishment Clause.

Hamburger points out that Jefferson's letter embodied a particular understanding of the relationship between church and state that was not even shared by the recipients of the letter. The Danbury Baptists, who were known as *dissenters*, opposed religious establishment but did not oppose the influence of religion on government.[7] According to Hamburger, "Jefferson's letter was not entirely a declaration of liberty. Separation was an idea first introduced into American politics by Jefferson's allies, the Republicans, who used it to elicit popular distaste against Federalist clergymen in their exercise of their religious freedom."[8] For the Federalist clergy had "inveighed against Jefferson, often from their pulpits, excoriating his infidelity and deism."[9] Although "[t]he religious dissenters, including the

---

[6]Thomas Jefferson, "Letter to the Danbury Baptists" (January 1, 1802), available at http://www.loc. gov/loc/lcib/9806/danpre.html (accessed June 1, 2004).
[7]Hamburger, *Separation of Church and State*, 163–180.
[8]Ibid., 109–110.
[9]Ibid., 111.

Baptists, sympathized with the Republicans and distrusted the Federalists, particularly the Federalist clergy . . . when invited by Jefferson to join the Republican demand for separation, the Baptists quietly declined."[10]

Because it was assumed that the moral ecology of a society could not be maintained without the influence of religion, dissenters had to constantly deal with the false charge that they were really separationists who wanted to remove any vestiges of religion from the public square. This is why, as Hamburger points out, "the Baptists who sought the support of the president [Jefferson] were silent about his letter. . . ."[11] For Jefferson's letter would have been counterproductive in quelling the fears of those who equated antiestablishment with separationism. As Hamburger notes, "[I]t may be useful to begin by considering the [Baptists'] awkward situation. . . . [E]stablishment ministers had long accused dissenters of advocating separation, whether of church from state or religion from government. . . ." But "Baptists merely sought disestablishment and did not challenge the widespread assumption that republican government depended upon the people's morals and thus upon religion."[12]

The Danbury Baptists, like most Americans at the time, maintained that the church and state were two separate spheres, but that the church, like other nongovernment institutions, played a vital role in civilizing the nation's citizens and instilling in them the notion that their rights were not derived from the fiat of governments but rather were stamped on them by their Creator. The role of government is to protect the people's God-given rights while the role of religion is to shape the moral understanding of the nation's people so that they may be upright citizens.

According to this view, the United States of America is a constitutional republic whose institutions presuppose, and entail, certain beliefs about the order and nature of things that are nonnegotiable in terms of maintaining the continuity and purpose of the nation, including the rights of its people and the powers of its governments (both state and federal). The philosophical infrastructure of the American Republic consists of a cluster of ideals, beliefs, practices, and institutions that are best sustained by a people who see this cluster as grounded in certain unchanging moral truths that are religious in nature.

Although the New Testament speaks very little about government and the Christian's responsibility as a citizen, there is one particular passage

---

[10]Ibid., 110.
[11]Ibid., 165.
[12]Ibid.

that may illuminate this Early American understanding. Jesus, in a familiar scene, is confronted by the Pharisees with an apparent dilemma:

> *"Tell us, then, what you think. Is it lawful to pay taxes to Caesar, or not?" But Jesus, aware of their malice, said, "Why put me to the test, you hypocrites? Show me the coin for the tax." And they brought him a denarius. And Jesus said to them, "Whose likeness and inscription is this?" They said, "Caesar's." Then he said to them, "Therefore render to Caesar the things that are Caesar's, and to God the things that are God's." When they heard it, they marveled. And they left him and went away. (Matt. 22:17–22, ESV)*

The most dominant reading of this passage is that Jesus is instructing his audience that the church and government have jurisdiction over different spheres of authority. Although I believe this reading is largely correct, those who present it often miss the subtle political implications of what Jesus is saying. He first asks whose image is on the coin. The answer, of course, is "Caesar's." But there is an unsaid question that begs to be answered: Who has the image of God on them?[13] If the coin represents the authority of Caesar because it has his image on it, then we human beings are under the authority of God because we have his image on us. Thus, good governments ought to be concerned with the well-being of their citizens, and these citizens correctly believe that their well-being is best sustained by a just government that protects their rights, including the right of religious liberty. Thus, both government and the church, though having separate jurisdictions, share a common obligation to advance the good of those who are made in God's image.

Given this understanding, the Danbury Baptists were troubled that their state, Connecticut, levied a tax to support the state's established religion, Congregationalism. Connecticut did allow Baptists and other citizens to request that the state redirect their tax money to their own churches. But the process required that "they first had to obtain, fill out, and properly file an exemption certificate." And because "Baptists were a harassed minority, some communities made it difficult for them to receive these exemptions."[14] This is why they shared their complaint with President Jefferson. But they,

---

[13]This is an insight offered by Luis Lugo in his essay "Caesar's Coin and the Politics of the Kingdom: A Pluralist Perspective," in *Caesar's Coin Revisited: Christians and The Limits of Government*, ed. Michael Cromartie (Washington, DC and Grand Rapids, MI: Ethics & Public Policy Center and Eerdmans, 1996), 14–15.

[14]Derek H. Davis, "Thomas Jefferson and the 'Wall Of Separation' Metaphor," *Journal of Church & State*, 45.1 (Winter 2003): 10.

like many Americans at the time,[15] did not see their resistance to religious establishment as inconsistent with a government that accommodates and sometimes encourages its people to embrace an account of rights and human institutions in which religion and its moral instruction are essential.

II. ANTI-CATHOLIC PREJUDICE AND THE TRIUMPH OF SEPARATIONISM

In the nineteenth century separationism surged to prominence, largely as a Protestant reaction against the influx of immigrants from predominantly Roman Catholic countries. Some of these immigrant groups, which included Irish and Italians, set up their own private religious schools. Many non-Catholic Americans believed that Catholic schools indoctrinated their students with superstitions that were inconsistent with the principles of American democracy. Take, for example, these comments by the great Baptist church-state separationist Joseph Martin Dawson:

> The Catholics, who are now [1948] claiming a near majority over all Protestants in the United States, would abolish our public school system which is our greatest single factor in national unity and would substitute their old-world, medieval parochial schools, with their alien culture. Or else they make it plain that they wish to install facilities for teaching their religion in the public schools. . . . Perhaps the burning issue has arisen soon enough to enable the friends of the native American culture to arrest the progress of the long-range plan of those who would supplant it. There can be no doubt about the Catholic plan. Having lost enormous prestige in Europe, the Church now looks to the United States as a suitable stage for the recovery of its lost influence. Here it would seek new ground, consolidate and expand, as compensation for its weakened position in bankrupt Europe, with the hope of transforming this continent, a Protestant country, into a Catholic citadel from which to exert a powerful rule. If this seems exaggerated and fanciful, the reader has only to open his eyes to what the Catholics are doing to achieve this end.[16]

In order to make sure that Catholic schools would not receive government funding of any sort, federal and state legislation was proposed to forbid the use of public resources for "sectarian" (read: Catholic) religious purposes. The most ambitious attempt to put this understanding into law was a proposed constitutional amendment by Representative James Blaine (R-ME). It read:

---

[15]Of course, establishment supporters did see antiestablishment dissenters as no different than separationists. See Hamburger, *Separation of Church and State*, 65–78.

[16]J. M. Dawson, *Separate Church & State Now* (New York: R. R. Smith, 1948), 96.

No State shall make any law respecting an establishment of religion or prohibiting the free exercise thereof; and no money raised by taxation in any State, for the support of public schools, or derived from any public fund therefore, nor any public lands devoted thereto, shall ever be under the control of any religious sect, nor shall any money so raised, or lands so devoted be divided between religious sects or denominations.[17]

Called the Blaine Amendment, it never became part of the Constitution. However, some individual states passed Blaine-type statutes or constitutional amendments that still remain on the books.

Hamburger astutely points out that by arguing that there was a need for these amendments, supporters of the Blaine Amendment and its progeny implicitly conceded that the First Amendment's Establishment Clause, by itself, does not prohibit the use of public resources for religious purposes. Of course, this would mean that separationist jurisprudence, which relies on a Blaine-type understanding of church and state, is likely not a proper reading of the First Amendment. This does not mean, of course, that some modest form of separationism, something like the traditional antiestablishment position of the Danbury Baptists, is not correct (as I believe is in fact the case). Rather, what it means is that a doctrine borne of anti-Catholic animus and a desire to declare an American Protestant hegemony as the *established understanding of public faith* is hardly the "neutral" and "separationist" creed its proponents have led us to believe. Ironically, as Hamburger points out, the underlying principles of separationism were picked up in the twentieth century by secularists hostile to *all religion in public life* who then applied these principles to the cherished practices of many (though not all) nineteenth-century anti-Catholic Protestant separationists—prayer[18] and Bible-reading in public schools.[19] These separationist principles were eventually applied critically by jurists and scholars to laws that reflected traditional moral understandings on abortion,[20] homosexuality,[21] and physician-assisted suicide.[22]

The most extreme application of this separationist point of view has to be the rejection on the part of some scholars of the American Founders'

---

[17]*Congressional Record*, 44th Congress, 1st session, December 14, 1875; http://www3.baylor.edu/Church_State/Blaine_Amendment.html (accessed June 2, 2004).
[18]See *Engel v. Vitale*, 370 U. S. 421 (1962); *Wallace v. Jaffree*, 472 U. S. 38 (1985).
[19]*Abington School District v. Schenpp*, 374 U. S. 203 (1963).
[20]See *Webster v. Reproductive Health Services*, 492 U.S. 490, 566–567, 569 (1989) (Stevens, J., dissenting).
[21]See D. W. Machacek and A. Fulco, "The Courts and Public Discourse: The Case of Gay Marriage," *Journal of Church & State*, 46.4 (Autumn 2004); *Bowers v. Hardwick*, 478 U.S. 186, 216 (1986) (Stevens, J., dissenting); *Lawrence v. Texas*, 539 U. S. 518, 525 (2003).
[22]David McKenzie, "Church, State, and Physician-Assisted Suicide," *Journal of Church & State*, 46.4 (Autumn 2004): 787–809.

notion that just government and constitutional jurisprudence presuppose that we can know and apply unchanging moral truths.[23] Take, for example, the words of separationist law professor Steven G. Gey:

> The establishment clause should be viewed as a reflection of the secular, relativist political values of the Enlightenment, which are incompatible with the fundamental nature of religious faith. As an embodiment of these Enlightenment values, the establishment clause requires that the political influence of religion be substantially diminished. . . . Religious belief and practice should be protected under the first amendment, but only to the same extent and for the same reason that all other forms of expression and conscience are protected—because the first amendment prohibits government from enacting into law any religious, political, or aesthetic orthodoxy. . . . [R]eligious principles are not based on logic or reason, and, therefore, may not be proved or disproved. . . . [R]eligion asserts that its principles are immutable and absolutely authoritative, democratic theory asserts just the opposite. The sine qua non of any democratic state is that everything political is open to question; not only specific policies and programs, but the very structure of the state itself must always be subject to challenge. Democracies are by nature inhospitable to political or intellectual stasis or certainty. Religion is fundamentally incompatible with this intellectual cornerstone of the modern democratic state. The irreconcilable distinction between democracy and religion is that, although there can be no sacrosanct principles or unquestioned truths in a democracy, no religion can exist without sacrosanct principles and unquestioned truths.[24]

Aside from raising the awkward question of whether the claim that "no religion can exist without sacrosanct principles and unquestioned truths" is an unquestioned truth about which Professor Gey is certain, one could point out that he seems unacquainted with the numerous works critical of this sort of crude relativism,[25] for he does not even engage any of them, let alone attempt to refute the arguments offered by their authors. Moreover, Professor Gey does not interact with any of the relevant academic literature on religious belief, morality, and rationality. Thus it is difficult to know how he would reply to the sophisticated and compelling arguments offered by members of the growing intellectual movement of theistic philosophers in Anglo-American philosophy published before 1990 (the year

---

[23]See Steven G. Gey, "Why Is Religion Special?: Reconsidering the Accommodation of Religion Under the Religion Clauses of the First Amendment," *University of Pittsburgh Law Review*, 52 (Fall 1990).
[24]Ibid., 79, 167, 174.
[25]See, for example, Hadley Arkes, *First Things: An Inquiry into the First Principles of Morals and Justice* (Princeton, NJ: Princeton University Press, 1986).

Gey's article appeared in print).[26] Given the enormity and sophistication of this movement and its literature, Professor Gey's stipulation of religion's irrationality without providing us any reason why we should put faith in this unsupported judgment is, on its own grounds, not based on logic and reason and thus should be rejected.

As America moved into the twentieth century, separationism was increasingly perceived as *the* American understanding of the Establishment Clause. Among its most vocal and public advocates were Baptists, Freemasons, the Ku Klux Klan, nativists, and secularists. One of the most ardent separationists of the twentieth century, Supreme Court Justice Hugo Black, was a Baptist and Freemason and, up until a little over a decade before his 1937 nomination to the Court, a member of the Ku Klux Klan. Although, as Hamburger points out, Black "in later years would discount his association with the Invisible Empire of the Ku Klux Klan" as an innocent membership in a fraternal organization, "Black's account of his participating in the Klan was, at best, understated."[27] Hamburger presents a detailed history of Black's Klan affiliation that leaves no doubt that Black was no nominal Klansman who wore his sheets only on holidays and for weddings.[28] According to Hamburger, "in September 1923 Black joined the powerful Richard E. Lee Klan No. 1 and promptly became Kladd of his Klavern—the officer who initiated new members by administering the oath about 'white supremacy' and 'separation of church and state.'"[29]

By the time the U. S. Supreme Court applied the Establishment Clause to the states in the 1947 *Everson* case, the separationist understanding was so widely accepted throughout the country that the Court could make it a fixed point in constitutional law without the need of anything like the Blaine amendment. And the Court did so in *Everson*, whose majority opinion was penned by Justice Black. The case concerned the question of whether the New Jersey Township of Ewing's payment to parents for the busing of their children to Catholic parochial schools violated the Establishment Clause. Black concluded that it did not, for three reasons: the payment was not given directly to a religious organization; the payment was available to chil-

---

[26]See, for example, Richard Swinburne, *The Existence of God* (New York: Oxford University Press, 1979); Alvin Plantinga and Nicholas Wolterstorff, eds., *Faith & Rationality: Reason & Belief in God* (Notre Dame, IN: University of Notre Dame Press, 1983); William Lane Craig, *The Kalam Cosmological Argument* (New York: MacMillan, 1979); Alvin Plantinga, *God and Other Minds: A Study of The Rational Justification of Belief in God* (Ithaca, NY: Cornell University Press, 1967); John Finnis, *Natural Law & Natural Rights* (Oxford, UK: Clarendon, 1980); John Finnis, *Fundamentals of Ethics* (Washington, DC: Georgetown University Press, 1983).
[27]Hamburger, *Separation of Church & State*, 423–424.
[28]Ibid., 422–434.
[29]Ibid., 426.

dren in all schools including non-religious private schools; and it was much like other services such as police, fire department, etc. Although many of Black's separationist allies both off and on the Court (four of his brethren dissented) did not like the fact that the wrong party, Township of Ewing, won the lawsuit, they would in coming years, upon reflection, realize that Black had delicately and cleverly placed into the arsenal of constitutional law adjudication, for the first time, the principles of separationism. Black writes in *Everson*:

> The "establishment of religion" clause of the First Amendment means at least this: Neither a state nor the Federal Government can set up a church. Neither can pass laws which aid one religion, aid all religions, or prefer one religion over another. Neither can force nor influence a person to go to or to remain away from church against his will or force him to profess a belief or disbelief in any religion. No person can be punished for entertaining or professing religious beliefs or disbeliefs, for church attendance or non-attendance. No tax in any amount, large or small, can be levied to support any religious activities or institutions, whatever they may be called, or whatever form they may adopt to teach or prac-tice religion. Neither a state nor the Federal Government can, openly or secretly, participate in the affairs of any religious organizations or groups and vice versa. In the words of Jefferson, the clause against establishment of religion by law was intended to erect "a wall of separation between Church and State."[30]

Hamburger writes that Black "understood what he was doing." For "only ten years before, when Black was appointed to the Court, Catholics vociferously condemned him for his Klan membership." What the facts and circumstances of *Everson* afforded him was "an opportunity to make separation the unanimous standard of the Court while reaching a judgment that would undercut Catholic criticism."[31]

Despite this victory and a few subsequent ones for the separationists,[32] the Supreme Court has not fully absorbed the premises of their jurispru-dence. In fact, the contemporary Court seems to be moving in a direction more accommodating of religion, especially in the areas of religious speech and public funding of schools when the funds are directed to the schools by private choice or when there is no evidence that the funds are being used for

---

[30]*Everson v. Board of Education*, 330 U.S. 15–16 (1947) (citation from *Reynolds v. United States* omitted).
[31]Hamburger, *Separation of Church and State*, 462.
[32]See, for example, *Aquilar v. Felton*, 473 U. S. 402 (1985); *School District of Grand Rapids v. Ball*, 473 U. S. 373 (1985).

indoctrination.[33] (Exceptions to this are free exercise cases involving states in which there are Blaine-like laws.)[34]

III. TAKING RELIGION SERIOUSLY

By making a convincing case that there are good historical and textual reasons not to equate separationism with being antiestablishment, Hamburger has provided a conceptual scheme by which courts may affirm the constitutionality of laws that are tied to religious understandings but are nevertheless not "state establishments." That is, a government within the United States may pass laws that provide public approval and sustenance to moral understandings that are consistent with, congenial to, or have their grounding in certain religious traditions but nevertheless are thought to advance the public good. Although not in line with the agenda of many contemporary separationists, this would have been well-received by their antiestablishment predecessors, such as the Danbury Baptists, who believed in the importance of religion and morality in the preservation of a Constitutional Republic. As Daniel Dreisbach notes:

> Although no friend of religious establishments, many evangelical dissenters resisted efforts to inhibit religion's ability to influence public life and culture, to deprive religious leaders of the civil liberty to participate in politics armed with political opinions informed by religious values, and to restrain the freedom of churches to define and advance their own mission and ministries, whether spiritual, social, or civic.[35]

In order to appreciate the contrast between contemporary separationism and the views held by eighteenth- and nineteenth-century dissenters, consider the current debate over abortion. Contemporary separationists generally support abortion-rights on antiestablishment and/or free exercise grounds. They argue that the pro-life position on abortion—that the fetus is a full-fledged member of the human community and thus a subject of

[33]See, for example, *Widmer v. Vincent*, 454 U.S. 263 (1981); *Lamb's Chapel v. Center Moriches Union Free School District*, 508 U.S. 384 (1993); *Zobrest v. Catalina*, 113 U.S. 2462 (1993); *Capitol Square Review Board v. Pinette*, 515 U.S. 753 (1995); *Rosenberger v. The University of Virginia*, 515 U.S 819 (1995); *Mitchell v. Helms*, 530 U.S. 793 (2000).
[34]See *Locke v. Davey*, 538 U.S. 1031 (2004).
[35]Daniel L. Dreisbach, *Thomas Jefferson & the Wall of Separation Between Church & State* (New York: New York University Press, 2002), 52. Hamburger writes: "In all probability . . . only a handful of Baptists, if any, and no Baptist organizations made separation their demand. Instead Baptists focused on other, more traditional, claims of religious liberty. What Baptists sought not only differed from separation of church and state but also conflicted with it. Tactically, dissenters could not afford to demand separation, for a potent argument against them had been that they denied the connection between religion and government—a serious charge in a society in which religion was widely understood to be the necessary foundation of morality and government." (Hamburger, *Separation of Church & State*, 177–178).

rights from the moment of conception—depends on a religious metaphysics. Writes Paul Simmons, a defender of this point of view:

> The fact that many people believe strongly that a zygote is a person is by now well established. The First Amendment allows people to believe as they will as a matter of conscience or religious belief. That is a matter of freedom of religion. But as a definition of personhood for constitutional protections in a pluralistic society, the zygote-as-person rationale is untenable in the extreme. . . . Abstract metaphysical speculation has its rightful place in theology; but it must finally be rejected as inappropriate to the logic necessary for democratic rule.[36]

Therefore, any law that prohibits abortion on those grounds would establish religion (thus violating the establishment clause) and/or impede the free exercise of women whose religious beliefs may permit them to obtain an abortion because the fetus is not a subject of rights (thus violating the free exercise clause).

Of course, it is no coincidence that opponents of abortion are generally more religious than those who support abortion-choice.[37] For abortion opponents usually accept a view of the nature of the unborn that is consistent with their religion's philosophical anthropology.[38] However, those who offer this point of view in the public square do not merely stipulate the veracity of their position, as one would expect from people whose purpose is to simply propound dogmas to condemn the "infidels."[39] Rather, they offer arguments that consist of reasons that are remarkably public. For these reasons are not extracted uncritically from a religious text or from the pronouncements of a religious authority, and they are fully accessible to even those who dispute their veracity and/or the conclusion for which they are conscripted.

Sophisticated pro-life advocates typically argue from the nature of the unborn in order to establish his or her standing as a rights-bearer who ought to be protected by our laws. This type of argument is meant to

---

[36]Paul Simmons, "Religious Liberty and Abortion Policy," *Journal of Church and State*, Vol. 42 (Winter 2000), 75.

[37]There are, of course, exceptions. For example, Doris Gordon (president, Libertarians for Life) and Nat Hentoff (writer, *The Village Voice*) are pro-life atheists. As far as I know, it is Doris Gordon who coined the term "abortion-choice," which I use in this essay and elsewhere. See her introductory essay in *International Journal of Sociology and Social Policy,* 19.3/4 (1999).

[38]See, e.g., Patrick Lee, *Abortion and Unborn Human Life* (Washington, DC: The Catholic University of America Press, 1996); J. P. Moreland and Scott B. Rae, *Body & Soul: Human Nature & the Crisis in Ethics* (Downers Grove, IL: InterVarsity Press, 2000).

[39]This is the stereotype advanced by Simmons when he writes that the pro-life view of the unborn is *merely* a claim of "Catholic dogma" and/or "special knowledge" that is neither "subject to critical analysis" nor rooted in "reason." (Simmons, "Religious Liberty and Abortion Policy," 75, 72, 71, 71).

rebut the typical abortion-choice argument that locates a human being's intrinsic value with whether it has the presently ability to exercise or exhibit certain functions—e.g., consciousness, self-awareness, ability to communicate, have a self-concept.[40] In a nutshell, pro-lifers respond to this sort of argument by arguing that there is a deep connection between our human nature and the rights that spring from it, which a just government is obligated to recognize. Because the unborn—from zygote to blastocyst to embryo to fetus—is the same being, the same substance, that develops into an adult, the actualization of a human being's potentials—that is, her "human" appearance and the exercise of her rational and moral powers as an adult (which abortion-choice advocates argue determine its intrinsic value)—is merely the public presentation of functions latent in every human substance, from the moment it is brought into being. A human may lose and regain those functions throughout her life, but the substance remains the same being.

Moreover, if one's value is conditioned on certain accidental properties, then the human equality presupposed by our legal institutions and our form of government—the philosophical foundation of our constitutional regime—is a fiction. In that case there is no principled basis for rejecting the notion that human rights ought to be distributed to individuals on the basis of native intellectual abilities or other value-giving properties, such as rationality or self-awareness. One can only reject this notion by affirming that human beings are intrinsically valuable because they possess a particular *nature* from the moment they come into existence. That is to say, what a human being *is*, and not what she *does*, makes her a subject of rights.

It is not surprising, therefore, that supporters of abortion-choice rebut the pro-life case by offering their own philosophical anthropology. That is, they present arguments to show that the unborn, though a human being, does not possess the requisite characteristics that would entail that the government ought to protect it as a subject of rights.[41]

The pro-lifer and the abortion-choice advocate offer contrary accounts of the same being, the unborn. The former offers an account of the human person that is at home in a religious worldview, though it is certainly not unreasonable to accept the pro-life position while rejecting the religious tradition from which it sprang.[42] On the other hand, the abortion-choice

---

[40]See, e.g., David Boonin, *A Defense of Abortion* (New York: Cambridge University Press, 2002); Dean Stretton, "The Fallacy of Essential Moral Personhood" (May 2003), available at http://www.pcug.org.au/~dean/femp.html (accessed June 30, 2004).
[41]See Boonin, *A Defense of Abortion.*
[42]See note 37.

advocate offers an account of the human person that denies the soundness of the pro-life position. The abortion-choice position is widely held by citizens who are secular in their worldview and harbor an antipathy to the influence of traditional religion on public life. For example, the number of organizations and individuals that own web sites that advance a secular worldview while supporting church-state separation and the abortion-choice position are nearly limitless.

So the pro-lifer and the abortion-choice advocate present contrary answers to the same question: who and what are we? Yet, according to the separationist, only the pro-lifer is forbidden from shaping public policy because her point of view is "[a]bstract metaphysical speculation [that] has its rightful place in theology; but . . . must finally be rejected as inappropriate to the logic necessary for democratic rule."[43] But the abortion-choice advocate attempts to justify his position by offering a different metaphysical account, one that picks out certain presently exercisable abilities or functions that a being must have in order to be accorded the protections of our laws. There seems to be no good reason, except a type of crass philosophical apartheid, that would justify saying that this account has its rightful place in politics and law while its alternative "has its rightful place in theology."[44]

CONCLUSION

Hamburger writes that because "Americans . . . gradually forgot the character of their old, antiestablishment religious liberty," they "eventually came to understand their religious freedom as a separation of church and state."[45] Thus, despite its widespread acceptance, it lacks constitutional authority. For this reason and because of its roots in prejudice, "the idea of separation should, at best, be viewed with suspicion."[46]

Consequently, when one interprets antiestablishment as equivalent to total separation of religion from our political and legal institutions, we should not be surprised that this results in the unjustified public marginalization of citizens who have a religious understanding of certain political and moral issues. As Hamburger and others point out, the Danbury Baptists and most other dissenters did not understand antiestablishment in this way, and neither should we.

The courts should not be in the business of siding with a militant secu-

---

[43]Simmons, "Religious Liberty and Abortion Policy," 75.
[44]Ibid.
[45]Hamburger, *Separation of Church and State*, 492.
[46]Ibid., 483.

larism that seeks to have its metaphysics and morals firmly embedded in our laws while it suggests that the metaphysics and morals of its religious opponents, regardless of the quality of their arguments, should not even be considered by the citizenry simply because they flow from a religious worldview. If liberal democracy means anything, it should at least mean that all citizens—regardless of the religious or nonreligious source of their policy proposals—should be allowed to offer their best public arguments without first being required to undergo a metaphysical litmus test.

CHAPTER NINE

Aslan in the Public Square

Louis Markos

ACADEMIA IS A GREAT PLACE for dropping names. Indeed, many times a day, whether it be in a classroom, the faculty lounge, or the library, I will overhear the names of one or more of the great thinkers of the past. And when I hear those names, my mind generally makes a quick and singular association. I hear Plato, and I think Greek philosopher. I hear Tolstoy, and I think Russian novelist. I hear Shakespeare, and I think British playwright. Sometimes a name will conjure a double association (I hear Hemingway, and I think both American novelist and war correspondent), but generally the first image (novelist in the case of Hemingway) will quickly prevail over the second.

This mental phenomenon, however, does not occur when I hear the name of C. S. Lewis. With the invocation of that name, three separate and distinct images immediately rise up in my mind, each jockeying for position over the other: Christian apologist, sci-fi/fantasy writer, Oxbridge don. Who *was* this man who humbly referred to himself as Jack? Was he the popular writer of *Mere Christianity* and *The Screwtape Letters*, the ingenious creator of The Chronicles of Narnia and The Space Trilogy, or the scholarly author of *The Allegory of Love* and *The Preface to Paradise Lost*? Was he an evangelist, a novelist, or a lecturer? Saint, fantasist, or critic?

Of course, he is all three, but this commonsense observation does not release us from the obligation to at least try to reconcile the three aspects of his unique vocation. Although such a reconciliation could be effected in a number of different ways, I would like to offer in what follows one particular (and personal) way that rests upon those aspects of my own vocation that I share with Lewis. For, like Jack, I am a Christian English professor who divides his time equally between speaking and writing on apologetics and literature and who has written his own trilogy of children's novels. It is through such vocational eyes that I see the world, and when I cast those same eyes on the life and works of C. S. Lewis, I see a single, composite picture: that of a dedicated teacher who, with the same synthetic, shaping imagination he brought to Narnia, creatively integrated his public, academic role as professor and scholar with his private, personal identity as follower of Christ and defender of the faith.

In short, I see a professional who bravely and consistently refused to abide by the modernist (post-Enlightenment) notion of a professional as one who separates completely the public from the private sphere. That is not to say that Lewis shared the personal details of his life with his students or that he delivered sermons in the classroom (he did neither), but that he questioned the way the modern world *defined* the spheres of public and private. Increasingly since the eighteenth century, the western world has driven a (finally artificial) wedge between reason and revelation, between scientific facts, logical proofs, and secular institutions on the one hand and religious beliefs, spiritual values, and faith-based communities on the other. The former, we have all been taught to believe, must dominate the public arena (the "naked public square," to use Richard John Neuhaus's apt phrase), while the latter must remain safely walled up in the private, domestic sphere. The two must never be allowed to overlap. Indeed, anyone who brings his "private" religious beliefs into the "public" square (politics, education, media, etc.) risks being dismissed as nonprofessional, nonrational, nonobjective, and perhaps nonsensical. The claims of faith are all well and good behind church doors and in the sanctity of one's prayer closet—just make sure they do not (like radiation from a nuclear power plant) leak out into the public streets of the city. Recite your creed on Sunday morning, but don't let it follow you into the work week.

For Lewis, such an unnatural and arbitrary separation of the sacred from the secular, the Christian from the humanist, simply would not do. He would insist in his apologetics, in his fantasy novels, and in his scholarly work that the integrated Christian worldview that reigned in Europe for a millennium and a half was not only rationally and logically sound but deserved a voice in the public (and especially academic) arena. It is *this* Lewis that I spy at the core of his multifaceted vocation, a Lewis whom we desperately need to hear today.

Granted, much work has been done over the last several decades to encourage just such people not to compartmentalize their faith, but to carry it with them into the workplace: to be, that is, salt and light in the (secular) world. Still, what we can learn from Lewis is a more aggressive and coordinated method for bringing that integrated Christian worldview first into our own minds and hearts and then into the naked public square. What Lewis did from his academic chair, we must learn to do from within the confines of our own increasingly post-Christian culture: from within our government offices and our corporations, our classrooms and our libraries, our medical centers and our legal firms. We must start within ourselves a revolution, and let that revolution spill out into the world around us. We must, like the hippies of the 1960s and 1970s, question the things we have been taught, but that questioning must lead not to a deconstruction but to a reconstruction of who we are as heirs of a once-Christian Europe.

REHABILITATING THE PAST

First and foremost, if we are to follow in the footsteps of C. S. Lewis, we must learn to identify and resist what Lewis (after Owen Barfield) called "chronological snobbery." As should be clear to anyone who has eyes to see, we live in an age that is grossly self-satisfied with its own achievements and beliefs. True, every age likes to see itself as the culmination of all the ages that came before it, but what distinguishes our age (and the wider modernist age in general) is its tendency to dismiss all past ages as unenlightened, misguided, and "medieval." The problem is not our cocky claim that we know more facts and figures about the natural world than our forefathers or that we possess more gadgets than our pre-industrialized predecessors. The fact of the matter is we do. No, the problem is that *because* we know and have more "stuff," we (illogically) reason that our own philosophical, theological, and aesthetic views, our own prioritizing of divine, human, and civic virtues, and our own social, economic, and educational initiatives must necessarily be superior to theirs.

In Chapter 13 of his spiritual autobiography, *Surprised by Joy*, Lewis defines chronological snobbery as "the uncritical acceptance of the intellectual climate common to our own age and the assumption that whatever has gone out of date is on that account discredited." He then follows up this definition by challenging himself and his readers to question their "uncritical acceptance" of their own age by doing the following:

> You must find why it went out of date. Was it ever refuted (and if so by whom, where, and how conclusively) or did it merely die away as fashions do? If the latter, this tells us nothing about its truth or falsehood. From see-

ing this, one passes to the realization that our own age is also "a period" and certainly has, like all periods, its own characteristic illusions.[1]

It is a sad fact that college-educated Christians are often the *last* people to question the philosophical, theological, and aesthetic history presented in our textbooks. We accept (as unreflectively as our non-Christian counterparts) the "party line" that claims that our age no longer believes what our ancestors believed because those old beliefs were put to the test and found to be flawed and in error. It's not hard to see why we accept this line. After spending four years in undergraduate school (and often many more in various graduate programs) absorbing the modernist reading of history, we are often reluctant to take the time and effort to question the assumptions and presuppositions on which that reading rests. Our job, we feel, is simply to pass on that which was taught to us as a proven, objective thing; to do otherwise would cause uncomfortable cognitive dissonance and leave us open to the charge of unprofessionalism, non-progressivism, and (worst of all) naiveté. Yes, we will question some of the details, but we too often, and too quickly, accept as a given the overarching framework of the received reading.

Again, every generation has certainly been guilty to some degree of accepting without questions the official history, but our age has put a new twist on such uncritical acceptance of the reigning paradigm. Lewis explains it best in Chapter 12 of *Reflections on the Psalms*: "Between different ages there is no impartial judge on earth, for no one stands outside the historical process; and of course no one is so completely enslaved to it as those who take our own age to be, not one more period, but a final and permanent platform from which we can see all other ages objectively."[2] If there is one thing our age is guilty of, it is precisely this stubbornly-held belief that we have a clear vision of all the flaws of every age, including our own. Even Marxist-inspired critics (radical feminists, new historicists, etc.), who pride themselves on their ability to pierce through all bourgeois illusions to discern the "real" socioeconomic forces that determine thought and action, willfully ignore the fact that if their method is correct, then they themselves (and their method) are likewise products of socioeconomic forces over which they have no conscious control.

Much of the problem can be traced to a logical fallacy that lies at the very heart of our modernist self-delusion—namely, the argument that scien-

---

[1] C. S. Lewis, *Surprised by Joy* (New York: Harcourt, Brace and Co., 1955), 207–208.
[2] C. S. Lewis, *Reflections on the Psalms* (New York: Harcourt, Brace, 1958), 121.

tific progress parallels moral progress. The analogy asserted between these two types of progress is, of course, a false one, but it exerts a great deal of emotional and rhetorical force. "Look at the great medical and technological breakthroughs that have occurred during our age," the spiel goes. "We have found cures for countless diseases, greatly reduced the infant mortality rate, vastly increased the speed of transportation and communication, and multiplied a hundredfold the most basic creaturely comforts. Surely an age that has accomplished such things must also be morally advanced; surely the refinement in bodily pleasures achieved in our age suggests a concurrent refinement of aesthetics and spirituality." In order to give the lie to this line of thought, we simply need to remember that the foundations for all these advances were laid out in the decades *before* totalitarianism from the right and the left began its wholesale slaughter of a significant percentage of the "morally advanced" human race.

Professor Lewis devoted considerable time and energy to exploding the rampant chronological snobbery lurking behind such false analogies. In his scholarly work, his apologetics, and even his fiction he argued passionately that newer does not always mean better, that though progress may be the rule for evolution, technology, and consumerism, neither culture nor religion nor ethics can be so measured. For Lewis this argument invariably involved a defense of the Middle Ages, since the modern world more often than not defines its achievements (and its superiority) over against those of the so-called Dark Ages. By defending Medieval Christendom from its detractors (both inside and outside the church), Lewis would be defending as well the specifically Christian worldview on which that age rested and upon which modern Europe was built.

In mounting his defense of the Middle Ages, Lewis set himself two related tasks. First, in *The Discarded Image* (and elsewhere) he systematically exposed the obscurantist effect of Enlightenment propaganda on our view of the Medievals. Chief among these propagandistic victories was the "fact" (disseminated by Voltaire in Europe and Washington Irving in America) that all the Medievals firmly believed that the earth was flat. Lewis swiftly demolishes this false "fact"—one that is consistently taught in our schools, both public and private—by quoting passages from a host of ancient and medieval writers (Aristotle, Ptolemy, Boethius, Aquinas, Dante) who knew full well that the world was round. In a similar vein, Lewis also quotes the Medievals themselves on another subject obscured by Enlightenment propaganda—the relative size and value of the earth. Though modern teachers, in unwitting collusion with the eighteenth-century *philosophes*, continue to inform their students that the men of the "Dark Ages" thought the universe was a small, cozy place dominated by the all-important earth, the fact is that they knew the universe was vast (though not infinite) and that in relation to that vastness the earth was but an insignificant point. Furthermore, the medieval belief, based on empirical observation, that the earth was at the center of the universe was not put forth as proof of human superiority (they left *that* claim to the more arrogant, egocentric thinkers of our modern world), but as a sobering reminder that we are the darkest, heaviest, coldest point in the cosmos, the drainage ditch of the universe.[3] (If you don't believe me—or Lewis—on this point, just read your Dante!)

Lewis was not appointed honorary head of the Oxford Socratic Club for nothing. Like Plato's great teacher, Lewis knew how to crush baseless arguments and wrestle logical fallacies to the ground. He did not, however, confine himself to such negative criticism. There was a positive side as well to Lewis's two-pronged defense of the Middle Ages. Not content merely to point out the flaws in our modern perception of that misunderstood age, Lewis sought (again, in his academic work, his apologetics, and his fiction alike) to rehabilitate the medieval cosmological model as a thing of beauty worthy of contemplation. He offered, that is, a counter-vision, an alternate narrative to the one taught in our colleges and schools. Just as Charles Dickens used his beloved *A Christmas Carol* to breathe new life and joy into the dull Yuletide celebrations of the overly utilitarian Victorians, so did Lewis use his equally beloved Chronicles of Narnia to help revive in us jaded, overly materialistic moderns a sense of wonder, humility, and, yes, thankfulness before the awesome majesty of God's creation.

Should we not, as modern Christians, join Lewis in his mission to restore to our world a lost sense of its own sacred past? I would argue that we must. How long can we go on trying to convince ourselves and our colleagues that the teachings of Christ and the Church are both true and universally valid, while passively perpetuating the Enlightenment myth that the long age during which Christendom reigned in Europe was dark, brutal, and superstitious? To be more specific, if we are Catholic believers, then we must stop being embarrassed by all the bad press and seek to recapture the rich cultural, intellectual, and aesthetic heritage of the Latin Church.

We might start by learning to approach the Middle Ages from the inside rather than from the outside. That is to say, let us learn (and

---

[3]C. S. Lewis, *The Discarded Image* (Cambridge, UK: Cambridge University Press, 1964), 97–100, 139–142.

encourage others to learn) to read Dante's *Divine Comedy* and Chaucer's *Canterbury Tales* not just as literary relics of a bygone era, but as windows on a world both wondrously strange and strangely familiar. Let us learn to see, *really* see, that the Christians who lived back then were real people who fought real struggles, and that it was out of their struggles that Europe was born. And while we're at it, we just might try to reclaim as well America's brief experiment with Christendom—the Puritan Age. For over a century now, we have been indoctrinated by Nathanael Hawthorne, Perry Miller, and Max Weber into viewing the Puritans as neurotic, hypocritical prudes driven to succeed by their own spiritual and psychological insecurities. When will "thinking" Christians muster enough courage to at least question this monolithic view? These God-inspired and Christ-haunted Puritans were as much Founding Fathers of our democratic institutions and our national soul as were Washington, Jefferson, Adams, or Franklin. Yet they continue to remain outsiders, sullied, in great part, by a single event—the Salem Witch Trials—that has been blown out of all proportion. Yes, some very good work has been done on Jonathan Edwards, but American Christians have yet to challenge in any real way (in a way, that is, that affects how our children are taught and how our nation views itself) the official, *Scarlet Letter*-view of the Puritan Age.

THE RENAISSANCE NEVER HAPPENED

Once we have given ourselves permission to look upon the past with sympathetic eyes, we are ready to follow Lewis one step further in his vocation of rehabilitation. Lewis knew that if he was to secure for Europe's Christian heritage a legitimate voice in the modernist arena, he would have to question not only the status of the Medieval Age itself but of its relative position and function in the stages of European history. This Lewis did brilliantly in the inaugural lecture he delivered at Cambridge University in 1954 to initiate his tenure there as the Chair of Medieval and Renaissance Literature. In the address (anthologized under the title *"De Descriptione Temporum"*), Lewis critiques the firmly held (indeed, unquestioned) belief that with the birth of the Renaissance, Europe left behind her ignorance and obscurantism and moved forward into the modern world. In opposition to this view and the prejudices that underlie it, Lewis boldly proclaimed that the Renaissance, far from parting company with the Middle Ages, never really happened. What we call modernism did not begin in 1500 but in the eighteenth century. It was the secular ideals of the Enlightenment, not the rebirth of classical culture, that defined Europe's break with her Christian and classical past. In fact, if truth be told, the Renaissance stands closer to the Medieval and Classical world in its view of God, man, and the universe than any of these ages do to our modern, post-Enlightenment world. Or, to put it another way, Michelangelo, Cervantes, Shakespeare, and Milton have more in common with Dante, Virgil, and Plato than with Voltaire or John Stuart Mill or Darwin. Even free thinkers like Galileo, Bacon, and Montaigne would surely have found greater kinship with the Medievals than with the moderns.[4]

We do not necessarily have to agree fully with Lewis in his contention that the Renaissance never happened to second him in his attempt to re-envision the historical dynamics that shaped the western world. But if we wish to be true to his legacy, then we must be willing to give each age its due, to see it as it was in itself, rather than to view it through the distorting lens of a later age that was hostile to it. If we are feeling in a bold mood, we might start by challenging ourselves and those with whom we share an office or a reading group or a club membership to take a second look at the Spanish Inquisition. As more of the records documenting that period have come out, it has become increasingly clear that the Inquisition (at least the part overseen by the Church) was nowhere near as bloody as long-standing Protestant and secular Enlightenment propaganda (not to mention Monty Python) has led us to believe. The death count was, in fact, quite low (especially when compared to the atrocities perpetrated in England and France in the name of religion). But the myth persists, perhaps in part because the period that includes the Inquisition marks a decisive moment when Spain was asserting her Catholic identity over against Moorish oppression from the south. As Spanish philosopher Julián Marías has pointed out, Spain is one of the few countries in Europe that made a direct and self-conscious decision to be a Christian nation defined in part by her Christian creeds.

And speaking of Christian self-identity, where shall we find educated, professional Christians who are brave enough to revive, as a positive thing, the image of the Christian Knight risking his life in defense of Christendom and the Holy Land? No, we should not cover over the atrocities perpetrated during the Crusades, but it is high time we remembered who exactly the aggressors were. The Knights were there to liberate lands that had been seized by Muslim conquerors. Simply consider the fact that the armies of Islam had seized control of all seven cities mentioned in Revelation 2–3

---

[4]C. S. Lewis, "De Descriptione Temporum," Selected Literary Essays (Cambridge, UK: Cambridge University Press, 1969), 1–14.

(that is, the original, most ancient centers of Christianity), and you will begin to see what an outrage the Muslim occupation of the Holy Land meant to the medieval Christians. Lewis reminds us in Part I, Chapter 2 of *Mere Christianity* that the reason we no longer kill witches is not because we are more moral than our ancestors, but because we no longer believe in witches. If we did believe in them, writes Lewis, "if we really thought there were people going about who had sold themselves to the devil and received supernatural powers from him in return and were using these powers to kill their neighbors or drive them mad or bring bad weather, surely we would all agree that if anyone deserved the death penalty, then these filthy quislings did."[5] In the same way, let us not consider ourselves less violent than the Crusaders because we no longer believe it a valid thing to fight for the honor of sacred ground.

I mention the Spanish Inquisition and the Crusades in particular since those two events have for the last two hundred years functioned in secular humanist circles as handy justifications for dismissing out of hand the true legacy of Christendom. Indeed, these two events (along with ritual invocations of the bad Popes) have been used to blacken Christianity's reputation vis-à-vis the sociopolitical realm in the same way that the trial of Galileo and the Scopes Monkey Trial have been used to blacken Christianity's reputation vis-à-vis science. In this arena, the church has, thankfully, raised up a handful of crusading scholars and teachers to remind us that the so-called war between science and religion is a modern and finally artificial thing. If not orthodox Christians, all the great early modern scientists (from Galileo to Newton to Kepler) were at least theists who shared a theistic worldview. Indeed, they would not have devoted their lives and careers to discovering (or, better, uncovering) the laws of nature if they had not believed that the universe was a rational, ordered system created by a rational, ordered God. There is no such thing as an indigenous Hindu or Buddhist science, not because the holders of those religions lacked critical thinking skills or technological know-how, but because they did not share the Christian faith *in* a rational universe.[6]

Too often, Christians grow timid and weak-kneed when the Crusades or the trial of Galileo is mentioned. Rather than confront these events head-on and seek to place them in a wider context, we either accept (passively) the standard view or reject (defensively) the whole issue and withdraw into

---

[5]C. S. Lewis, *Mere Christianity* (New York: Macmillan, 1960), 26.
[6]See Stanley L. Jaki, *The Road of Science and the Ways to God* (Chicago: University of Chicago Press, 1978).

our Christian subculture. And the reason we do this is because we can't take on the individual events themselves without first wrestling with the received interpretation of how these events fit into the stream of history. Just as Thomas Babington Macaulay saw all of pre-Victorian history as leading inexorably to the ascension of the Whig Party, so do the majority of post-Enlightenment scholars see European history as evolving, step by grueling step, toward the triumph of secular institutions, rational science, and the autonomous individual. As long as we leave that interpretation unquestioned, we will have little success in restoring the Christian world-view to its rightful place in the public square. In the same way, Lewis, until he boldly proclaimed that the Renaissance had never happened, could not fully reclaim the great thinkers of the Renaissance as culminations of a vital Christian humanist strain dating back to the Medieval and Classical periods rather than as proto-secular modernists who were stifled from speaking their mind by an oppressive church.

DINOSAURS IN THE CLASSROOM

And this leads in turn to the third thing that Lewis can teach us: the need for Christians to immerse themselves in the life and spirit of pre-modern Europe. We may succeed in rehabilitating the past from its detractors and even in championing the role played by those past ages, but if we ourselves cannot sympathize and identify with the ages we are defending, then all our work will have been in vain. To defend the past merely as a thing to be studied is like defending Christian doctrine as nothing but a set of rational propositions. To do either is to capitulate (whether we realize it or not) to one of the core elements of the modernist worldview—namely, that the only things to be taken seriously (*really* seriously) are those things that can be observed, calculated, and adumbrated. In modern academia, the past is something to be studied and dissected, not something to be known and appreciated. Modern critics no longer learn at the feet of the great bards and philosophers of the past. More often than not, it is *they* who stand on the dais looking with scorn (or at least suspicion) on the writers of the Great Books.

Not so Lewis, for whom pre-modern Europe (and especially the Middle Ages) was a place he knew and loved intimately. As he explains it to his scholarly Cambridge audience in "*De Descriptione Temporum*":

> I myself belong far more to that Old Western order than to yours. I am
> going to claim that this, which in one way is a disqualification for my task,

is yet in another a qualification. The disqualification is obvious. You don't want to be lectured on Neanderthal Man by a Neanderthal, still less on dinosaurs by a dinosaur. And yet, is that the whole story? If a live dinosaur dragged its slow length into the laboratory, would we not all look back as we fled? What a chance to know at last how it really moved and looked and smelled and what noises it made! . . . It is my settled conviction that in order to read Old Western literature aright you must suspend most of the responses and unlearn most of the habits you have acquired in reading modern literature. And because this is the judgment of a native, I claim that, even if the defense of my conviction is weak, the fact of my conviction is a historical *datum* to which you should give full weight. That way, where I fail as a critic, I may yet be useful as a specimen. I would even dare to go further. Speaking not only for myself but for all other Old Western men whom you may meet, I would say, use your specimens while you can. There are not going to be many more dinosaurs.[7]

As a scholar, Lewis had a full and rich understanding of the medieval world, but as a man, he had something more: he was one who believed, embodied, and felt in his bones the moral and aesthetic values of Old Western culture. He knew what it meant to look upon the cosmos not as our house but as our home. He knew what it felt like to live in a meaningful, sympathetic universe, one in which nature was not a textbook to be studied, but a poem to be marveled at. He understood, "firsthand" as it were, how hierarchy could uplift and define rather than crush and delimit, how religion could be the glue that held society together rather than the cause of division, how the classical virtues of prudence, justice, temperance, and courage, and the theological virtues of faith, hope, and love could lie at the core of sociopolitical-clerical rule rather than the dictates of realpolitik.

In this Lewis was special, but he need not be unique. There are many educated Christian professionals out there who could become dinosaurs if they would only spend the requisite time reading, relishing, and *absorbing* the great works of the past. We must open ourselves to what another great Christian English professor and author, T. S. Eliot, called the mind of the past; we must let the tradition sink in past those watchful dragons that would devour anything that smells even faintly of hierarchy, elitism, clericalism, or superstition. The best place to start, of course, is with Dante and Chaucer; to this, add Boethius, Augustine, St. Francis, and Aquinas, and you will be off to a great start. But again, don't just read—absorb; enter into the lives of the authors. Extend to the Medievals the same sympathetic

---

[7]C. S. Lewis, "De Descriptione Temporum," *Selected Literary Essays*, 13–14.

imagination that you would give to a reading (or viewing) of The Lord of the Rings. And as you read, remember one vital thing about Old Europe: pre-modern writers were *not* hung up about being original. They saw their task as that of carrying on a tradition that was much older than themselves and that would continue on long after they were dead.

You might also remember this sage advice from one of C. S. Lewis's closest friends, Charles Williams. In chapter 8 of *The Figure of Beatrice*, Williams informs us that Dante, being a good Medieval, "believed it to be less important that men should think for themselves than that they should think rightly."[8] When we read the Medievals, we do not encounter men for whom self-expression was the be-all and end-all of art. We encounter instead men and women who believed that truth existed and who sought in their professions and in their lives to approximate that truth.

May God give us the grace to do the same!

---

[8]Charles Williams, *The Figure of Beatrice* (New York: Noonday Press, 1961), 126.

CHAPTER TEN

Abortion, Research Cloning, and Beyond: New Challenges for Pro-Lifers in a Brave New World

Scott Klusendorf

I'LL NEVER FORGET THE DEBATE AT Orange Coast College in the spring of 1994. I was a relatively new pro-life advocate, and I was on campus to debate a pro-abortion attorney whose public credentials far outmatched my own at the time. That should have concerned me, but I felt ready. However, had I known before the debate who was watching from the stands, I would have been really nervous. Let me explain.

To help prepare for the event, I listened to a mock abortion debate between Francis J. Beckwith and Gretchen Passantino. Ever since I read her book *Answers to the Cultist at Your Door* while in college, I knew Gretchen was a top-notch Christian apologist. As expected, Dr. Beckwith convincingly defended his pro-life position, but Gretchen, posing as an abortion-choice advocate, put up quite a fight. In fact, she made the case for elective abortion better than anyone I'd ever heard! No surprise, then, that she, rather than my actual debate opponent, became my imaginary sparring partner as I prepped for that event at Orange Coast College.

So picture my surprise when at the conclusion of my own debate a pleasant woman congratulated me and said, "Scott, you did a terrific job handling your opponent tonight. You represented our side very well. Thank you for making a persuasive defense of the pro-life position." Then she introduced herself: "My name is Gretchen Passantino, and I'm here with some of our students."

Gretchen will never know how those few words impacted me as a young pro-life advocate. She was the first well-known apologist to affirm my work, and I drove home that night thinking that maybe, just maybe, I could make it as a full-time pro-life advocate. Twelve years and many debates later, I'm still on the job.

BIOETHICS WITHOUT ETHICS

Today, however, the stakes are much higher as pro-life advocates face horrors never imagined in 1994. The deception surrounding embryonic stem cell research (ESCR) is a case in point.

Until recently, ESCR advocates have flatly denied any intention of implanting cloned embryos in order to harvest tissues or organs from later-term fetuses—a practice known as fetus farming. But researchers are growing impatient. Stem cells from early embryos have yet to deliver one promised cure, and their tendency to form dangerous tumors could render them therapeutically useless. Indeed, throughout the scientific community there's a growing concern that usable cells will not be obtained unless cloned humans can be gestated well past the embryonic stage. Fearing a public backlash, "big biotech" is trying to legalize fetus farming on the sly with a series of phony cloning bans. In each case, what's banned is the *live birth* of cloned human beings, not their *creation* for destructive research. And just when you thought the deception couldn't get worse, cloning advocates are busy telling Americans that cloning is not cloning, that embryos are not really embryos, that morals are mere preferences, and that some humans are not really persons. If you think this is all science fiction, look no further than January 4, 2004.

On that date, then New Jersey Governor James McGreevey signed into law the most permissive stem-cell legislation in the United States, Senate Bill 1909.[1] Ironically, Garden State residents were told they were getting an anti-cloning bill. It was anything but that.

The new law makes it legal to create a cloned embryo, implant it in a woman's womb, then gestate it through the ninth month of pregnancy—so long as you kill the embryo before birth, the point at which it magically becomes a new human individual.[2] Thanks to the new law, there's nothing to stop researchers from fetus farming. In short, New Jersey's alleged anti-cloning bill not only fails to ban cloning—it sets the stage for fetal harvesting at taxpayer expense.

---

[1] See text of bill at http://www.njleg.state.nj.us/2002/Bills/S2000/1909_I1.PDF.
[2] Kathryn Jean Lopez, "State of Cloning," *National Review Online,* January 5, 2004; http://www.national review.com/lopez/lopez200401051346.asp.

"S-1909 has blown the cover off of the true agenda of the biotechnology industry," says Wesley J. Smith, author of *The Culture of Death* and *The Consumer's Guide to a Brave New World.* "Rather than restricting therapeutic cloning to the harvesting of stem cells from early embryos, as the industry often pretends in the media, the Biotechnology Industry Organization's (BIO) enthusiastic support of the New Jersey bill proves that [pro-cloning types] want an unlimited license to harvest cloned human life from inception through the ninth month."[3]

Smith is not the only one concerned. "The New Jersey legislation expressly encourages human cloning for, among other things, the harvesting of 'cadaveric fetal tissue,'" writes Robert P. George of Princeton University and a member of the President's Council on Bioethics. "The bodies in question are those of fetuses created by cloning specifically to be gestated and killed as sources of tissues and organs."[4]

Other states are considering similar laws. Douglas Johnson, legislative director for National Right to Life, says we're headed toward using fetuses for spare parts. "Elements of the biotech industry are definitely moving toward fetus farming and Congress must act to prevent that before it's too late."[5]

SIZE MATTERS: THE DRIVE TOWARD FETUS FARMING

Despite all the hype about promised cures, the problems with embryo cell treatments are legion. Advocates of ESCR know this. First, embryonic stem cells, though allegedly more flexible than their adult counterparts, are hard to control once implanted. They sometimes form tumors instead of usable tissue.[6] Second, the cloning procedures needed to produce embryos for research are quite expensive. As Wesley Smith points out, The National Academy of Sciences claims that "it could take about 100 human eggs per patient—at a cost of $1,000 to $2,000 apiece—just to derive one cloned embryonic-stem-cell line for use in regenerative therapy."[7] If true, it would be next to impossible to secure the billions of human eggs needed for widespread therapeutic cloning. And even if the biotechnology could be developed, "it would either be available only to the super rich or so

[3]Cited in ibid.

[4]Robert P. George, "Fetal Attraction: What the Stem Cell Scientists Really Want, *The Weekly Standard*, October 3, 2005.

[5]Cited in "Fetal Farming Is on the Horizon," *Citizen Link*, September 27, 2005; http://www.family.org/cforum/news/a0038045.cfm.

[6]Rick Weiss, "Embryonic Stem Cells Found to Acquire Mutations," *Washington Post*, September 5, 2005.

[7]Wesley J. Smith, "Cell Wars: The Reagans' Suffering and Hyped Promises," *National Review Online*, June 8, 2004; http://www.nationalreview.com/comment/smith200406081105.asp.

costly that it would have to be stringently rationed."[8] Third, noncontroversial adult stem cells are currently treating seventy known diseases while their embryonic counterparts are treating none, leading some scientists to wonder if embryo cells have any therapeutic value whatsoever.[9] Fourth, prospective investors have so far failed to pony up the cash for highly speculative research that might not cure anyone for years to come, if at all. Finally, there's good reason to suppose that cloning technology may never yield substantial treatments unless cloned humans are developed well past the embryonic stage.[10]

Indeed, experiments are already underway in which cloned cow embryos are implanted, gestated to the early or late fetal stage, and then killed so their organ tissues can be harvested.[11] Among the many benefits, cells extracted from later-term fetuses are stable, allowing researchers to get around the tumor problem associated with embryo cells. "We hope to use this technology in the future to treat patients with diverse diseases," said Robert Lanza, who coauthored one of the bovine studies.[12] Legally, he has a green light: the New Jersey law—and others styled after it—permit this same cloned organ farming to be done with humans.

THE CASE FOR LIFE: SIZE DOESN'T MATTER

Pro-life advocates contend that elective abortion and embryonic stem cell research (ESCR) unjustly take the lives of defenseless human beings. This simplifies the controversy over both issues by focusing public attention on just one question: Is the unborn a member of the human family? If so, killing him or her to benefit others is a serious moral wrong. It treats the distinct human being, with his or her own inherent moral worth, as nothing more than a disposable instrument. Conversely, if the unborn are not

---

[8]Ibid.

[9]"Benefits of Stem Cells to Human Patients: Adult Stem Cells v. Embryonic Stem Cells," published by Do No Harm; http://www.stemcellresearch.org/facts/treatments.htm.

[10]Robert Lanza et al, "Regeneration of the Infarcted Heart with Stem Cells Derived by Nuclear Transplantation," *Circulation Research*, 94 (April 2, 2004): 820–827; http://circres.ahajournals.org/cgi/reprint/94/6/820. In this study, usable cells were produced only after researchers placed the cloned mouse embryos in "surrogate mother" mice, grew them to the late *fetal* stage (the equivalent of the fifth to sixth month of pregnancy in humans), then aborted them for their heart tissue. See also Robert Lanza et al., "Generation of Histocompatible Tissues Using Nuclear Transplantation," *Nature Biotechnology*, 20 (July 2002): 689–696. The authors clearly state that "the cloned cells were derived from early-stage fetuses," not embryos. Both sources above are cited in "Research Cloning and Fetus Farming," Report of the Catholic Bishops; http://usccb.org/prolife/issues/bioethic/cloning/farmfact31805.shtml.

[11]Ibid.

[12]Advanced Cell Technology, "Somatic Cell Nuclear Transfer Gives Old Animals Youthful Immune Cells," June 29, 2005; www.advancedcell.com/press-release/somatic-cell-nuclear-transfer-gives-old-animals-youthful-immune-cells. Cited in Catholic Bishops, ibid.

members of the human family, elective abortion and ESCR require no more justification than having a tooth pulled.

Pro-life advocates defend their case using science and philosophy. Scientifically, they argue that from the earliest stages of development, the unborn are distinct, living, and whole human beings. True, they have yet to grow and mature, but they are whole human beings nonetheless. Leading embryology textbooks affirm this view.[13]

Philosophically, there is no morally significant difference between the embryo you once were and the adult you are today. As Stephen Schwarz points out using the acronym SLED, differences of size, level of development, environment, and degree of dependency are not relevant in the way that abortion advocates need them to be:[14]

> Size: Yes, embryos are smaller than newborns and adults, but why is that relevant? Do we really want to say that large people are more human than small ones? Men are generally larger than women, but that doesn't mean they deserve more rights. Size doesn't equal value.
>
> Level of development: True, embryos and fetuses are less developed than you and I. But again, why is this relevant? Four-year-old girls are less developed than fourteen-year-old ones. Should older children have more rights than their younger siblings? Some people say that self-awareness makes one human. But if that is true, newborns do not qualify as valuable human beings. After all, six-week-old infants lack the immediate capacity for performing human mental functions, as do the reversibly comatose, the sleeping, and those with Alzheimer's disease.
>
> Environment: Where you are has no bearing on who you are. Does your value change when you cross the street or roll over in bed? If not, how can a journey of eight inches down the birth canal suddenly change the essential nature of the unborn from nonhuman to human? If the unborn are not already human, merely changing their location can't make them valuable.
>
> Degree of dependency: If viability makes us valuable human beings, then all those who depend on insulin or kidney medication are not valuable, and we may kill them. Conjoined twins who share blood type and bodily systems also have no right to life.

In short, pro-life advocates contend that although humans differ

---

[13]See T. W. Sadler, *Langman's Embryology*, fifth edition (Philadelphia: W.B. Saunders, 1993), 3; Keith L. Moore, *The Developing Human: Clinically Oriented Embryology* (Toronto: B.C. Decker, 1988), 2; Ronand O'Rahilly and Pabiola Muller, *Human Embryology and Teratology*, second edition (New York: Wiley-Liss, 1996), 8 29.

[14]Stephen Schwarz, *The Moral Question of Abortion* (Chicago: Loyola University Press, 1990), 18. The SLED test was initially suggested by Schwarz, but I have modified and expanded on it here.

immensely with respect to talents, accomplishments, and degrees of development, they are nonetheless equal because they all have the same human nature.

Despite the clarity of the pro-life case, five troubling developments within bioethics are clearing the way for the brave new world of cloning and fetus farming. Each is a serious challenge to the dignity of all humans.

CHALLENGE #1: JUNK SCIENCE

In a February 2006 *New York Times* op-ed piece, Michael Gazzaniga, the director of the Center for Cognitive Neuroscience at Dartmouth and member of the President's Council on Bioethics, chided President Bush for allegedly misstating the facts about cloning:

> Calling human cloning in all its forms an "egregious abuse" is a serious mischaracterization. This makes it sound as if the medical community is out there cloning people, which is simply not true. The phrase "in all of its forms" is code, a way of conflating very different things: reproductive cloning and biomedical cloning.[15]

Very different things? How so? Gazzaniga's alleged distinction between "biomedical cloning" and "reproductive cloning" is totally misleading because *all* cloning is reproductive. So-called "reproductive" cloning means allowing the cloned human to be born alive. "Biomedical" (or therapeutic) cloning means creating him for research, but killing him before birth. In either case, *the act of cloning is exactly the same* and results in a living human embryo. I'll say more about this later; suffice it to say for now that a cloned human being is created when the nucleus is removed from a human egg and is replaced with genetic material from a donor. Once this occurs, the act of cloning is complete. After that, the only question is how we will *treat* the cloned human being—kill him for research or allow him to grow and develop.

Gazzaniga replies that adults and children are human beings, while cloned embryos are mere "hunks" of cells in a petri dish. This is sloppy science. Living human embryos are not mere "hunks" of cells but distinct, self-integrating organisms capable of directing their own maturation as members of the human species. Dr. Maureen Condic, assistant professor of neurobiology and anatomy at the University of Utah, explains the important distinction between clumps of cells and whole human embryos overlooked by Gazzaniga:

---

[15]Michael Gazzaniga, "All Clones Are Not the Same," *The New York Times,* February 16, 2006.

> The critical difference between a collection of cells and a living organism is the ability of an organism to act in a coordinated manner for the continued health and maintenance of the body as a whole. . . . Embryos are not merely collections of human cells, but living creatures with all the properties that define any organism as distinct from a group of cells; embryos are capable of growing, maturing, maintaining a physiologic balance between various organ systems, adapting to changing circumstances, and repairing injury. Mere groups of human cells do nothing like this under any circumstances.[16]

Meanwhile, Senators Diane Feinstein (D-CA) and Orrin Hatch (R-UT), co-sponsors of a pro-cloning measure in the U.S. Senate, have taken junk science to a whole new level. Each insists that the embryos in question are not human organisms but stem cells (or eggs!) with the potential to become human beings.[17] This is an unabashed lie. Embryos don't come from stem cells; they are living human beings that *have* stem cells. And extracting these cells is lethal for the tiny human subject. To say anything different is not science. It's political propaganda.

But if politics can explain away embryos, it can explain away fetuses. All we need are a few promised cures.

CHALLENGE #2: PHONY CLONING BANS

The relationship between fetus farming and cloning is clear. First, cloning (theoretically) provides a rich supply of embryos that can be grown to the fetal stage where organs can be harvested. Second, cloning allows researchers to derive these organs from a fetus that's a genetic match of the patient, thus minimizing the potential for organ rejection. Bottom line: you can't pursue fetus farming if you don't first sell the public on embryo cloning. The problem is, when asked directly if tax dollars should be used to clone human embryos for destructive research, a majority of the public says, "No way!"[18]

Fearing public backlash, big biotech is trying to legalize cloning on the sly with a series of phony bans. Known more accurately as "clone and kill" laws, these alleged "bans" allow human embryos to be cloned provided

---

[16]Maureen Condic, "Life: Defining the Beginning by the End," *First Things,* May 2003.

[17]Feinstein assured viewers of the February 24, 2002 *Meet the Press* that her bill would "clearly make it illegal to inject one of these stem cells into a woman's uterus" to cause pregnancy. Cited in Wesley J. Smith, "Brave New Clarity," *National Review On-line,* July 16, 2002; http://www.nationalreview.com/comment/comment-smith071602.asp.

[18]Wilson Research Strategies did a poll for the National Right to Life Committee (August 2004) that found that 53 percent oppose using tax dollars for destructive embryo research, while 38 percent support funding. The complete poll can be viewed at http://www.nrlc.org/Killing_Embryos/NRLCStemCellPoll.pdf.

they are destroyed for medical research prior to birth. Shocking though it may seem, some "pro-life" advocates support these bills.

In Missouri, former GOP Senator John Danforth is honorary co-chair for the Missouri Stem Cell Research and Cures Initiative (sponsored by the Missouri Coalition for Lifesaving Cures), a ballot measure that would amend the state's constitution to permanently allow embryonic stem cell research. Danforth assures us that he is solidly "pro-life" and has "always voted pro-life" and that the initiative "respects the sanctity of life." But misleading cloning language is all over the group's "Setting the Record Straight" fact sheet and other web site documents.

We're told in the fact sheet, for example, that the initiative "clearly and strictly bans human cloning."[19] But in the "Frequently Asked Questions" section, we get this baffling statement:

> We believe that ALL types of stem cell research should be pursued in the effort to find lifesaving cures, including research involving adult stem cells, Somatic Cell Nuclear Transfer (SCNT) and stem cells from excess fertility clinic embryos (also called blastocysts or pre-embryos) that would otherwise be discarded. We also believe that human cloning should be banned.[20]

Several paragraphs later, SCNT is defined as "a process that uses a patient's own cell and an empty, unfertilized egg to create ES [embryonic stem] cells." The deception here is breathtaking.

First, Somatic Cell Nuclear Transfer (SCNT) *is* cloning, and Danforth knows it. (A decade ago, this exact same technique gave us Dolly, the first cloned sheep.) The process begins when a scientist removes the nucleus from a mature, unfertilized egg (an oocyte) and replaces it with donor DNA. Chemicals are then added, and a spark of electricity (hopefully) jolts the cell into dividing and growing into a cloned human embryo. At this point the act of cloning is complete, and we are faced with a choice—nurture the embryo until it's born or destroy it for research. *What Danforth's Missouri Cures proposal strictly forbids is the birth of a cloned human being, not its destruction for medical research.*

Second, there is no such thing as a "pre-embryo." As pro-cloning advocate Lee Silver points out, the term is scientifically misleading and is used to deliberately fool the public into accepting destructive embryo research and cloning. He says, "I'll let you in on a secret. The term pre-embryo has

---

[19]"Setting the Record Straight," http://www.missouricures.com/settingtherecord.php.
[20]"Frequently Asked Questions," http://www.missouricures.com/faq.php.

been embraced wholeheartedly by IVF practitioners for reasons that are political, not scientific."[21]

Third, SCNT does not make embryonic stem cells from unfertilized eggs. It creates living human embryos that will be destroyed so researchers can *get* stem cells. And just when the deception couldn't get worse, we're told the Missouri Cures initiative "resolves concerns about human cloning by strictly banning human *reproductive* cloning to create babies"[22] (emphasis mine).

Let's be clear: Cloning is cloning—period! As mentioned above, the alleged distinction between "therapeutic" cloning and "reproductive" cloning is totally misleading because all cloning is reproductive. In each case, what's banned is the *birth* of cloned human beings, not their creation for destructive research. For example, New Jersey's own clone bill (S-1909) was sold to the public as a strict prohibition on human cloning, but with a hidden lethal twist: the so-called strict prohibition was simply that all cloned embryos and fetuses *must* be killed before they have a chance to develop into more mature human beings. Meanwhile, California law bans initiating a pregnancy with a cloned embryo, but only if that pregnancy "could result in the *birth* of a human being."[23] In other words, human lives may be created with cloning technology if and only if technicians agree—under threat of law—to destroy any clones *prior to birth*. That's the proposed ethical safeguard that allegedly bans cloning. It's a sham.[24]

Moreover, pro-lifers don't oppose the destruction of cloned human embryos because it kills "babies"—we oppose it because it unjustly takes the life of a defenseless human being, regardless of his or her stage of development. For Danforth and a sympathetic press to pretend otherwise is shameful.

"The mainstream media still discusses these issues as if scientists only want to use embryos left over from IVF procedures," writes Smith. "But those days are long gone. It is now undeniable that Big Biotech and its politician and university allies do not even intend to restrict biotechnological research to early embryos situated in petri dishes." As bills in New Jersey and other states clearly demonstrate, "the ground is being plowed already

---

[21]Lee Silver, *Remaking Eden: Cloning and Beyond in a Brave New World* (New York: Avon Books, 1997), 39. Silver is a Princeton University biology professor.
[22]Press release, October 11, 2005; http://www.missouricures.com/rel_101105.php.
[23]California Health and Safety Code, §125300. Cited in Catholic Bishops (emphasis mine).
[24]For more on this point, see Wesley J. Smith, "Stealth Cloning," *National Review Online*, February 15, 2005; http://www.nationalreview.com/smithw/smith200502150746.asp.

to allow cloned fetal farming, the next, but certainly not last, step intended to lead us to a Brave New World."[25]

CHALLENGE #3: INTOLERANCE DISGUISED AS MORAL NEUTRALITY

In a 2005 *New York Times* editorial, John Danforth wrote that government restrictions on embryonic stem cell research (put plainly, the practice of cloning human embryos for destructive research) wrongly impose a particular religious view on a pluralistic society:

> It is not evident to many of us that cells in a petri dish are equivalent to identifiable people suffering from terrible diseases . . . the only explanation for legislators comparing cells in a petri dish to babies in the womb is the extension of religious doctrine into statutory law.[26]

Danforth is just plain wrong that pro-life advocates opposed to ESCR provide no rational defense for their position. Sure, they do. The problem, however, is that he takes no time to actually engage the sophisticated case that pro-life philosophers present in support of the embryo's humanity.[27] Even at the popular level, he can't bring himself to answer a basic pro-life argument based on science and philosophy. As stated above, pro-lifers contend that from the earliest stages of development, the unborn are distinct, living, whole human beings. True, they have yet to grow and mature, but they are whole human beings nonetheless. The facts of science confirm this.[28] Philosophically, pro-lifers argue that there is no morally significant difference between the embryo you once were and the adult you are today. Differences of size, development, and location are not relevant in the way that ESCR advocates need them to be. Pro-lifers don't need Scripture or church doctrine to tell them these things. They are truths even atheists and secular libertarians can, and sometimes do, recognize.[29]

Yet nowhere in his piece does Danforth present a principled argument explaining why pro-life advocates are mistaken on these points. He appeals to neutrality, but this really won't help because his own position, like the pro-lifer's, is grounded in prior metaphysical commitments. Indeed, the nature of the ESCR debate is such that all positions presuppose a metaphysical view of human value, and for this reason the pro-research

---

[25]Ibid.
[26]John Danforth, "In the Name of Politics," *New York Times*, March 30, 2005.
[27]See, for example, Francis J. Beckwith, "The Explanatory Power of the Substance View of Persons," *Christian Bioethics*, 10.1 (2004): 33–54.
[28]Condic, "Life: Defining the Beginning by the End."
[29]See Libertarians for Life (http://l4l.org) and Godless Pro-lifers (http://godlessprolifers.org).

position Danforth defends is not entitled to win by default.[30] At issue is not which view of ESCR has metaphysical underpinnings and which does not, but which metaphysical view of human value is correct, pro-life or pro-destructive research?

The pro-life view on ESCR is that humans are intrinsically valuable in virtue of the kind of thing they are. True, they differ immensely with respect to talents, accomplishments, and degrees of development, but they are nonetheless equal because they share a common human nature. Their right to life comes to be when they come to be, either at conception or at the completion of a cloning process. Danforth's own view is that humans have value (and hence rights) not in virtue of the kind of thing they are, members of a natural kind, but only because of an acquired property that comes to be later in the life of the human organism. Because the early embryo does not appear (to him) as a human being with rights, destructive research is permissible. Notice that Danforth is doing the abstract work of metaphysics. That is, he is using philosophical reflection to defend a disputed view of human value in his quest to defend ESCR. Put simply, Danforth's attempt to disqualify the pro-life view from public policy based on its alleged metaphysical underpinnings works equally well to disqualify his own view.

In the end it's hard to see how Danforth's case for moral neutrality wouldn't also justify the destruction of later-term fetuses. For example, during a 2004 presidential debate, Senator John Kerry defended his overall record on abortion—which includes, we should add, his refusal to vote against grisly partial-birth procedures—with language similar to Danforth's:

> First of all, I cannot tell you how deeply I respect the belief about life and when it begins. I'm a Catholic, raised a Catholic. I was an altar boy. Religion has been a huge part of my life. . . . But I can't take what is an article of faith for me and legislate it for someone who doesn't share that article of faith, whether they be agnostic, atheist, Jew, Protestant, whatever. I can't do that.[31]

Presumably, stabbing late-term fetuses in the head and sucking out their brains is a mere preference issue, something we should no more restrict than your right to choose chocolate ice cream over vanilla.

---

[30]Francis J. Beckwith, "Law, Religion, and the Metaphysics of Abortion: A Reply to Simmons," *Journal of Church and State*, 43.1 (Winter 2001): 19–33. I owe my thoughts in this section to Beckwith's analysis.
[31]John Kerry, Second Presidential Candidates' Debate, Washington University, St. Louis, Missouri (October 8, 2004), Commission on Presidential Debates, http://www.debates.org/pages/trans2004c.html.

CHALLENGE #4: PERSONHOOD ETHICS

Writing in the *New York Times,* Michael Gazzaniga attacks President Bush's cloning policy as follows:

> The president's view is consistent with the reductive idea that there is an equivalence between a bunch of molecules in a lab and a beautifully nurtured and loved human who has been shaped by a lifetime of experiences and discovery. . . . DNA must undergo thousands if not millions of interactions at both the molecular and experiential level to grow and develop a brain and become a person.[32]

Notice the unsupported claims here. Why should we suppose that brain development bestows value on a person? As usual with pro-cloning advocates, Gazzaniga does not tell us why development matters, nor does he say why certain value-giving properties are value-giving in the first place. True, he later appeals to one's immediate capacity to experience memories, loves, and hopes, but isn't that just question-begging since the issue is whether one is a human subject even if one does not have memories, loves, and hopes? Newborns lack all of these qualities—does it follow they are fitting subjects for destructive research?

Gazzaniga then says that it squares with our basic intuitions to accept that adults and children are people while clumps of cells in a petri dish are not:

> Look around you. Look at your loved ones. Do you see a hunk of cells or do you see something else? . . . We do not see cells, simple or complex—we see people, human life. That thing in a petri dish is something else. It doesn't yet have the memories and loves and hopes that accumulate over the years.[33]

There is a host of problems with the idea of personhood coming into existence only after some degree of bodily development. One is that you end up saying things like "I came to be after my body came to be." Or "I inhabit a body that was once an embryo." Yet nowhere in his essay does Gazzaniga defend his metaphysical assumption that personhood is an accidental (nonessential) property rather than something intrinsic to the human subject. I wonder: Other than the embryos he'd like to arbitrarily exclude, has he ever met a living human that wasn't a person? Have any of us?

---

[32]Gazzaniga, "All Clones Are Not the Same."
[33]Ibid.

Meanwhile, Gazzaniga's appeal to our intuitions—"these embryos don't look like your relatives" (my paraphrase)—is naive, though I agree that some people will not be impressed with a two-week-old human embryo. For them, it's counterintuitive to suggest that something the size of a dot is a human being. But intuitions can be mistaken (many people once thought it counterintuitive to say blacks were human) and are always subject to compelling evidence to the contrary. We have that evidence: the facts of science make clear that embryos are not mere "hunks" of cells but nascent human beings at the earliest stages of development. In short, Gazzaniga's appeal to intuition does not refute the strongly evidenced claim for the humanity of the embryo; it merely sidesteps it.

Princeton philosopher Peter Singer is correct: once society accepts that human beings have value only because of some acquired property like self-awareness, there remains no logical reason to exclude only embryos. Fetuses and newborns will also lose their right to life.

CHALLENGE #5: THE NEW RELATIVISM

Journalist Christopher Caldwell writes, "A pro-life regime is not really something Americans want—it's just something they feel they ought to want."[34] During a debate I had at U.C. Davis in June 2006, Dr. Meredith Williams, who occasionally performs abortions, repeatedly called abortion tragic and said that she, too, wanted to reduce the practice, provided no laws were passed restricting it. But why abortion is tragic and why she wants to reduce it she couldn't say. Seriously, if the unborn is just a "parasite" as she claimed more than once during our debate, isn't removing that parasite a great event rather than a tragic one? The more abortions the better! She can't have it both ways.

Throughout our exchange, Dr. Williams couldn't decide whether women had an absolute right to bodily autonomy or not. For the first part of our exchange, she more or less argued that they did. However, during the cross-exchange she backed off that claim when I pressed her with this question provided by physician Rich Poupard:

> Let's say a woman has intractable nausea and vomiting, and insists on taking thalidomide to help her symptoms. After having explained the horrific risks of birth defects that have arisen due to this medication, she still insists on taking it based on the fact that the fetus has no right to her body anyway. After being refused thalidomide from her

---

[34]Christopher Caldwell, "Why Abortion Is Here to Stay," *The New Republic*, April 5, 1999.

physician, she acquires some and takes it, resulting in her child developing no arms. Do we believe that she did anything wrong? Would we excuse her actions based on her right to bodily autonomy? The fetus after all is an uninvited guest, and has no right even to life let alone an environment free from pathogens.[35]

When Dr. Williams said the woman was wrong to do that, I replied, "So if the mother wants to *harm* her unborn child with drug use, that's wrong, but if she wants to *kill* it with elective abortion, that's fine?" Many of those present immediately grasped the absurdity of her position.

TWO THINGS THAT MUST BE DONE?

All is not lost, but pro-life Christians face a daunting task. Peter Singer writes, "By 2040, it may be that only a rump of hard-core, know-nothing religious fundamentalists will defend the view that every human life, from conception to death, is sacrosanct."[36] To thwart his prophecy in the short term, pro-life advocates must press for a federal ban on *all* human cloning. There's potentially good news here: A ban on cloning is a ban on fetus farming. The U.S. House passed such a ban in 2002, but the legislation failed in the Senate.

For the long term, pro-life advocates must follow Gretchen Passantino's lead and actively encourage (and mentor) young Christian apologists capable of defending the pro-life view. Greg Cunningham is right:

> There are more people working full-time to kill babies than there are working full-time to save them. That's because killing babies is very profitable while saving them is very costly. So costly, that large numbers of people who say they oppose abortion and embryo research are not lifting a finger to stop them. They do just enough to salve the conscience but not enough to stop the killing.[37]

That's a stunning indictment of our movement, and it's easy to think, "That's not me." But unless concerned Christians take seriously the challenges put forth by a culture that increasingly denies the value of human life, we'll be creating human beings as organ factories long before 2040. You can bet the farm on it. Just ask New Jersey.

---

[35]Rich Poupard, "Do No Harm (Except for the Killing Thing)," published at http://lti-blog.blogspot.com/2007/01/do-no-harm-except-for-that-killing.html..
[36]Peter Singer, cited in "10 Ideas on the Way Out by 2040," *The Dallas Morning News*, November 27, 2005.
[37]Gregg has made this observation in numerous presentations on abortion.

CHAPTER ELEVEN

The Value of Historical Theology for Apologetics

Alan W. Gomes

I RECALL BOTH WITH AMUSEMENT and chagrin an encounter I had with a student during my first semester of teaching, almost twenty years ago. I was in the midst of my doctoral studies, spelunking in Latin texts, writing a dissertation, and also voraciously consuming the best survey works in historical theology (HT) as I crafted my own lectures. But I was smitten, for to me the study of HT was the most wonderful of pursuits. I was stimulated intellectually as I rubbed shoulders with the brightest and best of the Christian tradition. I also relished the "thrill of the hunt," for every day I discovered some new and unexpected twist, some novel and unusual argument that seemed to lurk around the turn of every page. It was all so fascinating and exciting! How could I not love it? Who wouldn't?

And so as I began that first class session, filled with excitement and enthusiasm but also with the trepidation of a new prof finding his way, the student's hand shot up. "Professor Gomes," he queried, "how is your course on the history of doctrine relevant to my ministry?" Wow! What impertinence! My whole *life* was absorbed in the study of HT—including incalculable hours prepping for this very class—and the ingrate *dares* ask if *my* class is relevant to *his* ministry? He may just as well have asked, "Professor Gomes, what right do you have to exist?"

So adapting some comments from a discussion I'd had with one of my own professors, I shot back defensively, "Well, granting that my class is about what occupied the minds of the greatest Christians of all times, perhaps you should ask instead whether your ministry is relevant to my class!"

A clever and rapier rejoinder, that! But I now wince just a bit when I think of how I answered that student, who probably meant no offense and simply wanted to know why he should take a course on HT when there are so many other pressing skills for a budding minister of the gospel to acquire.

Now, my response, while sarcastic, certainly did convey some important truths. Sometimes we *do* make our own ministry or church experience the measure of all things and determine "relevance" against them. Sometimes we *do* engage in a "chauvinism of the present,"[1] in which we think the latest is also automatically the greatest. Many *will be* surprised someday—perhaps on the last day—to find that their "great and unprecedented move of God" was but a side eddy, a meaningless whirlpool in which the enthusiasts swirled round and round and yet accomplished little of lasting value for the kingdom.[2] And so it could well be that we are the ones who need a "reality check," and there may be no better way of doing this than by studying the great thinkers of ages past.[3]

At the same time, I now believe that the student's query about the relevance of HT for our ministries was a fair one, and one that no doubt crosses more than a few students' minds, including those who may be too timid to ask it. So I make it a point to raise the question myself in the first session of my survey classes. The history of Christian doctrine *is* relevant for "practical" Christian ministry. There is indeed something that you can *do* with this knowledge.

As I discuss with my classes the specific ways in which a knowledge of the history of doctrine is practically relevant to ministry, I find that several of the illustrations come from the area of apologetics. Some of the illustrations are "negative" or "defensive." That is, they show how a knowledge of HT can deflect the false and sometimes even crackpot claims of those who would attack the faith or substitute a counterfeit version of it in place of the true. But the field of HT is "positive" also. Even beyond providing specific arguments to refute this or that cultic error or false teaching, the discipline of HT can inculcate intellectual disciplines and habits of mind that pay rich dividends for defenders of the faith.

---

[1]As one of my professors at Fuller Theological Seminary used to call it.
[2]I am indebted to W.G.T. Shedd for this poignant metaphor, which I have adapted slightly for this purpose.
[3]C. S. Lewis made this point nicely in his well-known essay "On the Reading of Old Books," in *God in the Dock: Essays on Theology and Ethics* (Grand Rapids, MI: Eerdmans, 1970).

PLAYING DEFENSE: DEFEATING SPURIOUS HISTORICAL CLAIMS

I was working on a writing project when the phone rang. It was Greg Koukl, a former student of mine who heads an excellent apologetics ministry called Stand to Reason. Our conversation went something as follows:

"Hi, Alan. Greg Koukl here. I'm writing an article that deals with the claims of *The Da Vinci Code*. The movie is coming out in a few weeks, and I'm getting lots of questions about it. I wanted to run by you some statements in the book and get your opinion. They have to do with the Council of Nicea and also the canon of Scripture."

"Glad to, Greg. But you should know that I'm probably one of the few people on the planet who hasn't really paid much attention to this thing—yet."

"No problem," Greg replied. "Let me just read to you some quotes from the book, and you can give me your response. They come out of this one particular chapter[4] from a character named Sir Leigh Teabing, who is a former 'British Royal Historian.' I want to hear your reaction to them."

"Fire away," I said.

What followed was a kind of Tourette's barrage of historiographical lunacy. Among the many "facts" that, according to Teabing, "the vast majority of educated Christians know," were the following:

• The Bible is strictly a human product and not from God. "Man created it as a historical record of tumultuous times, and it has evolved through countless translations, additions, and revisions. History has never had a definitive version of the book."

• "More than *eighty* gospels were considered for inclusion in the New Testament, yet only a relative few were chosen for inclusion—Matthew, Mark, Luke, and John among them [*sic*]."

• "Nothing in Christianity is original. The pre-Christian God Mithras—called the *Son of God* and the *Light of the World*—was born on December 25, died, was buried in a rock tomb, and then resurrected in three days. . . . Even Christianity's weekly holy day was stolen from pagans."

• At the Council of Nicea, called by Constantine, the bishops voted on the divinity of Jesus. "Until *that* moment in history, Jesus was viewed by His followers as a mortal prophet . . . a great and powerful man, but a *man* nonetheless. A mortal . . . Jesus' establishment as 'the Son of God' was officially proposed and voted on by the Council of Nicea." When Sophie, the interlocutor in this exchange, queries, "Hold on. You're saying Jesus' divinity was the result of a *vote*?" our learned British

---

[4]I.e., Chap. 55 in Dan Brown, *The Da Vinci Code* (New York: Doubleday, 2003). In the following quotes all italics are in the original.

Royal Historian replies, "A relatively close vote at that." Constantine's purpose in this, Sophie is told, was to make Jesus "into a deity who existed beyond the scope of the human world, an entity whose power was unchallengeable." And by virtue of its association with the Christian religion, the Roman Catholic Church now found itself in the position of superiority over any pagan challenges. "It was all about power," Teabing declared.

• "Because Constantine upgraded Jesus' status almost four centuries *after* Jesus' death, thousands of documents already existed chronicling His life as a *mortal* man. To rewrite the history books, Constantine knew he would need a bold stroke. . . . Constantine commissioned and financed a new Bible, which omitted those gospels that spoke of Christ's *human* traits and embellished those gospels that made Him godlike. The earlier gospels were outlawed, gathered up, and burned." Some of the gospels in question, Teabing relates, were then rediscovered in the Dead Sea Scrolls in the 1950s [sic] and at Nag Hammadi in 1945. The Vatican did what it could to suppress the release of these gospels, showing, as they did, that the modern Bible was compiled and edited by men who possessed a political agenda: to promote the divinity of the man Jesus Christ and use his influence to solidify their own power base.

"So, Alan . . . what do you think?"

What did I think? Teabing's riff was chock-a-block full of historical errors, portraying the first four centuries of ecclesiastical history as they might look in a fun house mirror. I scarcely knew where to begin.

"This is nuts!" I blurted out, exasperated. "Surely no one is taking this seriously!"

"Actually," Greg replied, "this book is having quite an impact, and not just among unbelievers. I've talked to quite a few Christians who are really shaken by its claims."

"Wow! What a great argument for knowing something about the history of the Christian tradition!" I exclaimed. "Anyone with even a cursory knowledge of how Christian doctrine developed wouldn't fall for this stuff. My students, and certainly you, Greg, can refute this without breaking a sweat. No student making the kinds of logical leaps and historical errors of this 'British Royal Historian' would get out of my survey classes alive!"

As I continued my discussion with Greg, it was clear that he already knew what was wrong with these assertions. All I did was suggest a few other book titles for him to share with his readers who might want to do further study. I then wished him the best.

Since my discussion with Greg I've read *The Da Vinci Code*, have seen the movie, and also looked at a few of the now considerable number of books and articles refuting it. Because *The Da Vinci Code* has already been decimated *ad infinitum,* there is no point in belaboring all its manifold problems. But I do wish to explore how different kinds of challenges require a knowledge and use of HT in somewhat different ways. An attack such as *The Da Vinci Code* is probably best handled by laying bare its many specific factual errors. But there are other sorts of assaults where a more nuanced or systemic knowledge of the history of doctrine may be required.

The Da Vinci Code contains a plethora of inaccuracies, in a variety of fields. Truly Dan Brown has shown himself a Renaissance man of error, mangling adroitly an impressive range of disciplines (both real and imagined[5]), as he perverts art history,[6] architecture, geography, linguistics, and, of course, the varied branches of early and medieval history (both sacred and profane) with astonishing ease. And it is on the level of particular errors of fact that many of the rejoinders by Christian apologists have sought to undermine it, and successfully so. The vote at Nicea was hardly "close" (over 300 to 2, though the exact numbers vary slightly). *Everyone* at Nicea already believed that Jesus was "the Son of God," though the Arian party defined that to mean that Jesus was a created divine being who took on flesh, while the orthodox party affirmed that he was literally God. In other words, both sides of the debate regarded Jesus to be "divine," with *neither* regarding him to be a *mere* man.[7]

Neither Constantine in general nor the Council of Nicea in particular had anything whatever to do with defining the biblical canon.[8] There never were "eighty gospels," even when one tabulates the various Gnostic and other pseudepigraphical productions. The Dead Sea Scrolls were discovered in 1947, not 1950, nor were any "gospels" included in these documents. The canonical Gospels in fact say a great deal about Jesus' genuine human traits, such as his human birth and growth (e.g., Luke 2:52); clearly Constantine's henchmen made quite a blunder by including these. Christians living long before the Nicene Council—men such as Ignatius of Antioch, Tertullian of Carthage, Irenaeus of Lyon, and a host of others[9]—vigorously affirmed the deity of Christ. Solid scholarship

---

[5]Robert Langdon is said to be a "Professor of Religious Symbology" at Harvard. While an academic may certainly study the meaning of symbols in the context of a particular discipline, there is no such discipline, per se, as "symbology."

[6]See, for example, Fred Sanders's fine piece at http://www.go.family.org/davinci/content/A000000099.cfm.

[7]Indeed, the Arian party that lost the purportedly "close vote" did not believe in the true humanity of Christ at all. While they taught that he had a human body, they denied that he had a human soul. Instead, the "Son Logos," a created, divine, angelic-like creature, simply inhabited a body.

[8]For an excellent treatment of canonicity, see Norman L. Geisler and William E. Nix, *A General Introduction to the Bible,* revised and expanded (Chicago: Moody, 1986).

[9]On this, see, e.g., E. Calvin Beisner, *God in Three Persons* (Wheaton, IL: Tyndale House, 1984).

exists to show that Mithrianism actually ripped off Christianity and not the reverse.[10] The so-called "Gnostic Gospels" of Nag Hammadi are quite late (i.e., mid-second century or later) compared to the canonical ones, thus fatally undermining their claims to authenticity. And these very Gnostic gospels, even if we were to accept them, tended much more to downplay or even outright deny Christ's genuine humanity, stressing instead his "divine" status (albeit in a heretical way, incompatible with biblical orthodoxy).[11] I could readily expand the list of discrete errors of fact just from the few snippets from Teabing cited above, and if one sought to tabulate *all* such errors of fact from the variegated disciplines touched upon in *The Da Vinci Code,* the list might well exceed the length of the book itself.

Now, I believe that on the level of highlighting egregiously erroneous factoids, the responses to *The Da Vinci Code* that I've seen do a creditable job.[12] And I certainly think this is a good way to torpedo a book so rife with such errors. After being confronted with the first dozen or so blatant falsehoods, the reader soon realizes that Dan Brown is utterly untrustworthy and that *nothing* in the book is to be believed. The reader comes to understand in short order the truth of what Irenaeus of Lyon (c. 135–c. 203) declared while refuting some of the *Da Vinci Code*-like teaching of his own day: "It is not necessary to drink up the ocean in order to learn that its water is salty."[13]

We have all heard the well-worn maxim that those who do not learn from the mistakes of the past are doomed to repeat them. But that maxim assumes a state of historical awareness often greater than what obtains today in society and in our churches. These days it is more aptly said that those who don't even *know* the past are fair game for the hucksters who would rewrite it. As a professor of HT, I can in a sense agree with a remark that Lee Strobel made to the Talbot faculty at a recent luncheon, where he said that Dan Brown has actually done a favor for those of us who wish Christians would take doctrine and HT more seriously. Many Christians who never before had an awareness of Christian history or the development of Christian doctrine are now clamoring for answers. Insofar

---

[10]See Edwin Yamauchi, "Easter—Myth, Hallucination, or History," *Christianity Today* (March 15, 1974): 5.

[11]Indeed, if Constantine truly wanted to upgrade Jesus' status from a mere man to a Godlike being, while at the same time getting quit of his human characteristics, he ought to have included the Gnostic gospels and suppressed the canonical ones.

[12]See chapter 17 in this volume entitled "The New Testament, Jesus Christ, and *The Da Vinci Code*" by Richard G. Howe. Also, Josh McDowell has catalogued a good number of problems with the book. See his *The Da Vinci Code: A Quest for An-wers* (Holiday, FL: Green Key Books, 2006). The Answers in Action web site also has some fine information refuting the book (http://www.answers.org/book reviews/davincicode.html).

[13]Irenaeus of Lyon, *Against Heresies*, 2.19.8.

as Christians are now digging into the roots of their faith as they seek to refute such challenges as *The Da Vinci Code*, it may well be that what Dan Brown perhaps meant for evil (or at least only to make a buck) God meant for good (Gen. 50:20).

Sometimes, however, the use of historical materials in combating error is better accomplished with greater attention to the overall flow or shape of Christian theology. That is, an adequate response may require more than pointing simply to errors in dates and persons and places and events and quotes. Some errors are more subtle than this and so may require responses with greater nuance.

In 1991 I moderated a debate at Biola University between Mormon and Christian apologists. Kurt Van Gorden of Jude 3 Mission and Bob Passantino of Answers in Action represented the historic Christian position, and Van Hale (a popular Mormon apologist) and Bill Forrest (a member of the Mormon "Seventy") contended for the LDS view. Among the propositions debated was, "Can man progress to Godhood?" A basic tenet of LDS theology is that through faithful obedience to the principles of the gospel (i.e., the teachings of Mormonism) a person may attain "exaltation," becoming a God[14] or Goddess in their life beyond this mortal existence. Furthermore, God and man are of the same species: God (or, to be more precise, "the Gods") once had a mortal existence just like our present one and attained Godhood through the same obedience that Mormons strive to accomplish. Human beings in their mortal state, therefore, are "Gods in embryo." The LDS doctrine is succinctly captured by the oft-quoted couplet of Lorenzo Snow, the fifth president of the Mormon Church: "As man is, God once was; as God is, man may become."[15]

"Anti-Mormons," as the LDS call us, have, of course, vigorously rejected such patently heterodox teaching. But in an attempt to impart the patina of historic orthodoxy to this monstrous error, some Mormon apologists have begun citing certain early church fathers, who they claim made the same or a fundamentally similar point to what the Mormons are making, employing language not unlike what one finds in Joseph Smith and in other Mormon General Authorities. Specifically, there is a teaching

---

[14]Though it might appear preferable to retain the upper case *G* when speaking only of the God of the Bible and not the "Goodhood" of which Mormons speak, I have chosen to maintain the capital *G* throughout. To switch between upper and lower case might imply that Mormons themselves make some kind of ontological distinction between the God of the Bible and their own Godhood, when in fact they do not. This will become clear in the discussion that follows.

[15]For some very fine treatments of the Mormon doctrine of God, see James White, *Is the Mormon My Brother?* (Minneapolis: Bethany House, 1997); Kurt Van Gorden, "Mormonism," in *The Zondervan Guide to Cults and Religious Movements*, ed. Alan W. Gomes (Grand Rapids, MI: Zondervan, 1995).

found in certain Church Fathers[16] that is called "theosis" or "deification." According to this teaching, the glorified Christian is destined to become "divinized" or to "become god." As Athanasius, Bishop of Alexandria (c. 296–373), put it, "For he [the Word] was made man that we might be made God."[17] Similarly, Theophilus of Antioch stated, "If man should incline to the things of immortality, keeping the commandment of God, he should receive as reward from him immortality, and should become God."[18]

And so the Mormons cry, "Foul." "Anti-Mormons," they say, practice a double standard. When Mormons say that man can progress to Godhood, we excoriate them as heretics. When Athanasius says it, we call him the "Father of orthodoxy," or at the very least give him a pass. And likewise for a vast number of other church fathers who also made statements of this kind.

So back to our debate. Van Hale used his opening remarks to quote a bevy of impressive Christian personages—men such as Justin Martyr, Theophilus of Antioch, Irenaeus, Novatian, Tertullian, Clement of Alexandria, Maximus, John of Damascus, Basil, Theodore, Augustine, Gregory Nyssa, Gregory Nazianzus, Origen, Athanasius, and Hippolytus— as making the same point as the Mormons: man can become God. This list of such citations, Hale informed his audience, is impressive, and time permitted him to offer but a handful of references from the four to five hundred pages of material he brought with him to the debate.

In this case it would not do to charge that the Mormons had falsified or concocted these quotations Dan Brown style, for they had not. Athanasius had indeed said what they quoted him as saying. And so had all the others. Mr. Hale had quoted them accurately, and he had all of the references lined up, should anyone challenge him.

Kurt Van Gorden and Bob Passantino had done their historical homework, however, and were well prepared for these citations. Unlike the Mormons, they grasped the overall theological shape of the early Christians' doctrine of God (i.e., theology proper), the place of *theosis* within it, and even the specific context of the texts cited by Mr. Hale.[19] They also were able to point to some telling qualifiers within the very same documents that he cited—qualifiers that utterly rule out the Mormon understanding of their words.

---

[16]I.e., particularly in the Fathers of the Eastern Church, though one finds it in the writings of some of the Western Fathers as well.

[17]Athanasius, *On the Incarnation of the Word*, 54.3.

[18]Theophilus to Autolycus, 2.27.

[19]I grant here for the sake of discussion that the Mormon apologists actually believed that their interpretation of these church fathers was correct, as opposed to knowingly misrepresenting their meaning.

In Kurt Van Gorden's reply, he observed that the Mormons who use this line of argument commit two logical fallacies in their handling of the historical materials: equivocation of terms and vicious abstraction. The Mormons equivocate terms when they claim that the words *God* and *divinization* mean the same thing for the church fathers that they do for the Mormons. The Mormons commit the fallacy of vicious abstraction when they rip a particular quotation out of its literary and historical context, sundering it from the overall thought of a thinker and from the proximate context of his remarks in a particular document.

It was easy for Kurt Van Gorden and Bob Passantino to show that these early fathers were strict monotheists who did not believe that man and God were of the same species, nor that God the Father had a Father before him, who had a Father before him, *ad infinitum* (as the Mormons teach). Nor did these early fathers believe that God attained Godhood in conformity with the law of eternal progression, as a reward for his faithful obedience. The god of Joseph Smith is as far from the God of Athanasius as Kolob is from earth.[20]

After Van Gorden's initial response, the Mormons were visibly shaken. So they attempted to regroup, with Van Hale pressing the following line of argument: "I'd like to ask you not what Athanasius, for example, is *not* saying, or not *what else* he might believe. But when Athanasius made the statement, which we find repeated dozens and dozens of times by other early Christians . . . when he made the statement that God became man so that men might become gods, *what was it* that he was conveying?"[21]

Because Van Gorden and Passantino had studied the doctrine of theosis and understood how it fit systemically in the Eastern Orthodox doctrine of God, they were well positioned to respond to this rejoinder. They replied that these fathers *did* believe in a communication of divine qualities to redeemed believers, but one that is relative, not absolute. The early fathers made it clear that there are certain *communicable* attributes that are consistent for God to impart to his creatures, such as holiness and immortality. At the same time, these fathers taught with equal clarity that there were certain unique, *incommunicable* attributes that would forever distinguish the believer from the God of the Bible,[22] ontologically speaking. Among these is the attribute of self-existence, or what is technically called aseity. That

---

[20]According to Mormonism, the star Kolob is purportedly where the head of the gods convened a council of the gods to agree upon a plan for the organization of the earth (Abraham 3:22–23, in the Mormon holy book, *The Pearl of Great Price*).

[21]I transcribed Mr. Hale's remarks verbatim from the audio tape of the debate. The tapes of this entire debate may be obtained from Answers in Action (www.answers.org).

[22]And, for that matter, the god of Mormonism!

is, God is not a contingent being, depending on anyone or anything for his existence. He exists from eternity and to eternity—complete, perfect, and fully actualized in and of himself. And it is of the biblical God alone that this can be predicated. In short, the early fathers were all strict monotheists, the LDS polytheists.

Now, the Mormon apologists did make some specific errors of fact, such as when Mr. Hale wrongly attributed the production of the Athanasian Creed to Athanasius himself, or when he took offense at the term "vicious abstraction," thinking it a personal insult and not (as it is) a technical term for a particular type of logical fallacy. But focusing on these errors would not have gotten at the fundamental falsehood at the bottom of their position. To do that, a broad grasp of the doctrinal shape of patristic theology proper was required. Because these evangelical apologists were prepared to conduct the battle at this level, they were able to cut off the false Mormon claims at their root.

THE POSITIVE BENEFITS OF HT FOR THE APOLOGIST

Until now our consideration of the use of HT has been mostly negative, in the sense of deflecting false claims. But I believe that the study of HT benefits the apologist positively in at least two ways. The first occurs by toning up the apologist's theological muscles through working out with the most intellectually powerful thinkers that the Christian tradition has to offer. The second way is through the development of a salutary historical method itself, which I believe pays rich dividends for the Christian apologist.

Pumping Some Intellectual Iron, or Running with the Big (Theological) Dogs

As I mentioned at the beginning of this chapter, one of the great joys of studying HT is the intellectual stimulation of hanging out with the brightest and best of the Christian tradition. This is not only fun but helps a person to develop ways of thinking and approaches to problems that he or she otherwise probably would not.

We can benefit enormously when we read the great debates between the heretics and the orthodox of yesteryear, for it is often true that these struggles were carried out between intellectual titans on both sides of the issue, the likes of whom we do not often see today. Just being in the company of such thinkers cannot but raise our own level of thinking. For the apologist this is especially useful, because in this way we may be able to spar vicariously with adversaries tougher than the ones we face in our day-to-day ministries. Now, we rightly laud the brilliance of Augustine and Athanasius and Calvin, but we sometimes do not stop to think about how formidable their opponents often were. I tell my students that they simply do not make heretics like they used to. For example, if one wants to see a really high-level denial of some of the cardinal doctrines of orthodoxy, one can scarcely find a more worthy opponent than Faustus Socinus (1539–1604). Here we encounter a mind well versed in the biblical languages, classical literature, logic, philosophy, exegesis, and theology, all pressed into the service of overturning the historic doctrines of the faith! If one can deal with Socinus's arguments against the Trinity, the deity of Christ, penal substitution, or God's foreknowledge of future contingents, then one can lay waste to the ruminations of the Watchtower or of Clark Pinnock without shifting out of first gear.

There is also a sense in which intellectual honesty would have us deal with the arguments against the faith in their *strongest* form. And we should not fear to do so, because orthodoxy is sufficiently robust to stand against the worst that heterodoxy can dish out. Perhaps few people modeled this intellectual honesty and serene confidence in the strength of biblical orthodoxy as effectively as Bob Passantino, mentioned earlier. I recall many occasions on which Bob would be dialoguing with cultists, during which he would help them craft a better argument for their heresy than they themselves could muster! He would, of course, then show the problems with even their position's strongest form. No doubt some of Bob's ability to do this could be attributed to his naturally fecund mind. But I also attribute a good deal of it to his wide reading in the best and brightest theologians of the tradition. Bob was accustomed to running with the big dogs, as it were, and this conditioned him to argue a position—any position—in the most robust way possible for it.

So, then, if we are to learn to think with such acuity that we can deal with the most formidable attacks against the faith, we must face those attacks squarely in the writings of the more intellectually nimble heretics of a bygone age. And we must also study carefully the impressive and formidable productions of the orthodox in countermanding them. Socinus may indeed have been brilliant, but John Owen was at least his equal and had the added advantage of arguing for the truth!

The writings of some of these theological greats may be tough sledding for the beginning apologist, and so one must take it in stride. One does not bench press five hundred pounds on the first trip to the gym. But given a consistent workout regimen of reading and carefully studying the writings of these powerhouses, one will soon enough be able to heft arguments of considerable intellectual weight.

The Value of a Proper Historiographical Method

The final value of the study of HT that I would like to mention occurs through the cultivation of a proper historical method per se. I am not here concerned with specific facts or arguments or data that one learns from historical personages, but rather the habits of mind and method that are requisite for the historical enterprise.

Leopold Von Ranke's famous maxim that the historian's task is to "tell it like it was" (*wie es eigentlich gewesen*) may be ridiculed by those who doubt the possibility or even the desirability of objective history, but I believe Von Ranke was fundamentally correct. In the case of intellectual history, this involves understanding a thinker on his or her own terms, in his/her own context. It is coming to grips with a document's meaning and penetrating what underlies the arguments being advanced. It is not about rehabilitating or castigating those long dead, but about grasping *objectively* what is being said and why.

While objectivity is the historian's goal, this does not mean that the historian is void of personal commitments, or that he or she must remain neutral as to the truth or falsity of the positions under consideration. The point is simply that history *qua* history is not about passing such judgments but is merely about getting the story straight, however the chips may fall. It is only *after* the position has been understood on its own terms and without bias that the historian may turn to apologetics and employ the fruits of his or her discovery in polemical or other theological application. But at that point the apologist has moved beyond the historical task *simpliciter* and into something else—something wonderfully valuable and necessary, perhaps, but something different nonetheless.

The objective habits of mind that characterize skilled historiography are consubstantial, as it were, with those of the skilled apologist. Whether the issue is dished up by an ancient or modern protagonist, the apologist must know truly what he or she is up against. We do well to attend carefully to the admonition of that great medievalist Etienne Gilson, who said that it is much easier to refute an opponent than it is to understand him. To this I would add that if one is to thoroughly refute an error, he must understand it as well as the one who holds it. To get into the head of someone who thinks quite differently from us requires the cultivation of an objective frame of mind. This mode of thinking is as necessary for the apologist as it is for the historian, the former typically dealing with a contemporary opponent, the later examining advocates long dead.

It will not do to misrepresent an opponent, living or dead, however much we may wish to justify it by some greater good. Bob and Gretchen Passantino of Answers in Action have formulated a "golden rule" of apologetics that bears repeating. We should do unto other's arguments and texts as we would have them do unto ours. None of us appreciates being misunderstood or deliberately misrepresented, and we must take care to treat others with the same respect. We can do nothing less as lovers of the truth. And truth is, after all, what both apologetics and historiography are all about.

CHAPTER TWELVE

Open Theism

Chad V. Meister

INTRODUCTION

Suppose that you had a friend from college—we'll call her Suzanne—who was raised in a wonderful Christian home and from her youth had passionate aspirations to be a missionary somewhere in Asia. Suppose also that Suzanne wanted to marry a man with a similar vision—one who longed to raise a family in the midst of following the onerous call of missions life. You prayed with your friend Suzanne for many years, both about her "calling" and about a particular young man whom she began dating her freshman year. After several years you and Suzanne and this man and many others felt a "yes" that they should move ahead in marriage, and shortly after college they did so. Following their call, they went to missionary training school to prepare for their career in Southeast Asia.

All was going well until, in one horrifying moment, Suzanne discovered that her husband was involved in an adulterous relationship with another woman at the school. After being discovered, he repented. But alas, in a few short months he was unfaithful again, and then again, and then again, and this state of affairs continued on for the next three years. During those years Suzanne's husband became hostile to Suzanne to the point of being verbally and physically abusive. In one fit of rage he struck her face and actually broke her cheekbone. He then left her, three months pregnant, divorced her, and moved in with his lover.

Suzanne is emotionally crushed, dejected, and terribly lonely. She is also angry—angry with her former husband, angry with herself, and especially angry with God. How could God have set her up with such a man? In her depression, she turns to her pastor for answers, and he comforts her with these words: "Don't be mad at God, Suzanne. It wasn't his fault. He gave you the best and wisest advice he could. He just didn't realize what kind of a monster your husband would become. If he had known, he would have told you so. Take comfort in the fact that God *is* looking out for you and that he did his best given what he knew at the time."

This scenario, now famously known as the "Suzanne Story" in theological circles, is presented in Gregory Boyd's book, *God of the Possible*.[1] It is based on a true story, one in which Boyd suggests that his response—of God's not knowing the future actions of Suzanne's husband—was a very helpful way to resolve this terrible tragedy in the life of a woman in his church. It is a view about God and the future typically referred to as the "Openness of God" view or "Open Theism," and it is rapidly growing in many circles in the United States and Europe.[2] It is not merely an ethereal theological position held by a few high and lofty theologians in seminaries and graduate schools, but one that a number of pastors and laypeople in multiple denominations now espouse in some form.

In this essay I intend to provide a fair and balanced overview and analysis of this view. Given that, I should mention that I realize my own epistemological limitations—that I am fallible and that most likely not everything I believe to be true is in fact true. I could be mistaken.

Be that as it may, as I reflect on this issue and search the Scriptures and the thoughtful work of others, it seems to me that there are multiple problems and concerns with the Openness view. As you examine the arguments and evidences presented here, judge for yourself what is true and right and good.

A BRIEF OVERVIEW OF OPENNESS DOCTRINE

To begin, then, it is important to first describe what open theists espouse. There are differing points of view among the various Openness theologians and philosophers, so I'd like to hone in on a *central* issue that unifies them all. *All Open Theists allege that God does not know which future contingent events will occur.* Now we need to clarify several issues at this point. Openness proponents are not claiming that God knows no future events. He does know several kinds of things regarding the future. He knows how he will respond to certain human actions such as sin and love. He knows future events that are *causally determined* from previous ones (e.g., future earthquakes based on his infallible knowledge of plate tectonics and other

---

[1]Gregory Boyd, *God of the Possible* (Grand Rapids, MI: Baker, 2000), 103–106.
[2]The book that put the issue center stage in the U.S. is *The Openness of God: A Biblical Challenge to the Traditional Understanding of God*, eds. Clark Pinnock, Richard Rice, John Sanders, William Hasker, and David Basinger (Downers Grove, IL: InterVarsity Press, 1994).

factors); he knows his own future actions (e.g., "I will rescue my people Israel in four hundred years," etc.); because he has infallible knowledge of all present and past events, he knows everything that can be known about the future that can be *inferred* from the past and present (e.g., he knows that Saddam Hussein will not be President of the United States in 2012 and that Madonna will not be President of Russia after a surprise marriage to Vladimir Putin); and he knows many other things that can be inferred from his infallible present knowledge.

What God does not know for sure, according to Openness proponents, are *future contingent events*. But what are they? Future contingent events are future events that are not causally determined by present events. Future human actions would be prime examples of future contingent events. For example, God does not know for sure what I will have for dinner tonight, or what John Edwards will decide to do about inflation if elected President, or which terrorists will attempt to bomb a major U.S. city in 2015 (if at all), and so on.

God not only does not know for sure what *will* happen in such situations as these, but he also does not know for sure what *would* happen given other conditions in such situations. This latter kind of knowledge is knowledge of what is referred to as "conditional future contingent events." An example of this that not only does God not know for sure who will win the next presidential election, he does not know what a person who is not elected would do in a given situation if he or she would have been elected. At best, God knows what he or she *could* do in future situations, but not what that person *would* do if faced with them.

As a result of what God does and does not know, he is ignorant of virtually all of humanity's future. He knows future possibilities but not future realities; he knows what *could* happen but not what *will* happen. He is a very good guesser, no doubt, and his guesses or predictions are based on infallible present knowledge, but he sometimes gets things wrong. Thus he can make assessments about our future actions based on our present character, but sometimes he is mistaken and surprised (as in the Suzanne story). Now God's being surprised is taken by Openness proponents as an asset, not a liability. For since God does not know the future, he must take risks, and on their view, a risk-taking God is better than a non-risk-taking God.

THE CASE FOR DIVINE FOREKNOWLEDGE

We will evaluate three types of evidence in order to determine the plausibility of the Openness position in contrast to the traditional or classical view of God's infallible foreknowledge—biblical, historical, and philosophical. The order of these three is not random. For evangelicals, biblical evidence, it seems to me, should be given more weight than the other two. After all, evangelicals maintain that the Bible is the inspired Word of God, and while our interpretations of it are fallible, it is the basis of our theological knowledge.

Evangelicals also maintain that God has been working through his Church from its inception—he is leading her, and his guiding hand has been directing her all along. He led the councils and discussions that agreed upon the canon, and he raised up men and women to protest theological corruption—e.g., Christian Fathers such as Justin Martyr, Athanasius, Augustine, Anselm, Aquinas, John Calvin, Martin Luther, John Wesley, and many others. That doesn't mean they were right about everything, but they were generally unified about the central issues regarding the nature and work of God. If we are to veer from views upon which they agreed, it should be done with tremendous caution, trepidation, and substantial rationale.

Finally, we'll examine the question of which view of foreknowledge is most philosophically plausible. Openness proponents typically maintain that there is a dichotomy here such that if God foreknows our future actions, then they cannot be *free* actions. But since we do have free will on their account, God must not know what those future actions/decisions will be. So the philosophical evidence for the Openness position will also be evaluated.

Let's begin, then, with the biblical evidence.

Biblical Evidence

God's foreknowledge, as mentioned in the Bible, can be divided into two kinds—his knowledge of what *will* happen and his knowledge of what *would* happen.[3] First, we shall examine several passages dealing with God's foreknowledge of the former kind, and we will begin in the Old Testament. Consider the first four verses of Daniel 11:

> In the first year of Darius the Mede, I arose to be an encouragement and a protection for him. And now I will tell you the truth. Behold, three more kings are going to arise in Persia. Then a fourth will gain far more riches than all of them; as soon as he becomes strong through his riches, he will arouse the whole empire against the realm of Greece. And a mighty king

---

[3]For more on the distinction between different kinds of knowledge that God might hold, see William Lane Craig, "The Middle Knowledge View," in James K. Beilby and Paul R. Eddy, eds., *Divine Foreknowledge: Four Views* (Downers Grove, IL: InterVarsity Press, 2001), 119–143.

*will arise, and he will rule with great authority and do so as he pleases.
But as soon as he has arisen, his kingdom will be broken up and parceled
out toward the four points of the compass, though not to his own descen-
dents, nor according to his authority which he wielded, for his sovereignty
will be uprooted and given to others besides them.*[4]

Notice the variety of free-will activity in this prophetic passage. There
are many examples in the Old Testament of God foreknowing the future
actions of human beings—actions that were freely accomplished and yet
were prophesied to happen.

The prophet Isaiah uses this kind of knowledge as a demonstration that
God is, in fact, the true God. For example, Isaiah 44:6–8 says:

Thus says the LORD, *the King of Israel and his Redeemer, the* LORD *of
hosts: "I am the first and I am the last, and there is no God besides Me.
And who is like Me? Let him proclaim and declare it; Yes, let him recount
it to Me in order, from the time that I established the ancient nation. And
let them declare to them the things that are coming and the events that
are going to take place. . . . Have I not long since announced it to you and
declared it? And you are my witnesses.*

In another passage, the prophet notes that idols are not real gods, for
they can do nothing, neither good nor evil, let alone tell what future events
are to come. That ability falls to Yahweh alone; he's the one true God (Isa.
41:21–24). The future isn't moving along here haphazardly based merely
on the whims of free creatures with God unawares. Rather, God establishes
nations and rulers, and he knows the future in such a way that he is both
involved in it and can declare what is to come.

But God's knowledge of the future is not limited to only what *will*
happen. It isn't merely what is referred to as "simple foreknowledge."[5]
He also knows what *would* happen given different future scenarios. For
example, in 1 Samuel 23:6–13 the prophet describes a scenario in which
Saul was intending to attack David and his men at a city called Keilah.
David then inquires of God, through Abiathar the priest, whether the
people of the city will surrender David into Saul's hand if and when Saul
attacks. God informs him that they will indeed do this if he remains in
the city. So we see here that God knew that if David *were* to remain in

---

[4]All scriptural references are taken from the *New American Standard Bible*. Of course, some critical
scholars won't be happy with reference to Daniel as being literally prophetic. But this essay presupposes
that God can and has given predictions about the future through Old Testament prophets.
[5]For more on simple foreknowledge, see David Hunt, "The Simple Foreknowledge View," in Beilby and
Eddy, eds., *Divine Foreknowledge*, 65–118.

Keilah, then Saul and his men *would* come after him, and if Saul *were* to come after him, then the men of Keilah *would* hand David over to Saul. These events did not happen, for David fled Keilah. So it was not that God foreknew merely what was going to happen, but what would happen given the various future possibilities.[6] This kind of foreknowledge is incredible, to say the least.

In the New Testament we also see the notion of God's foreknowledge mentioned and described on a number of occasions. For example, in 1 Peter 1:10–11 Peter notes that the Old Testament prophets foretold the sufferings and glory of Christ. Peter also refers to groups of believers in Asia, Galatia, and elsewhere as being "chosen according to the foreknowledge of God the Father" (1 Pet. 1:1–2). Likewise, Paul states in Romans 8:29 that "those whom He foreknew, He also predestined to become conformed to the image of His Son." Jesus himself has foreknowledge of future events that entail human freedom. For example, in his Olivet Discourse (Matt. 24:1–25:46) he tells his disciples about the times and signs of the destruction of the Temple. During the Passover meal, he also foretells his betrayal—a free and sinful future action by Judas.[7]

There are many other examples of God's foreknowledge of both future contingent events and conditional future contingent events scattered throughout the Old and New Testaments, but this is ample evidence to demonstrate that the Bible does teach that God has such knowledge.[8]

Historical Evidence

While the biblical evidence should be the primary focus of theological issues such as this one, the views of the Church Fathers, as they are often called, should also be taken into consideration and included as providing either evidential support or detriment. Regarding the issue of divine foreknowledge, the early church was not silent. For example, Justin Martyr (c. 100–165),[9] in reference to prophecy, refers to "God foreknowing *all* that shall be done by all men"[10] (italics added). Irenaeus (c. 120–202), in

---

[6]See also Jeremiah 38:17–18.

[7]For other examples of foreknowledge in the New Testament, see William Lane Craig's *The Only Wise God: The Compatibility of Divine Foreknowledge and Human Freedom* (Eugene, OR: Wipf and Stock, 2000), 31–37.

[8]For more on this, see Millard J. Erickson, *What Does God Know and When Does He Know It: The Current Controversy over Divine Foreknowledge* (Grand Rapids, MI: Zondervan, 2003), Chap. 2. See also William Lane Craig, *The Only Wise God*.

[9]All dates are A.D.

[10]Justin Martyr, *First Apology*, 44, in *Ante-Nicene Fathers*, Vol. I, Alexander Roberts and James Donaldson, eds. (Peabody, MA: Hendrickson, 1994), 177. Thomas Oden makes reference to many of the early and medieval theologians on the issue of divine foreknowledge in his *The Living God: Systematic Theology, Volume One* (San Francisco: Harper and Row, 1987), 69–77, 293–297. Many of the references

his *Against Heresies*, emphasizes that God foreknows all things, including those people who would not believe.[11] Tertullian (c. 150–212) proclaims that God foreknows all events and that this foreknowledge "has for its witness as many prophets as it inspired."[12] He's right, for we could include Cyprian, Clement of Alexandria, Athanasius, Origen, Hippolytus, and many others from the first several centuries of the church.[13]

The later medieval theologians and apologists were also united in holding that God knows all past, present, and future events. Augustine (354–430), often referred to as the greatest and most influential theologian after the apostle Paul, wrote prolifically about the nature and knowledge of God. Regarding God's foreknowledge, he states, "His vision is utterly unchangeable. Thus, He comprehends all that takes place in time—the not-yet existing future, the existing present, and the no-longer-existing past."[14] Augustine also argues that God's knowledge of the future "cannot be deceived," and yet human beings have freedom of will to act sinfully.[15] Similarly, Anselm of Canterbury (c. 1033–1109) defended both God's *absolute foreknowledge of all future events* and maintained that many of these future events occur through the free will of human agents.[16] And ol' Aquinas (1224–1274) should not be forgotten. He argued that not only does God know what *will* happen, but what *would* happen given different scenarios.[17]

This view of God's infallible foreknowledge continued on through the Reformation era as well. Both Luther (1483–1546) and Calvin (1509–1564), for example, were in full agreement with the earlier theologians that God foreknows all events, as were Jacob Arminius (1560–1609) and Jonathan Edwards (1703–1758).[18] The list goes on and on. Detractors

---

here come from his work as well as from Norman Geisler's and H. Wayne House's finely researched work, *The Battle for God: Responding to the Challenge of Neotheism* (Grand Rapids, MI: Kregel, 2001).

[11]Irenaeus, *Against Heresies*, 4.29.2.

[12]Tertullian, *Against Marcion*, 2.5.

[13]Interestingly, God's foreknowledge, as described by many of these seminal figures of early church history, does not imply divine determinism. Rather, it is based on knowing what his free creatures *will* choose to do and what they *would* choose to do given different circumstances. See, for example, Justin Martyr, *First Apology*, XLV–LIII; Athanasius, *Four Discourses Against the Arians*, III.30; Irenaeus, *Against Heresies*, XXXVII, 4.29. In their excellent work *God's Strategy in Human History* (Eugene, OR: Wipf and Stock Publishers, 2000), Paul Marston and Roger Forster note that the pre-Augustinian theological tradition was united in holding to freedom of the will, and they quote numerous theologians from the first several centuries of the church to support their claim.

[14]Augustine, *City of God*, 11.21.

[15]Ibid., 5.10.

[16]See Anselm's *Trinity, Incarnation, and Redemption: Theological Treatises*, ed. J. Hopkins and H. Richardson (New York: Harper and Row, 1970), 153–163.

[17]Thomas Aquinas, *Summa Theologica* (any edition), I, Q14.

[18]See Martin Luther's *Bondage of the Will* (Grand Rapids MI: Revell, reprint, 1990), 80–81; John Calvin's *Institutes of the Christian Religion* (Philadelphia: Westminster Press, 1960), 3.21–22; Jacobus Arminius's *The Works of Arminius* (Grand Rapids, MI: Baker, reprint, 1986), 2.28; and Jonathan Edwards's *The Works of Jonathan Edwards*, T. Edwards, ed. (New York: Garland, 1987), 11.4.111.

are rare and are usually described as unorthodox, if not something worse. Thus, within the historic Christian church until recent times, there has basically been universal agreement among theologians and philosophers on the idea that God's absolute and infallible knowledge covers all past, present, and future events. Again, the unanimity on this issue does not guarantee its truthfulness, but it should at least cause us to be wary of its denial.[19]

Philosophical Evidence

Having considered biblical evidence for God's foreknowledge as well as noting the widespread agreement of the Church Fathers on the topic, we will next explore philosophical reasons for believing in divine foreknowledge. It has been held by nearly all Christian theologians from the beginning of the Church that God is omniscient, meaning that he knows all things that are proper objects of knowledge—that is to say, he knows all truths. No doubt, to maintain that God is ignorant of some truth or set of truths seems oxymoronic, if not downright blasphemous. And since there are truths about future contingent events (e.g., truths about future free human actions), God must know those truths. An argument for God's knowing future free human actions, then, can be put succinctly in the following format:

1. God is omniscient.
2. An omniscient being knows all truths.
3. Therefore God knows all truths.
4. There are truths about future contingent events (e.g., future free human actions).
5. Therefore, God knows all truths about future contingent events.[20]

This argument is valid, which means that if steps 1–4 are true, then the conclusion must also be true.

Openness proponents deny the conclusion that God knows all truths about future free human actions. But to deny this, one must deny one of the four steps. Typically those in the Openness camp will not deny God's omniscience; they will not deny, that is, steps 1–3. So this leaves step 4, that there are truths about future free human actions, and this *is* in fact the step most frequently challenged. The argument takes a number of forms, but the most persuasive of them goes something like this: "God is omniscient,

---

[19]Even the early Christian creeds, which are definitive for orthodoxy, express God's infallible foreknowledge. For more on this, see Norman Geisler's essay in this volume ("The Essentials of the Christian Faith") as well as *The Battle for God*.
[20]A variation of this argument is offered by William Lane Craig in his *What Does God Know?* (Norcross, GA: RZIM, 2002), 18–19.

which means that God knows all truths. But future free human actions are not truths. Since the future does not yet exist, there are no truths about the future. So, while God does not know future free human actions, that does not mean that he isn't omniscient. *He is omniscient, for he knows every-thing that can be known.* Since the future doesn't exist, it cannot be known, even by an omniscient being."

The response to this challenge to the traditional view of God's omni-science quickly leads into a philosophical jungle that one should enter slowly, wielding the weapons of an unwearied mind and a wary eye. Upon entering this jungle, it will be helpful to first probe into the meaning of the word *true.* We can begin with a familiar example. The statement that "George W. Bush is President of the United States on March 10, 2007" is true. But what does it mean to say that this statement is true? It means that the statement (more precisely, the proposition represented by the statement) corresponds to the fact that George W. Bush is President on this day. Truth is thus a correspondence between a statement (proposition) and a fact.[21]

Further, statements are either true or false, and they are either past tense, present tense, or future tense. So, it is either true or false that George W. Bush is President of the United States on March 10, 2007. And, of course, we know that it's true. So far so good. But what is interesting is that facts—those things that make statements (propositions) true—can refer to issues of the past, the present, or the future. Consider this statement: "John Kerry did lose the presidential election in 2004." Is this statement true? Of course it is. But notice that it is a *past fact* that makes it true. Similarly, con-sider this statement: "Iraq will have a Communist government in 2025." This statement, too, must be either true or false. Obviously *we* don't know whether it's true or false, but that is beside the point. It is one or the other. And what makes it either true or false is what form the future government of Iraq turns out to be—a *future fact.*

Openness proponents have challenged the view that future-tense con-tingent statements are either true or false. They argue that such statements are neither true nor false but indeterminate. Since the future is not here yet, there are no future facts. So, for example, it is neither true nor false that Iraq will have a Communist government in 2025; it is simply indeterminate.

But this view that there are no future facts leads to a number of diffi-culties. First, if future-tense statements are neither true nor false, then past-tense statements cannot be true or false either, for what makes the one true

---

[21]This is referred to as the "correspondence theory" of truth. For an advanced treatment of truth theories, see Richard Kirkham, *Theories of Truth* (Cambridge, MA: MIT Press, 1992).

(or false) is the same thing that makes the other true (or false)—namely, *a fact referring to the past* or *a fact referring to the future*. The past *no longer* exists, and the future *is yet to* exist. We can't consistently affirm that past facts now exist but future facts do not. One is simply in the past, and the other is simply in the future. To give up on the one is to give up on the other. But surely no one wants to claim that it is neither true nor false that John Kerry lost the election in 2004! Consider another example to clarify the point:

1. "It will rain tomorrow" (asserted on April 12).
2. "It did rain yesterday" (asserted on April 14).[22]

Notice that both 1 and 2 make the same claim about the facts—rain on April 13. Philosopher William Lane Craig comments: "If 'It is raining today' is now true, how could 'It will rain tomorrow' not have been true yesterday? The same facts make a future-tense statement *asserted earlier*, a present-tense statement *asserted simultaneously*, and a past-tense statement *asserted later* all true" (italics mine).[23]

Further, to deny that future-tense truths are either true or false leads to other problematic consequences. Consider the following example: "It is the case that Hilary Clinton either will or will not run for the presidency in the 2012 election." Does it make sense to maintain that this statement is neither true nor false since it is a future-tense statement? Clearly not. It is true. But what makes it true? That Hilary either *will* or *will not* run for the presidency.[24]

So what have we gained here? We've demonstrated that it is more reasonable than not to believe that there are truths about future contingent events, which is step 4 in our argument. Given, then, that we agree with steps 1–4, the conclusion, step 5—that God knows all truths about future contingent events (such as future free human actions)—must also be true.[25]

PRACTICAL AND THEOLOGICAL CONCERNS

Having sketched out Open Theism and examined reasons for affirming God's foreknowledge, we shall now look briefly at several concerns that

---

[22]This example is taken from Nicholas Rescher, *Many-Valued Logic* (New York: McGraw Hill, 1969), 2–3, as quoted in William Lane Craig, *The Only Wise God*, 58.
[23]Ibid.
[24]A response to this argument could be that what makes it true that Hilary either will or will not run for the presidency is a law of logic called "the law of excluded middle" (every proposition is either true or not true; "P or not-P"). This seems problematic, however. For in this case it would be a *law of logic* that makes a future free action true! But the law of logic isn't what's causing her future decision to run or not run for the presidency; it is *Hilary* who will be the cause of her future decision about the presidency.
[25]Craig insightfully addresses these issues in his *The Only Wise God*, 58–65.

arise from Openness Theology. The concerns focused on here fall into four categories, the first two having to do with practical issues and the latter two having to do with theological ones.

Lack of Confidence in Divine Guidance

On the Openness view, God does not know our future. Not only does he not know where you will have dinner tonight, for example, but he does not know for sure where you'll be next week, or what your life and career will look like in the next five, ten, or twenty years. On such a view of God, how can we be assured that he will give us the right advice about any future matter of significance? Just as he was wrong about Suzanne's husband, we cannot be assured that he will be right about *any* particular future situation that involves human beings (as most of them do!).

Suppose, then, that you are in the midst of making a life-changing decision. Perhaps it has to do with your job or your family or a friendship. You're wondering what the best direction is in a given scenario—which of two jobs you should choose, for example. As you consider your decision, you ask God for help. But he doesn't know how things are going to turn out either. Perhaps in a year your boss at job #1 is going to dislike you for whatever reason and fire you without warning, even though God doesn't want this to happen and has no idea that it will. Suppose that boss is also going to make up wicked and shameful lies about you—lies that will seriously damage your character and career and even create stress and difficulty in your marriage. As a result, your effectiveness significantly decreases. If you take job #2, however, in one year your boss is going to promote you to another level and express kindness toward you and your family, and your effectiveness at work and elsewhere will continue to increase.

Now, of course God, being God, could force the boss at job #1 to like you against his free will and to not fire you. On the Openness view God could start overriding people's free will to accomplish his purposes in your life. But now we're back to denying free will, which is something that Openness defenders have been attempting to avoid (and for good reason). On this view of God, for him to accomplish many (if not most) things he may want to accomplish, he is going to have to ride roughshod over people's choices and decisions. He would have to do this, that is, unless he's like the God of the deists and sits back and watches the world unfold. But how could we trust a God who either doesn't know the future or who merely watches our lives from a distance?

One leading Open Theist responds to the problem this way: "Accordingly we must acknowledge that divine guidance, from our perspective, cannot be considered a means of discovering exactly what will be best in the long run."[26] Imagine a God who could not be trusted about giving us sure guidance for the future, a God who is doing the best he can but simply makes mistakes when it comes to future judgments.[27] This is, I think, a view of God that is much less than the one portrayed in the Bible.[28]

Loss of Divine Comfort

Not only does such a view of God's foreknowledge seem to be a diminishing of what he truly knows, but it also tends to create a feeling of uneasiness, uncertainty, and even a sense that God cannot really help me. Rather than comforting Suzanne, for example, it seems that the view that God makes mistakes would create even more discomfort in her. I can imagine her thinking to herself, *I thought I could pray to God for guidance about the man I should marry, but even he gets things wrong!*

After giving a brief overview of Open Theism to the faculty and staff of the college where I teach, one of the campus counselors came up to talk with me about this issue. She has been counseling for a long time, and here are her words to me: "I've met with people for many years who have very deep wounds and hurts, and the last thing they need is a lesser God!" She told me that this Openness view of God's not knowing our future, from a practical counseling perspective, is extremely unhelpful and potentially dangerous.

Contrary to Open Theism, we needn't worry that he might be mistaken when we seek guidance from our great and glorious God. He simply doesn't make mistakes.

Denial of Certain Biblical Prophecies

One of the most difficult issues for Openness proponents is the long list of biblical prophecies that appear to clearly entail God's knowing the future. A few were mentioned earlier, but I'd like to focus on one that is problematic on the Openness account for several reasons. In Luke 22:34 Jesus prophecies to Peter: "I say to you, Peter, the rooster will not crow today until you have denied three times that you know Me." This prophecy

---

[26]David Basinger, "Practical Implications," in Clark Pinnock, et al., *The Openness of God*.

[27]John Sanders, in his *The God Who Risks*, 205, writes, "Is it possible for God to have mistaken beliefs about the future? The traditional theological answer is that God cannot, but there are several biblical texts that seem to affirm that what God thought would happen did not come about (for example, Jeremiah 3:7, 19–20)." Boyd makes a similar inference in his *God of the Possible*, 60.

[28]For more on this issue, see Bruce A. Ware, *God's Lesser Glory: The Diminished God of Open Theism* (Wheaton, IL: Crossway Books, 2000), 177–189.

poses an interesting dilemma for the Openness adherent, for how did Jesus know this information? One response could be that God knew Peter's inner character so well that he simply inferred how Peter would respond.[29] But this answer is problematic for several reasons. First, how did Jesus predict that there would be *three* temptations before the rooster crowed? How did he know that the people who did tempt Peter would tempt him, and tempt him at the very times in which they did tempt him? One could say that God caused them to tempt Peter those three times, but the Bible says that God tempts no one (Jas. 1:13). Since the free will of the tempters is also involved, on the Openness view God could not have known where they would be at those very times and precisely how they would respond to Peter as he approached them (or even whether Peter would approach them).

Second, how did God know that Peter would *deny* Jesus rather than simply run away from his tempters? After all, Peter had just run away that very night when the mob came and took Jesus to the chief priests and elders. One could hold that a person's character so determines how he or she will act that since God knows our present character, he can predict infallibly our future actions. And so, with Peter, God simply predicted infallibly what he would do based on Peter's character. But this leads to two further problems.

First, such a view of character is deterministic, and determinism is a position that Openness defenders wish to avoid. One of the central elements of Openness theology is a strong view of the freedom of the human will, what's referred to as "libertarian freedom." But the view that our actions are *determined* by our character is contrary to a libertarian view of free will. A second problem here is that this view of the determinative power of one's character causes difficulties for Openness theologians in another passage in the Bible. In Genesis 22:12, after Abraham lifted the knife to offer his son Isaac as a sacrifice on the altar in obedience to God, it says this: "[God] said, 'Do not stretch out your hand against the lad, and do nothing to him; for *now I know* that you fear God, since you have not withheld your son, your only son, from Me'" (emphasis added). Openness theologians frequently use this passage as an example of God not knowing the future. But how can they say, on the one hand, that God knows our character so well that he can predict our actions (as in the Peter case), and yet maintain that God needs

---

[29]This is, in fact, Boyd's view. See his *God of the Possible*, 35–37. Sanders, in his *The God Who Risks*, 135–136, holds that this prophecy of Jesus is conditional; that is, Peter could have chosen not to betray Jesus those three times even given Jesus' claim that he would. Sanders here also mentions as a possibility for Openness proponents the view that God foreordained the temptations to occur. This concession is quite surprising given the arguments frequently leveled against Calvinists by Open Theists for holding such a position.

to see us act before he knows our character and before he knows what we will do (as in the Abraham case)? They cannot have it both ways. Either (1) our character determines our actions, and God knows our character so well that he can infallibly predict our actions based on our character, or (2) God knows our character very well, but since we have free will we can freely choose to act contrary to our character. If the Openness proponent chooses answer (1), then he can explain Peter's denials of Jesus, but he will have to give up libertarian free will and the argument from Genesis 22 that God did not know Abraham's inner character or how he was going to act regarding his son Isaac until he actually raised the knife to kill him.

On the other hand, if the Openness proponent chooses answer (2), then he can explain how God did not know whether Abraham was faithful until he actually took the knife in his hand and lifted it up to kill his son. But he cannot then explain how God knew for sure that Peter was going to deny Jesus, and deny him three times, until he was actually in the process of denying him.[30]

It seems very clear. Either we have libertarian free will (i.e., the power of contrary choice) or we do not. If we do, then we are not deterministically bound by our character; we can act contrary to our character if we so choose. If this is true, then God can know our future actions only through divine foreknowledge, not through an inference or deduction based on our current character states. It seems that the most plausible explanation for Jesus' knowing that Peter would freely deny him three times is that he had foreknowledge of what Peter was going to do.

At this point, a question is likely looming in your mind: "What about the passage just cited in Genesis 22 about God 'now' knowing that Abraham fears him *after* he raised the knife to kill his son?" Does this mean that God really did not know what Abraham was going to do? This leads to the last concern that I'd like to raise regarding Open Theism.

Faulty Hermeneutic

It is recognized by virtually all theologians that the Bible, on occasion at least, uses what's called anthropomorphic language. Anthropomorphic language is language that describes God as having human characteristics, but the language is not meant to be taken literally in such cases. Rather, God is using human-like terms that are often contextually relative to the culture of

---

[30]This appears to be Boyd's view since he argues vociferously that God tests people in order to know what is in their heart. See his chapter "The Open Theism View," in Beilby and Eddy, eds., *Divine Foreknowledge*, 31–33.

those with whom he is communicating, and he is doing this for the purpose of communicating in ways people can understand.

Mormon theologians, however, often take such passages literally in order to make their case that God the Father is an exalted man. They use, for example, passages such as Exodus 7:5 where the Lord says, "I stretch out My hand on Egypt," Numbers 6:25 ("the LORD make His face shine on you)," and Psalm 34:15, which proclaims that "the eyes of the LORD are toward the righteous." Given these passages and others like them, Mormons argue that it is evident that God has a face, hands, eyes, and feet. God is an exalted man! But interestingly, they don't use Psalm 57:1 where the psalmist pleads, "Be gracious to me, O God, be gracious to me, for my soul takes refuge in You; and in the shadow of Your wings I will take refuge. . . . " Now God becomes a chicken? Of course, God doesn't have wings, and neither does he have hands, eyes, and feet. He is not a physical being; he is "spirit" (John 4:24). But he uses language that we understand to communicate to us. The references to his having eyes are, of course, to let us know that he is aware of our actions—he is watching us and is watching out for us. As noted earlier, the Bible uses many anthropomorphisms in describing God and his actions. But we must use the greatest care in ascribing to him literal characteristics that weren't meant to be taken literally.

It seems that Openness theologians make a hermeneutical mistake similar to the Mormon error when they take as literalisms passages in the Bible that were meant to be anthropomorphisms. God doesn't literally need to test people to see what they will do before he knows it. The passage in Genesis 22 in which God says, "Now I know that you fear God" after Abraham raises the knife may well be just such an example of an anthropomorphism. It's not that God was unaware of Abraham's faithfulness before he raised the knife; God knows our very thoughts before we speak them or act on them (Ps. 139:1–6). So this may be anthropomorphic language in which God is telling Abraham that he knows quite well that Abraham is faithful. Abraham has demonstrated his faithfulness by his readiness to offer the life of his son.

There is also another possibility of interpretation here. To "know" something in the Hebrew culture typically meant to have experiential awareness of the thing. Thus Genesis 4:1 literally says that Adam "knew" (NASB; ESV, "had relations with") his wife, meaning that he had intimate experience with her. Similarly, after Abraham raised the knife to offer his son, God at that point had experiential awareness of Abraham's faithfulness to him. Whether anthropomorphic language or merely the language of the Hebrews, it is clear that God was aware of what Abraham would do long before his actions with Isaac and that he would be faithful to God, for much earlier in Genesis 12:2–3 God states that through Abraham he will make a great nation.

Openness theologians maintain that the model of God in which he doesn't know future free actions better meshes with the biblical texts that refer to God in these anthropomorphic ways. But once it is noted that there are, in fact, anthropomorphisms throughout the Bible, and that they are there for the purpose of communicating to human beings in human language, the traditional view emerges as the most reasonable and sensible view of God given the Bible as a whole.

To their credit, Openness proponents have significantly brought to light the view that there is a relational aspect of God with his human (and nonhuman) creatures. God isn't the great cosmic stare, standing eternally frozen and unmoved toward the world, as some theologies tend to intimate. He is a loving Father who, in cooperation with his children, is advancing his kingdom throughout the earth. Contrary to Openness claims, though, he can truly interact with us and at the same time be eternally aware of what we *will* do and what we *would* do. That is part of what it means to be God, and such a view is both biblical and reasonable. In short, God is *interactive* with his creatures without being *reactive*. Since he knows the end from the beginning (Isa. 46:10), he can be proactive by planning in advance what he will do in accordance with his infallible foreknowledge.

CONCLUSION

In this essay I've offered three basic strands of evidence for the traditional view of God's foreknowledge and several concerns regarding its denial by Open Theists. I believe that one should be open to *examining* any revisionist claim to the traditional view of God, especially when it is held by respectable, qualified, and Christ-following people. We are fallible creatures and may well have gotten things wrong. But I also believe that the Openness proponents are the ones who have gotten things wrong here, especially regarding divine foreknowledge. I challenge you now to study these things for yourself and to follow the words of the apostle Paul in 1 Thessalonians 5:21: "Examine everything carefully; hold fast to that which is good."[31]

---

[31]Thomas Oden goes so far as to call Openness theology "a heresy that must be rejected on biblical grounds" in his article entitled, "The Real Reformers and the Traditionalists," *Christianity Today*, February 9, 1998, 46.

PART THREE

Defending
Christian Theism

CHAPTER THIRTEEN

The Cosmological Argument

Winfried Corduan

PLEASE ALLOW ME TO BEGIN this essay with a truly bizarre story that I hope you will find enlightening.

A PARABLE

By the time Jason showed up at the doctor's office, he was in evident agony. A thin film of perspiration glistened on his flushed face; his steps had the deliberate precision of someone who is barely keeping his balance; each shallow breath felt like a vial of acid penetrating his chest. One glance at Jason was enough for the physician to make a good guess as to what the problem was.

"Looks to me like you have pneumonia," he said. "That's an infection caused by a bacillus, you know. Let's see if we can confirm my diagnosis."

With no further delay the doctor reached for a large magnifying glass, told Jason to hold still, and started to examine his skin, square inch by square inch. After an hour or so, which seemed like days to Jason, he said he had not found anything yet, asked the nurse to bring him a more powerful glass, and went through the whole process again, this time even more carefully and twice as slowly. Finally he put his instrument down, glowered at Jason, and said, "I know you will find this very frustrating, but I can't see any pneumonia germs anywhere. You must have something else."

A METHODOLOGICAL APPLICATION

What a weird story! You don't confirm pneumonia by looking for the bacillus outside of a person. If you want to know if someone has pneumonia, you look at the respiratory tract to find evidence for the effects of the germ.

The same logic applies to evidence for God's existence. Don't bother trying to invent some kind of a spiritual magnifying glass to try to see God. God's own nature keeps this from becoming a possibility; after all, if he exists he must be an infinite, invisible spirit, just the kind of being who is impossible to detect directly. But what you can do is to look at the world to see if it is put together in such a way that it must have been created by God. In fact, someone who believes in God is very likely going to say:

Unless there were a God, there could not be any world.

Someone who expresses this sentiment is not just looking for one specific attribute of the world. It is the very existence of the world that leads a person to realize there must be a God who created it.

This is the heart of the cosmological argument. More specifically, among the number of versions of the cosmological argument, this is the argument based on existential causality, which has its roots most prominently in Aristotle and Thomas Aquinas.[1]

For many people, the above statement is not even really an argument, but the assertion of a truism. An argument needs to have premises and a conclusion, and many people might say that there is no inference here at all, but simply a declaration of something that should be obvious to anyone. Other thinkers dispute this way of seeing the matter and say that if this insight is supposed to be helpful at all, then it must be formulated as an argument. In that case, the premises must be clarified (the nature of the world) in order to see if the conclusion (the existence of God) truly follows. In order to prepare this statement for the argument that is to follow, I need to rephrase it somewhat with slightly different terminology, though I consider the new version to be synonymous with the previous one:

Unless there were an infinite being, there could not be any finite beings.

---

[1]The most famous exposition of the cosmological argument by Aristotle is in *Metaphysics*, Book A, reprinted in many places including Hippocrates G. Apostle, *Aristotle's Metaphysics* (Bloomington, IN: Indiana University Press), 197–212. Thomas Aquinas's "Five Ways" are in the *Summa Theologica*, Vol. 1, q. 2, art. 3. Contemporary versions of this argument are given among other places in Norman L. Geisler and Winfried Corduan, *Philosophy of Religion*, second edition (Grand Rapids, MI: Baker, 1988), 175–207, and Winfried Corduan, *No Doubt about It: The Case for Christianity* (Nashville: Broadman & Holman, 1997), 102–122.

THE INEVITABILITY OF METAPHYSICS

Now, there is no way around the fact that what follows is going to be metaphysical. Then again, contrary to a widespread misunderstanding, that fact should not put us off. When people hear the term *metaphysics* they immediately fear that they are about to be exposed to something strange, esoteric, and incomprehensible—something far beyond the world in which we actually live. But that does not have to be the case at all. Metaphysics simply asks the question, What is real? And I am even willing to go out on a limb and declare that once we have properly looked at the nature of reality, the conclusion of the argument will follow in pretty straightforward fashion. Thus this essay is going to focus almost entirely on the metaphysics involved, and God will barely get a mention at the end.

Unfortunately, as surprising as this may sound, there have been numerous attempts either to state or to refute the cosmological argument without doing metaphysics. Consider the following statement made by Antony Flew in the course of criticizing Thomas Aquinas's argument to the effect that there must be an "Unmoved Mover," namely God:

> Aquinas here labored to derive this conclusion from the Aristotelian notions of potentiality and actuality. These panting labors I omitted ... partly because they would be felt as paralyzingly technical, but chiefly because they could at best show only—what at this late hour no longer needs to be shown—the scientific inadequacy of these and other Aristotelian concepts.[2]

It obviously depends on the industriousness or indolence of the individual philosopher whether it is too much of a hardship to retrace the metaphysical basis of any argument.

One thing is for sure, however: he cannot possibly do justice to the argument if he is uninterested in pursuing the metaphysics underlying the argument. A critique of a metaphysical argument without the metaphysics can never yield anything more than a straw man. (As a matter of fact, even though Aristotle and Newton may disagree on their physics, they do actually agree on their metaphysics, as we shall show below.)

---

[2]Antony Flew, *An Introduction to Western Philosophy: Ideas and Argument from Plato to Sartre* (New York: Bobbs-Merrill, 1971), 193. The fact that Flew has recently changed his mind to a certain, not clearly delineated, extent concerning the existence of God is, of course, no reason not to engage with the argument he has presented here. It is the idea, not the man, that is the focal point here, and it is not possible prior to engaging with any person's philosophy first to make contact and check whether he still believes what he wrote.

THE METAPHYSICS OF REAL LIFE

The metaphysics that I will employ is one I believe to be grounded in the realities of life as we encounter them on a day-to-day basis. In other words, when I invoke *metaphysics*, I am not about to send you into a new world of heretofore undiscovered, abstract entities. Rather I invite you to follow along using the basic insights of life that most of us (I dare say, all of us) already share.

For example, it is a commonly accepted supposition that events and things have causes. Take the case of a murder mystery. Imagine that in a dark Scottish castle, the corpse of the Lord of the Manor has been discovered with a dagger of strange exotic design protruding from his back. Rational people infer that something happened that brought about this state of affairs, and so they call in the police or a private detective. Nobody believes that this death just happened. Changes have causes.

To go one step further, ordinary things have causes. Or, to be more precise, finite things have causes. It is here that metaphysics becomes important because I have to clarify what I mean by *a finite thing*. A finite thing is something that meets any one of the following conditions:

1. It is restricted by time and space.
2. It can be changed by something other than itself.
3. It has a beginning in time.
4. It needs things other than itself to continue existing.
5. Its attributes, whether essential or accidental, are to some extent influenced by other things.

Another term that we can use for a *finite* thing is that it is a *contingent* being. It is a contingent being simply because it could not exist without all of the factors that bring about its existence, sustain its existence, and shape its nature. To say that a thing is contingent is to say that it is finite and dependent. There is no separate category of contingency. In other words, we should not think of a thing as being caused, sustained, shaped, influenced by other things, and also contingent. It is the first four attributes that make it contingent. Consequently, I am puzzled by the following statement by William Lane Craig:

> The problem with appeal to the Thomist argument, however, is that it is very difficult to show that things are, in fact, contingent in the special sense required by the argument. Certainly, things are naturally contingent in that their continued existence is dependent upon a myriad of factors

including temperature, pressure, entropy level and so forth, but this natural contingency does not suffice to establish a metaphysical contingency in the sense that being must continually be added to their natures or they will be spontaneously annihilated.[3]

Of what "special sense" could Craig be thinking here? What would be "metaphysical contingency" in contrast to "natural contingency"? The contingency in which we are interested is precisely the natural contingency that Craig acknowledges. If it were not for the factors that Craig brings up, the thing would, indeed, not exist. The rest is just a matter of nomenclature to generalize this ordinary understanding of how things work. And, needless to say, it makes no difference whether we are talking about a single finite thing, a number of finite things, or a cosmic collection of finite things. If their being is dependent on other things, then they are finite and contingent. This label applies just as much to something as ephemeral as a thought I may have had a few moments ago as to something as imposing as the entire universe. It is either finite or infinite.

There is no question that it is very difficult to imagine anything that does not meet at least one of these criteria. In fact, it may seem as though there is nothing left that would not meet these criteria of finitude.[4] A nonfinite (or better, an infinite) being would be a highly unusual entity, one that we would not usually expect to encounter in our daily lives, and that is precisely the point of the argument.

THE PUZZLE OF CHANGE

Given the nature of a finite being as enumerated in our list above, it becomes apparent that it must be subject to change. Either it has experienced change in the past, or it is liable to experience change in the future. So let us examine the nature of change. I am stipulating here that change is something with which we are all familiar and that theoretically one should not have to defend the reality of change, though for some philosophers an explanation of change can be an insurmountable obstacle.

Richard A. Purdy takes the easy way out. He asserts that "change in being is indefinable. . . . The antithesis between Being and Nothing is

---

[3]William Lane Craig, "Cosmological Argument," in W. C. Campbell-Jack, Gavin McGrath, and Stephen Evans, eds., *New Dictionary of Christian Apologetics* (Downers Grove, IL: InterVarsity Press, 2006), 179–180.

[4]As a matter of fact, it is not possible to meet one of these criteria without meeting all of the other ones. However, this point is not required for this argument to hold up. Put briefly, the reasoning behind this fact is that when something either comes into being or is changed while it exists, this means that it receives a new or changed form because a thing cannot *be* without *being something*. Therefore, the being of a thing and the nature of the thing are mutually intertwined.

absolute."[5] In making this statement he has isolated his philosophy from everyday life, but he is not the first person to have done so. He has also aligned himself with the philosophical position of Parmenides of Elea, who more than two thousand years ago claimed that being is all there is, and that nonbeing by definition cannot exist. Consequently, there cannot be any change either. He stated:

> It is, and that it is impossible for it not to be, is the way of belief, for truth is its companion. The other, namely, that It is not, and that it must needs not be,—that is the path that none can learn at all.[6]

The problem with this enticingly simple solution is that it dispenses with all movement, change, and particularity, all of which we experience on a daily basis. With this starting point Parmenides was forced to advocate all of the bizarre ideas that are infamous for leading undergraduate students to reject philosophy after the first few weeks in an introductory course: neither the particularity of things nor change nor motion are real. Of course, the fault does not lie with philosophy in general, but with the philosophy that Parmenides advocated.

The differentiation between two individuals requires that one is not the other; the nature of change mandates that a thing will become what it is not; and motion implies that a thing will change location from where it is now to where it is not yet. For example, it would not be possible for Fred not to be George or for George not to be Fred, and thus they can each only be one and the same individual. It would not be possible for Fred as an infant not to be six feet tall or as an adult not to be less than two feet tall, so he could never have changed in size. Finally, if George cannot not be at the store before he leaves home, and if he cannot not be at home once he is at the store, George cannot move from one place to another.

On the other extreme, his contemporary, Heraclitus of Ephesus, strayed into the opposite direction by viewing the whole world as one large process of change. For him, there never was any absolute distinction between being

---

[5]Richard A. Purdy, "Norman Geisler's Neo-Thomistic Apologetics," *Journal of the Evangelical Theological Society*, 25/3 (September 1982): 358. The sentence I have left out above states: "To speak of potentials as intrinsically nothing but extrinsically something is contradictory no matter how you juggle the terms." Why should one even have to juggle the terms to avoid a contradiction? There is none, and we can save any juggling for the next carnival. Under most circumstances you do not commit a contradiction when you state that something has a property extrinsically but does not have the same property intrinsically. For example, I currently have the property of being three feet away from my computer extrinsically, but I do not have that property intrinsically. (I am saying "under most circumstances" because it is possible to say that having extrinsic properties is an intrinsic property and then create a neat little paradox in the process, but that is hardly the point in question here.)

[6]Parmenides, Fragment 4, translated in John Burnet, *Early Greek Philosophy*, fourth edition (London: A. & C. Black, 1948), 173.

and nonbeing; it all gave way to constant change within the universe. "You cannot step into the same river twice; for fresh waters are overflowing and upon you."[7] In another fragment he contended that the world, "was ever, is now, and ever shall be an everlasting fire, with measures of it kindling, and measures going out."[8] Thus, one could never say that anything *is* anything; it is nothing but *becoming*.

Plato attempted to reconcile the paradox that being and nonbeing appear to be mutually exclusive in theory, while change is a constant reality in everyday life, by introducing the world of Ideas or Forms. Even though we may perceive constant change within our ordinary existence, there is a realm of Forms above this world where the distinction between being and nonbeing applies strictly. Thus, for example, if Fred becomes tall, he first has the Form of "Shortness," which absolutely excludes a Form of "Tallness"; but then the Form of "Tallness" replaces the Form of "Shortness" utterly, without any residue.[9] Even though in our everyday world Fred changes from short to tall, in the world of the Forms there is no change; there are only two absolute, mutually exclusive Forms switching on and off. Still, even Plato himself realized that he was not really solving the problem, but only relocating it into the realm of the Forms, where the question of why one Form leaves and the next one arrives remained as intractable as ever.[10]

Aristotle proposed a metaphysical scheme that provided a solution to the problem, at least insofar as it coincides with the way in which people usually think of change. First of all, there is no question that there is a categorical difference between being and nonbeing. However, as explained above, as long as we accept the realities of particularity, change, and motion, there must be a gradation of being that makes change possible. Since absolute nonbeing per se really does not exist, then, given the reality of change, change cannot take place on the side of nonbeing[11] but has to occur somewhere within being.

It follows then that, given the above two realities—change is real, and change occurs in the realm of being—there must be two kinds of being: being that currently is, and being that will be when the change occurs. We

[7]Heraclitus, Fragments 41, 42, in ibid., 136.

[8]Fragment 20, ibid., 134.

[9]Plato, *Phaedo*, 78d–79d, in Edith Hamilton and Huntington Cairns, eds., *The Collected Dialogues of Plato*, trans. Hugh Tredennick (Princeton, NJ: Princeton University Press, 1963), 61–63.

[10]Plato, *Parmenides*, 129a–135b, in ibid., trans. F. M. Cornford, 923–929.

[11]Aristotle, *Metaphysics*, in Apostle, *Aristotle's Metaphysics*, 146–159. For a thorough study of how this understanding was incorporated by Thomas Aquinas, see Mary Consilia O'Brien, *The Antecedents of Being* (Washington, DC: Catholic University, 1939).

can call the latter category being-in-potentiality, which refers to something that can become actual being, but has not yet made its appearance. As the change takes place, it moves from being-in-potentiality to being-in-actuality. Thus there are both being and becoming—Parmenides and Heraclitus were both right—and there is no contradiction between the two; actual being does not arise from absolute nonbeing, but from potential being. Aquinas summarized, "potency and act divide common being."[12]

Admittedly, there is a point of confusion here in the nomenclature that both Aristotle and Aquinas used. They frequently referred to the change from potentiality to actuality as "motion," a point that even the followers of Aristotle forgot by the time of René Descartes.[13] But "motion" in this sense dovetails entirely with Isaac Newton's laws as well. Aquinas said, "Whatever moves is moved by another."[14] Newton's first law of motion is: "Every object in a state of uniform motion tends to remain in that state of motion unless an external force is applied to it."

On the surface, these two statements seem to be contradictory because apparently Aristotle and Aquinas are saying that a thing will only remain in motion so long as it is forced to be in motion, while Newton seems to say that a thing will remain in motion on its own so long as there is no force to stop it.

But these two statements do not contradict when you understand that for Aristotle and Aquinas "motion" refers to change. In the case of Newton's law, we stipulate the actuality of an object in an ideal environment in constant motion. The object also has the potential to stop moving, but that potential will not be actualized until there is a cause that brings about the stoppage. Consequently, for Newton just as much as Aristotle, a thing will change only if it is changed from outside itself. Whatever changes (that is to say, whatever "moves" in Aristotelian terminology) must be changed by some external factor. It is true that Aristotle's physics did not extend to ideal environments, but both Newton and Aristotle agree that change (Aristotle's "movement") will not take place until another factor interferes. Newton and Aristotle subscribed to the same principle of causality.

HOW MODAL LOGIC HELPS

Let us take a further look at the nature of potentiality by making reference to recent discussions in the area of modal logic. Modal logic distinguishes

---

[12]Thomas Aquinas, *On the Truth of the Catholic Faith: Summa contra Gentiles*, Vol. 2, ch. 54, art. 10.
[13]Sarah Byers, "Life as 'Self-Motion': Descartes and the Aristotelians on the Soul as the Life of the Body," *Review of Metaphysics*, Vol. 59, No. 4 (June 2006): 723–755.
[14]Aquinas, *Summa Theologica*, Vol. 1, q. 2, art. 3.

between the four ways ("modes") in which a statement can be true: something is actually true; something is possibly true; something is necessarily true; or something is necessarily false. Note that there is some overlap; if something is actually true, it must be possibly true; or if something is necessarily false, it is necessarily true that it is false. These distinctions apply both to the sentences and to the objects in the sentences to which they refer. For example, the sentence "there exists water" is actually true, and we can also talk of the actual existence of water.[15] Similarly, the sentence "I will live to see my 100th birthday" is possibly true, and thus we are saying that I have the potential being of a centenarian.

For the last few decades, philosophers using modal logic have come to express the nature of possibility by imagining logically possible worlds in which some statements are true even though they are not true in the actual world. So, to stick to the latter example, we can say that in the actual world I am currently fifty-seven years old, and if it is possible for me to be a hundred years old, we can conceive of a logically possible world in which I am a centenarian. Let us follow a widely adopted convention and refer to the actual world as *?* and to other logically possible worlds as sequences of *W*'s, beginning with *W*, followed by *WW*, followed by *WWW*, and so forth.

So, if there is a logically possible world *W* in which I am a hundred years old, where in the world is that world? Some philosophers[16] believe that these logically possible worlds exist in their own right and that there is no intrinsic difference with *?*, our present actual world. Most people would find that idea a little strange, though, because it would blur the all-important distinction between what is actual and what is merely possible.

Then where do these logically possible worlds exist? The point is that they don't exist in their own right at all; they exist only as potentials in the actual world.[17] When I am saying that it is possible for me to be a hundred years old, or that there is a world *W* in which I am a centenarian, I have not left the actual world. It is in the actual world that I have the potential to be something else, assuming that it is logically possible.

Then we have an analog here to the Aristotelian idea of potentiality. When we say that something is potential, we are saying that there is an

---

[15]Philosophers distinguish between the modal categories *de dicto*, which refers to the verbal expression (sentences, propositions), and *de re*, which refers to the subject of the sentence. It is not always possible to make the carryover from *de dicto* to *de re*, but frequently the two go hand in hand.

[16]E.g., David Lewis, "Possible Worlds" and "Counterparts of Double Lives?" in Michael J. Loux, ed., *Metaphysics: Contemporary Readings*, Contemporary Readings in Philosophy (Oxford, UK: Routledge, 2001), 160–167, 188–217.

[17]This understanding has been advanced particularly strongly by Alvin Plantinga. See his "Actualism and Possible Worlds," in Loux, *Metaphysics*, 168–187.

unactualized possibility and that this is a possibility that is real as a possibility in the actual world. Possibilities are not free-floating ideas or beings that somehow all of a sudden become true or actual, but they are already embedded in the actual world. I have the potential, at least to the best of my knowledge, to live to be a hundred. It may not be likely, and the probabilities may even be stacked against it, but the logical possibility and the potential are there. On the other hand, there is no possibility, neither logical, nor metaphysical, nor physical, that I will become a thumbtack. This is an impossibility because it does not comport with the state of affairs in *a*—the actual world. My essential nature in *a* is such that it logically prevents my becoming an actual thumbtack, and so I do not have the potential being of a thumbtack.

The point of all of this is to show that the idea of potentiality is not some outlandish concept that philosophers dreamed up when they got bored with the way in which the real world functions, but it is a way of saying something that is true about the real world. The square root of four is two—necessarily. My pickup truck has four-wheel-drive—actually. You will finish reading this essay—potentially. A circle has four corners—impossibly. All of these assessments are based on what I have learned to be true in *a*. In other words, here is another roundabout way of saying that what is potential is based on what is actual, or that potential being is something that comes with actual being.

CHANGE AS THE ACTUALIZATION OF A POTENTIAL

What happens, then, when a thing is changed? Let us take the easy example of a potter turning a lump of clay into a bowl. We begin with an actual entity, the lump of clay, which has the potential to become a bowl. We wind up with another actual entity, the bowl, which in turn may have other potentials, such as to become a pile of broken pottery shards. More specifically, what actually occurred when the potential of the clay to become a bowl was actualized? The potter took the clay, gave it a shape, and performed those chemical processes (such as heating it in a kiln) that gave the clay this new identity. This idea is not strange or mysterious, and Aristotle did not invent it. This is what the actualization of a potential is all about: a causal agent imposes a different form on a substance. This can be very straightforward, such as in this case of a lump of clay being given a new physical form, or it can be extremely complex, such as in the birth of a living human being. However, simple or complex, the basic process is the same. In each case, the material substance with whatever attributes it may have at the moment is being given a new nature that has certain different attributes. The same principle also applies to the differentiation between two particular individuals (they have two different forms), the change that a substance may undergo, such as growing taller (there is an alteration in the form), or physical motion (the geographic coordinates of the form in its union with the material substance are changed).

Thus there are two clear requirements for there to be the actualization of a potential. First of all, there has to be some actuality already. You cannot realize the potential of something that does not exist, nor can something that does not exist alter the form of something that does. And second, it is clear that in order for a potential to be actualized, something that is already actual must function as a cause. In the case of the bowl of clay, it was necessary for there to be a potter who imposed the new form on the lump of clay. Potentials do not actualize themselves.

Sometimes it looks as though some entity actualizes its own potential. If you follow along with the following example, I promise that I will let it remain purely a thought experiment. Imagine that I have the potential to become a great tuba player. Now, in one sense it is obviously I who needs to actualize that potential. I need to hold the tuba, blow into it properly, push the right valves, and practice until I have attained sufficient skill. But still, the potential does not actualize itself. It is the rest of me, which is already actual, that needs to put in the study and practice in order to actualize that potential, and that part of me has to be actual. I could not suddenly from one moment to the next become a tuba player. First I need to have the potential, and second, that potential needs a cause to become actualized, just as any other potential.

CAUSALITY

Thus we have arrived at the idea that finite beings are actualized potential and that it takes a cause, which is an actual being in its own right, to actualize the potential. Unfortunately, in the history of modern philosophy the nature of causality has been drastically misunderstood and consequently misapplied to the cosmological argument. The fundamental flaw, which has become ingrained in modern philosophy, is that causality has been portrayed as a sequence of two events. Allegedly, we recognize causality when event A has been consistently followed by event B. Somehow in the transition between the two events, a causal action has taken place. David Hume, as is well known, demonstrated that such a mysterious transition cannot be discerned empirically, but Immanuel Kant rescued it by consigning it to the *a priori* categories of the mind. But thereby Kant merely closed the door on ever becoming clearer on what causality actually is because, according to his philosophy, one cannot treat the synthetic *a priori* categories as objects of knowledge themselves. However, not only is such metaphysical skepticism unnecessary, it is actually rooted in this fundamental misunderstanding.

How many events occur when causation takes place? One can follow the modern scheme and recognize two events, one before and one after the causation. Thus, to use Hume's illustration, when billiard ball A causes billiard ball B to move, you see two events. First, billiard ball A moves, and then billiard ball B moves. But these two events surround the causation; they are not actually the causation. When does the real causation take place? It is at one particular moment in time—namely, at that precise point when billiard ball A transfers some of its momentum and kinetic energy to billiard ball B. At that moment the actuality that is a part of the first moving ball activates the potential of the second ball by shifting its form from being at rest to being in motion. Therefore, there is only one event, the actualization of the potential, which is metaphysically equivalent to a shift in forms.

Let us look at a second example to illustrate the same point. Timothy McDermott uses the idea of a Bunsen burner heating a beaker of water. McDermott says, "But what we call the Bunsen burner heating the water is nothing more than the water being heated by the Bunsen burner."[18] This innocuous statement has clear implications for the theory of cause and effect; for the cause acts only insofar as there is a change in the being of the effect. McDermott clarifies,

> The existence of the cause expresses itself in activity, but that activity is the coming to existence of the effect. Causality, then, should not be given its modern reading as involving a sequence of two changes: it is one change in the effect as seen from the cause.[19]

By contrast, C. J. Ducasse would take exception with McDermott's last statement. He analyzes causality as a three-term relation: There is a state of affairs prior to causation, S; at a given time, T_1, the cause, C, is introduced; this produces a change in S at a later time, T_2, to give us the effect E. Thus,

---

[18]Timothy McDermott, "Existence and Causality," Appendix 3, ST, Blackfriars edition, Vol. 2 (New York: McGraw-Hill, 1964), 184.
[19]Ibid.

there are three terms, S, C, and E, and two changes, the introduction of C and the subsequent change of S to E. A causation is then "a change in E in S by an earlier change C in S."[20]

To apply Ducasse's analysis to McDermott's example, S would be the beaker of water before the Bunsen burner has become heated. At time T_1, the burner, designated as C, starts to heat the water. Then at T_2 the water starts to be heated, which is E. Thus there were two changes: the heating by the Bunsen burner, and an instant later the being-heated by the water.

But this analysis is out of keeping with reality. The water does not become heated after the Bunsen burner is heating it, and the Bunsen burner is not heating water before the water is becoming heated; by the very language used it becomes obvious that the two occurrences take place simultaneously. Nor may it be said that C stands for the Bunsen burner as it is lit but has not yet begun to actually heat the water. As long as the water has not yet started to become heated, it is unwarranted to label the burner as the cause of its being heated. A cause without an effect is an absurdity. Hence, we may, with McDermott, think of the causation being one change occurring at one time: the impartation of being.[21]

Thus, this is the situation. A contingent being is one that requires a cause to exist. Since it never stops being contingent, it never ceases to require a cause. A cause actualizes a being simultaneously with the potential being actualized. In other words, you don't first have the causation and then later have the effect. Thus, whatever contingent beings exist require causes for their existence as long as they exist. Again, without invoking anything that we have contrived apart from our experience, we see that a contingent being is never free of its need for a cause. This fact is the idea that seems to have Craig stymied—namely, that "being must continually be added to their natures or they will be spontaneously annihilated."[22] This is an awkward way of putting it, as though being were a type of fuel that needs to be placed into an entity's tank to keep it going, but it catches the idea. If a thing does not retain the causes on which it is dependent, it will no longer exist. Surely this is not a surprising insight.

GOD

And thus we finally get to God. Let us recall our initial statement:

---

[20]C. J. Ducasse, *Nature, Mind, and Death* (LaSalle, IL: Open Court, 1951), 105.

[21]It is clear that Ducasse has confused temporal priority with logical priority. The human observer will reason from the burner to the heating of the water or vice versa, but such a sequence interpreted in terms of time is illusory. In the realm of temporal being, there is only one instantaneous event.

[22]Craig, "Cosmological Argument," 180.

Unless there were an infinite being, there could not be any finite beings.

In the chain of contingent beings that are mutually dependent on each other, there are only two options. Either there is a cause outside of the chain that actualizes the potential without being actualized by it, or there simply are no contingent beings.

Think of the following illustration. Imagine a computer spreadsheet in which the cells (labeled by letters and numbers) have no initial values. You would like cell *A1* to have the value of "1." You can type a "1" on the keyboard, hit "enter," and be done with it. But instead you decide to get the value from another cell, say *B1*. So, you give *A1* the formula "= *B1*" and see what happens. Of course, nothing happens because *B1* does not have any value. So you can either give *B1* directly the value of "1" or you can derive it from yet another cell, say *C1* and enter "= *C1*." But that doesn't help either since *C1* doesn't have any value. The fact is that no matter how long you make the chain of cells referencing each other, unless you input a value from outside the chain, none of the cells will have any value.

Nor does it help to link the cells to each other in a circle. Say that you have gone all the way back to cell *Z256*, and you decide that you're tired of the game. So, you tell *Z256* that its value is that of *A1*, where you started. What will you get? You will get an error message. You will still get no numerical value. To repeat, unless you provide a value from outside the circle of cells, none of them will yet have any value.

The same principle applies to contingent beings. If an entity is dependent for its being on another entity, which is itself dependent on another entity, it does not matter how long a chain of mutually dependent entities you create or whether you link all of these things in a circle; unless there is an entity outside the chain that actualizes the potential of the chain without being actualized by the chain, you will never get any actual being. And since we know that contingent beings exist, there must be such a being.

Thus, in order for there to be contingent beings, there must be a being

1. that is not restricted by time or space;
2. that cannot be changed by anything other than itself;
3. that did not have a beginning in time;
4. that does not need things other than itself to continue existing;
5. whose attributes are not influenced by other things (which means that it has only essential attributes, no accidental ones).

In short, it is an infinite being, precisely the kind of being that we usually refer to as *God*.

There are, of course, more questions, but there will also be more answers.[23] For our purposes, we have shown that if you understand the nature of finite beings, you have to realize that there is also an infinite being.

---

[23]For example, an obvious question is why this infinite being should properly be called *God* and whether he is identical with the God of the Judeo-Christian tradition. Sometimes, in fact, critics of the argument point to this as a serious flaw in the argument. Much has been made of the fact that Aquinas ends each of his "five ways" with the conclusion, "and this all men understand to be God," which seems both abrupt and unwarranted. However, this criticism also ignores the fact that Aquinas spends another forty questions (more than three hundred pages in my small-print Latin edition) developing the attributes of the First Cause/First Mover. See also Geisler and Corduan, *Philosophy of Religion*, 186–191, and Corduan, *Handmaid to Theology: An Essay in Philosophical Prolegomena* (Grand Rapids, MI: Baker, 1981), 118–127.

CHAPTER FOURTEEN

The Design Argument

Miguel Angel Endara

THE ARGUMENT FROM DESIGN, also called the teleological argument, has a long and somewhat scarred history, falling into general disfavor for the last two centuries upon encountering David Hume's devastating pen.[1] Nonetheless, in recent times we have seen a resurgence of life in this argument. The argument from design is once again back on the discussion table.

In its long history, the argument appears in two modes. In the first mode, the argument appears as an inference from design based on the harmonious regularity, balance, and/or order of the universe. We may, for example, argue that nature displays a sense of harmonious regularity that we may compare to the geometric regularity of Islamic art or the heavenly harmony of "*Gloria in Excelsis.*" Thomas Aquinas gives us a good example of this first mode, arguing that many diverse things in the world work together in harmony, thereby necessitating a Power to account for this design quality of the world. This *Power* we call God.[2] More recent incarnations of this mode of argument include support from scientific data that have come to light primarily within the last thirty years. Reasoning inductively from the scientific data, some argue that the presence of the necessary preconditions for the possibility of one planet in the universe to sustain life is miniscule. Therefore, the regularity and harmony of these preconditions to accommodate life on earth warrants the existence of a divine designer. This is the fine-tuning argument from design. Notable efforts among those

---

[1]David Hume critiques the argument from design in his *Enquiry Concerning Human Understanding*, The Harvard Classics, Vol. 37 (New York: P.F. Collier & Son, 1910). http://etext.library.adelaide.edu.au/h/hume/david/h92e/ (accessed March 16, 2007), and *Dialogues Concerning Natural Religion*, second edition (Indianapolis, IN: Hacket Publishing Company, Inc., 1998).
[2]See Thomas Aquinas, *Summa Contra Gentiles*, ed. Joseph Rickaby (London: Burns and Oates, 1905), I.13; http://www2.nd.edu/Departments/Maritain/etext/gc.htm (accessed March 16, 2007).

who provide this mode of argument are those of astronomer Hugh Ross and philosopher Robin Collins.[3]

In this chapter I provide an argument from design, henceforth called the *teleological argument*, which pertains to the second mode of the argument. This mode is also an inference from design, but unlike the first mode, it relies on the ostensible features of the world that display purpose, function, end, or *telos*. Alternatively stated, there are features within the world that seem designed to achieve some purpose. By means of these features, we infer that the world is the handiwork of an intelligent designer, God.

William Paley gives us the classical example of this mode of argument in his *Natural Theology*.[4] Here Paley imagines finding a watch on the ground. He proceeds to examine it, discovering its complex and intricate design characteristics that seem to exist for a purpose, and this leads him to infer the existence of a watch designer. Analogously, the seemingly purposeful characteristics of the world lead Paley to infer a divine designer, God.

In our own time, intelligent design theory gives us powerful theoretical tools by means of which we may construct more compelling and robust teleological arguments. Hence, in this chapter I present an example of this second mode of argument, based on intelligent design theory, which, as I will demonstrate, is a viable argument worthy of consideration.

AN ANOMALOUS IDEA IN NEO-DARWINIAN SCIENCE?

In his explanation of the causes of things Aristotle includes the *teleological* or *final* cause.[5] The teleological cause is *that for which a thing exists*. We may clearly see examples of this in artifacts. The chair was made for the purpose of sitting, the knife was made for cutting, and the closet was made to provide space to hang clothes. However, teleological causes are not exhausted with artifacts, for Aristotle also thought that all beings, including biological organisms, and even their characteristics, exist for certain

---

[3]See, for example, Hugh Ross, *The Creator and the Cosmos: How the Latest Scientific Discoveries of the Century Reveal God*, third edition (Colorado Springs: NavPress, 2001), 145–168. See also "Fine-Tuning for Life in the Universe" (2004), http://www.reasons.org/resources/apologetics/design_evidences/200412_fine_tuning_for_life_in_the_universe.shtml (accessed May 7, 2006); Robin Collins, "A Scientific Argument for the Existence of God: The Fine-Tuning Design Argument," in Michael J. Murray, ed., *Reason for the Hope Within* (Grand Rapids, MI: Eerdmans, 1999), 47–75, and Robin Collins, "The Teleological Argument," in Paul Copan and Paul Moser, eds., *The Rationality of Theism* (New York: Routledge, 2003), 132–148.
[4]William Paley, *Natural Theology* (Houston: St. Thomas Press, 1972).
[5]See Aristotle, *Metaphysics*, trans. W. D. Ross, I.3; http://etext.library.adelaide.edu.au/a/aristotle/metaphysics/ (accessed March 16, 2007).

purposes. Biological beings have an intrinsic or built-in, goal-directed plan of development, an *entelechy*. Entelechy-guided development results in mature organisms that possess teleological or purposeful functions. Due, to a large extent, to the work of Thomas Aquinas, Christianity also embraced Aristotelian teleological explanations, crediting the God of the Bible as the one who supplied the intrinsic teleological causes of living beings. Nonetheless, with the advent of the Age of Enlightenment and Newton's mechanical description of the universe, teleological explanations began to fall into disfavor.

In our own time most scientists work exclusively from a naturalistic framework, embracing *methodological naturalism*.[6] Since appealing to teleological causes implies that some kind of supernatural entity or force is behind the teleology, science eschews this notion, except for biology. Curiously, biology is unique among the sciences in allowing the legitimacy of teleological statements, including statements about design and function or purpose. Though most biologists and philosophers of science embrace methodological naturalism, they agree that teleological explanations are foundational to arrive at a proper understanding of the complex behavioral patterns and morphological structures of biological organisms.

In order to understand complex biological traits, one must ask what these are for. In other words, one must ask what are the "goals," "purposes," or "ends" of these traits? In the context of this type of discussion, the term *function* takes a prominent role, where function is the characteristic action or purpose of an organism's structure or trait. For example, the function of the heart is to pump blood, the function of eagle wings is to fly, and the function of fish flippers is to swim. However, according to the fears of some, a possible anomaly or incongruity exists. Recognizing that certain traits have *functions* seems to imply that some supernatural entity or force somehow "planned" the trait in question for a future purpose or end. How, then, do philosophers of biology and biologists understand the concept of *function* or *purpose*? There are many proposed rival naturalistic theories that attempt to resolve the anomaly under consideration. However, as of yet, no theory seems to be universally

---

[6]*Methodological naturalism* (MN) is the philosophical presupposition that stipulates that scientific explanations of natural phenomena may only have empirical causal explanations. Of course, this means that any kind of supernatural explanation is ruled out *a priori*. However, some philosophers and scientist dub this as *strong* MN and opt for a weaker version, where empirical causal explanations of natural phenomena are primarily assumed, but where supernatural explanations are not ruled out. For an excellent anthology that challenges the philosophical legitimacy of strong methodological naturalism, see William Lane Craig and J. P. Moreland, eds., *Naturalism: A Critical Analysis* (New York: Routledge, 2000).

embraced. Thus, herein lies a significant contemporary debate within the philosophy of biology.[7]

In this chapter we examine a proposed solution to this anomaly given by a prominent contemporary philosopher of science, Michael Ruse.[8] In what follows, then, we analyze Ruse's evolutionary functional analysis arguing, contra Ruse, that the biological traits in question were in fact planned by a divine designer for a future purpose, as intelligent design theory reveals.

MICHAEL RUSE'S BIOLOGICALLY-BASED EVOLUTIONARY FUNCTIONAL ANALYSIS

Working strictly within a naturalistic framework, Ruse explains distinct ways of understanding design and purpose in biology. Prominent among these are the following two *functional analyses*:

1) Some functional explanations offer a causal account of a trait's existence. This is the *etiological analysis* offered by philosopher Larry Wright.[9] Here the causal arrow points both ways, for the trait and its function exist due to each other. The trait and the function, in other words, are both cause and effect of each other. "A leads to B, but in turn B leads to A."[10] So, according to this account, the heart exists because it has the function of pumping blood, and the function of pumping blood is the cause of the heart's existence. Or, to use one of Ruse's examples, "The lens is there because it focuses the light. The light is focused because the lens is there."[11]

2) Another functional explanation offers a causal account of how a particular trait enhances a whole organism. Here particular traits exist because they confer the ability or capacity to aid a system or organism to do its overall task. This is the *capacity analysis* account offered by philosopher Robert Cummins.[12] According to this account, the heart functions as a pump in order to deliver blood through the entire organism, thereby sustaining its life. Thus, the function of pumping blood aids in conferring the capacity of an organism to survive and reproduce.

---

[7]The chapters in the following well-received anthologies evince this contemporary debate. See, for example, David Buller, ed., *Function, Selection, and Design* (New York: SUNY Press, 1999) and Collin Allen, Marc Bekoff, and George Lauder, eds., *Nature's Purpose: Analyses of Function and Design in Biology* (Cambridge, MA: The MIT Press, 1998). The chapters of these anthologies also confirm that naturalistic explanations are the only ones seriously considered by most philosophers of biology and biologists.
[8]Michael Ruse, *Darwin and Design: Does Evolution Have a Purpose?* (Cambridge, MA: Harvard University Press, 2003), 250–289.
[9]See, Ruse, ibid., 260.
[10]Ibid., 269. However, we ought not to assume that A leads to B every time. See ibid., 260.
[11]Ibid., 263.
[12]See ibid., 260–262.

Ruse's own evolutionary analysis takes into account both of these explanations. However, according to Ruse, one must first understand *function* in terms of "adaptation."[13] Adaptation refers to traits that confer fitness to an organism and/or it refers to the process by means of which the mechanism of natural selection retains these traits. Undoubtedly, there are innumerable adaptations that may confer fitness on an organism. The significant question, then, is, "How is it that some traits are adapted into an organism and some are not?" Traits arise or experience modification through chance gene mutations, reproduction, and competition, among other things. Here Wright's etiological analysis helps us begin to understand why particular traits in organisms exist or become adapted. Particular traits in an organism exist due to the function they perform, and in turn its function exists due to the existence of the trait. The mechanism of natural selection, then, provides for a cyclical cause and effect of traits. Still, according to Ruse, Wright's analysis is incomplete in that it is missing a critical piece of the explanatory puzzle. Traits exist for certain *beneficial* ends, which make these ends *valued* or *desirable*.[14]

Specifically, natural selection retains traits that confer *benefits* to the organism while weeding out those that do not. Here we see an aspect of Cummings's capacity analysis. The function of adapted traits is to beneficially contribute to the capacity of the entire organism to do its overall task. Specifically, Ruse measures the overall task of a biological organism in terms of the benefits or values that aid in the capacity for survival and reproduction. However, we still have a problem, for, we may ask, "What does science and, in particular, biology have to do with terms like *desirability* and *values*?" Is science not supposed to be "neutral" regarding *values*? According to Ruse, one may legitimately employ value terms in biology when these do not refer to transcendent or absolute values but instead refer to values relative to the well-being of biological organisms. As Ruse states, we ought to judge the traits of an organism "in terms of the overall benefit or good of the organism."[15] These relative values linked to the well-being of a biological organism, then, are necessary and commonplace.[16] Hence, natural selection adapts traits that possess functions that confer the value of fitness, understood in terms of survival and reproduction, to an organism.

According to Ruse, organizationally complex or design-like traits and

---

[13]See ibid., 262.
[14]Ibid., 265.
[15]Ibid., 282.
[16]Ibid., 287.

functions also arise through natural selection.[17] As time passes, by means of natural selection beneficial accidental traits that add to the capacity of an organism to do its overall task accumulate, while detrimental or non-beneficial traits diminish. Through this process, complex biological traits arise from simple ones through several evolutionary stages. So we may imagine simple biological traits that possess a simple function that, through several evolutionary stages, have lost their original value, thus becoming obsolete. We may further imagine the fortuitous confluence of these simple traits with other simple, but now obsolete, traits, resulting in organized complex traits that possess respectively complex functions. Some call this natural evolutionary process that beneficially exploits traits "co-option." Ruse gives us an artifactual analogy of how the co-option process might work.[18] We may consider building an arched stone bridge without cement by first building a supporting structure and removing it when the bridge is done. Analogously, we may imagine several simple traits collaborating to form a new and novel organizationally complex trait, while natural selection weeds out other, now obsolete, traits. Once natural selection produces an organism with traits that successfully aid in its survival and reproduction, it continues to replicate the result to achieve the same end. Surviving biological organisms with adapted organizationally complex traits and functions, then, result from the accumulation of accidental variations guided by natural selection over millions of years.

Natural selection, then, produces organized complex biological systems that we may understand and explain through the employment of intentional terms such as *purpose* and *design*. Nonetheless, we should not lose sight that these traits only *seem* designed. As a result, Ruse contends that we must understand *design* in a metaphorical sense.[19] Although strictly speaking the metaphorical term is false, it nonetheless possesses a heuristic function. That is, using *design* in a metaphoric sense allow us to see the biological traits in question in a novel mode that sparks our thinking, allowing us to better understand the function or purpose of the trait. Therefore, in Ruse's view the design metaphor is powerful in that it leads to fruitful questions while it stimulates responses. However, we must understand seemingly designed complex traits as adaptations brought about by means of the mechanism of natural selection in order to

---

[17]Ibid., 274–276.
[18]See ibid., 320. Specifically, Ruse uses this analogy in his discussion of sequential biochemical processes that result in the formation of new organizationally complex molecular organisms. However, the principle behind this analogy also seems to fit the formation of biological traits.
[19]See ibid., 265–267.

confer greater value or enhance the survival and reproduction advantages of the organism.

THE SEEMINGLY DESIGNED DEFENSE MECHANISM OF THE BOMBARDIER BEETLE

Given Ruse's evolutionary analysis, we begin to see why most biologists and philosophers of science do not eschew the need for *design* language. These people admit that particular biological traits and organisms indeed seem to be *designed*. Instead, the term *design* is merely a metaphor, all the while recognizing that *design* is the product of protracted naturalistic causes. Here, then, it seems that we have a replacement for the classical design argument, for we no longer need to appeal to a "God" or any other noumenal entity to account for *design* in living organisms. The naturalistic mechanism of natural selection seems to work just fine. Nonetheless, we might ask, can this philosophically sophisticated explanatory framework account for all seemingly designed organizationally complex biological traits? Let us briefly look at the seemingly designed biological defense mechanism of the bombardier beetle and ask whether Ruse's analysis may properly account for it.

The bombardier beetle is a type of ground beetle. These beetles are the subject of much marvel and wonder because they possess a complex, intricate, and effective defense mechanism. They repel their predators—ants, spiders, and frogs—by squirting them with a high-pressure, rapid-fire jet, about five hundred pulses per second, of boiling liquid, 100 degrees Celsius, in virtually any direction.[20] How does this tiny creature accomplish this amazing task? The beetle's glands produce two chemicals, storing them in a reservoir within the abdomen. When threatened, the muscles surrounding the reservoir push the chemicals into a heart-shaped reaction chamber that then secretes an element that breaks down and catalyzes the chemicals, causing a reaction.[21] The beetle's predators now begin to receive rapid-fire

---

[20]See Brad Harrub and Bert Thompson, "Bombardier Beetles and Airplane Engines" (2003); http://www.apologeticspress.org/articles/2102 (accessed April 5, 2006) and Thomas Eisner and Daniel J. Aneshansley. "Spray Aiming in the Bombardier Beetle: Photographic Evidence," *Proceedings of the National Academy of Sciences of the United States of America*, Vol. 96 (August 17, 1999): 9705–9709; http://www.pnas.org/cgi/content/full/96/17/9705 (accessed April 6, 2006).

[21]Here is the technical explanation:

Two chemicals, hydroquinones and hydrogen peroxide, are produced in glands, and then stored in a large reservoir housed within the beetle's abdomen. When the animal feels threatened, muscles surrounding the reservoir contract, pushing the chemicals through a muscle-controlled valve into a heart-shaped reaction chamber lined with cells that secrete peroxidases and catalases—oxidative enzymes. The enzymes quickly break down the hydrogen peroxide, and catalyze the oxidation of the hydroquinones into p-benzoquinones—compounds that are well known for their irritant properties. This chemical reaction results in a release of free oxygen, and causes a substantial liberation of heat. Harrub and Thompson, "Bombardier Beetles and Airplane Engines."

doses of boiling irritating liquid, forcing them to quickly alter their plans of attack. This incredibly effective form of combustion is so amazing that researchers are attempting to reproduce the mechanism for possible use within the aircraft industry.[22]

Biochemist and intelligent design theorist Michael Behe would see the bombardier beetle's defense mechanism as an example of an *irreducibly complex* biochemical system. Behe uses the term *irreducible complexity* to describe biochemical systems that contain diverse parts conjoined in such a way that if only one part is taken out, the system no longer functions.[23] So it is with the beetle's defense mechanism. We may imagine that if one of the compound traits of the mechanism fails or is taken out, the mechanism no longer functions.

How might Ruse explain this marvel of seemingly complex organized design? Undoubtedly, the mechanism of natural selection working on the bombardier beetle's ancestors, through millions of years, must have produced the beetle's defense mechanism. Specifically, we may imagine that beneficial traits—traits that added to the beetle's ancestors' overall benefit—slowly accumulated. Some of the defense mechanism's original or proto-traits might have functioned for other purposes that also conferred survival and reproductive advantages to the beetle's ancestors. As the beetle biologically evolved, these proto-traits might have been co-opted for the defense mechanism. Here we are reminded of Ruse's arch analogy where several traits piggyback on each other to form a new and novel trait that starts functioning independently.[24] Further, natural selection took care of weeding out the original and now obsolete leftover traits.

We see, then, in accord with the *etiological analysis* of function that the defense mechanism of the bombardier beetle exists to ward off predators, and the function of warding off predators exists because the defense mechanism exists. Furthermore, in accord with the *capacity analysis* of function, the defense mechanism exists because it possesses value, benefiting the beetle *qua* beetle in its capacity to survive and reproduce. Without the defense mechanism, the bombardier beetle might have become extinct long ago.

The above is but a very general outline of how the bombardier beetle might have evolved according to Ruse's evolutionary analysis. Still, there

---

[22]"An Insect's Knack for Combustion," *Mechanical Engineering Design*, "News & Notes" (2004); http://www.memagazine.org/supparch/medes04/newsnotes/newsnotes.html (accessed April 6, 2006).
[23]For a full treatment on the topic of irreducible complexity, see Michael J. Behe, *Darwin's Black Box: The Biochemical Challenge to Evolution* (New York: Free Press, 1996).
[24]See Ruse, *Darwin and Design*, 320.

are tremendously large explanatory gaps in the evolution of the beetle that may not have recourse to naturalistic evolutionary accounts.[25] As one of my former philosophy professors used to say, "The devil is in the details." Is this co-option process a suitable one to explain irreducibly complex traits?

In order to provide a viable evolutionary pathway of how the defense mechanism of the bombardier beetle evolved based on co-option, a plausible explanation must be given regarding the original function of each of the irreducible components or traits of the mechanism. Did each of these components exist prior to the time that the defense mechanism existed? If so, what was the function for each of these original components? Furthermore, if we are dealing with an irreducibly complex system or trait, we need to have a precise set of sequential assembly instructions (DNA-based instructions) for the defense mechanism.[26] Regarding these instructions, we may ask where they come from. Could natural selection or other evolutionary mechanisms have manipulated the DNA so as to provide such a set of instructions? If so, what was the benefit for such an instruction set prior to the time that it was wholly in place? Was the assembly set of instructions itself co-opted? In other words, taking Ruse's route, we may imagine that the instruction set itself has many parts or components and that these components might have had some kind of *value* prior to the time the instructions were finalized. What was their value? In sum, we see that the evolutionary pathway story itself seems to be organizationally complex. Thus, the question becomes, "Are the mechanisms of natural selection working on competition, reproduction, and random gene mutation robust enough to account for the defense mechanism as well as the DNA information of the bombardier beetle?"[27] Could biologi-

---

[25]Many theists have been challenged with a "God-of-the-gaps" objection—an attempt to get around scientific explanatory gaps by appealing to God. For example, before we know why the planets move, we might appeal to God, claiming that he directly moves them. In our own time, intelligent design theory is sometimes charged with this objection: We cannot, as of yet, explain the causal origins of the bacterial flagellum, for example, so an intelligent designer (God) is appealed to. One problem with this objection is that it is a double-edged sword. If we are ignorant about the origins of a natural phenomenon, we may err not only in prematurely appealing to God but in prematurely appealing to chance or biological evolution. We may get around this objection by appealing to an intelligent designer only when our appeal is based on what we know rather than what we do not know. Intelligent design theory legitimately appeals to a designer because it bases its appeal on a reliable empirical marker of design, *specified complexity* (explained in the next section). See William Dembski, *The Design Revolution* (Downers Grove, IL: InterVarsity Press, 2004), 116–126 for a detailed explanation.

[26]In order for the beetle's mechanism to function, its component parts must be constructed according to a precise biochemical sequence. The deoxyribonucleic acid (DNA) molecules, which exist inside cells, contain the genetic information or blueprint for all the physical traits of the organism, including the precise biochemical sequences for the construction of these traits. See the documentary *Unlocking the Mystery of Life: The Scientific Case for Intelligent Design*, Illustra Media, 2002; http://www.illustramedia.com/productions.htm.

[27]See the comments and criticism on the co-option theory by Scott Minnich in *Unlocking the Mystery of Life*.

cal evolutionists even begin to imagine a plausible pathway to account for irreducible complexity?

In his Internet article "Bombardier Beetles and the Argument of Design," Mark Isaak responds to this last question in the affirmative.[28] According to Isaak, "a step-by-step evolution of the bombardier system is really not that hard to envision."[29] Isaak proceeds to give us the eighteen steps by means of which he envisions how the bombardier beetle might have evolved. Still, Isaak seem to dismiss crucial necessary steps in the beetle's evolutionary process. As Harrub and Thompson note, among other things, Isaak fails to explain the evolution of the unique set of muscles that compress in order to send the chemicals into the reaction chamber as well as failing to explain how the male and female genders of the beetle evolved different muscles and mechanisms.[30]

Furthermore, in the case of the evolutionary pathway that Isaak gives us and the one we might imagine that Ruse would give us, there is no accounting for the genesis of the information necessary in developing and assembling the component parts of the defense mechanism at the level of DNA instructions.

We have a third option that accounts for the information-rich, irreducibly complex defense mechanism of bombardier beetles—intelligent design theory.

SPECIFIED COMPLEX INFORMATION AS A MARKER OF DESIGN

Whenever we observe artifacts such as hieroglyphs etched out in stone—the figures on the side of Mount Rushmore in South Dakota or the stone figures on Easter Island—we immediately infer design from an intelligent source.[31] Inferences to design from an intelligent source are a normal part of the human thinking process. But just how, exactly, do we infer design? We normally infer design by viewing complex improbable objects that match a recognizable pattern. We recognize, for example, that nature in the form of wind and erosion provides unsuitable mechanisms to create the figures on Easter Island and Mount Rushmore. Why? We normally do not see anything like these complex figures on rocks in the process of being created without the involvement of intelligent intervention. Moreover, these

---

[28]Mark Isaak, "Bombardier Beetles and the Argument of Design" (2003), http://www.talkorigins.org/faqs/bombardier.html (accessed April 7, 2006).
[29]Ibid.
[30]Harrub and Thompson, "Bombardier Beetles and Airplane Engines."
[31]These examples were taken from *Unlocking the Mystery of Life*.

figures match recognizable patterns, that of bodies and faces. In particular, these figures:

> a) are not accountable by physical laws,
> b) match a recognizable pattern (are *specified*), and
> c) are *complex,* possessing many distinct parts or features.

In short, *specified complexity* evinces design.

As William Dembski points out, the plot of Carl Sagan's novel-turned-into-movie, *Contact,* was built around the discovery of extraterrestrial intelligence based on distant radio signals that matched the prime numbers between 2 and 101.[32] Here we have another example of *specified complexity*, for the radio signals possess many and distinct features that match an independently recognizable pattern, the prime numbers from 2 to 101, which are hardly accountable by means of physical laws. Thus, Dembski claims that we may infer design by means of identifying *specified complexity*.[33]

However, we may ask, is specified complexity a reliable criterion for inferring intelligent design?[34] According to Dembski, the justification for this criterion proceeds from a practical inductive generalization argument, where for every instance where we know the cause of specified complexity, we discover that it is an intelligent designer. As Dembski himself explains,

> . . . in very instance where specified complexity is present and where the underlying causal story is known (i.e. where we are not just dealing with circumstantial evidence, but where, as it were, the video camera is running and any putative designer would be caught red-handed), it turns out

---

[32]Dembski, *The Design Revolution*, 34–35.

[33]For a more in-depth explanation of the detection of design from specified complex patterns, see William Dembski, *The Design Inference* (Downers Grove, IL: InterVarsity Press, 1999) and *No Free Lunch* (Lanham, MD: Rowman & Littlefield Publishers, 2002).

[34]Ruse critiques Dembski's theoretical argument by claiming that while natural selection cannot produce *designed* organisms, it can, in principle, produce complex *design-like* organisms. To demonstrate his point, Ruse gives us the example of a computer program called Tierra, created by Thomas S. Ray, which attempts to simulate biological evolutionary processes. Tierra seems to successfully demonstrate that complex and even novel organisms that seem designed may arise merely through natural selection working on competition, reproduction, and mutations. Ruse concludes that this program demonstrates that Dembski is wrong in principle (see Ruse, *Darwin and Design*, 326–328). Given that Tierra does not attempt to simulate the origin of life, the main question regarding Tierra and similar simulation programs is whether the simulated biological processes, conditions, parameters, and functions actually simulate those of Earth and its organisms. Many people may be able to create a virtual world where biological evolution produces a variety of new and novel seemingly designed, specified complex organisms, given non-Earth-like processes, conditions, parameters, and functions. However, the trick is to create a realistic simulation. Robert C. Newman makes this very criticism regarding Tierra and other such simulations. Specifically, among his other criticisms, Newman questions whether the self-reproducing automata of these simulators actually simulate the function, biochemistry, and reproduction of real multicellular organisms. Bereft of a realistic simulation, Ruse fails to demonstrate his point. See Robert C. Newman, "Artificial Life and Cellular Automata" (2000), http://www.arn.org/docs/newman/rn_artificiallife.htm (accessed April 20, 2006).

design is present as well. . . . *Where direct, empirical corroboration is possible, design actually is present whenever specified complexity is present.* [italics in the original][35]

As an application of Dembski's principle, we discover that the sequencing of the DNA bases that gives rise to the construction of the bombardier beetle's defense mechanism as well as the mechanism itself are examples of specified complex information.[36] Both possess numerous and distinct features that match recognizable patterns. In particular, DNA bases match the pattern of a complex computer program with functions, while the defense mechanism matches the complex pattern of a combustion chamber. Given the detection of specified complexity and the failure of Ruse's analysis to account for such a pattern, we can properly infer an intelligent source.[37]

Furthermore, we infer that this intelligent source transcends our natural world. How so? First, we know that human beings are the only intelligent source in our natural world. Second, we also know that human beings are not the intelligent source behind the bombardier beetles. Third, the beetle's defense mechanism is only an example of numerous other specified complex traits and functions found in the animal and plant kingdom.[38] Therefore, the intelligence transcends our physical world. As such, we claim that this transcendent intelligence is God.

At this point, someone may inquire about the identity of this intelligence that we call *God*. Though the argument from design just proposed does not give us the God of the Bible, it does give us a being whose attributes of intelligence and transcendence are compatible with the attributes

---

[35]Dembski, *The Design Revolution*, 95–96. Also, on page 36 Dembski refers us to Parts Two and Three of *The Design Revolution* as well as his *No Free Lunch* in order to obtain a full theoretical justification for his claims.

[36]I previously claimed that the defense mechanism of the bombardier beetle is an example of *irreducible complexity*. Irreducible complexity is a species of specified complexity, for all irreducibly complex systems are also specified and complex, but irreducibly complex systems possess the additional feature of *irreducibility*. For a thorough treatment of irreducible complexity and its relationship to specified complexity, see Dembski, *No Free Lunch*, 239–310.

[37]A significant distinction between intelligent design theory and arguments from design must be made at this point. The conclusion of intelligent design theory is not the existence of *God*. Instead, the "intelligent designer" of the theory is a pragmatic, conceptual intelligence that resolves scientific anomalies or privations of explanatory power within evolutionary biology. Intelligent design theorists, then, say nothing regarding the objective existence (they do not deny or affirm it) or the identification of the intelligence behind specified complexity. The silence of intelligent design theory regarding the ontological status (the existence or nonexistence) and the identification of this intelligence in no way thwarts the possibility of the natural philosopher to create an information theoretic teleological argument employing the criteria for detecting design used by intelligent design theory. For more information regarding the distinctions and similarities of the intelligent design theory and the design argument, see Dembski, *The Design Revolution*, 37, 64–71.

[38]Michael Behe give us many examples of irreducibly complex traits at the molecular level, including "aspects of protein transport, blood clotting, closed circular DNA, electron transport, the bacterial flagellum, telomeres, photosynthesis. . . ." See his "Molecular Machines: Experimental Support for the Design Inference" (1996); http://www.arn.org/docs/behe/mb_mm92496.htm (accessed June 9, 2006).

of the God of the Bible. We recognize that the above teleological argument is limited in that it cannot supply many of the attributes the God of the Bible possesses. Other arguments to God's existence, such as cosmological arguments, also possess this limitation. Thus some propose that we take a cumulative case approach to the identification of the God who is the conclusion of these types of arguments.[39] Through such an approach we may discover more divine attributes, allowing us to make a stronger identification with the God of the Bible.

CONCLUSION

We may briefly summarize the above-explained teleological argument in the following manner:

1) Specified complexity is a reliable detector of design.

2) The bombardier beetle's defense mechanism is an example of irreducible complexity, which is a species of specified complexity.

3) The naturalistic mechanism of natural selection, working on random gene mutation, reproduction, and competition, cannot account for the information-rich specified complexity of the defense mechanism.

4) We infer an intelligent and transcendent designer as the source for the existence of the bombardier beetle and other biological organisms who exhibit specified complexity.

5) This intelligent and transcendent designer we call *God*.

---

[39] As an example of a recent cumulative case approach written for a popular audience, see Lee Strobel, *The Case for a Creator* (Grand Rapids, MI: Zondervan, 2004), 273–291. In these pages Strobel sums up his cumulative case based on the previous chapters of his book, arguing that: a) God is an immaterial personal being with free will, b) God has enormous power, c) his existence does not have a prior cause and he is without a beginning, existing outside of time, d) God is an intelligent being who continued his relation with his creation after the Big Bang, e) God endowed human beings with the curiosity and power to explore the world, by means of which he might be discovered, f) God is an incredibly creative being, and g) God is omnipresent.

CHAPTER FIFTEEN

The Transcendental Argument[1]

Sean Choi

IN RECENT YEARS, a theistic argument that goes by the name *the transcendental argument for God's existence* (TAG for short) has gained much attention and critical scrutiny. TAG is an argument that is prominent in presuppositional apologetic circles (even to this day), and it can be traced (at least as far) back to the writings of Cornelius Van Til.[2] More relevantly for the purposes of this essay, TAG was featured prominently in the famous debate between Christian apologist Greg Bahnsen and atheist advocate Gordon Stein. This debate took place at the University of California, Irvine, on February 11, 1985.[3] Over the years, the Bahnsen-Stein debate has attained legendary status—at least in Reformed circles—and may very well be the high-water mark for TAG. There is nearly unanimous agreement on all sides that Bahnsen won that debate: he clearly outmatched Stein. There is less of an agreement, however, about what Bahnsen *actually proved* (if he proved anything) during that debate. Speaking from personal experience, I have met many people from Reformed circles who think that Bahnsen not only "won" the debate (in the sense of outmatching Stein's

[1]I dedicate the present essay to the following group of people: Bob Passantino (who is the subject of the Festschrift to which my essay contributes), the members of the Van Til List (cf. footnote 25), especially James Anderson, Aaron Bradford, David Byron, and Greg Welty, as well as the "regulars" at the Mars Hill Club (you know who you are). In order not to ensnare myself in the paradox of the preface, I hereby announce that I fully endorse the arguments (and claims) advanced in this essay.
[2]For a good sampling of Van Til's statement on the matter, see Greg Bahnsen, *Van Til's Apologetic: Readings and Analysis* (Phillipsburg, NJ: P&R, 1998), 516–529.
[3]An audio recording of this debate is available through Covenant Media Foundation; www.cmfnow.com.

Some members of Providence Orthodox Presbyterian Chapel have performed a labor of love by transcribing the entire debate (complete with numbered lines for easy reference) and making it available for free download. Throughout this article, I will be quoting from "version 1.2" of the transcribed text. (This text is permanently archived on the web at web.archive.org/web/20060627133134/http://www.popchapel. com/Resources/Bahnsen/GreatDebate/.) In what follows, when referring to the content of this debate, I will do so by way of referencing the text of the above transcription. Future references to the transcribed text will take, for example, the following form: BSD, 11–23 (shorthand for Bahnsen-Stein Debate, line numbers 11–23).

rhetorical skills), but that he successfully demonstrated in that debate the utter, rational ineluctability of Christian theism.[4] Given this high esteem that Bahnsen's performance in his debate with Stein has had in the oral tradition, I think it is high time that Bahnsen's actual argument (TAG as he understood it)[5] in that debate be given a critical analysis, and I seek to offer one in this essay.

This essay proceeds as follows. In section I, I present a brief characterization of the nature of transcendental arguments in general and say what I think is the proper logical form of such arguments. In section II, I reconstruct and analyze Bahnsen's formulation of TAG that he presented during the Bahnsen-Stein debate. I will argue that Bahnsen's actual argument in that debate—insofar as it can be reconstructed so as to be deductively valid[6]—fails to establish Bahnsen's purported claim for his TAG—i.e.,

---

[4]Just for the record, I also have met plenty of people in Reformed circles who think that Bahnsen did not actually prove what he intended to prove. But my overall impression is that there are more supporters of Bahnsen than dissenters in the Reformed tradition. Also for the record, although much of what I say below about Bahnsen's apologetic argument, TAG, might seem overly critical, I have a very high appreciation for the commitment he showed to Christ, both in writing and in his life.

[5]Although I will not discuss them here (due to both the announced, limited aim of this article and space limitations), it is worth noting that there are alternative ways that TAG (or a TAG-like theistic transcendental argument) has been formulated by Reformed thinkers. The most sophisticated formulation that I know of—one that shows an astute awareness of contemporary epistemology—is James Anderson's "If Knowledge Then God," in *Calvin Theological Journal*, Vol. 40, No. 1 (2005), 49–75.

Even outside the Reformed circle, theistic arguments that are "transcendental" in spirit abound. For example, some construe C. S. Lewis's "argument from reason" (cf. his *Miracles* [New York: Collier, 1960], Chap. 3) as a transcendental argument for theism *simpliciter* (vis-à-vis philosophical naturalism), as opposed to Christian theism. (I personally remember Bob Passantino construing Lewis's argument in this way. Bob was particularly fond of Richard Purtill's argument in *Reason to Believe* [Grand Rapids, MI: Eerdmans, 1974], Chap. 3.) For a sampling of contemporary philosophical developments and discussions of the argument from reason, see the symposium (on that argument) in *Philosophia Christi*, Vol. 5, No. 1 (2003), as well as the relevant articles in the following issues of *Philo*: Vol. 2, No. 1 (1999) and Vol. 3, No. 1 (2000). Also see Victor Reppert's contribution in *In Defense of Natural Theology: A Post-Humean Assessment*, eds. James Sennett and Douglas Groothuis (Downers Grove, IL: InterVarsity Press, 2005), as well as his more popular statement of the argument in *C.S. Lewis's Dangerous Idea: In Defense of the Argument from Reason* (Downers Grove, IL: InterVarsity Press, 2003). William Hasker's *The Emergent Self* (Ithaca, NY: Cornell University Press, 2001), Chap. 3 also provides a sophisticated defense of the argument from reason.

An influential contemporary theistic argument that purports to be a rational reconstruction of Lewis's argument from reason is Alvin Plantinga's "evolutionary argument against naturalism" (EAAN); cf. Plantinga, *Warrant and Proper Function* (Oxford, UK: Oxford University Press, 1993), Chap. 12, and *Warranted Christian Belief* (Oxford, UK: Oxford University Press, 2000), Chap. 7. Plantinga's argument is critically analyzed (by distinguished contemporary philosophers) in *Naturalism Defeated? Essays on Plantinga's Evolutionary Argument Against Naturalism*, ed. James Beilby (Ithaca, NY: Cornell University Press, 2002). (Plantinga also provides a response to his critics in that book.)

Finally, Stephen Parrish's *God and Necessity: A Defense of Classical Theism* (Lanham, MD: University Press of America, 2001) deserves to be mentioned. Parrish incorporates the insights of contemporary modal metaphysics in arguing for the transcendental necessity of theism.

[6]Bahnsen at times stated that his TAG is not a "deductive" (nor an inductive) argument, but rather a different form of argument altogether—a transcendental argument. Here is an example of his making this claim:

Years ago Van Til realized that opponents of presuppositionalism tend to think that there are only two kinds of reasoning: inductive and deductive. Deductive reasoning stands opposed to inductive. However, there is also transcendental reasoning, in which the preconditions for the intelligibility of what is experienced, asserted, or argued are posed or sought. It, too, stands opposed to a purely inductive approach to knowledge. Critics seem to think that, since presuppositionalism does not

that *Christian* theism is the necessary precondition for proving anything at all. In section III, I raise a more general worry for a Bahnsen-style TAG that has come to be known as "the Fristianity objection" and argue that a recent attempt by Michael Butler to dispose of that objection is unsuccessful.

I

TAG is not supposed to be transcendental in name only, but it is supposed to be a true *transcendental* argument for the existence of God. So let us briefly inquire about the nature of transcendental arguments (henceforth TAs) in general. TAs are deductive (though not *merely* deductive; cf. footnote 6) in nature, and they exhibit a particular form. In order for any argument to be considered transcendental, it must at the very least have the following feature noted by Robert Stern:[7]

> [P]erhaps the most definitive feature . . . [of TAs] is that these arguments involve a claim of a distinctive form: namely, that one thing (X) is a necessary condition for the possibility of something else (Y), so that . . . the latter cannot obtain without the former. In suggesting that X is a condition for Y in this way, this claim is supposed to be metaphysical and a priori, and not merely natural and a posteriori: that is, if Y cannot obtain without X, this is not just because certain *natural* laws governing the *actual* world and discoverable by the empirical sciences make this impossible (in the way that, for example, life cannot exist without oxygen), but because certain metaphysical constraints that can be established by reflection make X a condition for Y in every *possible* world (for example, existence is a

---

endorse pure inductivism, it must favor deductivism instead. This logical fallacy is known as false antithesis. (*Van Til's Apologetic*, 176, n. 55)

In claiming that Bahnsen's TAG is offered as a "deductive" argument, all I have in mind is that he offers it as an argument that has the following property: it *purports* to be a valid argument (where a *valid* argument is any argument having the following formal property: it is necessary that if its premises are true, then its conclusion is true). Thus understood, transcendental arguments form a *subclass* of deductive arguments (since transcendental arguments purport to be valid). That is, transcendental arguments do not differ from "normal" deductive arguments in the purported *inferential connection* between their premises and conclusion, but rather (if anything) in their *aim* or *goal*. For example, transcendental arguments have as their goal (which need not be shared by an argument *qua* deductive argument) elucidating the conditions under which intelligible experience is possible. But the inferential claim made by a (non-transcendental) deductive argument and a transcendental argument is of the same kind: in both types of arguments it is *claimed* to be *necessary* that if their premises are true, then their conclusion is true. And *that* is what makes an argument deductive in nature. So, I do not think that I am guilty of any kind of fallacy here. It should be noted that in claiming that Bahnsen's TAG is, contrary to Bahnsen's assertion, deductive, I am not suggesting that his entire "approach to knowledge" (or epistemology) is deductive.

[7]Some other features commonly thought to be essential to TAs include: elucidating the conditions for the possibility of experience and being anti-skeptical in nature; cf. *Transcendental Arguments: Problems and Prospects*, ed. Robert Stern (Oxford, UK: Clarendon Press, 1999), 3–5. For a good recent overview of various attempts to define a TA, see Ronney Mourad, *Transcendental Arguments and Justified Christian Belief* (Lanham, MD: University Press of America, 2005), Chap. 1. A good examination of these (and other) features specifically in connection with TAG can be found in Michael Butler's "The Transcendental Argument for God's Existence," in *The Standard Bearer: A Festschrift for Greg L. Bahnsen*, ed. Steven M. Schlissel (Nacogdoches, TX: Covenant Media Press, 2002), 65–124, esp. 77–81, 90–94.

condition for thought, as the former is metaphysically required in order
to do or be anything at all).[8]

So the general form of TAs can be stated as follows:

> (TA1) q.
> (TA2) It is necessary that: if not-p, then not-q.
> (TA3) So, p.

As it occurs in (TA1) and (TA2), q is a variable that takes as its value
propositions concerning some phenomenon that can be asserted, without
much controversy in the philosophical context in question, to obtain and
thus to be a fact. I will refer to the premise that corresponds to (TA1) in any
given transcendental argument as the *granted* premise of that argument. As
it occurs in (TA2) and (TA3), p is a variable that takes as its value propositions concerning some other phenomenon that is claimed to be a fact
and that is such that it is a necessary precondition for the obtaining of the
phenomenon mentioned in q. I will refer to the premise that corresponds to
(TA2) in any given transcendental argument as the *transcendental* premise
of that argument. The transcendental premise of a TA asserts that there is
a conceptual or metaphysical connection between the phenomenon mentioned in q and the phenomenon mentioned in p such that the latter is a
condition for the possibility or intelligibility of the former. If this claim is
true, then one (e.g., a skeptic about the phenomenon mentioned in p) who
asserts (TA1) while denying (TA2) is caught in self-contradiction. For he
both asserts that a certain phenomenon obtains while denying that a necessary precondition for that phenomenon obtains—which is incoherent.

So if it is understood as conforming to the schema (TA1)–(TA3), TAs
can be given a *valid* form: any argument corresponding to the above argument schema is such that it is impossible for all of its premises to be true
but for its conclusion to be false. But it is not an easy matter to establish the
truth of all of its premises and thus to refute the skeptic. That is, establishing the *soundness* (i.e., formal validity plus all true premises) of TAs is a
much more difficult matter. In particular, although (if it is well chosen) the
truth of the granted premise will be fairly obvious to the parties in dispute,
it is a difficult task to establish the truth of the transcendental premise. So
the premise that usually does most of the work in a transcendental argument is the transcendental premise—the premise asserting the necessary

---

[8]Stern, *Transcendental Arguments*, 3.

connection between the uncontroversial phenomenon mentioned in q and its alleged preconditional phenomenon mentioned in p. As we will see below, this is also the case with TAG.

As a paradigm example of a sound TA, consider Descartes's famous *Cogito* argument:

(C1) I am thinking.
(C2) It is necessary that: if I do not exist, then I am not thinking.
(C3) So, I exist.

It is necessary that if (C1) and (C2) are true, then (C3) is also true. To grant the truth of (C1) and (C2) while denying (C3) would land one in inconsistency. Furthermore, both (C1) and (C2) seem to be true. One can try to weaken (C1) to

(C1*) It only seems to me that I am thinking

but to no avail—for what is this activity of "seeming to think" if it is not *itself* thinking? For example, if one *doubts* that his activity of seeming to think really is thinking, then in virtue of doubting this he is thinking—for doubting simply *is* a form of thinking. Also, denying (C2) entails that it is possible for one not to exist and yet to actually think—which just seems incoherent.[9] So, the *Cogito* seems to be a TA that is not only valid but sound.

Now TAG is (at minimum) a *theistic*, transcendental argument. Accordingly, its general form is to argue that God exists as "a necessary precondition" of some fundamental and uncontroversial phenomenon. There are three such fundamental phenomena that are often appealed to in discussions of TAG: logic, science, and objective moral standards. As it is usually presented, TAG is an argument that purports to show that without God, logic, science, and objective morality would not be possible.[10] In this essay I will limit myself to assessing the merits of TAG as that argument pertains to the possibility of logic, but what I say about logic can be applied, with appropriate modifications, to the issues of science and morality as well. So the general schema of TAG might be formulated as follows:

---

[9]That various fictional characters (e.g., Hamlet) seem to think and act is no counterexample to this claim. For such claims regarding fictional characters is *elliptical* in nature; e.g., "Hamlet thinks he sees a dagger" is elliptical for "*According to the* Hamlet-*story* Hamlet thinks he sees a dagger." Properly speaking, Hamlet does not think or do anything, but the play *Hamlet* depicts him as thinking and so on.

[10]Bahnsen emphasized these three phenomena in his debate against Stein. Also cf. *Van Til's Apologetic*, 110, n. 65.

(TAG1) LOGIC.

(TAG2) It is necessary that: if God does not exist, then not-LOGIC.

(TAG3) So, God exists.

As it occurs in (TAG1) and (TAG2), LOGIC is a variable that takes as its value propositions concerning some phenomenon concerning logic or rationality, which can be asserted to obtain without much controversy in the philosophical context in which the specific formulation of TAG occurs. (Depending on which phenomenon is chosen, we will get slightly different formulations of TAG.) Thus, as mentioned before, the real workhorse premise—as well as the premise that is hardest to establish—in any particular formulation of TAG will be the premise corresponding to (TAG2) in the above schema.

Thus lightly armed regarding the nature and logical form of TAs, let us now examine the formulation of TAG that Greg Bahnsen presented in his debate against Gordon Stein.

II

In the aforementioned Bahnsen-Stein debate, Greg Bahnsen presented a formulation of TAG to argue for distinctively Christian theism, rather than "theism in general."[11] Bahnsen's central claim in that debate is that the "presuppositional conflict" between the atheistic worldview and the Christian worldview can be resolved in favor of Christian theism by arguing "from the impossibility of the contrary."[12] That is, "[t]he transcendental proof for God's existence is that without Him, it is impossible to prove anything."[13] That is indeed a bold and ambitious claim. How does Bahnsen go about arguing for that claim?

To begin, Bahnsen simply takes for granted (i.e., he takes as his granted premise) that there are laws of logic (e.g., the laws of identity—*p is identical to p*), excluded middle (*p or not-p*), and noncontradiction (*not-[p and not-p]*)) and that there is a rational justification for them. The question is, how are we to *account* for this fact? Which worldview, atheism or Christian theism, offers a better account of these laws? As far as I can see, Bahnsen's most fully developed case for believing that only Christian theism can account for the laws of logic is presented during his opening speech of seg-

---

[11]Cf. BSD, 37–51. In that portion of the debate he presents three different reasons why he argues for *Christian* theism.

[12]BSD, 240–242. As is well known, in saying this, Bahnsen is taking his cue from Cornelius Van Til; cf. *Van Til's Apologetic*, 492, 621.

[13]BSD, 244–245. Unless I specify otherwise, by "God" I shall have in mind the God of Christian theism.

ment two of his debate with Stein. I think it is worth quoting him at some length here. Says Bahnsen:

> What are the laws of logic, Dr. Stein, and how are they justified? We still have to answer that question from a materialist[14] standpoint. From a Christian standpoint, we have an answer obviously; they reflect the thinking of God. They are if you will a reflection of the way God thinks and expects us to think.[15] But if you don't take that approach, and want to justify the laws of logic in some a priori fashion, that is apart from experience . . . then we can ask why the laws of logic are universal, unchanging, and invariant truths. . . . [I]f you want to try to justify all of them in that way, we have to ask, "why is it that they apply repeatedly in a contingent realm of experience?" Why in a world that is random . . . is it that the laws of logic continue to have that success-generating feature about them? Why should they be assumed to have anything to do with the realm of history, or why should reasoning about history or science or empirical experience have these laws of thought imposed upon it?[16]

> Now if you want to justify logical truths along a posteriori lines, that is rather than arguing that they are self evident; but rather arguing that there is evidence for them that we can find in experience or by observation . . . people will say we gain confidence in the laws of logic through repeated experience, and then that experience is generalized.

> Of course some of the suggested logical truths it turns out are so complex or so unusual that it's difficult to believe anyone has perceived their instances in experience. But even if we restrict our attention to the other more simple laws of logic, it should be seen that if their truth cannot be decided independently of experience, then they actually become contingent. That is, if people cannot justify the laws of logic independent of experience, then you can only say they apply as far as I know in the past

---

[14]Though it will not be crucial to my forthcoming analysis of his argument, it needs to be pointed out that Bahnsen mistakenly assumes throughout his debate with Stein that *if one is an atheist he must be a materialist*. This is just false, and I really cannot think of any good reason why he might have thought that conditional is true.

[15]During cross-examination, Stein asks, "Saying that logic reflects the thinking of God is to make a non-statement. How is that an answer to anything that's relevant in this discussion?" (BSD, 1339–1341), which Bahnsen answers by saying:

> It answers the general metaphysical issue of how there can be universal, invariant, abstract entities in a particular person's worldview. . . . [T]he statement that the laws of logic are intelligible within a Christian theistic universe, has meaning because there are things which are in fact, spiritual, immaterial and have a universal quality such as God's thinking, and those standards that he imposes on people. (BSD, 1343–1351; cf. *Van Til's Apologetic*, 235–241)

[16]BSD, 1123–1130, 1136–1142. In this and the following quotations, I have slightly altered the grammar of the transcribed text in certain places. Much of the following quotations are, it seems, taken from his unpublished article, "Science, Subjectivity and Scripture" (1979). That article is available online through Covenant Media Foundation at www.cmfnow.com/articles/pa044.htm. (This article is permanently archived on the web at web.archive.org/web/20030113022227/http://www.cmfnow.com/articles/pa044.htm.)

experience that I've had. They are [then] contingent, [and] they lose their necessity, universality and invariance.

Why should a law of logic, which is verified in one domain of experience by the way, be taken as true for unexperienced domains as well? Why should we universalize or generalize about the laws of logic?[17]

Now it turns out if the a priori and the a posteriori lines of justification for logical truths are unconvincing as I'm suggesting they both are, perhaps we could say they are linguistic conventions about certain symbols. Certain philosophers have suggested that. The laws of logic would not be taken as [inexorably] dictated, but rather we impose their necessity on our language. They become therefore somewhat like rules of grammar . . . [but] the laws of grammar, you see, are just culturally relative. If the laws of logic are like grammar, then the laws of logic are culturally relative too. Why then are not contradictory systems deemed equally rational? If the laws of logic can be made culturally relative, then we can win the debate by simply stipulating a law of logic that says, "anybody who argues in this way has got a tautology on his hands, and therefore it's true."

Why are arbitrary conventions like the logical truths so useful if they are only conventional? Why are they so useful in dealing with problems in the world of experience?[18]

Bahnsen concludes his case by saying:

Dr. Stein has wanted to use the laws of logic. I want to suggest to you one more time that Dr. Stein in so doing is borrowing my worldview. He is using the Christian approach to the world, so that there can be such laws of logic . . . [b]ut then he wants to deny the very foundation of it.[19]

How shall we understand Bahnsen's argument here? I offer the following rational reconstruction of his argument. Bahnsen, as noted above, takes for granted that there is a rational justification for the various laws of logic. Thus, the following might be suggested as the granted premise of his TAG:

(1) There is a rational justification for the laws of logic.

In keeping with the TAG schema (TAG1)–(TAG3) presented above, Bahnsen can be taken to argue in turn for a premise such as:

(2) It is necessary that: if Christian theism is false, then there is no rational justification for the laws of logic.

---

[17]BSD, 1152–1170.
[18]BSD, 1173–1188.
[19]BSD, 1223–1226.

The extended passage from his debate with Gordon Stein quoted above can be taken to be his argument on behalf of a premise such as (2). How should we construe *that* argument? Here is a preliminary way of reconstructing Bahnsen's argument for (2):

> (2a) If there is a non-Christian theistic way to justify the laws of logic, then it will be either the a priori way or the a posteriori way or the conventionalist way.
>
> (2b) Neither the a priori way nor the a posteriori way nor the conventionalist way will justify the laws of logic.
>
> (2c) So, there is no non-Christian theistic way to justify the laws of logic.

Although it can be debated whether Bahnsen provides sufficient argumentation to establish the truth of (2a) or (2b), I will not quibble with that here.[20] For the purpose of my analysis, I can simply grant him this point. Even granting this contentious point, I think it can be seen that Bahnsen's strategy (employed in his debate with Stein) is insufficient to establish the truth of (2). Here is a way of bringing out the difficulty. For Bahnsen's style of argumentation (reconstructed above) to have even a ghost of a chance of successfully establishing the truth of (2), he needs an *additional* premise that would fill an inferential gap left over by that argument. The following seems to be a plausible candidate for such a premise:

> (2d) Necessarily: if there is a rational justification for the laws of logic, then it will be either Christian theistic or non-Christian theistic.

It might thus be thought that once we add (2d) to (2a)–(2c), we will be able validly to derive the needed (2).

However, that would be mistaken. Although (2c) does follow from (2a) and (2b) by *modus tollens* (*if p then q*; *not-q*; so, *not-p*), the larger inference from (2a), (2b), (2c), and (2d) to (2) is simply invalid. The problem is that even with the plausibly necessarily true premise (2d), there is no way

---

[20]Besides, Bahnsen himself offers the following qualification in his unpublished article: . . . the preceding discussion only suggests a *program* for cross-examining various alternative ways of justifying logical truths . . ." ("Science, Subjectivity and Scripture"). Curiously, Bahnsen then goes on to endorse in that article the following form of inference: "there is substantial disagreement among the experts that p. Therefore, the experts lack justification concerning p." Consider: "[T]his issue [of offering a justification for logic] is not an absolutely clear and certain matter in philosophy, and it does remind us that the approaches taken to the question are far from uniform"—on the basis of which he goes on to conclude, "Is this *really* the paradigm of objective, settled, rationality?"

to derive the necessary proposition (2) as a conclusion as long as (2a) and (2b) are themselves *contingent*.

To remedy this modal defect, premises (2a) and (2b) must be taken to be *necessary* truths, as follows:

> (2a*) It is necessary that: if there is a non-Christian theistic way to justify the laws of logic, then it will be either the a priori way or the a posteriori way or the conventionalist way.
>
> (2b*) It is necessary that: neither the a priori way nor the a posteriori way nor the conventionalist way will justify the laws of logic.

From (2a*) and (2b*) it now follows by *modal modus tollens* (*it is necessary that: if p then q*; *it is necessary that not-q*; so, *it is necessary that not-p*) that

> (2c*) So, it is necessary that there is no non-Christian theistic way to justify the laws of logic.

More importantly, from (2a*), (2b*), (2c*) and (2d) it now validly follows that (2). And given the granted premise (1) and the newly derived transcendental premise (2), it follows that

(1) Christian theism is true,

which is the desired conclusion of TAG, as Bahnsen conceives of it (i.e., a TA for Christian theism).

So, if Bahnsen has provided good reasons (in his debate with Stein) to believe both (2a*) and (2b*) to be true (i.e., to believe that (2a) and (2b) are both *necessarily* true), he will have offered a successful defense of TAG. But has he?

I do not think Bahnsen has shown such a thing. Consider once more (2b*):[21]

> (2b*) It is necessary that: neither the a priori way nor the a posteriori way nor the conventionalist way will justify the laws of logic.

Even granting (for the sake of argument) that the options mentioned in (2b*) are *not* a false trilemma, for all Bahnsen has said, (2b*) might be false. For example, it can be argued that since Bahnsen has not *exhaustively* examined (and refuted) *every possible* a priori, a posteriori, and conven-

---

[21]Bahnsen's prospects of establishing the truth of (2a*) will be examined in the next section.

tionalist way of justifying the laws of logic, he is only entitled to conclude, *at best*, that:

> (2b**) All the a priori, a posteriori, and conventionalist ways of justifying the laws of logic *thus far examined* have failed.[22]

But the truth of (2b**) is consistent with the falsity of (2b*); that is to say, (2b**) does not entail (2b*). But Bahnsen needs the truth of (2b*) to get his TAG off the ground. So, unless Bahnsen has an argument as to why, *in principle*, every possible a priori, a posteriori, or conventionalist way of justifying the laws of logic must fail, he cannot get his TAG off the ground. Since Bahnsen does not present such an "in principle" argument for (2b*),

---

[22]In this connection, the following portion of Bahnsen's cross-examination of Stein (and Bahnsen's subsequent commentary on that exchange) is instructive:

Bahnsen: What is the basis for the uniformity of nature?

Stein: I went through this, but I'll be glad to reiterate it.

B: Okay.

S: The uniformity of nature comes from the fact that matter has certain properties which it regularly exhibits. It's part of the nature of matter: electrons, oppositely charged things attract, the same charges repel. There are certain valences that can fill the shell of an atom, and that is as far as it can combine. . . .

B: Do all electrons repel each other?

S: If they are within a certain distance of each other, yes.

B: Have you . . . tested all electrons?

S: All electrons that have ever been tested repel each other. I have not tested all.

B: Have you read all the tests on electrons?

S: Me personally or can I go on the witness of experts?

B: Have you read all of the witnesses about electrons?

S: All it takes is one witness to say "no" and it would be on the front pages of every physics journal, and there are none, so therefore I would say "yes" in effect, by default.

B: Well, physicists have their presuppositions by which they exclude contrary evidence too; but in other words, you haven't experienced all electrons, but you would generalize that all electrons under certain conditions repel each other?

S: Just statistically, on the basis of past observation.

B: And we don't know that it's going to be that way ten minutes after this debate then?

S: No, but we see no evidence that things have switched around either. (BSD, 1401–1442)

Commenting on this exchange during his closing statement, Bahnsen says:

Dr. Stein said the laws of science are law-like because of the inherent character of matter. But Dr. Stein doesn't know the inherent character of matter. Now if he were God, he might reveal that to us as I think God has revealed certain things to us about the operation of the universe. But he's not God; he doesn't even believe that there is a God. Since he hasn't experienced all the instances of matter and all of the electron reactions—all of the other things scientists look at—, *since he hasn't experienced all of those*, he doesn't *know* that those things are *universal*. He doesn't know that the future is going to be like the past. (BSD, 1776–1782, emphasis added)

It seems that the proverbial saying, "What's sauce for the goose is sauce for the gander" applies here. If it is true that Stein is not justified in believing the universal statement

(S) All electrons repel each other *precisely because* he has not experienced *all* interactions between electrons, then it likewise seems true that Bahnsen is not justified in believing in the universal statement.

(B) All the a priori, a posteriori, and conventionalist ways of justifying the laws of logic fail because *he* has not read and refuted *all* the instances of the aforementioned ways of justifying the laws of logic. (Bahnsen was well-read, but not *that* well-read.) In short, if Bahnsen's line of reasoning above as to why Stein is not justified in believing in (S) were sound, then it seems that a similar line of reasoning would show that Bahnsen is not justified in believing in (B). If Bahnsen's argument against Stein were sound, a similar line of reasoning would show that all that Bahnsen is entitled to believe is (2b**) above.

he has failed to show that his TAG is sound and *thereby* has failed to show that his TAG is a successful proof of the rational ineluctability of Christian theism.[23]

III

Recall that Bahnsen's TAG basically takes the following form:

(1) There is a rational justification for the laws of logic.

(2) It is necessary that: if Christian theism is false, then there is no rational justification for the laws of logic.

(3) Christian theism is true.

We have seen that the key premise (and the one that does the real work in the above argument) is (2). Given that (1) is the granted premise, if the truth of (2) can be successfully established somehow, then (3) follows validly from (1) and (2). Bahnsen's TAG would then be established as a sound TA for Christian theism. But establishing the truth of (2) turned out to be a difficult matter. I have suggested the following as a plausible rational reconstruction of a valid argument in support of (2):

(2a*) It is necessary that: if there is a non-Christian theistic way to justify the laws of logic, then it will be either the a priori way or the a posteriori way or the conventionalist way.

(2b*) It is necessary that: neither the a priori way nor the a posteriori way nor the conventionalist way will justify the laws of logic.

(2c*) So, it is necessary that there is no non-Christian theistic way to justify the laws of logic. [From (2a*) and (2b*)]

(2d) Necessarily: if there is a rational justification for the laws of logic, then it will be either Christian theistic or non-Christian theistic.

(2) So, it is necessary that: if Christian theism is false, then there is no rational justification for the laws of logic. [From (2a*)–(2d)]

In the previous section I argued that Bahnsen has failed to establish the truth of (2b*). In this section I will consider the prospects (and difficulties) of defending premise (2a*).

To begin, consider the negation of (2a*) (in an equivalent form):

---

[23]As noted above (cf. footnote 20), by Bahnsen's own admission the argumentation contained in the extended quotation at the beginning of section II is only meant to be a "program" for showing the inadequacy of the a priori, a posteriori, and conventionalist ways of justifying the laws of logic. And whatever a "program" (in Bahnsen's sense) for p exactly amounts to, it seems clear that it falls short of being a principled argument for p. (At best, it might be taken to be an *outline* of such an argument—one that needs to be filled out in great detail—which neither Bahnsen nor any of his contemporary followers ever did.)

(2a*) It is possible that: there is a non-Christian theistic way to justify the laws of logic and it is neither the a priori way nor the a posteriori way nor the conventionalist way.

No one sympathetic to Bahnsen's TAG has yet provided any good reason against believing that (2a*) is true. Indeed, if (2a*) is even *possibly* true, that will be sufficient to show that (2a*) is false.[24] However, I will not argue that (2a*) *is* possibly true. I will concern myself in this section with the more modest project of showing that nothing Bahnsen, nor any of his sympathizers, have said gives us any reason to believe that (2a*) is *impossible*. That is, *for all that Bahnsen and his sympathizers have said*, (2a*) is possibly true. The possibility of (2a*) is, as we might put it, *epistemically* possible (roughly possible given all that we know, or perhaps better, possible given all of our evidence), for all that Bahnsen and his sympathizers have said.

One way of arguing that the possibility of (2a*) is epistemically possible is by arguing that there is no evidence against the following proposition:

(F) It is possible that: there is a worldview distinct from Christian theism and which is such that if it *were* true, it *would* provide a *sufficient* justification for the laws of logic.

As a specific illustration of such a worldview, consider Fristianity, which is a theistic worldview that holds to the doctrine of the quadrinity (one God in four persons) and is otherwise identical to Christianity, or as similar to Christianity as possible (given its qaudrinitarian tenet).[25] And more relevantly for our purposes, *in whatever way* that Christian theism is supposed to account for the laws of logic, Fristian theism would account

---

[24]We can see this as follows. (2a*) is basically of the form *necessarily p*. The form of (2a*) is thus *not-necessarily p*. That is in turn equivalent to *possibly not-p*. (2a*) is thus equivalent in form to *possibly not-p* (the form it takes in the text above). To argue for the *possibility* of (2a*) is thus to argue for the truth of *possibly possibly not-p*. In the widely accepted system of modal logic, S5 (indeed, in the weaker system S4), *possibly possibly not-p* is equivalent to *possibly not-p*, which is in turn equivalent to *not-necessarily p*. And *that* is just the negation of the form that (2a*) takes. So, if (2a*) is even possibly true, then (2a*) is false.

Some philosophers might object to the above derivation on the ground that there seems to be successful counterexamples to the general validity of S4 (and thus S5); cf. Nathan Salmon's "The Logic of What Might Have Been," in his *Metaphysics, Mathematics, and Meaning* (Oxford, UK: Oxford University Press, 2005). However, it is worth noting that all the "Salmonesque" counterexamples to S4 essentially concern *de re* modality (e.g., the essentiality of origins for artifacts like a wooden table), whereas the above derivation is strictly concerned with *de dicto* modality. Hence Salmon's counterexample to S4 gives us no reason to think that the derivation provided in the previous paragraph is suspect.

[25]Fristianity is a hypothetical worldview made (in)famous by David Byron in the now defunct Van Til List. Fortunately, all of its many posts are archived online at web.archive.org/web/20041030013242/ http://www.ccir.ed.ac.uk/~jad/vantil-list. Byron offers a nice summary of the history and subsequent development of the Fristianity objection at web.archive.org/web/20000118153717/http://www.ccir.ed.ac. uk/~jad/vantil-list/archive-Jul-1999/msg00049.html. (The hyphen after "Jul" is not due to the computer's hyphenation function but is a necessary part of the URL.)

for them *in like manner.*[26] There are differences, of course: in Christian theism, it is the trinitarian God (Father, Son, and Holy Spirit) who does the trick, whereas in Fristian theism it is the quadrinitarian God (Father*, Son*, Holy Spirit*, and a fourth divine person whom I will dub Fred) that would do the trick.

Of course, Fristianity is not an *actual* worldview or religion, as is, for example, Islam. But no one—certainly not I—is claiming this. In any case, objecting to Fristianity on the ground of its non-actuality is beside the point. Bahnsen's TAG, recall, is supposed to establish the *rational necessity* of Christian theism. And to defeat a necessity claim such as that, *possible* worldviews (as much as actual worldviews) are fair game.[27]

As far as I can see, Bahnsen never provided a good defeater against a possible worldview such as Fristianity.[28] The best (and at the time of this writing, the only) attempt to defeat the Fristianity objection in print, written by someone largely sympathetic to Bahnsen's TAG, is due to Michael Butler. His defense of TAG against the Fristianity objection is worth quoting in full:

---

[26]For example, in his closing statement, Bahnsen hints at how a Christian theistic account of logic is supposed to go:

> The [Christian] answer [to how logic is justified] is that God created the world, and this world reflects the uniformity that he imposes on it by his governing, and our thinking is to reflect the same consistency or logical coherence that is in God's thinking. (BSD, 1606–1608)

I see no reason to think that a Fristian could not give basically the same answer *if Fristianity were actual.*

[27]To his credit, Michael Butler acknowledges this point, contra Bahnsen; cf. "The Transcendental Argument for God's Existence," 87.

[28]As far as I can see, the closest he comes to doing so is in the following passage of *Van Til's Apologetic:*

> It is absolutely crucial that transcendental argumentation begin by positing that Christian theism is either true or false. . . . Van Til's defense of the faith does not require the apologist to be aware of and refute every single variation of unbelieving philosophy, but *only the presupposition common to them all* (namely, *the rejection of Christian theism*). Many apologists mistakenly imagine that there are really three options available: one may accept Christianity, reject it, or be "undecided." But, as Van Til recognized, to be undecided about the claim that Christian theism is the presupposition necessary to make sense out of any reasoning whatsoever, is to begin one's reasoning on the operational assumption that this claim is false (and can be laid aside as one proceeds to research and develop one's views). Since there are *only two options* at the most fundamental level—the truth or falsity of Christian theism as a presupposition—the refutation of *the* unbelieving one (in whatever illustrative variation it appears) is an indirect proof of the other. (277, n. 39, emphasis added)

The reason why this argumentative strategy—i.e., either the Christian worldview is true or the non-Christian worldview is true; the non-Christian worldview is not true; so, the Christian worldview is true—fails to dispose of the Fristianity objection is because Bahnsen's adopted criterion for individuating non-Christian worldviews and grouping them all as *"the* one worldview" (i.e., their common rejection of Christian theism) is far too crude. For example, on the same basis the hypothetical Fristian could argue as follows: "There are only two worldviews, Fristian theism and *the* unbelieving one"—which is to say, any worldview that has as its presupposition the rejection of Fristian theism. All the alleged worldviews (and here we would have to include Christian theism) are really just variations on a common presuppositional theme that Fristian theism is false. It seems that Bahnsen's argument in the passage cited above is totally ineffective against this *tu quoque.*

In this connection it should be mentioned that there is a good discussion of Bahnsen's defense of TAG in Butler's "The Transcendental Argument," 76–89. It is noteworthy that, as regards the Fristianity objection, Butler's conclusion is that Bahnsen has failed to fully defeat that objection to TAG (cf. "The Transcendental Argument," 86–87).

The only way we know that God is a Trinity is that He revealed it to us—mere speculation or empirical investigation would never lead us to this conclusion. But the Fristian worldview, which is, ex hypothesis, identical to Christianity in every other way, asserts that its god is a quadrinity. But *if Fristianity is otherwise identical to Christianity, the only way for us to know this would be for the Fristian god to reveal this to us.* But there is a problem with this. Supposing Fristianity has inspired scriptures (which it would need to have since it is in all other ways identical to Christianity), these scriptures would have to reveal that the Fristian god is one in four. But notice that by positing a quadrinity, the Fristian scriptures would be quite different from the Christian Scriptures. Whereas the Christian Scriptures teach that, with regard to man's salvation, God the Father ordains, God the Son accomplishes, and God the Spirit applies, the Fristian scriptures would have to teach a very different order. But exactly how would the four members of its imagined godhead be involved in man's salvation? More fundamentally, whereas in the Christian Trinity we read that the personal attribute of the Father is paternity, the personal attribute of the Son is filiation, and the personal attribute of the Spirit is spiration, what would be the personal, distinguishing attributes of the members of the Fristian quadrinity? What would their relationship be to each other? *Further questions* flow out of this. How would the quadrinity affect the doctrine of man and sin? How would redemptive history look different? What about eschatology? This all needs to be spelled out in detail. This illustration reveals a general problem. One cannot tinker with Christian doctrine at one point and maintain that other doctrines *will not be affected.*[29] It does no good for the proponent of Fristianity to claim that the only difference between his worldview and the Christian worldview is over the doctrine of the Trinity. Christian doctrine is systemic, and a change in one area will necessarily require changes in others. It is necessary, therefore, that the advocate of Fristianity spell out how this one change in doctrine affects all other doctrines. But once this is done, *there is no guarantee that the result will be coherent.*

Thus, without providing the details of Fristian theology, this objection loses its punch. It can only be thought to be a challenge to Christianity if it, like Christianity, provides preconditions of experience. But without knowing the details, we cannot submit it to an internal critique. Until this happens, we can justifiably fall back on the conclusion that there is no conceivable worldview apart from Christianity that can provide the preconditions of experience.[30]

---

[29]The Fristian objector is surely not committed (nor need he be) to this *strong* claim. He need not claim that changing one Christian doctrine (and one so central as the Trinity) will have *no effect* on all the other doctrines. All he needs is the much more modest claim that there is no guarantee forthcoming that the changes that will have to be made (e.g., once the Trinity is replaced by a quadrinity), as a matter of principle, can only lead the Fristian objector to an incoherent worldview.

[30]"The Transcendental Argument," 118–119, emphasis added.

Has Butler disposed of the Fristianity objection with the above response? I do not think so. First, consider the following conditional asserted by Butler:

> (*) If Fristianity is otherwise identical to Christianity, the only way for us to know [that its God is a quadrinity] would be for the Fristian god to reveal this to us.

Butler offers (*) as being true, but I think there are good reasons for thinking it is false. That the Fristian God is a quadrinity is something we know to be true in virtue of *stipulation*. Indeed, recall how *I* introduced Fristianity earlier in this section: "consider Fristianity, which is a theistic worldview that holds to the doctrine of the quadrinity (one God in four persons) and is otherwise identical to Christianity, or as similar to Christianity as possible (given its quadrinitarian tenet)." (Indeed, that is how *Butler himself* introduced the concept of Fristianity.[31]) Butler is suggesting that there is mystery here when there is none. "Fristianity" has come to mean what it does *precisely because* in the course of offering a possible defeater to TAG, Fristianity was *defined* as a possible worldview that includes a quadrinitarian God. *Voila!* Thus, we do not need some mysterious revelation[32] to teach us that the Fristian God, a God of a merely possible worldview Fristianity, is a quadrinity. Also, that the content of Fristianity is identical to the content of Christianity (*modulo* the former's commitment to the doctrine of quadrinity) does not entail that the means by which we know about the (attributes of the) God of the one worldview is the same as the means by which we know about the (attributes of the) God of the other. For in the case at hand, one worldview (Christianity) is actual, while the other (Fristianity) is merely possible: and in general our methods for knowing about actuality are different from our methods for knowing about (non-actual) possibility.

Second, as concerns Butler's many questions (many of them good questions), I would like to ask a question of my own: how exactly does a series of (unanswered) questions amount to an *argument* (for anything)? My question is largely rhetorical, to which there is an obvious answer: it doesn't. In any case, since many of his questions concerning Fristianity are predicated on the *erroneous* assumption that that worldview needs a (cf. footnote 32) revelation, they are largely irrelevant.

---

[31]Ibid., 86.
[32]If Butler intends by this *actual* revelation, then, of course, his objection is confused. No God of a merely possible worldview can be the author of any actual revelation—any more than a merely possible angel can dance on a head of an actual pin.

Finally, consider Butler's claim that once the specific contents of Fristianity are "spelled out" (i.e., once it is specified in detail how its adherence to the doctrine of quadrinity will affect its other doctrines), "there is no guarantee that the result will be coherent." In saying this, however, Butler mischaracterizes the dialectical situation between TAG and Fristianity. It is the job of TAG to show that all worldviews (actual and possible) incompatible with Christian theism are incoherent. If TAG (as Bahnsen and Butler conceive of it) is *successful* in establishing what it purports to establish, then *there should be a guarantee* that "the result" in question will be *in*coherent. It is the defender of TAG who needs to show that all possible ways of tinkering with the contents of Christian theism so as to develop Fristianity's distinctive commitment (to a quadrinitarian God) into a full-blown worldview are, as a matter of principle, bound to fail due to incoherence. The Fristian objector to TAG need not provide a positive proof of the coherence of such a fully developed Fristianity; all she needs (to defeat TAG) is to argue that *for all we have reason to believe*, a fully developed Fristianity seems coherent. To be sure, the resulting, fully realized Fristian theology might very well sound bizarre and strange—especially to *Christian* ears! But judgments about bizarreness and strangeness are largely governed by one's *presuppositions* and are not necessarily reliable indicators of incoherence. Thus I conclude that Butler's attempted refutation of the Fristianity objection fails.

There is a negative and a positive way to state the general lesson to be learned from the preceding sections. Stated negatively, the lesson is that a formulation of TAG that purports to establish the rational inescapability of *Christian* theism (like Bahnsen's and Butler's) seems too ambitious and doomed to fail. Stated positively, the lesson is that if a Christian wishes to include a TAG-like, "transcendental" theistic argument in his apologetic arsenal, he would be better advised to seek it in its more modest incarnations (like the arguments mentioned in footnote 5).

CHAPTER SIXTEEN

God and the Evidence of Evil[1]

R. Douglas Geivett

THE REALITY OF SUFFERING AND EVIL[2]

It certainly is not difficult to identify examples of concrete evils that provoke us to wonder, Why is there evil in the world? The enigma of evil is a prominent theme in great literature. Though literature portrays imaginary worlds, it is a powerful tool for expressing the realities and nuances of human experience. Consider Victor Hugo's depiction of human suffering in the following passage from *Les Misérables*:

> Man overboard! Who cares? The ship sails on. The wind is up, the dark ship must keep to its destined course. It passes on . . . he hollers, stretches out his hands. They do not hear him. . . . .What a specter is that disappearing sail! He watches it, follows it frantically. It moves away, grows dim, diminishes. He was just there, one of the crew. . . . Now, what has become of him? He slipped. He fell. It's all over! He is in the monstrous deep . . . the voracious ocean is eager to devour him. The monster plays with his agony. It is all liquid hatred to him. He tries to defend, to sustain himself; he struggles; he swims. . . . There are birds in the clouds, even as there are angels above human distresses, but what can they do for him? They sing, fly, and soar, while he gasps. . . . Men are gone. Where is God? He screams, "Help! Someone! Help!" He screams over and over. Nothing on the horizon. Nothing in the sky. He implores the lofty sky, the endless waves, the reefs; all are deaf. He

---

[1]This essay is a modified version of "How Can a Good God Allow Evil and Suffering?" in *Philosophy: Christian Perspectives for the New Millennium*, eds. Paul Copan, Scott B. Luley, and Stan W. Wallace (Addison, TX: Christian Leadership Ministries and Norcross, GA: Ravi Zacharias International Ministries, 2003), 123–148.
[2]I remember my first encounter with Bob and Gretchen Passantino, to whom this chapter and this book are dedicated. They were legendary among aficionados of Christian apologetics. When I met them, I understood why. They had an infectious enthusiasm for all things apologetical. They were models of Christian humility. And they loved people, especially students, almost as much as they loved Jesus. They were ambassadors more than they were culture warriors. We need more like them.

begs the storms; but impassive, they obey only the infinite. . . . What can he do? He yields to despair. Worn out, he seeks death, no longer resists, gives up, lets go, tumbles into the mournful depths of the abyss forever. . . . The soul drifting in that sea may become a corpse. Who shall restore it to life?[3]

Is this not poignant? How does Hugo describe in such psychologically rich detail an experience that he himself has not had? Clearly, it is not autobiographical, as the man in the story does not live to describe the experience. How then does the novelist translate his character's inner world with such uncanny depth of insight? His tale is a symbolic representation of the many different ways in which men and women experience loss, disappointment, disillusionment, frustration, silence, and alienation from God.

Hugo's drowning man initially cries out, hoping against hope for some assistance. He first calls out to his shipmates. But they do not hear him. He then casts about for some other source of salvation. The birds fly overhead, yet they are powerless and oblivious. Their carefree spirit is an insult to his deplorable condition. What about the elements themselves that engulf him? Is salvation to be had there? No, they are the immediate *problem*. And God—where is God? Might *he* yet deliver? Time goes by. The man swims and treads water, conserving his strength as much as possible, and God does nothing to intervene. And so the man's thoughts turn from the hopeless prospect of survival to the possibility that when he dies, all will not be lost. He may yet be raised.

What powerful images Hugo offers—of ways that humans cling to anything that would give them hope, even as the world falls apart around them. I might have chosen an example of suffering or evil from the front page of any newspaper or told of my own griefs or of those close to me. But isn't it also revealing to have a passage from literature that speaks of an experience foreign to all of us that nonetheless parallels things we do know experientially.

THE SPECTACLE OF MISERY

Let us consider another masterful depiction of suffering in literature—one that is, I believe, an account of actual historical events. The biblical narrative of Job recounts the trials that intruded, by divine permission, into the life of a righteous man. God instructed Satan: "Everything he has is in your

---

[3]Victor Hugo, *Les Misérables*, trans. Lee Fahnestock and Norman MacAfee (New York: Signet, Penguin Books, 1987), 94–95.

hands, but on the man himself do not lay a finger" (Job 1:12, NIV). And so Satan did everything in his power to induce despair and dissolve faith. In a single day, the wealthy Job was reduced to utter destitution and informed that all his sons and daughters had died in a natural disaster. In the words of Puritan author Thomas Watson, "Job was a spectacle of misery."[4] His wife, an exasperated victim of all of these events as well, counseled her husband with these querulous words: "Curse God and die" (Job 2:9, ESV).

I have often wondered about the significance of that statement. What thoughts and feelings did she mean to express? One possibility is that her desperation had convinced her that cursing God was the only thing now that made sense, that this was the most natural and appropriate, even the inevitable, response to the siphoning of all that was significant in her life. Surely she realized the terrible consequences of literally cursing God: anyone who does that is treading on thin ice and had better be prepared to die. But does she care? In light of her losses, God did not seem to care a great deal. So what if cursing God led to punishment by death? Job's better half no longer believed God was worthy of her trust. Thus it was immaterial whether God would punish her resentment by killing her. He had utterly failed to earn her respect. This anguished interpretation may be summarized in this way: "In light of our wretched circumstances and God's betrayal, we may as well die."

An alternative interpretation of her peevish declamation highlights the consequences of abandoning faith: "If you curse God and turn your back on him, acting as if there is no God [which is in part what it would signify to curse God], then you might as well die. For who can live without God?"

Both interpretations illustrate attitudes that individuals sometimes adopt as they think about evil and its theological implications. And that is our theme here: *What is the religious significance of evil and suffering in the world?*

EVIL IS BOTH AN INTELLECTUAL AND AN EXISTENTIAL PROBLEM

I'm often invited to address the problem of evil from one of two distinct perspectives. At times I'm asked to speak about the intellectual obstacle that evil presents to religious conviction. Even when this *intellectual* problem of evil is the focus of my message, I always assume what is generally the case—that there are those in the audience for whom intellectual doubts are

---

[4]Thomas Watson, *All Things for Good* (1663; Edinburgh, Scotland and Carlisle, PA: The Banner of Truth Trust, 1986, reprint), 27.

not the major concern. Usually there is someone present who is threatened with disillusionment by some overwhelming circumstance, some deep disappointment, some instance of pain, evil, or suffering. It is very little help to those who are actively suffering to address the concerns of the intellect and offer a solution to some *philosophical* problem of evil. And yet—with some trepidation—I want to suggest that even in the abstract theoretical realm of philosophical discussion there may be something of substance for the weary sufferer that would reach her even in her hour of pain.

On other occasions I'm invited to speak on the role of adversity in spiritual formation. At such times I recognize there are those in the audience who struggle mightily with the intellectual dimensions of the problem of evil. They are most eager to find a solution to the logical and evidential problems in order to get on with believing in God. In these circumstances, my chief concern—to make sense of how evil actually plays a constructive role in our spiritual development and in fostering confidence in God—may not speak to the intellectual needs of some in the audience.

The problem of evil then has two important dimensions—the intellectual-apologetic and the existential-pastoral. These dimensions of concern seem, on the surface, to be entirely unrelated. And yet, I believe, they are actually complementary because of the intimate connection between our spiritual and our intellectual formation.

There are three distinct types of arguments from evil that sabotage conviction that God exists or that God is worthy of our affection. The first two arguments are primarily *intellectual* in nature. The third is more broadly *spiritual* and *existential*. While the first two are philosophical, they are not so narrowly philosophical that non-philosophers cannot be moved by them. The third is more personal and pastoral. And yet even the most rigorously intellectual of sufferers requires a pastoral response. In this chapter we shall focus only on the intellectual or philosophical challenge of evil.

DEFINING THE PROBLEM OF EVIL

You may wish to follow through a series of questions: Do you think that God exists but that this God is neither trustworthy nor worthy of our affection? Or do you view belief in God as irrational? If so, why? How does the reality of suffering imply the nonexistence of God or the irrationality of belief in God?

It is a good exercise for both parties to invite the objector to spell out the argument he envisions. And the believer needs to anticipate the possible responses to that invitation. One objector may say, "I can't really offer a straightforward argument." Another may fumble and piece together the lineaments of an argument, while voicing a sense of inadequacy: "I'm not doing this very well, but it goes something like this." Yet another type of response may come from the highly prepared person who immediately produces premises and conclusions, with everything nicely laid out, neatly revealing the precise logic of the argument.

Suppose an objector struggles unsuccessfully to articulate an argument. With all diplomacy, you might then suggest that what is supposed to be obvious (namely, that evil implies the irrationality of belief in God) is not so obvious after all. Then you might offer your own clear formulation of the objection and ask, "Is that what you have in mind? Is that what is bothering you?" In other words, the best course of action may be to help the objector formulate the argument more precisely.

What does your willingness to help your partner in dialogue really communicate? It reflects integrity—not to mention credibility, preparation, and graciousness. And it opens doors. We break down barriers when we confess from our own human experience, "You know, I've thought a lot about this issue too. And I have to be honest with you, I've been bothered by this myself. So I can certainly understand your objection."

The beauty of this approach is summarized in the title of an older book on popular apologetics that I read as a college student: *I'm Glad You Asked.*[5] I've always loved that title; it's so at odds with our normal inclinations. How often do we secretly hope our non-Christian peers will *not* ask the questions they have because, after all, we are still processing the questions and answers ourselves? With adequate preparation, though, we can be glad when they ask, especially if the questions they raise ultimately provide a platform for presenting the gospel. One welcome aspect of the problem of evil is that it does invite an intelligent articulation of God's solution to the human predicament. We can speak of the hope of eternal life in Jesus and the divine solution to the problem of pain and suffering. Our attitude often betrays our doubts: "Why proclaim the gospel? Why bother? Nobody's listening. Nobody cares. Nobody wants to know." However, questions such as "Why is there evil in the world?" or "How could God be real?" or "If God exists, what's he doing about pain and suffering?" throw open the door for us to share what we prematurely assume our listeners do not want to hear. So relish the questions for the opportunities they present.

---

[5]Ken Boa and Larry Moody, *I'm Glad You Asked* (Wheaton, IL: Victor Books, 1987, reprint).

Suppose your objector is able to lay out a compelling form of the argument from evil. What then? You must know what counts as a plausible form of the argument. For this purpose, it is helpful to turn to the literature in the philosophy of religion. There we have a record of the formulations of the argument that are taken seriously by those who have thought most deeply and persistently about the problem of evil.

Most philosophers of religion—atheists, agnostics, and theists alike—divide the major versions of the argument from evil against the existence of God into two categories: the *logical* and the *evidential* arguments. The relationship between these two terms needs some explanation, for the evidential argument is not *il*logical (as though *logic* and *evidence* were opposing terms). Rather, the terms simply refer to the manner in which each argument is constructed. Both methods are represented as plausible and compelling by their respective proponents.

THE LOGICAL ARGUMENT FROM EVIL

What is *logical* about the logical argument from evil? *Logical* here refers to the deductive structure of this argument form. The argument is alleged to be formally valid, such that if the premises are true, the conclusion follows with such logical force that it also must be true. By the rules of logic, this is an argument of the strongest possible form. Syllogisms are common versions of deductive arguments. One type of syllogism is called *modus ponens*, which has the form:

> If P, then Q.
> P.
> Therefore, Q.

Or we could substitute for P and Q to give a concrete example of this form:

> Premise 1: If Socrates is a human being (P), then Socrates is mortal (Q).
> Premise 2: Socrates is a human being (P).
> Conclusion: Therefore, Socrates is mortal (Q).

Here's a syllogism of a slightly different form called *modus tollens*:

> If P, then Q.
> Not Q.
> Therefore, not P.

With the same substitutions as before, we get the following argument:

> Premise 1: If Socrates is a human being (P), then Socrates is mortal (Q).
> Premise 2: Socrates is not mortal (not Q).
> Conclusion: Therefore, Socrates is not a human being (not P).

Deductive arguments like these are logically impressive. If their respective premises are true, then their respective conclusions are necessarily true (i.e., they *cannot* be false). The formal strength of such arguments makes them quite daunting logically. If one accepts the premises of an argument where the conclusion follows validly from the premises, then the jig is up. One must accept the conclusion.

The ambition of the logical argument from evil is to demonstrate that God does not exist. However, as we'll see, the logical argument is so ambitious that this proves to be its Achilles' heel.

What does the logical argument from evil actually look like? Let me illustrate with a story, an experience I had when I was a college student. I was enrolled with about a hundred other students in an elementary course in physics that we affectionately called "bonehead physics" (because not much brainpower was required to succeed in the course). I thought of the professor as a cordial, gregarious sort of person, fairly popular with the students, even though I had never had a personal conversation with him. After class he would stand in the doorway and greet the students as they filed by, sort of like a Baptist minister following the Sunday sermon.

As I left class one day I overheard this professor talking with another student about religion. This piqued my curiosity. After listening from across the hall, I could tell that this professor of physics was genuinely and enthusiastically interested in religious questions. Standing there I thought, *I'm going to have to ask him about this.* When the conversation concluded, I introduced myself and said, "You know, I overheard your conversation about religion. May I ask what is the nature of your interest in these questions?"

He answered, "I'm very sincere in seeking religious truth. I've been looking for religious reality and studying the major world religions for quite some time. It's been a major personal project for me, and I take the question of religious truth very seriously. But at this point I'm agnostic. I haven't reached any conclusions, and my quest continues." And then he corrected himself. "Actually," he said, "I have made some progress. I've narrowed the field slightly by eliminating one of the options. One major religious perspective I've considered just isn't reasonable. It's not plausible at all."

When he announced that it was Christianity that had failed the test of rational scrutiny, I thought it might be best just to drop the subject. But somehow the words just came out. "Really?" I said, "I'm a Christian, and I think I have some pretty good reasons for my beliefs. Would you be willing to tell me how you've concluded that Christianity can't be true?"

His answer was predictable and compact. "It all comes down to the problem of evil. First, Christians believe that God is all-powerful, or omnipotent. Second, they believe that God is morally perfect. Putting these together, if God is omnipotent he could prevent evil if he wanted to, and if he is morally perfect he would desire to prevent evil if he could. Since the Christian God has both the desire to prevent evil and the power to fulfill that desire, there shouldn't be any evil at all. But obviously there is evil in the world. So the Christian God doesn't exist. It's that simple. That's why I'm not a Christian."

His statement of the problem was a version of the logical argument from evil. As he stated it, it is a *modus tollens* argument:

> Premise 1: If God (a being who is both omnipotent and perfectly good) exists, then there should be no evil.
> Premise 2: But there is evil (i.e., it is not the case that there is no evil).
> Conclusion: God does not exist.

In effect, my professor of physics was arguing in a way made famous by Oxford philosopher J. L. Mackie.[6] He asserted that there is a *logical inconsistency* within the following set of three propositions accepted by most Christians: (1) God is omnipotent, (2) God is perfectly good, and (3) evil exists. The implications are severe. If these three propositions are logically incompatible, then the believer who seeks to be rational must abandon at least one of them in order to recover consistency in his beliefs. However, the Christian believer cannot abandon any one of these three propositions without ceasing to be fully Christian in what he believes. To deny evil, for example, would make mincemeat of the doctrine of the atonement of Jesus Christ in his death and resurrection. Without God's simultaneous love and power the death of Jesus would be a meaningless symbol. And what, after all, would the crucified one be atoning for if not the evil that is so real and pervasive in human experience? The other propositions about

---

[6]See J. L. Mackie, "Evil and Omnipotence," *Mind*, 64 (1955), and Chap. 9 in his *The Miracle of Theism* (Oxford, UK: Clarendon Press, 1982).

divine omnipotence and moral perfection refer to major components in the Christian understanding of God's nature. They cannot be jettisoned either. Thus, proponents of the logical argument attempt to corner the believer into a logical "no-good-options" zone.

You may wonder what I said in response to my teacher. It was a moment of decision for me, and sometimes I think my philosophical career was launched during that conversation. With sincere respect for the superior firepower of my professor, I acknowledged that I probably could not answer his objection to his satisfaction. Of course, he agreed. But he did say he would be interested in what I thought. For two hours we talked. My growing confidence peaked when this professor remarked at the end, "To be honest, some of this I really haven't thought through very well. You've raised some interesting questions, and you've given me some food for thought. Would you be willing to meet with me and a group of my university colleagues? I think they, too, would be interested in what you have to say." In total disbelief, the words fell from my trembling lips: "Okay, sure."

I was never more anxious in my life than during my preparations for the day of the planned gathering. But again God was gracious. My professor friend, after introducing me at the outset of the meeting, announced that we should all first agree about *what evil is* exactly. From that point the entire conversation focused on disagreement about the nature of evil. I never even had the opportunity to share what I had prepared to say! As I listened to sophisticated unbelievers first propose and then dispose of conflicting conceptions of evil operative in any plausible argument from evil against theism, it occurred to me that would-be objectors have their work cut out for them.

As for me, I resolved to wrestle further with this perennial objection in pursuit of the most compelling response. I've had twenty years to think about what I would say if I could sit down again with those gentlemen.[7]

How should we respond to the logical argument from evil, which charges Christian belief with logical inconsistency? There are several steps for dealing with the charge that a given set of propositions is inconsistent. On the face of it, these three propositions—asserting God's omnipotence, God's moral perfection, and the reality of evil—appear to be incompatible. The key question here is, Is there any way to dispel the impression of inconsistency?

---

[7]My first published book grew out of this experience. See *Evil and the Evidence for God* (Philadelphia: Temple University Press, 1993).

A first step in dispelling the impression of inconsistency is to invite the objector to *demonstrate* the inconsistency of these propositions. Most thoughtful philosophers of religion acknowledge that the three propositions in question are not explicitly contradictory. They concede that in order for the argument to be fully successful, it must be augmented with auxiliary premises. Additional propositions, acceptable to the Christian theist, are needed to draw out the alleged inconsistency. The needed supplements must specify what it means for God to be omnipotent and what it means for God to be morally perfect.

It turns out that producing the needed amplification is a daunting task in its own right. In fact, as most philosophers now agree, no objector has yet succeeded. We'll see why in a moment. But the point to grasp here is that the saber of the logical argument must have its edges sharpened with auxiliary propositions if it is to cut to the quick of theistic belief. Otherwise the argument goes limp.

A second step, when confronted with the charge that a given set of propositions is logically inconsistent, is to offer reasons in support of the credibility of each individual proposition. If there is good reason to accept each proposition, then this is *prima facie* justification for affirming their conjunction. If our three propositions—God is omnipotent, God is morally perfect, and evil exists—are all independently plausible for good reasons, then the good reasons for believing each proposition *in isolation* are also good reasons to believe them *in conjunction*. And reasons to believe them in conjunction are reasons also to suppose that the appearance of contradiction is no more than *appearance*.

This consideration greatly reduces the impression of inconsistency. If an objector is made to *struggle* to support the charge of inconsistency, the point is even more powerful. For into the vacuum created by the difficulty of rigorously demonstrating a logical inconsistency one may insert evidence and credible reasons for taking each of the three propositions. This strategy also strengthens the believer's resolve to preserve commitment to orthodox belief rather than to adopt the compromising expedient of softening his position regarding the nature of God. Armed with evidence for the existence of God, the believer has a powerful means of parrying the thrust of this objection.[8]

A third step in dispelling the impression of inconsistency is most decisive. Here the goal is to demonstrate that the original set of three proposi-

---

[8]For a detailed argument on this point, see ibid.

tions is actually consistent.[9] Earlier I suggested that the Achilles' heel of the logical argument from evil is that it attempts the maximally ambitious project of demonstrating the nonexistence of God. But to demonstrate the nonexistence of God in this way, one must specify what is meant by divine omnipotence and divine moral perfection and show that the conjunction of these properties entails the nonexistence of evil.

Let us consider each property in turn. The objector interprets divine omnipotence to mean that *God could prevent evil if he wanted to*. But is this a satisfactory characterization of divine omnipotence? Is it possible that there are worlds that God cannot create under certain conditions? Suppose God desires to create a world with free creatures who are capable of morally significant action. It is at least logically possible that even an omnipotent God may not be able to create such a world without also permitting evil. For in creating a world of creatures with freedom to do either good or evil, God leaves it up to them whether or not they will choose evil. Of course, because God is omniscient, he will know in advance whether a world with free creatures, able to do evil, would in fact be a world with evil in it. If God desires not to have a world with evil in it, he might choose not to create a world with free creatures. But having a world with free creatures may be a great enough good to justify God's creation of such a world, even if it is a world that he knows will contain evils caused by free creatures. The point is, if it is God's purpose to create a world with free creatures, his omnipotence does not entail that he can prevent free creatures from doing evil without violating their freedom. This broadening of the field of discussion through the exploration of logical possibilities challenges the assumption that an omnipotent God could prevent evil if he wanted to.

Next let us consider God's absolute moral perfection. The objector commonly interprets this to mean that *God would want to prevent evil if he could*. In response the theist may propose the following clarification of the doctrine of omnibenevolence: It is logically possible that a morally perfect God has *a morally sufficient reason for permitting all of the evils that exist*. The objector does not know that it is *not possible* that God has a morally justifiable reason for allowing every instance of suffering. What the absolute moral perfection of God actually implies is not that God must absolutely prevent evil, but that if God permits evil there must be some moral justification for his permission of it.

Notice, the theist is not required to *know* the specific "morally sufficient

---

[9]Portions of the discussion that follows parallel Alvin Plantinga's treatment of this argument in his book *The Nature of Necessity* (Oxford, UK: Clarendon Press, 1974), Chap. 9.

reasons" that would justify God's permission of evil. For the purposes of defusing the logical argument from evil, it is enough that the availability of morally sufficient reasons is a *logical possibility*. We need only propose that an all-powerful, all-loving God may in fact be morally justified in permitting every evil in the quantity that we actually find in the universe. The logical argument purports that divine moral perfection is logically incompatible with divine omnipotence and the reality of evil, on the grounds that moral perfection entails the desire to prevent evil. But moral perfection only entails the prevention of evil that is not morally justified by some competing desire.

Here's an alternative way to make the same point. Suppose God is morally perfect. Suppose further that this entails that God (who is also omnipotent) would not permit any evil without having a morally sufficient reason for doing so. Then it follows that any actual evil is such that God is morally justified in permitting its occurrence. Again, this is true even if we cannot imagine what goods would justify God's permission of evils that occur. (Of course, we infer on the same grounds that God will see to it that worse evils—evils that would not be justified at all—never have and never will occur.)

Recall that the logical argument from evil is an *all-or-nothing* affair: either it is completely successful or it is an utter failure. Given the more plausible conceptions of divine omnipotence and divine moral perfection proposed in response to this objection, and the logical possibilities that these conceptions indicate, it follows that the logical argument does not demonstrate inconsistency among the three propositions in question. Thus the argument fails completely. For the past three decades proponents of the logical argument have been an endangered species. Noted philosopher of religion William Rowe—himself an atheist—writes: "Some philosophers have contended that the existence of evil is *logically inconsistent* with the existence of the theistic God. No one, I think, has succeeded in establishing such an extravagant claim."[10]

The objector who still maintains that evil somehow counts against the rationality of Christian belief must abandon the logical argument in favor of a more promising line of attack.

THE EVIDENTIAL ARGUMENT FROM EVIL

The above rebuttal of the logical argument from evil does not settle the question of rational belief in God. The skeptic may yet complain, "If God

---

[10]William L. Rowe, "The Problem of Evil and Some Varieties of Atheism," in *Contemporary Perspectives on Religious Epistemology*, ed. R. Douglas Geivett and Brendan Sweetman (New York: Oxford University Press, 1992), 41, n. 1.

has morally sufficient reasons for permitting all the evils there are, we certainly do not know what those reasons are. In fact, it looks as if there are certain evils that simply are not morally justified."

This brings us to the evidential argument from evil. The chief premise of this argument is that *some evils are so bad that they (probably) are not morally justified.*[11]

Consider the multiple faces of evil and suffering. Some varieties may be regarded as just retribution for wrong actions; some persons are made to suffer because they deserve to be punished for wrong deeds. Other varieties of suffering may produce a good that could not be achieved by any other means, fostering in the sufferer greater faith in God, courage, compassion toward others, and so forth. In these instances, we see how the evil permitted may be justified.

However, no matter how many different principles are set forth to explain the evils of our world, there will still remain a residue of evil, comprised of what we might consider the truly horrendous evils in the universe, that no one can explain. If there is some morally sufficient reason for God's permission of the greatest atrocities of human experience, it remains firmly hidden in the mind of God. We cannot conceive of goods that would justify such horrendous evils as those catalogued by Marilyn Adams: "individual and massive collective suffering . . . the rape of a woman and axing off of her arms, psycho-physical torture whose ultimate goal is the disintegration of personality, betrayal of one's deepest loyalties, child abuse of the sort described by Ivan Karamazov, child pornography, parental incest, slow death by starvation, the explosion of nuclear bombs over populated areas."[12] Worse, it is unthinkable that any good could justify such evils; it is repugnant to us even to suppose that God's permission of the worst evils is somehow morally justified. Thus, even if it is logically possible that every instance of evil is permitted on morally sufficient grounds, our inability to make sense of certain evils is evidence that no such morally justifying reasons really exist. Even if we are mistaken in thinking that no morally sufficient reason justifies God's permission of truly horrendous evils, we are nevertheless rationally obliged to believe there are none *on the basis of the evidence we have.* Our evidence indicates that a morally sufficient reason

---

[11]For a seminal exposition of the evidential argument, see Rowe, "The Problem of Evil and Some Varieties of Atheism." For a sampling of sophisticated reflection on the evidential argument by prominent figures in philosophy of religion, see *The Evidential Argument from Evil*, ed. Daniel Howard-Snyder (Bloomington, IN: Indiana University Press, 1996). An excellent and accessible treatment of the evidential argument is James Petrik's *Evil Beyond Belief* (Armonk, NY and London: M. E. Sharpe, 2000).

[12]Marilyn McCord Adams, *Horrendous Evils and the Goodness of God* (Ithaca, NY: Cornell University Press, 1999), 26.

does not exist. Since it is unlikely, as far as we can tell, that God has a morally justifying reason for permitting the worst kinds of evil, it is unlikely that an omnipotent and morally perfect being exists.

How are we to respond to this evidential argument from evil?

First, we may start by accounting for some classes of evil. Most people will grant that certain explanatory principles do adequately account for some of the evils in the world. There are certain goods that would not exist if evil were not permitted, even if the good of permitting certain other particular evils is unimaginable. How is this point helpful if the evidential argument appeals exclusively to the inexplicable evils of human experience? If, over time and in response to criticism, we develop a track record of offering plausible explanations for particular evils, then the residue of horrendous evils may be regarded as anomalies that have their own explanation even if we do not know what that explanation is. While this is not the strongest kind of response to the evidential argument, it is a helpful beginning.

Second, it is hardly surprising that there should be considerable mystery about the purposes of God. God himself declares, "My thoughts are not your thoughts" (Isa. 55:8, ESV). God's nature and ways are beyond our complete comprehension. It would be most unreasonable to expect to achieve perfect clarity about his purposes, his character, and his relationship to the world using the comparatively puny capacity for reflection that we have as finite creatures. If after our most sophisticated deliberations, there remains some mystery that shrouds God's reasons for permitting some of the evils in the universe, does the lack of human comprehension really constitute a reason for believing that God has no morally sufficient reason for permitting those evils? The question answers itself.

Third, we must distinguish between *gratuitous evil* and *inscrutable evil*. Inscrutable evil is evil whose moral justification is beyond our (present) understanding. Gratuitous evil is evil that, as a matter of fact, occurs in the absence of any morally justifying reason.[13] The major premise in the evidential argument is that there is (or probably is) gratuitous evil in the world. But what is the evidence for this? The only evidence for the existence of gratuitous evil is the evidence of inscrutable evil. But the existence of inscrutable evil certainly does not entail the existence of gratuitous evil. But perhaps inscrutable evil *is* good evidence for the existence of gratuitous evil. Let us consider this suggestion.

We have already noted the finitude of human understanding in judg-

---

[13]Some philosophers speak of "pointless evil" rather than "gratuitous evil" when discussing the evidential argument from evil.

ing God's purposes and actions. We have a limited capacity for discerning between *genuinely* gratuitous evil and only *apparently* gratuitous evil. Most skeptics know better than to claim that the existence of actual gratuitous evil can be demonstrated. The evidential argument from evil is thus built upon the *appearance* of gratuitous evil. But is that not at least a guide to rational belief on the part of cognitively limited human beings? Are we not dependent on how things appear or seem when we seek to make rational choices about what to believe? If we are not able, by our best efforts, to conceive of a plausible explanation for God's permission of horrendous evils, what can we do but conclude that there is no adequate explanation?

Certainly appearances sometimes are adequate grounds for things we believe. This is generally the case in sensory perception, where how things appear in our visual field, for example, is a good indication of how things actually are. If I peer through the window and it seems visually to me that there is a white-headed pigeon on the telephone wire, then I probably am justified in believing that there is a pigeon on the wire. I am not justified in believing that there is a rhino on the wire. There are at least two reasons for this. First, I am not being appeared to in this way. It does not seem to me that there is a rhino on the wire. Second, even if I was appeared to in this way, I would have independent reason for thinking that there is something wrong with this appearance such that it is not a reliable indicator of the truth. For starters, rhinos are unknown to this part of Southern California. Furthermore, rhinos generally do not take much interest in scaling telephone poles (so, at least, I suspect). Nor do they have the capability of climbing telephone poles (of this I am certain).

But visual appearances are not always reliable grounds for belief. What if I report that it seems visually to me, from a distance of thirty meters, that there is an inchworm on the telephone wire? You would be right to doubt that I have the requisite powers of observation and that I jest when I offer such a report. It is doubtful that I should ever be appeared to in just that way. There may well be an inchworm on the wire. But if there is, it is highly unlikely that it would appear to me that there is. That is not the sort of thing I would be able to detect with the naked eye from a distance of thirty meters. In fact, as far as appearances are concerned, it (visually) appears to me that there is not an inchworm there.

Am I, then, justified in believing (as I now do, actually) that there is not an inchworm on the wire? Well, I am justified in believing this, but not on the basis of appearances. The belief policy I adopt with respect to the proposition that there is an inchworm on the telephone wire is grounded in other factors. In this case, the fact that I spontaneously and arbitrarily imagined the existence of an inchworm on the wire for the purposes of illustration is a major factor supporting my belief that the proposition is false. It would be a striking coincidence, would it not, if there actually was an inchworm right there, on precisely that spot on the wire, as I peer through the window while deliberately imagining just that circumstance? There may be other factors supporting my belief. But again, appearances have nothing to do with my judgment about the matter. The nonappearance of an inchworm is not evidence in support of my judgment that there is no inchworm there. You would be incredulous if I reported seeing an inchworm there; you should be equally incredulous if I report, "I believe there is no inchworm there because it visually appears to me that there is no inchworm there." On the other hand, if I say, "I believe there is not a pigeon on the wire because it visually appears to me that there is no bird of any sort on the wire," you may think me reasonable.

Now let us take the appearance of gratuitous evil. Is this more like the appearance that there is not a pigeon on the wire or more like the appearance that there is not an inchworm on the wire? The skeptic assumes that the appearance of gratuitous evil is more like the appearance that there is no pigeon on the wire. But what is his basis for assuming that? The mere inscrutability of evil is not enough to warrant this assumption. The skeptic must have some conception of the powers of human understanding and the faculties appropriate to the discernment of gratuitous evils that permits his judgment that the appearance of evil is a reliable indicator of the actual existence of gratuitous evil. He would also have to know enough about the limits of moral justification for permitting evils to be sure that appearances of the absence of justifying reasons is an adequate indicator that there are no justifying reasons. He will be justified in believing there are no morally sufficient reasons for God's permission of apparently gratuitous evils only if appearances in this case are a reliable indication of the way things are. It begins to look like the skeptic must have God-like powers of cognition.

I believe it is question-begging even to assert, without more evidence than the mere inscrutability of evil, that there are *apparently* gratuitous evils in the world. We must be careful not to confuse the inability to discern a justifying reason with it seeming that there is no justifying reason. It is perfectly coherent for a theist to claim that it does not seem to him that any evil, no matter how inscrutable it may be, is gratuitous. It may, in fact, seem to the theist that no evil is gratuitous, even though some evils are admittedly inscrutable. His judgment that inscrutable evils do not appear to him to be gratuitous may rest on the confidence he has that God exists, that God is all-powerful and perfectly good, and that "in all things God works for the good" (Rom. 8:28, NIV). An unbeliever, lacking this conviction, is at most entitled to a cautious agnosticism about whether inscrutable evils are in fact gratuitous. But this sort of agnosticism will not permit the confident denial that the existence of the worst evils makes the existence of God unlikely and belief in God irrational. The force of the evidential argument evaporates.

REMEMBERING GOOD FRIDAY

We have explored the two most prominent forms of the argument from evil against God's existence. As it happens, there is a little-appreciated argument from evil *for* the existence of God. It begins with the question that stumped my physics professor and his cohorts: What is evil? I think the most intuitively plausible, non-question-begging answer is that evil is *a departure from the way things ought to be.* We call certain events evil because they seem to be a breakdown in the way things ought to be. When we hear of the brutal, senseless, and intentional slaying of an innocent person, we naturally recoil in horror and insist, "That's just not right!" We do not feel that we are merely expressing an opinion or a preference. We are making a judgment about objective reality. But if evil is a departure from the way things ought to be, then it follows that there is a way things ought to be in order for there to be evil. But here's the rub for the unbeliever: How can there be a way things *ought* to be unless there is a *design/plan* for the world? And how can there be a design/plan without a suitably talented, intelligent, powerful, resourceful designer and fashioner of reality? We humans can be very smug about the theological implications of evil because it makes us wonder if God really cares. But what does it mean to insist that God does not exist if our conviction that evil exists is so irresistible? Atheists and agnostics have their own problem of evil to contend with.

Furthermore, those who repudiate religious belief because of evil trivialize suffering and the admirable and enviable faith of those who suffer, especially when those who suffer remain faithful and find reason for hope in the face of suffering on account of God's presence and goodness to them. It is rather more puzzling when a person of naturalistic orientation suffers with grace and courage. To what do they attribute their endurance in suffering? What is the source of their strength? Is it not easier to make sense of the source of courage, comfort, and grace for a believer in God who suffers? The skeptic who ridicules the conviction that God exists and that God has morally sufficient reasons for permitting horrendous evils tacitly mocks the vibrant, authentic faith of true believers who experience horrendous evils and yet come to love and trust God even more. Perhaps the depth of conviction among believers who suffer is a signpost pointing to a reality that the unbeliever has yet to experience.

The crowning consideration in our response to the problem of evil is that God has done something about evil. He himself passes through it, experiences it, and defeats it. In Peter Kreeft's book on popular Christian apologetics, *Yes or No: Straight Answers to Tough Questions About Christianity*, a Christian and an unbeliever are engaged in dialogue about the truth of Christianity. Addressing the problem of evil, the Christian remarks:

> Jesus Christ. He came right down into our trap and died to free us. The One who asks us to trust Him to solve the problem of evil already did the greatest thing to conquer it. He suffered every kind of evil with us. He was hated by the people He loved. He was nailed to a cross and died. He even felt His father leave him horribly alone on the cross when He said, "My God, my God, why have You forsaken Me?" *That's* evil. All the evil in the world is there, and there He is in the middle of it. You think of God up in Heaven controlling things down here and you wonder why He doesn't do a better job. You wonder if He really cares, and how He can be good if He just stays there and turns away and lets terrible things happen. But it's not like that. He didn't stay away. He came down into evil. That's the Christian answer to the problem of evil. Not a tricky argument, but Christ on the cross, God on our side, the side of the innocent sufferer.[14]

And then he says these most memorable words: "How can you resent a God like *that*?"

Some time ago I debated the question, Does God exist? with an agnostic philosopher. During the question-and-answer period afterward, one woman approached the microphone and with obvious rage began to explain why her experience with pain and suffering prevented her from believing that God exists. It was as if she blamed me for this because I believed in God.

As tactfully as I could, I said to her, "I can't help but notice that you seem very angry. But with whom are you angry if God does not exist? Are you angry at me for believing in God? How does that help you? Are you

[14]Peter Kreeft, *Yes or No? Straight Answers to Tough Questions About Christianity* (Ann Arbor, MI: Servant Books, 1984), 41.

sure you don't believe in God? Perhaps it isn't that you don't believe in God, but that you're angry with God. But consider what God has done for you through Jesus Christ. Can you really resent a God like that?"

When we reach this level of dialogue with co-sufferers in the human community, we begin to touch the deepest existential problem of all and connect our own universal human experience of suffering and evil with God's redemptive purposes.

We saw earlier that the evidential argument from evil is an argument from the reality of gratuitous evil, which is incompatible with the existence of God. The argument allows for the possibility that none of the evil around us is truly gratuitous. But we must judge on the basis of how things appear. And since there are evils that are so horrendous that we cannot conceive of a justification God could have for permitting them, we should conclude that there probably are gratuitous evils. We should, in conclusion, consider Christianity's distinctive answer to this claim.

Inscrutable evil is inherently mysterious. If we knew what divine purpose is served by every instance of evil, there would be no inscrutable evil. For any instance of evil that is inscrutable, we would like to know whether it is also gratuitous. But it seems that is something we could never know. Or is it?

We should recall, first, that evidence for the existence of God is evidence that inscrutable evils are not gratuitous. But there's more we can say in light of the crucifixion and resurrection of Jesus Christ. By all accounts, death by crucifixion was slow and agonizing. There is strong historical evidence that Jesus was crucified and that his crucifixion was a miscarriage of justice.[15] The film *The Passion of the Christ* is a painfully vivid portrayal of the suffering of Jesus. He was, to borrow the words of Isaiah the prophet, "despised and rejected by men; a man of sorrows, and acquainted with grief" (Isa. 53:3, ESV). Consider the passion of Jesus—the hours between his arrest and the moment he died—and ignore everything that happened next. What was done to Jesus, what Jesus experienced, is a horrendous evil. Without the benefit of divine revelation, we should conclude that this evil is as inscrutable as they come. And who can say that any individual has suffered more than Jesus did on the day of his execution?

At the heart of Christianity is an event that, from a strictly human point of view, is utterly senseless. If the story had ended with Jesus' burial, his crucifixion would simply be another heart-rending example of gratuitous evil. But something happened that challenges this verdict. Jesus was raised from

---

[15]See Martin Hengel, *The Crucifixion* (Minneapolis: Augsburg Fortress, 1977).

the dead![16] This resurrection demonstrates that there is a divine purpose in all that Jesus suffered. That purpose is recounted in the New Testament. In a chapter on the resurrection, the apostle Paul states this purpose simply and directly: "Christ died for our sins" (1 Cor. 15:3, ESV). This was, he says, "in accordance with the Scriptures." This includes what that ancient prophet Isaiah wrote: "Surely he has borne our griefs and carried our sorrows . . . he was wounded for our transgressions; he was crushed for our iniquities; upon him was the chastisement that brought us peace, and with his stripes we are healed" (Isa. 53:4–5, ESV). It is for this reason that we call that day of horrendous evil "*Good* Friday."

If we have ears to hear, we learn from this that human sin is serious business. What would otherwise be an utterly gratuitous evil is filled with meaning: it holds the promise of human redemption. This is called the "mystery of our salvation." And if God has revealed to us the extraordinary purpose that makes sense of the suffering of Jesus, then we have reason enough to believe that no suffering is genuinely gratuitous.[17]

---

[16]For a fuller treatment of miracles and of the evidence for the resurrection of Jesus, see R. Douglas Geivett and Gary R. Habermas, eds., *In Defense of Miracles* (Downers Grove, IL: InterVarsity Press, 1997).
[17]I wish to thank John Kwak for his help in preparing the manuscript for this chapter.

CHAPTER SEVENTEEN

The New Testament, Jesus Christ, and *The Da Vinci Code*

Richard G. Howe

THE DA VINCI CODE: ANATOMY OF A PHENOMENON

The novel *The Da Vinci Code* took the nation by storm for the next few years after its 2003 release.[1] Its impact can be seen not only in the vast number of copies sold, but in the number of television interviews that its author, Dan Brown, has participated in, the number of television magazines dealing with several controversial topics introduced by the novel, and the number of books that have come out in response to it.[2] While at least one of its controversial claims was not unique to Brown's novel,[3] no other book in recent history has caused the level of scrutiny and reaction that *The Da Vinci Code* has. Because the issues are so important and because the truth of these matters is so readily accessible, it behooves Christians to set the record straight in order to "walk in wisdom toward outsiders . . . so that you may know how you ought to answer each person."[4]

---

[1] The movie was not a wild blockbuster as anticipated, but it certainly did very well on its opening weekend, grossing over seventy million dollars. Its opening weekend was exceeded by only two other movies in their respective openings—*Star Wars: Revenge of the Sith* and *Spiderman*.

[2] A sampling of books that have come out refuting the claims of the novel include: Richard Abanes, *The Truth Behind the Da Vinci Code* (Eugene, OR: Harvest House, 2004); Darrell L. Bock, *Breaking the Da Vinci Code: Answers to the Questions Everyone's Asking* (Nashville: Thomas Nelson, 2004); James L. Garlow, *The Da Vinci Codebreaker* (Minneapolis: Bethany House, 2006); James L. Garlow and Peter Jones, *Cracking Da Vinci's Code: You've Read the Fiction, Now Read the Facts* (Colorado Springs: Victor Books, 2005); Hank Hanegraaff and Paul Maier, *The Da Vinci Code: Fact or Fiction?* (Wheaton, IL: Tyndale House, 2004); Erwin W. Lutzer, *The Da Vinci Code Deception: Credible Answers to the Questions Millions Are Asking about Jesus, the Bible, and The Da Vinci Code* (Wheaton, IL: Tyndale House, 2006); Josh McDowell, *The Da Vinci Code: A Quest for Answers* (Holiday, FL: Green Key Books, 2006); Ben Witherington III, *The Gospel Code: Novel Claims About Jesus, Mary Magdalene, and Da Vinci* (Downers Grove, IL: InterVarsity Press, 2004).

[3] The thesis that Jesus was married to Mary Magdalene and fathered a bloodline that continues to today was advanced by Michael Baigent, Richard Leigh, and Henry Lincoln, *Holy Blood, Holy Grail* (New York: Delacorte Press, 1982). For a critical review of the book, see Brian Onken, "Searching for the Holy Grail—Again: A Summary Critique," *Christian Research Journal*, Vol. 27, No. 1 (2004): 48–51.

[4] Col. 4:5–6. Unless otherwise indicated, Scripture quotations in this chapter are taken from *The Holy Bible: English Standard Version*.

WHY ALL THE FUSS?

Some have responded to the many critics, saying that their reaction is unwarranted since *The Da Vinci Code* is only a novel. As such, they say, it was never intended to be taken seriously. For sure, there is a popular literary genre known as historical fiction that allows a writer to weave a fictional story around historical events. Usually, however, the distinctions between the historical context of the story and the fictional elements of the story are clear. But Dan Brown's novel crosses the line in a number of serious ways.

Before one even begins reading the story, Brown makes the bold assertion that "all descriptions of artwork, architecture, documents, and secret rituals are accurate."[5] Further, when one takes a closer look at what Dan Brown himself says both about the claims of the novel and other things about his own worldview, it becomes clear that as far as he is concerned, this is more than an entertaining novel.

In response to an interview, Brown commented, "When I started researching [*The*] *Da Vinci Code*, I really was skeptical and I expected on some level to disprove all of this history that's unearthed in the book. And after three trips to Paris and a lot of interviews, I became a believer."[6] One must ask, "A believer in what?" When asked by Charlie Gibson on *Good Morning America* how the book might have been different if Brown had written it as a nonfiction book, Brown repeated the same sentiment: "I don't think it would have. I began the research for *The Da Vinci Code* as a skeptic. I entirely expected as I researched the book to disprove this theory. And after numerous trips to Europe, about two years of research, I really became a believer. And, it's important to remember that this is a novel about a theory that has been out there for a long time."[7] Matt Lauer of *The Today Show* asked Dan Brown how much of the book is based on reality. Brown answered, "Absolutely all of it. Obviously Robert Langdon is fictional, but all of the art, architecture, secret rituals, secret societies—all that is historical fact."[8]

In an address to a gathering of writers in his native New Hampshire, Brown revealed a number of things both about his view of the novel itself and his own worldview. "I wrote this novel as part of my own spiritual quest. I never imagined a novel could become so controversial. . . . *The Da Vinci Code* describes history as I have come to understand it through

---

[5]Dan Brown, *The Da Vinci Code* (New York: Doubleday, 2003), 1.
[6]Video interview with Dan Brown, downloaded from http://www.danbrown.com/novels/davinci_code/breakingnews.html.
[7]Ibid.
[8]Ibid.

many years of travel, research, reading, interviews, exploration."[9] Such comments are nested in a worldview characterized in the same speech by historical skepticism, religious relativism, epistemological relativism, a mischaracterization of science and religion, and a non-Christian view of the relationship between faith and reason.

Space and design do not allow a thorough examination of these matters here. But it is important to bear these in mind in order to dispel the criticism that it is unnecessary to go to any trouble in responding to *The Da Vinci Code*. There clearly is an agenda here. These matters are much too important for Christians to sit quietly by and let the claims of the novel go unchallenged.

THE DA VINCI CODE: ITS CLAIMS

There are a number of criticisms to be made regarding the false claims in the novel about artwork and other points from history.[10] While many of these mistakes are somewhat trivial, they serve as an indicator of the poor historical research that went into the work, despite Brown's claims to the contrary. When it comes to a more in-depth analysis, it is Brown's claims about documents that interest me. Remember that on his "Fact" page, Brown asserts that all his descriptions are accurate. But what, according to Brown, do these documents say? Through the mouth of the novel's historian Leigh Teabing, the novel makes a number of claims about who Jesus is, based upon the contrasts between the New Testament Gospels and other ancient documents. Specifically, the novel makes the following four claims:

1. The Christian doctrine of the deity of Christ was the result of a close vote among church leaders convening at the Council of Nicea in A.D. 325.[11]

2. The Bible as we know it was collated by Constantine at the Council of Nicea in A.D. 325.[12]

3. The story of Jesus is more accurately contained within the Gnostic documents than in the New Testament and shows a mere human Jesus.[13]

4. This story also shows that Jesus was married to Mary Magdalene and fathered children.[14]

---

[9]Audio speech by Dan Brown, downloaded from ibid.

[10]For comments regarding the novel's mistakes about the artwork of Leonardo Da Vinci, see Garlow, *The Da Vinci Codebreaker*, 122–124, 125–127, 137–138. For comments on other historical mistakes, see the DVD *The Da Vinci Delusion* (Fort Lauderdale: Coral Ridge Ministries, 2006).

[11]*The Da Vinci Code*, 233.

[12]Ibid., 231, 234, 244.

[13]Ibid., 234, 235, 245–246, 248, 255–256.

[14]Ibid., 244, 245, 246, 249.

The punch line of the novel is that the true identity of the Holy Grail is none other than Mary Magdalene herself. Just as in the traditional legend the grail was reputed to be the repository of the blood of Jesus collected as it dripped from him on the cross, in a literal way Mary Magdalene is reputed to be the true repository of the blood of Jesus inasmuch as she carried his child, the progenitor of his royal bloodline.

The title of the novel comes from the idea that this "truth" (that Jesus and Mary Magdalene were married and gave rise to a blood-line that continues to the present) was originally suppressed by male-dominated church authority because Jesus fathered a daughter who was supposed to lead the church. Having been suppressed, the knowledge of this bloodline has been protected throughout the centuries by a secret society whose leadership included such luminaries as Sir Isaac Newton and Leonardo da Vinci. According to the theory, Leonardo hid a number of clues about this "truth" in his artwork, most notably *The Last Supper* and *Mona Lisa*.

Does the historical evidence support such a claim? More specifically, can we know anything about the likelihood that Jesus was married to Mary Magdalene? How are such historical inquiries conducted? How does the New Testament evidence stack up against other ancient documents regarding what we can know about Jesus? It is to these questions I would now like to turn my attention.

THE DA VINCI CODE: RESPONSES TO THE ARGUMENTS

I would like to unpack the novel's arguments for the above four claims and respond to each of them.[15] The evidence will show that not only is it sometimes the case that the claims are unsupported, but often the exact opposite of what the novel has to say is actually the case. As it turns out, Dan Brown (through the mouth of Leigh Teabing) is not the historian that he would want you to think.

The Deity of Jesus and the Historical Evidence

The novel claims: The Christian doctrine of the deity of Christ was the result of a close vote among church leaders convening at the Council of Nicea in A.D. 325.

Response: The divinity of Jesus was affirmed long before Constantine and the Council of Nicea. The Council of Nicea was the first of several

---

[15]Probably the best critique of the claims of the novel is the Bock book cited in note 2. I am especially indebted to him for some of what I have to say in my responses.

ecumenical church councils.[16] It was convened June 19, 325, by the Roman Emperor Constantine in Nicea in Bithynia (now Isnik, Turkey). There were around three hundred church leaders present to try to settle the dispute between the followers of Arius (who regarded Jesus as a subordinate god and of a *similar* substance to the Father) and Athanasius (who regarded Jesus as coequal and of the *same* substance as the Father). Notice that for the most part none of the leaders present denied the deity of Christ. Rather, the dispute was regarding the exact nature of that deity. Further, there was no vote on the deity of Christ. The church leaders were asked to sign the final conclusion of the council, which affirmed the view of Athanasius and the full deity of Christ, and only two out of the three hundred or so refused. This is far from the "close vote" that *The Da Vinci Code* claims.

The historical evidence shows that the Council of Nicea only confirmed what was already fairly well established within the majority of the church at the time—namely, that Jesus was divine and coequal with the Father.[17] This can be seen by a look at what some of the early Christian leaders had to say about the identity of Christ. It is important to note that all these church leaders lived well before the Council of Nicea.

Justin Martyr (A.D. 100–165), in his *First Apology*, claimed that . . . the Father of the universe has a Son; who being the logos and First-begotten is also God."[18] Ignatius (A.D. 105) said, "From that time forward every sorcery and every spell was dissolved . . . when God appeared in the likeness of man unto newness of everlasting life."[19] Irenaeus (A.D. 130–202) wrote,

---

[16]An ecumenical church council was a gathering of church officials that dealt with particular doctrinal issues, the results of which were adopted by the entire Christian church. The first instance of such a gathering was when the apostles gathered at Jerusalem to address the matter of circumcision and the Gentile Christians (Acts 15). After the apostolic era, the first of a number of gatherings was at Nicea. For a helpful summary of these early councils and the doctrinal creeds that arose from them, see chapter 6 by Norman L. Geisler in this book entitled "The Essentials of the Christian Faith." Another helpful discussion of the development of early Christian doctrine is John D. Hanna, *Our Legacy: The History of Christian Doctrine* (Colorado Springs: NavPress, 2001).

[17]Interestingly, this is one of several places where the movie differs markedly from the novel. In the movie the main character, Harvard Professor of Religious Symbology Robert Langdon, disputes the claim by the novel's historian, Leigh Teabing, about Nicea and argues that the council only sanctioned what was already widely held in the churches. Other notable departures of the movie from the novel include: changing the number of alleged murders of women by the church from five million (*The Da Vinci Code*, 125) to fifty thousand (according to Langdon; "millions," according to Teabing); creating more of a distance between Opus Dei and the Vatican on the one hand and the rogue murderers seemingly acting in their names on the other; eliminating the reference to Aramaic in the discussion about the quote from the Gnostic *Gospel of Philip* (since the extant copy is a Coptic translation of the original Greek); and adding several expressions of skepticism on the part of Langdon (in addition to the one noted above about Nicea) regarding the reality of the Priory of Sion and whether Mary Magdalene actually penned the Gnostic gospel that bears her name.

[18]*First Apology of Justin Martyr*, 63:15. The writings of these early Christian leaders are easily accessible both in print and online. See, for example, J. B. Lightfoot, *The Apostolic Fathers* (Grand Rapids, MI: Baker, 1976) and L. Russ Bush, *Classical Readings in Christian Apologetics: A.D. 100–1800* (Grand Rapids, MI: Zondervan, 1983).

[19]Ignatius, *Epistle to the Ephesians*, 19.

"The Church . . . has received from the apostles and their disciples this faith: [She believes] in . . . Christ Jesus, *the Son of God*, who became incarnate for our salvation . . . and His [future] manifestation from heaven in the glory of the Father 'to gather all things in one,' and to raise up anew all flesh of the whole human race, in order that to Christ Jesus, *our Lord, and God*, and Savior, and King, according to the will of the invisible Father, 'every knee should bow.'"[20]

We can see here that Jesus was understood to be the Son of God and our Lord and God. Many other quotes could be given from this time period attesting to the fact that the divinity of Jesus, far from being invented by Constantine at the Council of Nicea, was held by Christians more than a century before.[21]

The Early Attestation of the New Testament Documents

The novel claims: The Bible as we know it was collated by Constantine at the Council of Nicea in A.D. 325.

Response: The four Gospels of the New Testament were attested to long before Constantine and Nicea. The early attestation of the four canonical Gospels of Matthew, Mark, Luke, and John can be seen in several early writings.[22] The *Muratorian Canon* was discovered in 1740 by Italian historian Ludovico Antonio Muratori. It is an eighth-century copy of a document dated around the late second century. The first few lines are missing, but the text reads "The third book of the gospel is that according to Luke. . . . The fourth of the gospels is that of John, one of the disciples."[23] It names only four Gospels and names the writings of Valentinus, who was an important Gnostic writer of that time, as being excluded from the Church.[24]

The Church Father Irenaeus has an extended discussion for why there are four Gospels.[25] Other early Christian writers or writings that attest to, quote, or make allusions to the Gospels include Origen's *Homily on Luke*

---

[20]Irenaeus, *Against Heresies*, I, 10, 1, emphasis added.
[21]See, for example, Mathetes (c. A.D. 130), *Letter to Diognetus*, 7, 9; Clement of Alexandria (A.D. 150–215), *Christ the Educator*, 3.1; Tertullian (A.D. 150–225), *Against Praxeas*, 2; Hippolytus (A.D. 170–236), *Against the Heresy of One Noetus*, 14.
[22]The term *canonical* means that a given document was recognized by the Christian community as having apostolic authority and as being inspired by God. As such, it was included in what we now refer to as the Bible. The term *canon* means "standard" or "rule." For a discussion of the process of canonicity, see Norman L. Geisler and William E. Nix, *A General Introduction to the Bible*, revised and expanded edition (Chicago: Moody Press, 1986), 203–317.
[23]Cited in Bock, *Breaking the Da Vinci Code*, 112. See also Geisler and Nix, *General Introduction to the Bible*, 288.
[24]Bock, *Breaking the Da Vinci Code*, 112.
[25]Irenaeus, *Against Heresies*, 3.11.7. See also 3.11.8 and 3.1.1.

(A.D. 185–254), *Epistle of Barnabas* (c. 70–79), the *Didache* (c. 70–130), Papias' *Interpretation of the Oracles of the Lord* (c. 70–163), Marcion (c. 140), the Epistles of Ignatius (c. 110–117), and Clement of Rome's *Epistle to the Corinthians* (c. 95–97).[26]

It is important that one does not misunderstand the argument here. These early attestations do not, in themselves, prove that what the New Testament says about Jesus is true. What they do show, however, are the early views of the Christians regarding which documents were authoritative at an early date. Thus the novel is wrong when it says that such decisions were not made until the Council of Nicea. By the time the council convened, much of the New Testament (certainly the four canonical Gospels) was already well-established and recognized as authoritative.

The Jesus of the New Testament vs. the Jesus of the Gnostics

The novel claims: The story of Jesus is more accurately contained within the Gnostic documents than in the New Testament and shows a mere human Jesus.

Response: A comparison of the Jesus of the New Testament with the Jesus of the Gnostic gospels reveals some very interesting contrasts. But the contrasts do not follow the description that Teabing gives us in the novel. Let us first take a look at the Jesus of the Gnostic gospels.

Teabing makes a great deal out of the Nag Hammadi documents. What exactly are these documents? They were discovered in 1945 in a cave in the Egyptian desert. The documents are eighth-century Coptic[27] translations of original Greek documents dating from the second to the fourth centuries, consisting of twelve codices (books) and eight leaves from a thirteenth. Eliminating duplication, there are forty-five separate titles. Some of them have strange names like *The Hypostasis of the Archons,* *The Concept of Our Great Power,* and *The Discourse on the Eighth and Ninth.* Others have titles that contain names of biblical characters such as *The Apocryphon of James, The Gospel of Thomas,* and *The Sophia of Jesus Christ.*[28] These documents have been translated into English and are easily accessible through libraries and bookstores.[29]

---

[26]Geisler and Nix, *General Introduction to the Bible,* 288–289.
[27]Coptic was basically an ancient Egyptian language that utilized Greek letters.
[28]It is important to note that none of the Gnostic documents bearing the name of a biblical figure were actually written by that biblical figure. These documents were written more than a century after the period of the New Testament.
[29]The standard English translation is James M. Robinson, ed., *The Nag Hammadi Library: The Definitive Translation of the Gnostic Scriptures Complete in One Volume,* third revised edition (San Francisco:

Interestingly, much of the teaching contained in these documents has been known to modern scholars by way of the critics who wrote in early church history—particularly Ireneaus in his *Against Heresies*. But with the discovery of the primary sources, it allows us to read these teachings in the words of those who held them. The doctrines are a combination of Christian themes and Gnosticism; thus they are often referred to as the "Gnostic Gospels" or "Gnostic writings."[30]

But just what is Gnosticism? The term comes from the Greek word *gnosis*, meaning "knowledge." The term refers to a religious movement that began to flourish toward the end of, or soon after, the apostolic era. The movement taught that one is saved not because of any atoning work of a Savior but through a secret knowledge. Some tenets of Gnosticism include:

• The true God is a pure, immaterial fullness of light, removed from the creation.
• The material world is evil and is not a subject of ultimate redemption in the end.
• The one who suffered on the cross was not Jesus but a physical substitute.

In order to evaluate the claims of the novel, it is necessary to see the picture of Jesus that these documents actually portray. In the novel Teabing said, "And, of course, the Coptic Scrolls in 1945 at Nag Hammadi . . . in addition to telling the true Grail story . . . speak of Christ's ministry in very human terms."[31] But do they? Most of the documents are very strange and sometimes border on the incoherent (e.g., "Jesus said 'Blessed is he who came into being before he came into being'"[32]). Thus, it is difficult to glean a consistent picture of anything, though most of the teachings fall within the Gnostic worldview. Several points, however, do come through regarding the nature of Jesus. First, in the Gnostic documents there is a distinction between the living Jesus and the fleshly Jesus, the latter being the one who was crucified.[33] Second, the true identity of the Gnostic Jesus seems to reside in his transcendence apart from his incarnation.[34] In other words, the *real* Jesus was an immaterial essence, not a physical human being. This comes through to such an extent that it shows how absurd Teabing's claim actually is. Third, the Gnostic Jesus is an exalted being and an associate of

---

Harper San Francisco, 1988). All of my citations come from this edition.
[30]Other Coptic Gnostic documents have been found apart from the Nag Hammadi documents and are sometimes grouped together with them in translations (e.g., *The Gospel of Mary*, discovered in Cairo in 1896.) This document is also referenced in the novel.
[31]*The Da Vinci Code*, 234.
[32]*The Gospel of Thomas*, 19.
[33]*Apocalypse of Peter*, 81:4–21; *Second Treatise of the Great Seth*, 56:6–19.
[34]*The Letter of Peter to Philip*, 136:16–23.

the unknowable creator.[35] Fourth, the Gnostic Jesus seemingly had little regard for women.[36] This point is significant since the tenor of both the novel and Dan Brown's worldview is that Christianity is largely responsible for the repression of women and that women were much more liberated within the culture and worldview depicted by the Gnostic documents. Fifth, the Gnostic Jesus seemingly had little regard for human sexuality.[37] This is especially interesting in light of the novel's emphasis on the sacred feminine and the role of human sexuality in religious experience. Sixth, the Gnostic Jesus seemingly had little regard for decency.[38]

In stark contrast to the bizarre picture of Jesus portrayed in the Gnostic Gospels, the New Testament gives a picture of a very human Jesus.[39] We find that Jesus had a human ancestry (Matt. 1:20–25), a human birth (Luke 2:4–7), human flesh and blood (John 19:34), and a human childhood (Luke 2:21–22, 41–49, 52). In addition, Jesus experienced human hunger (Luke 4:2), human thirst (John 4:6–7), human fatigue (John 4:6), human sorrow (John 11:35), human temptation (Heb. 4:15), human pain (Matt. 26:38; 27:34, 46), and human death (Matt. 16:21).

Further, the New Testament also gives a picture of a divine Jesus. Jesus claimed to have had glory with the Father (John 17:5; cf. Isa. 42:8; 48:11) and to be the I AM (John 8:55–59; cf. Exod. 3:14). He spoke with absolute authority (Matt. 7:24–29). He claimed that God was His Father (John 5:17–18). He claimed to be one with the Father (John 10:30–33). He claimed to come forth from God (John 8:42–47). He claimed to be the only access to the Father (John 14:6). He claimed to be able to forgive sins (Matt. 9:2–7). He claimed to deserve absolute allegiance (Luke 14:26–27). He claimed to be the judge of all mankind, and that to dishonor him is to dishonor the Father (John 5:21–23). He also accepted worship (John 20:28–29; Matt. 28:9; Luke 24:52).[40]

We see from these and many other references that could be marshaled that it is the New Testament that acknowledges the reality of the humanity of Jesus,

---

[35]*The Second Treatise of the Great Seth*, 69:22–26; 70:4–7.

[36]*The Gospel of Thomas*, 114.

[37]*The Book of Thomas the Contender*, 144.9; *The Testimony of Truth*, 30:19–31:6.

[38]*The Gospel of Thomas*, 37. In the passage, Jesus talks about disrobing and not being ashamed. In all fairness, the reference here likely has to do with shedding one's physical body. But even this is in contrast to Teabing's characterization since this would show that the Gnostic Jesus had little regard for the physical body.

[39]The following points on the humanity of Jesus were adapted from Norman L. Geisler, *Baker Encyclopedia of Christian Apologetics* (Grand Rapids, MI: Baker, 1999), s.v., "Docetism," 202–203.

[40]All of these points were recognized by Jesus' contemporary critics as claims to deity. The reason some critics today say that Jesus never claimed to be divine is because they are expecting Jesus to claim deity the way they themselves would claim deity in the western culture of the twenty-first century. But that is not at all how a first-century Jew would claim deity.

not the Gnostic gospels. Further these same early descriptions, and the very words of Jesus himself, show that Jesus was also God in the flesh. If Teabing had really been interested in advancing a human Jesus, he could have done no better than the Jesus of Matthew, Mark, Luke, and John. But by placing his faith in the Nag Hammadi documents, he undermined some of the very points about Jesus' humanity that he sought to advance. Since Teabing was interested in denying a divine Jesus, it is understandable that he would want to eliminate the earliest and most reliable historical evidence, since that is exactly the picture of Jesus that the New Testament portrays. But once again he ends up being scandalized by the Nag Hammadi documents since the picture of Jesus there ends up being one of a strange metaphysical being.

The Alleged Marriage of Jesus and Mary Magdalene

The novel claims: This story also shows that Jesus was married to Mary Magdalene and fathered children.

Response: Jesus was not married. The novel advances several arguments to show that Jesus was married to Mary Magdalene. The novel's main character, Harvard Professor of Religious Symbology Robert Langdon, argues that it would have been unseemly for a first-century Jewish man to be unmarried. Further, it is sometimes argued that even if certain men were unmarried, it would have been unheard of for a Jewish rabbi to be unmarried.

In response, it needs to be pointed out that celibacy was not unheard of in first-century Judaism. We see from the writings of the Jewish historian Josephus that the sect of the Essenes celebrated celibacy.[41] Further, Jesus was not, technically speaking, a rabbi. Though he was referred to as such on occasion by his disciples, this was more of a generic term for "teacher" rather than an indication that Jesus was officially installed as a Jewish rabbi. Thus, any argument that Jesus must have been married that is based on the assumption that he was a rabbi is faulty.

Besides the supposed social demands that Langdon thinks require one to conclude that Jesus was married, Teabing advances an argument from the Gnostic Gospel of Philip:

> Flipping toward the middle of the book, Teabing pointed to a passage. "The Gospel of Philip is always as good place to start." Sophie read the passage. *And the companion of the Saviour is Mary Magdalene. Christ loved her more than all the disciples and used to kiss her often on her*

---

[41]Josephus, *Antiquities*, Book XVIII, 1, §5; *The Wars of the Jews*, II, 8, §2.

mouth. The rest of the disciples were offended by it and expressed disap-
proval. They said to him, "Why do you love her more than all us?" The
words surprised Sophie, and yet they hardly seemed conclusive. "It says
nothing of marriage." "*Au contraire.*" Teabing smiled, pointing to the
first line. "As any Aramaic scholar will tell you, the word *companion*, in
those days, literally meant *spouse*."[42]

There are several observations to make regarding Teabing's argument.
First, regarding the quote, the text does not say that Jesus kissed her on
the mouth. Teabing's translation is actually an embellishment. In actuality
it reads: "And the companion of the [. . .] Mary Magdalene. [. . . loved]
her more than [all] the disciples [and used to] kiss her [often] on her [. . .].
The rest of [the disciples . . .]. They said to him 'Why do you love her more
than all of us?'"[43] While one may safely conclude that it is saying that Mary
Magdalene was the companion of Jesus,[44] it is not at all certain that Jesus
would kiss her on the mouth.

Second, if kissing hints that they were married, what are we to make of
Judas kissing Jesus in Matthew 26:49? The fact is that, culturally, kissing
was a common gesture of hospitality and affection among friends (Rom.
16:16). Even in the Gospel of Philip, kissing seems to have a more spiritual
connotation.[45]

Third, Teabing says, "as any Aramaic scholar will tell you," but the
Gospel of Philip as we have it today is a Coptic translation of a Greek document. Thus, there is no Aramaic word to translate. Even if one argued that
it was likely that Jesus spoke Aramaic, there is no way to know what the
Aramaic word was that Jesus used.[46]

Fourth, in this passage the disciples seem to be offended that Jesus
would kiss Mary Magdalene. But if Jesus and Mary were married (as surely
the disciples would know), why would they be offended at a man kissing
his own wife?

Fifth, the disciples ask, "Why do you love her more than all of us?"
But if Jesus and Mary Magdalene were married, then this seems to be a
ridiculous question to ask a man regarding his wife. They would in effect
be asking, "Why do you love your wife more than us—a group of men?"
These last two points show that the disciples were offended that Jesus

---

[42]*The Da Vinci Code*, 246, emphasis in original.
[43]*The Gospel of Philip*, 63:34–64:2. The brackets indicate holes in the manuscript. Words within the
brackets are supplied by the translator based on several considerations including context and the constraint
upon the suggested word length based on the size of the hole.
[44]Cf. 59:9.
[45]See 58:26–59:8.
[46]As mentioned in note 17, the movie eliminates the reference to Aramaic.

seemed to show favoritism to Mary Magdalene. Clearly, even in the Gospel of Philip, in the disciples' minds there was no good reason for him to do so, and thus in their minds there was no special relationship between Jesus and Mary Magdalene.

Another reason to conclude that Jesus was not married is that it is conspicuous that Paul, in 1 Corinthians 9:4–5, when defending the right of the apostles to be accompanied by their believing wives, refers to the other apostles and even the Lord's brothers but does not mention Jesus. Surely if Jesus was married, Paul would have appealed to this fact to seal his argument. The most likely reason that he did not is because Paul knew that Jesus was not married.[47]

A closer look at Mary Magdalene reinforces the conclusion that Jesus was not married to her. It is reasonable to think that Mary Magdalene was not married at all. Though she was part of a group of women who traveled with Jesus, Mary Magdalene is never singled out as being anything special, as surely she would have been if she were the wife of Jesus. She is not tied to any male in Scripture, unlike other women (e.g., Mary, the mother of Jesus, or Mary, the wife of Clopas). Rather, this Mary is designated by her geography (Mary of Magdala). Further, while she was present at the cross, Jesus shows no special concern for her. Rather, he addresses his mother Mary and the disciple John. Thus, it seems certain that Jesus was not only not married to Mary Magdalene, but neither she nor Jesus was married at all.

CONCLUSION

Each of the four important claims of *The Da Vinci Code* has been refuted: 1) the doctrine of the deity of Christ was not the result of the Council of Nicea; 2) the Bible as we know it (particularly the four Gospels) was not collated by Constantine; 3) the story of Jesus is not more accurately contained in the Gnostic documents; and 4) Jesus was not married. What we find with the historical evidence is that the divinity of Jesus was affirmed long before Constantine and the Council of Nicea. The four Gospels of the New Testament were attested to long before Constantine and Nicea. A comparison of the Jesus of the New Testament with the Jesus of the Gnostic gospels reveals that the Gnostic Jesus is a bizarre metaphysical being with some strange views, whereas the Jesus of the New Testament is both human and divine. Finally, Jesus was not married to Mary Magdalene.

The Jesus of historic Christianity stands unscathed.

---

[47]Bock, *Breaking the Da Vinci Code*, 42–44.

CHAPTER EIGHTEEN

The Resurrection of Jesus and Recent Agnosticism

Gary Habermas

THIS ESSAY FITS LIKE A COG into a larger case that I have been developing for many years. Since I[1] along with others[2] have set forth full defenses of the historicity of Jesus' resurrection, such attempts will not be reconstructed here. Rather, I will zero in on a critique of a noteworthy trend that has appeared in recent years, albeit one that has been addressed very rarely.

CURRENT SCHOLARSHIP AND AGNOSTIC DEFAULT POSITIONS

The vast majority of critical scholars allow for a surprisingly strong basis of known historical data surrounding the end of Jesus' life and the birth of the Christian church. For example, virtually all scholars, whatever their personal beliefs, espouse or at least concede that Jesus died by Roman crucifixion and that his disciples experienced grief and disillusionment at

---

[1] For some of my most recent examples, see Gary R. Habermas, *The Risen Jesus and Future Hope* (Lanham, MD: Rowman and Littlefield, 2003); with Antony G.N. Flew, *Resurrected? An Atheist and Theist Dialogue* (Lanham, MD: Rowman and Littlefield, 2005); "Resurrection Research from 1975 to the Present: What Are Critical Scholars Saying?" *Journal for the Study of the Historical Jesus*, Vol. 3 (June 2005), 135–153; "Experiences of the Risen Jesus: The Foundational Historical Issue in the Early Proclamation of the Resurrection," *Dialog, A Journal of Theology*, Vol. 45 (2006), 289–298; "Mapping the Recent Trend Toward the Bodily Resurrection Appearances of Jesus in Light of other Prominent Critical Positions," in *The Resurrection of Jesus: John Dominic Crossan and N.T. Wright in Dialogue*, ed. Robert B. Stewart (Minneapolis: Fortress, 2006), 78–92; "The Late Twentieth-Century Resurgence of Naturalistic Responses to Jesus' Resurrection," *Trinity Journal*, Vol. 22 (2001), 179–196; for a popular treatment, with Michael Licona, see *The Case for the Resurrection of Jesus* (Grand Rapids, MI: Kregel, 2004).

[2] Many of the major examples include N.T. Wright, *The Resurrection of the Son of God* (Minneapolis: Fortress, 2003); William Lane Craig, *Assessing the New Testament Evidence for the Historicity of the Resurrection of Jesus* (Lewiston, NY: Mellen, 1989); *The Historical Argument for the Resurrection of Jesus During the Deist Controversy* (Lewiston, NY: Mellen, 1985); Stephen T. Davis, *Risen Indeed: Making Sense of the Resurrection* (Grand Rapids, MI: Eerdmans, 1993); Richard Swinburne, *The Resurrection of God Incarnate* (Oxford, UK: Oxford University, 2003).

his death, usually allowing that Jesus' burial tomb was later found empty. Then, due to experiences that they believed were appearances of the risen Jesus, the disciples were transformed, even to the point of being willing to die for their faith. At a very early date they began to proclaim the death and resurrection of Jesus Christ, and the church was born shortly afterward, founded on this gospel message. Even a few former skeptics, such as James, the brother of Jesus, and Paul, became believers after they, too, believed that they had seen the risen Jesus.

These developments in recent critical thought are intriguing. On the surface, they appear to support quite strongly the New Testament teaching that Jesus was raised from the dead. At the very least, they point to exceptionally important events that cannot be either dismissed easily or ignored. One such indication is that only a minority of scholars actually hold that any naturalistic hypotheses can account for the data.[3]

If my recent survey of well over two thousand scholarly sources in German, French, and English is accurate, a fairly strong majority of recent scholars accept not only that Jesus' disciples actually saw him in some sense after his death by crucifixion, but many scholars now even favor bodily appearances![4] While surveys, of course, do not mean that any particular position is correct, that this is the contemporary theological state provides at least some clues as to where recent scholars think the data point.

During the last two hundred or more years of theological trends, this is perhaps the closest that the predominant view has come to embracing at least the general New Testament teaching on this subject.[5] One obvious question is why more scholars do not willingly and openly seem to acknowledge their recognition or belief that Jesus was raised from the dead and that he actually was seen afterward. Why are so many caveats sometimes added to the discussion that one wonders if the scholars meant what they seemed to say in their works? Moreover, when pressed, why do some scholars at least appear to even take steps backward and end their comments by asserting something like, "Well, when all is said and done, we cannot really tell what happened. Sure, the disciples had real experiences of some sort, but we should perhaps just leave the issue there and not attempt to say what actually occurred"?

---

[3]This is in spite of the recent upturn of interest in these alternative theses. See Habermas, "The Late Twentieth-Century Resurgence of Naturalistic Responses to Jesus' Resurrection," especially 184–196.

[4]Habermas, "Mapping the Recent Trend toward the Bodily Resurrection Appearances of Jesus in Light of Other Prominent Critical Positions," in Stewart, *Resurrection of Jesus*, especially 82–92.

[5]One may, of course, disagree with my survey of recent scholars or otherwise dispute these trends. But it should be noted that if my count is anywhere close to being accurate, I would have to be mistaken by quite a large margin in order for these general observations to be overturned.

My suggestion is that this latter move is sometimes made for a variety of reasons, many of which seem to be closely related. Some scholars simply do not want to be "pinned down" to a particular view. Others perhaps do not want to sound overly conservative, especially when they are in the presence of their colleagues. On the other hand, maybe still others do not wish to be known as "liberals" either! Peer pressure of various kinds is always a very strong motivator. Other scholars do not want faith or theology to be linked too closely to historical findings, even if they actually believe in the resurrection. And perhaps some simply think that the evidence cannot be pressed beyond the initial recognition that the disciples had real experiences.

One last puzzle piece needs to be added. Rather intriguingly, in spite of these caveats that are often heard in public dialogue or in private conversation, comparatively few scholars publish that their position is agnostic, at least overtly so.[6] To return to the question of why some scholars do not appear to be more enthusiastic in their endorsement of the resurrection, even when this seems to follow from their own research, I will venture a suggestion. It is certainly arguable that while agnosticism may not be the first option, it may serve well as a fallback statement for those who perhaps feel that they have gone as far as they can in the direction of historicity, for reasons such as those just given. In other words, when scholars are pushed for specific details that indicate where they stand, some more clearly defend the historicity of the resurrection appearances, while others migrate to an agnostic response. For the latter, then, the agnostic position often functions as a sort of default setting.[7] I will present here an overview of the agnostic position, followed by a general critique.

THE AGNOSTIC POSITION ON JESUS' RESURRECTION

In keeping with these comments, it may not be surprising that relatively few developed agnostic positions on the resurrection appearances have appeared during the last few decades. More frequently, we find a brief comment here or there that may indicate such a question.[8]

---

[6]Habermas, "Mapping the Recent Trend toward the Bodily Resurrection Appearances of Jesus in Light of other Prominent Critical Positions," in Stewart, *Resurrection of Jesus*, 81–82, 91.

[7]This is also my conclusion in ibid., 204, n. 60. As a rather incredible aside, it is always amazing that when this sort of specific clarification is requested, those who move to the conservative side are often called "apologists" or non-scholars, while those who take the agnostic stance are thought of as being "careful" or "scholarly"!

[8]G. T. Eddy pleads, "let us allow more room . . . for a reverent agnosticism about bodies and tombs," in "The Resurrection of Jesus Christ: A Consideration of Professor Cranfield's Argument," *Expository Times*, Vol. 101 (1990), 329. Sometimes it is even difficult to know if this is what the scholar is implying. One possibility is the comment by Richard A. Burridge and Graham Gould that they are not sure of the

One exception is the change of emphasis in Willi Marxsen's nuanced resurrection research. In older treatments that manifested Rudolf Bultmann's ongoing influence, Marxsen produced a rare example that favored a natural understanding of Jesus' resurrection.[9] Still, he hinted that there was room for an agnostic stance.[10] In a later volume, perhaps reflecting the changed scholarly climate more in favor of the resurrection, Marxsen concluded that he did not know whether Jesus appeared in a subjective or an objective manner.[11]

More recently, per Bart Ehrman, we can know a number of historical items such as those that we have outlined above. For example, "we can say with complete certainty that some of his disciples at some later time insisted that . . . he soon appeared to them, convincing them that he had been raised from the dead." Explaining further, "Historians, of course, have no difficulty whatsoever speaking about the belief in Jesus' resurrection, since this is a matter of public record. For it is a historical fact that some of Jesus' followers came to believe that he had been raised from the dead soon after his execution."[12]

Still, Ehrman thinks that as we address these crucial questions, we also get into areas that we *cannot* know about the resurrection appearances. For instance, "we cannot be completely certain, historically, that Jesus' tomb was actually empty." Further, as historians, "we cannot say that Jesus was actually raised from the dead." Yet, each of these beliefs can be affirmed by faith.[13] So here we find ourselves in a quandary between what we can know, what we cannot know, and what we can believe.

Peter Carnley's version of agnosticism is of a different sort. Like virtually all scholars today, he is sure that the disciples at least thought that they had seen Jesus, who they believed was alive after his death: "It seems clear enough that, on the basis of these alleged experiences, the disciples were convinced that they had seen the raised Christ."[14] Later he reaffirms this:

---

sense in which Jesus was raised; see their *Jesus Then and Now* (Grand Rapids, MI: Eerdmans, 2004), 208. They may simply be saying that Jesus *was* raised in some sense, but that they are not prepared to give details. Dale Allison muses on the sense in which it might be said that Jesus rose from the dead in his *Resurrecting Jesus: The Earliest Christian Tradition and Its Interpreters* (New York: T. and T. Clark, 2005), 364–375.

[9]Willi Marxsen, *The Resurrection of Jesus of Nazareth*, trans. Margaret Kohl (Philadelphia: Fortress, 1970), especially 88–97. An earlier essay by Marxsen was a forerunner, while featuring its own phase of development: "The Resurrection of Jesus as a Historical and Theological Problem," in *The Significance of the Message of the Resurrection for Faith in Jesus Christ*, ed. C.F.D. Moule (London: SCM, 1968), 5–50.

[10]Marxsen, *The Resurrection of Jesus of Nazareth*, 96, 119, 126, 152.

[11]Willi Marxsen, *Jesus and Easter: Did God Raise the Historical Jesus from the Dead?*, trans. Victor Paul Furnish (Nashville: Abingdon, 1990), 70–74.

[12]Bart Ehrman, *Jesus: Apocalyptic Prophet of the New Millennium* (New York: Oxford University Press, 1999), 230–231.

[13]Ibid., 229.

[14]Peter Carnley, *The Structure of Resurrection Belief* (Oxford, UK: Clarendon Press, 1987), 64.

"Meanwhile, there is no doubt that the first disciples interpreted the Easter visions or appearances as signs of the heavenly presence of Christ."[15]

However, while historical investigation does have some value,[16] it is ultimately inconclusive regarding the resurrection.[17] Still, Carnley thinks that Christians have internal confirmation of the resurrected Jesus, which is due, not to the rigors of historical research, but to the witness of the Holy Spirit.[18] So Carnley's agnosticism is with regard to the results of historical investigation rather than the truth of the resurrection itself.

Probably the most developed account of resurrection agnosticism is the thesis of A.J.M. Wedderburn, who begins his treatment of the question by clearly stating that many of the key resurrection questions *are* historical in nature.[19] Accordingly, he affirms a list of data very similar to that mentioned at the outset of this essay. For instance: "It is an indubitable historical datum that sometime, somehow the disciples came to believe that they had seen the risen Jesus."[20]

However, Wedderburn concludes his study by supporting the verdict of "a reverent agnosticism." While there are good data that favor the resurrection appearances, and the naturalistic alternatives are problematic, perhaps even clearly so, a supernatural event like a resurrection or the resulting afterlife are difficult barriers to overcome. The result is that skeptics will probably not be convinced by historical arguments. So the verdict is, "Not proven."[21]

He admits that this leaves a very difficult pastoral problem with those who need assistance in areas of guilt, suffering, bereavement, and fear of the unknown, given a faith that is agnostic and "vulnerable at all points." One might be tempted to tell such hurting persons that they will be reunited with their loved ones after death, but can this be affirmed in good conscience?[22]

These agnostic positions share several features. Historical study is deemed to be at least partially applicable and even able to establish a number of relevant data. For example, for each researcher, it is clearly the case that Jesus' disciples were convinced that they had seen the risen Jesus after his death. Yet, ultimately, history is judged to be deficient, either as an

---

[15]Ibid., 246.
[16]Ibid., 95, 225–226.
[17]Ibid., 72, 264.
[18]Ibid., 248–265, especially 248–249, 256, 259–265.
[19]A.J.M. Wedderburn, *Beyond Resurrection* (Peabody, MA: Hendrickson, 1999), 12–19, 21–22, 38.
[20]Ibid., 13.
[21]Ibid., especially 95–98, but also 134, 153, 218–219, 221, 225.
[22]Ibid., especially 221–226.

insufficient basis for exercising faith or at least as grounds for supporting the facticity of the resurrection. One common element here seems to be that Jesus' resurrection appears to require an acknowledgment of supernatural activity, and this remains problematic. Nonetheless, the resurrection can still be believed as a tenet of faith.

PROBLEMS WITH THE AGNOSTIC POSITION ON THE RESURRECTION

It will be no surprise that I find the agnostic position on the resurrection of Jesus to be rather problematic, and on multiple grounds. Here I will discuss an ascending series of six problems with this approach.

First, as often happens with responses to rival positions, occasionally the case against one's opponent is biased. Expressed popularly, the cards are frequently stacked in such a manner that the task of establishing the contrary position, from the outset, is more difficult than it need be. This is a less serious offense and can certainly be corrected.

Wedderburn provides a couple of examples here. He states that the historical defense of the resurrection would not convince a skeptic.[23] Further, the verdict against the supernatural positions of either resurrection or afterlife is "Not proven."[24]

But since when is convincing a person of the opposite persuasion a prerequisite for arguing that one's view is fairly indicated by the data? Is it not the case that the opposite could also be said with assurance? How likely is it that the argument constructed by a skeptic or agnostic would convince a believer against his/her position? I doubt that either side wants this to be a prerequisite for their rationality!

Moreover, virtually no scholar requires that one's position be "proven." In any inductive discipline, including history, probability is the guide for research. Thus, to label the position taken by an opponent as "Not proven" is to assume a standard that *no* historian can live by. Neither can the agnostic position be "proven," and this ought not even be required. Speaking evidentially, then, we need to be satisfied with a probable argument. That is all that is required. In our case, we therefore want to know if the resurrection is the most likely event.

Second, the agnostic position usually entails its own burden of proof. If a scholar is satisfied to assert that agnosticism is simply his private view, then that is, of course, his option. But if a stronger position is taken—that

[23]Ibid., 95.
[24]Ibid., 225.

neither we nor others are able to ascertain a cause for the origin of the disciples' faith—then this assertion assumes its own burden of proof. Now we are justified in asking *why* this stronger agnostic position is held. In this case, *both* the agnostic and the theistic assertions about the resurrection should be prepared to evidence their positions. The agnostic position is not established simply by the *claim* that we can go no further. How or why should the conclusion halt at precisely this point? *Why* is it the case that we cannot get behind the data and know what happened to the disciples?

But now agnostic scholars may have reached a dilemma. They can be satisfied with the very personal stance above and the resulting private view that it entails, devoid of evidential force. In this sense, their position might be comparable to those who say that they believe firmly in the bodily resurrection of Jesus but will not produce any data in its favor, since it is enough that it is true "in their hearts." Both are personal positions without confirmation. Or agnostics can accept their own burden of proof and provide *reasons* why no one is able to go any further.[25] Too often it is thought to be evidentially insufficient to "simply believe," while agnostics have the evidential privilege to "simply assert" their view. This frequent disparity in positions must change.

Third, at a deeper theoretical level than the previous point, until a philosophical position that questions or denies the supernatural realm is itself established, the agnostic begs the question by assuming the truth of that position. So are we justified in doubting miracles?

As a specific example, many have commented that the occurrence of a miracle is highly unlikely, if not impossible, since it involves a supernatural occurrence.[26] But as Stephen Parrish asks, "why are miracles widely accepted as extremely improbable?" If one *knew* that a particular philosophical position that basically disallowed miracles was true, "then one would be completely justified in assigning miracles a very low order of antecedent probability." But this is the very position that must be demonstrated, not assumed. Apart from such a heavily-evidenced case, one has begged the question against the possibility of miracles.[27] Thus, no matter

---

[25]Or they could, of course, try to dispute who has the burden of proof.

[26]Ehrman asserts that miracles "by definition, are infinitesimally remote" (*Jesus: Apocalyptic Prophet of the New Millennium*, 196; cf. 228). Here he confuses the unlikelihood that a miracle will happen *at any given moment* with the overall near-impossibility of miracles anytime, anywhere. But to hold that the latter is true by definition, as Ehrman clearly states, is more than a confusion. It also provides a good example of this error, for he must *assume* a particular philosophical stance in order to "know" this about miracles, for he has certainly not proven that miracles virtually never occur. And by assuming such a perspective, he ignores and begs the ery question that he is trying to address.

[27]Stephen E. Parrish, *God and Necessity: A Defense of Classical Theism* (Lanham, MD: University Press of America, 1997), 156–157; cf. 172.

how strongly such an agnostic stance is asserted, it still fails, having committed an informal logical fallacy.

Fourth, the agnostic scholars above argue or imply that a major problem with affirming that God raised Jesus is that such an event involves supernatural activity. But many researchers, including those who affirm the resurrection, note that it is problematic to argue *historically* that a particular event was a miracle. Arguably, history as a discipline is unable to show that *God* acted in a particular event. History may only be able to decide on the status of the event itself since, as historians, we may only be able to judge the evidence for what happens in the time-space world and decide on that.

On such a distinction, then, we can only study the historical ramifications of two events: did Jesus really die, and did his followers see him after that point? A real death for a historical figure and seeing a person in time and space are both matters that historical and other inductive research (such as documents, interviews, medical data, and so on) can determine. In other words, history *can* study the side of the issue that occurred in its own domain. But whether this event was a *miracle* or whether *God raised Jesus from the dead* are distinct philosophical questions and must be treated differently from historical questions.[28]

On this specific point, I actually *agree* with the agnostic scholars. We can view the historical portion of the miracle-*claim*, as Wedderburn states, by examining its this-worldly components. Therefore, for the purposes of this essay, all I want to know are these same two questions: 1) whether, according to the canons of historical probability, Jesus died, and 2) whether human witnesses saw him afterward. We can agree not to cloud the issue with other questions.[29] So we will therefore suspend judgment on the supernatural portion of the issue of the *cause* of the resurrection.

Wedderburn correctly recognizes this crucial distinction between historical investigation and one's philosophical and theological position.[30] Moreover, he also makes the same distinction between the historical portion of a claim and the philosophical part. Answering those who argue that history and revelation are sometimes so intertwined that we cannot

---

[28]I still think that the philosophical side of the question of whether God raised Jesus can be answered definitely. For many details, see Habermas, *The Risen Jesus and Future Hope*, Chaps. 2–3.

[29]For my discussions of this distinction between the historical and philosophical sides of an issue, see ibid., especially 4–5; see also Gary R. Habermas, *The Historical Jesus: Ancient Evidence for the Life of Christ* (Joplin, MO: College Press, 1996), 60–61.

[30]Wedderburn, *Beyond Resurrection*, 97; cf. 12–19, 21–22, 38. Ehrman agrees about the role of our beliefs but incorrectly seems to remove these items from anything but the realm of faith (*Jesus: Apocalyptic Prophet of the New Millennium*, 229).

investigate the claims at all, Wedderburn states that even such events "have a side, a dimension, which *is* open to history and the historian . . . the fact that it is supposed to be a revelation *in history* means that human eyes have seen something and human ears have heard something. . . .This side of the revelatory act is open to history . . . [and] must be scrutinized to ascertain its trustworthiness and credibility."[31]

How would this translate to a study of the resurrection? Here Wedderburn applies well his previous point: "The resurrection-event itself may be beyond the reach of historians, but they can still pass judgment on whether that event is needed at all to explain what *is* within their reach, namely the early Christians' claim that Jesus had been raised." So Wedderburn thinks that history cannot tell whether God was actually involved in the resurrection event, but is it still necessary to determine whether "some such event occurred and impinged upon and occasioned the more obviously human events of which we do know? This *is* a historical question to which the historian can attempt to give some sort of answer."[32]

Distressingly, Wedderburn seems to forget his own distinction later when he decides in favor of agnosticism. When discussing naturalistic alternatives to the resurrection, he judges that, "however unconvincing they may seem," these options have an advantage over supernatural origins for this event.[33] So even though natural hypotheses do not seem to explain the data that we have, they may be better than looking to the supernatural for an explanation. But we have agreed that the discipline of history cannot answer the supernatural portion of the question. So why bring it up again and prejudice the decision?

Thus, rather than keeping the clear distinction that he called for earlier between human observations in space and time and any possible supernatural cause of this event, Wedderburn crosses his own line and leaves the realm of historical investigation. He even decides that rather "unconvincing" natural options are probably better than supernatural explanations. So he crosses his own line of historical research and then opts for what he takes to be a less likely cause. But we should note that he does this *because* the miraculous possibility does not fit well with his own preconceptions!

I end this fourth critique by a call to reaffirm Wedderburn's own methodology. We cannot answer with historical tools whether *God* is the one who raised Jesus from the dead. Rather, our attention is on a smaller, more

---

[31]Wedderburn, *Beyond Resurrection*, 15 (emphasis in original).
[32]Ibid., 14–15 (emphasis in original).
[33]Ibid., 96–97.

focused goal: is agnosticism the best explanation for the death and later sightings of Jesus?

Fifth, in making a case for Jesus' resurrection by using only the recognized historical data that are conceded by virtually all critical scholars, including agnostics, we have the advantage of a factual cartel from which we might draw for our discussion. Agnostic questioning sometimes makes it appear that the scholar did not want to follow the evidence to its conclusion, functioning as a way to stop the proceedings before they ever begin pointing in the direction of the resurrection. However, it is certainly possible that these shared data could remove the agnostic question mark. If naturalistic theories have failed or are even less likely options, then perhaps we have plenty of evidence already to decide the case. The point, then, is that critical scholars ought not reject or pull up short of the results that proceed from their own research.

Instead of looking at less likely data, such as concentrating on textual conflicts that are not part of these recognized historical findings, perhaps it can be determined that more than an undefined "something" occurred to Jesus' disciples. The key here is to major not on what we think we *cannot* know, but on what our own methodology indicates that we *can* know. Do we *already* have an adequate foundation from which we might answer this question? Scholars need to address viably the results of their own research. Of course, they can *deny* the conclusion of the resurrection, but this is different from providing an adequate explanation.

So we may already possess precisely what we need. Since scholars readily concede that Jesus' disciples had experiences that they *thought* were appearances of Jesus after his death, these need to be explained. If naturalistic hypotheses do not viably do so, then we must look elsewhere for what *convinced them* of this. In other words, did the disciples *really* see him later or not? Anything less is an inadequate response. By using only those data to which scholars agree, we may already have adequate grounds to argue that Jesus' followers actually saw him alive after his death. So we need to stay focused precisely on this particular issue. If the resurrection appearances follow, then we have successfully made a historical case for them. We must account for our shared data.[34]

By pulling up short with an agnostic response, we may actually curtail the historiographical process, bypassing the very information that might

---

[34]This is the portion of the argument on which I have concentrated the most over the years, and where I think that the case is at its strongest. The interested reader is referred to the sources in footnote 1 above for examples of this research.

establish the appearances as the most likely explanation. Fuller is right in asserting that the factual situation "therefore requires that the historian postulate some other event" as an adequate reason for the disciples' conviction. We must have a "cause of the Easter faith. . . . outside of their belief."[35]

Sixth, regarding the frequent objection that such a conclusion might still involve a supernatural act, hence making it less likely, a last, potent suggestion needs to be made. This response potentially nullifies the objection that when faced with a supernatural event, we must draw back to the agnostic stance, strictly to avoid the miraculous claim.[36] Although the case definitely cannot be argued here, I have pointed out at length elsewhere that an exceptionally strong evidential case can be made for an afterlife, based on highly evidential near-death experiences (NDEs).

The sorts of cases that I have in mind are not the more popular, much publicized accounts of floating above one's body, proceeding down a tunnel, and seeing a light or deceased loved ones. I am referring to highly evidential reports of near-death individuals being able to recount surroundings as well as events, sometimes even those that occur a distance away from themselves, all of which are subsequently confirmed. Sometimes these reports occur in the absence of heartbeat (including flat EKG readings) or brain waves (including flat EEG readings) or where the patient is congenitally blind.[37]

I have argued that by far the most likely conclusion to be drawn is that at least the best of these cases strongly evidence what I have termed "minimalistic life after death," in that they indicate consciousness beyond the initial stages of death. While I do not think that NDEs are miraculous events, they do evidence a supernatural realm.

The relevance for the resurrection is that not only would a supernatural realm beyond this world exist, but the confirmation concerns the specific area of life after death.[38] The claim of agnostic doubt is that we cannot

---

[35]Reginald Fuller, *The Formation of the Resurrection Narratives* (Philadelphia: Fortress Press, 1980), 169, 181.

[36]We have already argued that such a response most frequently neglects its own burden of proof, begs the question by assuming the truth of its own worldview, and fails to distinguish the historical side of the miracle-claim.

[37]For many such cases and listings of relevant sources, sometimes from medical journals, as well as detailed arguments for an afterlife, see Gary R. Habermas and J. P. Moreland, *Beyond Death: Exploring the Evidence for Immortality* (Wheaton, IL: Crossway Books, 1998; Eugene, OR: Wipf and Stock, 2003), Chaps. 7–9. See also Habermas, *The Risen Jesus and Future Hope*, 60–62; Gary R. Habermas, "Near-Death Experiences and the Evidence—A Review Essay," *Christian Scholar's Review*, Vol. 26 (1996), 78–85; Gary R. Habermas, "Paradigm Shift: A Challenge to Naturalism," *Bibliotheca Sacra*, Vol. 146 (1984), 437–450, especially 444–449.

[38]It may be remembered that Wedderburn also links together these two topics (*Beyond Resurrection*, 129–134, 222–226).

decide on such *events or realm*. But if an afterlife is a reality, the popular objection against the resurrection that supernatural events are practically impossible loses a great deal of its force. And if an afterlife is a reality, the resurrection could be investigated strictly on its own grounds in order to ascertain if it is a unique instance of this reality. Since the evidence for the disciples seeing an appearance of Jesus after his death is so strong, this would be a final blow to the agnostic option.

A lingering agnostic concern might be that Jesus' resurrection would still be a unique event.[39] But according to the fourth critique above, at the very least we should not pursue the question of the miraculous side of the resurrection but rather investigate this-worldly, historical aspects of this event. Did Jesus die? Was he seen afterward? The way is now totally clear to pose and answer these questions.

Is there is a path by which we may move from the most secure historical facts to the historical appearances of Jesus? That Jesus died and that afterward his early followers thought they saw him again are both held by virtually all critical scholars, including agnostics. Most critical scholars also concede that natural alternative hypotheses are unable to explain these data. This scenario indicates that the best explanation for what occurred is that Jesus was seen by his disciples after his death. More succinctly, that the early disciples really thought that they had seen Jesus after his death, coupled with the failure of naturalistic alternative hypotheses, indicates that the early disciples probably did see Jesus again. The more thoroughly these natural options are disproven, the more probably Jesus' appearances are indicated. This is the inference to the best historical explanation.

CONCLUSION: TO PULL BACK OR MOVE AHEAD?

So where does this discussion leave us? We began this essay with a list of facts that is accepted as historical by the vast majority of scholars who comment on the issues, regardless of their personal beliefs or theological outlook. Other pertinent data could be added to the list too. The relevant question, then, is whether we ought to pull back and conclude that in spite of these data almost anything is preferable to Jesus' appearances after death, as Wedderburn does. Or ought we to move ahead and affirm that an examination of the historical portion of Jesus' resurrection-claim pushes us to the conclusion that it is indeed the best explanation of our data?

---

[39]To be sure, the resurrection was not an NDE, for several reasons. The relevant texts indicate that Jesus 1) was really dead, 2) was raised in his own (although now changed) body, and 3) would never die again. The apostle Paul taught that Jesus was the very first to be raised in this manner (1 Cor. 15:20).

Some scholars think that agnosticism has the advantage of always taking the natural path; hence its question marks regarding the supernatural. But I have argued that the agnostic alternative is seriously troubled by an ascending series of at least six problems, many of which are quite troublesome. For starters, besides some overstatements that need adjusting, taking the agnostic stance on the resurrection may be simply a private notion devoid of its own reasons. But if the position is asserted, the mere claim is insufficient; a burden of proof is entailed. *Why*, precisely, can we not get behind the data and know what happened to Jesus' disciples? Why are the data insufficient? Why should we stop exactly here?

Additionally, unless a deeper philosophical position that questions the supernatural is itself established, the agnostic begs the question against that realm. On what grounds are we justified in doubting the occurrence of miracles? What determines that this alternative outlook on the world is correct?

Further, I actually *agree* with the agnostic contention that historians are only able to investigate the historical side of a miracle-claim. Yet, research *still* may show both that Jesus died and that he was seen afterward by his followers. We could table the supernatural portion of the question regarding the *cause* of the resurrection. But the balance would be shifting well away from agnosticism, because its skepticism of the supernatural is now a moot point.

Moreover, if the historical facts on which scholars agree strongly favor the resurrection, then the central claim that Jesus was seen after his death would still obtain, and now agnosticism would be on the run! But lastly, if the many well-evidenced near-death experiences establish at least a minimalistic afterlife, it would appear that the nature of this reality drives a final nail in the agnostic coffin. For if life after death actually exists, we *now know* about the reality of a central, relevant tenet that agnostics have long questioned. So, pursuing only the historical side of the issue, Jesus could have lived after his death.

As just summarized above, the fact that the early disciples really thought that they had seen Jesus after his death, when juxtaposed with the failure of natural alternative hypotheses, indicates that the early disciples probably did see Jesus again. The more these natural options fail, the more Jesus' appearances emerge as the probable inference to the best historical explanation.

Therefore, the view that Jesus was indeed raised from the dead makes the best sense of the historical and other data. For those who already think that God exists or that there are other reasons to hold to a supernatural realm (see some examples in the other chapters in this volume), these would provide additional clinchers to the argument here.

The agnostic position on the resurrection exhibits the modern charm that is engendered by a scholarly shoulder shrug, accompanied by a verdict of, "We can't be sure." But it opts for the question mark without realizing that this maneuver exposes a position that is devoid of solid reasons that would establish its position. Exactly why can't we know the nature of the disciples' experiences? Further, how is the agnostic position itself established? And since we are only investigating the historical side of these claims, what about the strong evidence that Jesus was seen after his death, especially when NDEs indicate that agnostics are already mistaken regarding the cognate realm of an afterlife?

By championing the question mark, agnosticism works itself too quickly into a corner, opening itself up to the precise contrary data that can disprove it. Here it comes up very short on a number of crucial questions in areas where we already have plenty of data to draw positive conclusions.

PART FOUR

World
Religious Movements

CHAPTER NINETEEN

Mormonism

Kurt Van Gorden

INTRODUCTION

Dr. John Warwick Montgomery correctly argues for the integration of Christian apologetics in virtually every aspect of Christian thinking: "The 21st century Apologist needs to take Apologetics far more seriously. He needs to incorporate Apologetics into every aspect of his or her ministry: every sermon, every class, every evangelistic activity."[1] The church is besieged by hostilities on every side. She therefore has an inescapable scriptural duty to defend her faith, not just against atheism, agnosticism, and worldly philosophy, but also against cults,[2] sects, heresies, the occult, and world religions.

Mormonism[3] stands out among the cults that attack the church since Christianity is condemned in their canonized scripture. Joseph Smith's "first vision" in 1820 broadly condemned Christianity by saying that our churches are "all wrong," our creeds are "an abomination," and our members are "all corrupt."[4] Smith followed this with the proclamation that his church is "the only true and living church upon the face of the whole earth."[5]

In apologetics, the concern is not with those who throw rocks but rather with their publicized attacks against Christianity that, if left unan-

---

[1]John Warwick Montgomery, "Defending the Hope That Is in Us: Apologetics for the 21st Century," *Trinity Global Journal* 4(2); http://www.trinitysem.edu/journal/4-2/montgomery-budapest-essay.htm (accessed March 30, 2006), modified and republished in this volume.
[2]The term *cult* is used here as a non-pejorative theological description. The Christian church has used the term *cult* in this way since the late nineteenth century, when it was also first applied to Mormonism.
[3]The Church of Jesus Christ of Latter-day Saints is the official name for the Mormon Church. However, Joseph Smith used "Mormon" and "Mormonism" and declared that "Mormonism is truth" (*The Personal Writings of Joseph Smith* [Salt Lake City: Deseret, 1984], 420).
[4]*Pearl of Great Price*, 1:19.
[5]*Doctrine and Covenants*, 1:30.

swered, are potentially deceiving to multitudes of people. In defense of
the church, the apostle Jude wrote, "I found it necessary to write appealing to you to contend for the faith that was once for all delivered to the
saints."[6] Jude found this "necessary" because he faced precisely what we
face today—namely, sects and heresies springing up to deceive the unwary.
His use of the word "contend" is strong and cannot be translated with less
emphasis.[7] Jude is not alone in his convictions, for several passages of the
New Testament are dedicated to defending the person, work, and gospel
of Jesus Christ.

The modern church lacks this kind of apostolic apologetics. The world
wants to baptize the church in relativism, subjectivism, non-judgmentalism,
and pluralism that make all religions equally valid and Jesus by any other
description just as legitimate. Instead of mounting a courageous defense,
the church slumbers in passivity, forgetting that Christ's enemies do not
sleep. One who loves the gospel of the Lord Jesus Christ cannot help but
defend it in all quarters, among all people, and under all circumstances.

We cannot convert anyone to Christ—that is God's work alone. But
apologetics is a tool that God used both in New Testament times and
throughout the centuries to convince unbelievers of Christian claims. In
some cases, unbelievers see the argument and still reject Christ, just as King
Agrippa did when he said to Paul, "In a short time would you persuade me
to be a Christian?" (Acts 26:28). In other situations, as in Athens, Paul gave
his defense, and "some men joined him and believed" (Acts 17:34). Paul
realized that once the seed of God's Word is planted, the result is left to God
(1 Cor. 3:7; 2 Tim. 2:25). The same is true when evangelizing Mormons;
some will believe, and some will not, but we are to give a reasonable defense
of God's truth nonetheless.

Paul also tells us that the mind is the premier battleground for deception: "But I am afraid that as the serpent deceived Eve by his cunning, your
thoughts will be led astray from a sincere and pure devotion to Christ" (2
Cor. 11:3). Regarding this battle, G. K. Chesterton referred to "the suicide
of thought" that is occurring and noted that "the whole modern world is at
war with reason."[8] Today our ability to reason has not diminished as much
as our unwillingness to reason. Subjective feelings are too often preferred
to what is logical, sound, coherent, and cohesive. So it is with the subjective Mormon truth-test—the testimony or "burning in the bosom" (as my

---

[6]Jude 1:3. All biblical citations in this chapter are from *The Holy Bible: English Standard Version*, unless
otherwise noted.
[7]*The Good News Bible* translates this as "fight on for the faith."
[8]Gilbert Keith Chesterton, *Orthodoxy* (London: The Bodley Head, 1927), 54.

deceased Mormon grandmother used to call it)—which too frequently takes precedence over contradictions between the Bible and Mormon doctrine.

There exists yet another "war with reason" in terms of how Christians deal with Mormon heresy. Certain evangelicals have tried new approaches to interfaith relations with Mormons that stand apart from historic apologetics,[9] and apologetic methods employed by Christians in the past are abandoned as useless. Some have even called a truce and engaged Mormons in "common ground" dialogue.[10] Two kinds of conduct have emerged. One is total passivity, which is found in the "Johnson-Millet dialogue." Here Rev. Gregory C. V. Johnson represents the evangelical position in dialogue with a BYU professor, Robert L. Millet, who represents the Mormon position. The emphasis on theological differences is dropped in lieu of developing personal friendships that have value "beyond the ability to convert somebody."[11] Mormonism is no longer described as a false religion, sect, or cult but is viewed as a "culture and not a cult," a "Sacred Tribe," or our "Neighboring Faith."[12]

The second kind of conduct is reflected in the "New Mormon-Evangelical Dialogue,"[13] which pursues vigorous theological discussions but results in some evangelical participants inferring that Mormons are their brothers in Christ without a rejection of Mormonism or a confession of Christian doctrine.[14] This is strangely reminiscent of the ecumenism of the 1950s where several Utah Protestant churches followed the lead of the liberal theologian Marcus Bach in declaring Mormons their brothers and sisters in Christ.[15] Despite the well-meaning intentions of these Christians,

---

[9]In the 1990s Rev. Gregory C. V. Johnson encouraged his Ogden Valley Baptist Church to jointly meet with the local Mormon Church as an interfaith approach. A Provo Assembly of God pastor, Rev. Dean Jackson, also proclaimed "1998 [as the] year of repentance" toward Mormons. This included inviting a Mormon Area Authority to speak at his church service, even though 2 John 10 forbids such (cf. *Christianity Today*, February 7, 2000, 66).

[10]There is no argument here against common-ground discussions for evangelism. The problem is that common-ground apologetics is replaced by common-ground friendship, which puts off the question of personal salvation sometimes for years (see, for example, the Johnson-Millet dialogue, Boise, March 2004, where the question was put to Millet by another Christian some six years later).

[11]Johnson-Millet dialogue, The Rock Church (July 29, 2003) in Salt Lake City, Utah.

[12]Writer John Morehead states that Mormonism is not a cult but a "Sacred Tribe" or our "Neighboring Faith" (www.sacredtribes.com). Greg Johnson often refers to Mormonism as "our theological other" (Johnson-Millet dialogue, Boise, March 2004). Some try to call Mormonism a culture rather than a cult. However, nothing prevents it from being both a culture and cult.

[13]For a critical review of the inherent weaknesses, consult Dr. James A. Beverley's lecture at the Evangelical Theological Society, 2005, "The New Mormon-Evangelical Dialogue: The Zacharias Case and the Views of Robert Millet" (St. Louis: ACTS, 2005).

[14]Richard Mouw, in Robert Millet's *A Different Jesus* (Grand Rapids, MI: Eerdmans, 2005), wrote: "I think that an open-minded Christian reader of this book will sense that Bob Millet is in fact trusting in the Jesus of the Bible for his salvation. That is certainly my sense" (p. 183).

[15]Bach's chapter "The Mormon," from *The Faith of My Friends* (New York: Bobbs-Merrill, 1951), was so favorable to Mormonism from a Protestant minister's viewpoint that the Mormon press, Deseret Books, obtained rights to reprint it. Protestants also participated with Mormons in joint Thanksgiving, Christmas,

there remains a serious risk in providing a false security for Mormons who still reject the central tenets of Christianity.

Friendships of this nature, which do not draw clearly distinctive theological lines, are dangerous, particularly for weak Christians. I personally know of Christians who became baptized Mormons after attending the Johnson-Millet dialogue because they saw no difference between Mormonism and Christianity. In these dialogues, some of which I attended, Christianity was not defended and the differences between Mormonism were not delineated.[16]

Mormons and evangelicals cannot utter the word *God* without an ontological conflict arising between the notions of visible and invisible or material and spirit. God the Father in Mormonism is a man born on another planet[17] who worshiped a Father god before him,[18] who was also once a mortal man just as we are[19] and was therefore a contingent being dependent on food, water, and air for survival. God the Father in Christianity is invisible, eternal, the uncreated Creator, immaterial Spirit, immutable, omnipotent, omniscient, omnipresent, and does not progress from a lower state to a higher state of existence.[20] Once the distinctions between these two Gods are obliterated, the true God is lowered to the level of a common god. It seems clearer (and more biblical) to insist upon lucid definitions from the outset rather than try to repair mangled definitions later.[21]

Easter, choir, prayer, and worship services. The LDS *Church News* (Deseret News, Salt Lake City) is a good resource for tracking these joint activities in the 1900s.

[16]In the Johnson-Millet dialogues, Johnson admitted that listeners may not know "which guy was the Mormon or which guy was the evangelical," although he hopes otherwise (Boise, March 2004). He also posted an article from the Utah State University dialogue on his web site (June 2003) that stated, "Indeed, a striking trait of their public conversation was that it was hard to tell who was of which faith"; www.standingtogether.org/faithinteraction (accessed March 26, 2004).

[17]Joseph Smith wrote, "The Father has a body of flesh and bones as tangible as man's" (*D & C*, 130:22). Furthermore, "he was once a man like us; yea, that God himself, the Father of us all, dwelt on an earth, the same as Jesus Christ himself did" (Joseph Smith, *Documentary History of the Church*, 6:305). I refute this doctrine in my book *Mormonism* (Grand Rapids, MI: Zondervan, 1995).

[18]Joseph Fielding Smith, the tenth LDS prophet, wrote, "Our Father in heaven, according to the Prophet, had a Father." Joseph Fielding Smith, *Doctrines of Salvation* (Salt Lake City: Bookcraft, 1955), 2:47.

[19]Joseph Fielding Smith stated, "Evidently his Father passed through a period of mortality even as he [Jesus] passed through mortality, and as we all are doing." Ibid. Brigham Young claimed that God the Father was of the "same species" as man (*Journal of Discourses*, 4:217).

[20]Cf. invisible (Col. 1:15; Heb. 11:27), eternal (1 Tim. 1:17), the uncreated Creator (Gen. 1:1; John 1:3), immaterial Spirit (John 4:24; Hos. 11:9), immutable (Mal. 3:6), omnipotent (Rev. 19:6; 21:22), omniscient (Ps. 147:5; Isa. 40:28), omnipresent (1 Kings 8:27; Jer. 23:24), and does not progress from a lower state to a higher state of existence (Ps. 102:26–27).

[21]An example is found in the Johnson-Millet dialogues in reference to whether the atonement of Christ took place in the Garden of Gethsemane or on the cross. Millet said, "So if you were to ask a Latter-day Saint, 'Where did the atonement take place?' [and] he were to give, or she were to give, the correct Scriptural answer, they would say, 'What began at Gethsemane was finished on the cross.'" Johnson replied, "You know, I have no problem with what Bob just said. In fact, I too see great significance in what began in the Garden of Gethsemane as what was culminated on the cross." (Johnson-Millet dialogue, March 6, 2004). This, though, cannot be found in any Christian book on theology and clearly opposes

How is it that "relational" Mormons and evangelical Christians claim to worship together and pray together when the biblical God rejects mixture with other gods?[22] In the biblical showdown between Elijah and the prophets of Baal, Elijah never forgot that their god was ontologically different from his God.[23] He refused to join in worship with them or allow confusion of terms. Professor Ronald Huggins (Salt Lake Theological Seminary) claims that the promoters of relational dialogue are "pandering and slandering"; that is, they pander to the enemy of Christ's gospel and slander brothers in the Lord at the same time.[24]

STRENGTHS AND WEAKNESSES OF APOLOGETICS AMONG MORMONS

Christianity and apologetics are not amorphous studies awaiting new frameworks from external worldviews. Since genuine Christians share the essential doctrines of Christianity, we look to the Bible to eliminate ambiguity on these positions. Jude spoke of our "common salvation" and said that our faith was "*once for all* delivered to the saints." Paul admonishes us in Galatians 1:9, "[I]f anyone is preaching to you a gospel contrary to the one you received, let him be accursed." The gospel, then, received during the apostle's lifespan is the only one permitted by New Testament standards. No new gospel would be restored by Joseph Smith, Moroni, or the Mormon Church in later times.

As far as I know, there has been no study of the impact of traditional apologetic models (classical, evidential, presuppositional) on Mormonism. Some of the new postures taken by evangelicals in Utah are not new apologetic models as much as they are non-apologetic attitudes in sharing Christ. My proposition, and that of my deceased colleague Bob Passantino, is that a solid apologetic approach in answering the Mormon gospel is an effective tool for evangelism that has borne fruit in the lives of thousands of former Mormons. Until recent times with the new non-apologetic approach, the history of mission work among Mormons always included apologetics. In 1991 Bob Passantino and I demonstrated our defense of the gospel in a formal public debate with two Mormon apologists at Biola University where

---

Paul, who wrote of Christ "making peace by the blood of his cross" (Col. 1:20). Nowhere does Scripture make what happened in the garden part of Christ's atonement for our sins.

[22]At a Fuller Theological Seminary conference (April 2003) with evangelical and Mormon scholars, joint worship and prayer was conducted without reservation (Johnson-Millet dialogue, Fuller Theological Seminary, March 3, 2003). It is yet to be explained how joint worship and prayer of this kind is not sin, according to 2 Corinthians 6:14–15, when the Mormon god is a man and the Christian God is Spirit.

[23]See 1 Kings 18:24–40.

[24]Ronald Huggins, "An Appeal for Authentic Evangelical-Mormon Dialogue" (www.irr.org/MIT/authentic-dialogue.html).

we used the "Golden Rule of Apologetics."[25] Before commenting further on the debate, I will look at other models.

Anti-Apologetics

Anti-apologetics ignores or rejects the biblical passages that demonstrate and call for apologetics. This attitude was offensive to the imprisoned Paul who wrote that nobody stood with him at his first *apologia* (2 Tim. 4:16). We are to stand. Nonetheless, we find anti-apologetic advocates (or sometimes non-apologetic advocates) among those with newer approaches to Mormons.[26] Often these people either greatly fear defending the faith, or they attempted it once and believe that they failed in their effort, so they reason that it is invalid for everyone. They either despise apologetics or greatly minimize its value in evangelism.

Soft Apologetics

"Soft apologetics," a view that is gaining ground in the new evangelical approach to Mormonism, is a misnomer used by some to mean a softer, more compassionate apologetic.[27] The term "soft apologetics," as coined by philosopher Stephen T. Davis, however, does not mean a weaker form of apologetics as many of these people take it to be.[28] Utah evangelicals who falsely caricaturize the traditional Christian apologist as a shouting, red-faced, vein-popping, teeth-gritting Bible-thumper demonstrate their ignorance of genuine historic apologetics. In my thirty years of work among the Mormons, I have very rarely encountered any apologist of this nature. To advocate "soft apologetics" based upon this imaginary characterization is inappropriate.

Humble Apologetics

A recent twist in apologetic models is "humble apologetics," a term coined by John Stackhouse Jr. Claiming to practice this method, Rev. Greg Johnson

---

[25]See Bob Passantino, "The Golden Rule Apologetic"; http://www.answers.org/apologetics/goldenapol.html.

[26]A similar struggle occurred between conservative and liberal churches in the twentieth century. Liberals found little use for apologetics and insisted that our duty was merely to propagate the gospel. J. Gresham Machen refuted this theory in *Christianity and Liberalism* (New York: Macmillan, 1923).

[27]See the chapter "Soft Apologetics: Declaring the Uniqueness of Christ in a Postmodern and Religiously Plural World," in David Lundy, *Borderless Church: Shaping the Church in the 21st Century* (Waynesboro, GA: Authentic Media, 2006), 61ff.

[28]Stephen T. Davis coined "soft apologetics" not as a new field of apologetics, but as a description of how rational people can either affirm the evidence of Christ's resurrection (hard apologetics) or deny it and remain rational (soft apologetics). He argued for an apologetic by which we Christians must demonstrate the reasonableness of our claims to the world, even if we can't "prove" the claims true. His definition does not match what Utah evangelicals call "soft apologetics."

(Standing Together Ministry) invited Stackhouse to promote humble apologetics at a seminar in Sandy, Utah. In his message Stackhouse was quite rude and unnecessarily offensive and so demeaned other Christians that he contradicted his theory, lacking the humility he propounds as fundamental to an apologetic approach.[29]

In his book on the subject, Stackhouse is less insensitive than in his lecture but still offers no sound apology for Christianity.[30] He opens with skepticism: "We must not treat our views as if they were certainly right—even our most important views, including our religions. It will surprise some readers to find that I think there is much to say in favor of skepticism, even from (and particularly from) a Christian point of view."[31]

One has to ask what kind of defense humble apologetics is if Christianity may not be right and, in fact, may even be wrong. He ends with precisely the same conclusion on his final page: "For all we know, *we might be wrong* about any or all of this. And we will honestly own up to that possibility."[32] In my view, this book is not an apologetic but merely Stackhouse's treatise on how he lost respect for traditional apologetics.[33] Replacing true apologetics with personal skepticism and labeling it "humble apologetics" is no advancement in methodology.

Evidential Apologetics

In my experience, "evidential apologetics" is the most useful traditional apologetic model for evangelizing Mormons. I prefer this method because it supports and strengthens the response to errors found in Mormon theology. The frail apologetic attitudes previously mentioned have inherent weaknesses. We find no support for anti-apologetics, soft apologetics, or humble apologetics in Scripture. Instead, we find Jesus and the apostles regularly pointing to the evidence (which is the strength of classical and evidential apologetics). The new models bypass the methods of Jesus, Paul, Peter, Luke, John, and Jude in providing evidence to unbelievers for the truth-claims of Christianity.[34]

---

[29]Stackhouse shocked listeners by shouting "son of a b****" twice in a sermon illustration. There was no doubt that he challenged traditional apologetics when he demeaned the methods of Josh McDowell and others. Cf. John Stackhouse, "Humble Apologetics: Defending the Faith Today," Good Shepherd Lutheran Church, Sandy, Utah, cassette tape, January 21, 2005.

[30]John G. Stackhouse Jr., *Humble Apologetics: Defending the Faith Today* (New York: Oxford University Press, 2006).

[31]Ibid., 10.

[32]Ibid., 232, emphasis in the original.

[33]See the reviews of Stackhouse's book by Doug Groothuis (http://www.ivpress.com/groothuis/doug/archives/000011.php#more) and Dallas Miller (http://www.trinitysem.edu/journal/4-3/7_Bk_Review_Dallas_Miller_v4n3.htm).

[34]For more on apologetic models, see Chaps. 2, 3, and 4 in this volume.

Common-Ground Apologetic Dialogues

A good application of evidential apologetics is the common-ground approach. Apologetics is one thing, but how we apply it is quite another. Evangelism begins with a heart of love and prayer for the lost. Since 1976 I have trained Christians to listen and ask questions, never assuming that the person to whom you are speaking believes everything their church teaches, and then apply apologetics only when and where the occasion arises. We should focus on the differences that make a difference in one's eternal destiny—topics such as the nature of the Father, Son, and Holy Spirit, man's sinful nature, Christ's atonement, God's saving grace and his eternal retribution, to name a few. When one alters, for example, the nature of Jesus Christ by claiming that he was born in heaven of Heavenly Parents, was our elder spirit-brother in a preexistence, was a spirit-brother to Lucifer, was in a contest with Lucifer to become mankind's savior, was chosen by a council of gods to be our savior, was sired by the Father (a resurrected man) with Mary, and had a temple marriage (these are all crucial to Mormon doctrine),[35] it is evident that we have an ontological distinction between the Mormon Jesus and the Christian Jesus.

Therefore, in discussions with Mormons, we cannot agree every time they utter the name "Jesus," since it is impossible for them to speak of Jesus and mean what we Christians mean by that name. The apostle Paul warned the church about those with "another Jesus than the one we proclaimed" (2 Cor. 11:4). They use the name "Jesus" but define his nature entirely differently.[36] Jesus also spoke of those who knew his name and called him Lord, but he did not know them (Matt. 7:21–23). This certainly is a difference that makes a difference.

Mormonism is a distorted branch of theism; in fact, it teaches polytheism. Unlike evangelizing atheists, where we need to first present theism, Mormons do not have to be first convinced of theism. The central questions are what kind of being God is and perhaps how many gods exist. The genesis of a common-ground apologetic dialogue begins with the recognition that some being exists who is greater than we are. I find that a common-ground approach like this forms a good basis for discussion.[37]

---

[35]I devote a number of pages to this in *Mormonism*, 44–51.

[36]Greg Johnson and others claim that Mormons are thinking of the same historical Jesus as Christians do when they speak of Jesus, although there are theological differences (Johnson-Millet dialogue, Boise, 2004). This is not true. One cannot separate the historical Jesus from the biblical theology concerning him. Likewise, Mormons cannot speak of their Jesus outside of their extrabiblical revelation.

[37]Part of our mission work is an annual booth at the Utah State Fair. Through that event we have developed friendships with specific Mormons who have visited us annually since 1986. From our first meeting, there is no question in their minds that they have a different god, different Jesus, different Spirit, different gospel (2 Cor. 11:4) from us. But they are not so offended by these truths that they do not return year after

In contrast to this, it is popular among certain evangelical Christians in Utah to promote "common-ground relationships" with Mormons that include little or no apologetics. In their writings they are critical of traditional apologetics that, it should be noted, has been used by the church since the apostolic age. This approach is a step backward to the ecumenism of the 1890s, when Christian leaders met in common-ground dialogue with world religion leaders not to defend Christianity but to put aside their differences in the name of tolerance. When you enter into community worship with non-Christians for the sake of inclusiveness, civility, respect, or friendship, you have entered into ungodly ecumenism that leaves the true Christ behind. Paul appropriately asks us, "what fellowship has light with darkness?" (2 Cor. 6:14).[38]

Apostolic Apologetics

Jesus and the apostles provided evidences, in an apologetic format, for his messiahship, fulfilled prophecy, and other historical events. Dr. William Lane Craig effectively argues for the apologetic methods of Jesus and the apostles:

> Jesus appealed not only to his miracles as evidence of his divine mission, but, as the Gospels portray him, also to fulfilled prophecy (Luke 24:25–27). . . . Similarly, the apostles, in dealing with Jewish audiences, appealed to fulfilled prophecy, Jesus' miracles, and especially Jesus' resurrection as evidence that he was the Messiah (Acts 2:22–32). This was probably also Paul's typical approach (Acts 17:2–3, 17; 19:8; 28:23–24). When they confronted Gentile audiences who did not accept the Old Testament, the apostles appealed to God's handiwork in nature as evidence of the existence of the Creator (Acts 14:17). Then appeal was made to the eyewitness testimony to the resurrection of Jesus to show specifically that God had revealed himself in Jesus Christ (Acts 17:30–31; 1 Cor. 15:3–8).[39]

Any teaching, be it Mormon or other, that pits itself against clear biblical passages must be challenged and discarded. Our greatest strength

---

year, if for no other reason than to greet us. Each year we offer our newest gospel tracts, and they take them—literally thousands of them annually. So the concept that you can't make friends, and keep them, after you have "fully preached the gospel" (Rom. 15:19, NKJV) just isn't true. Interestingly, the critics of missions like ours have never worked with us to see this firsthand.

38One progressive evangelical church in Utah, for example, invited a Mormon instrumentalist to be part of the evangelical worship team on Sunday mornings. No repentance or salvation was required. The congregation had an unregenerate Mormon who believed in many gods leading them, in part, in their worship of the true God. This not only fosters confusion among Christians but involved no conversion of the man, who left the worship team several months later.

39William Lane Craig, *Five Views on Apologetics*, Steven B. Cowan, ed. (Grand Rapids, MI: Zondervan, 2000), 41–42.

as apologists is to emulate Jesus, the apostles, and the kind of apostolic apologetics we see in the New Testament for defending the truth.

THE EARLY APOLOGIES AGAINST MORMONISM

The first apologetic article written against Mormonism was ironically published one month *before* the Book of Mormon and two months *before* the Mormon Church was founded! Dr. Cornelius C. Blatchly, who regularly wrote articles about heresies in New York, obtained sixteen pages (pages 353–368) of the Book of Mormon prior to its publication and submitted an apologetic article to the *New York Telescope,* published February 20, 1830.[40]

Blatchly revealed that Martin Harris, who funded the printing of the Book of Mormon, said that Joseph Smith would translate the plates "by placing the spectacles in a hat and looking into them." Blatchly was a qualified scholar who compared the style of the Book of Mormon to the Bible and noted that if the same God wrote both books, then there should be some uniformity. He pointed out the Book of Mormon's redundancy and inferior grammar. For example, "yea," "it came to pass," "now," and "behold" occurred some 162 times in sixteen pages. He discovered a double negative in which Smith said the opposite of what he intended: "*yea*, the devil would *never* have *no* power over the hearts of the children of men: [*never* to have *no* power, is *ever* to have *some* power]."[41] Even with this scant information, Dr. Blatchly warned his Christian readers that a new heresy was on the horizon—one that required a biblical defense.

Alexander Campbell, who lost preachers and members to the Mormon Church, wrote a second and more thorough apology. He published his essay on February 7, 1831, just ten months after Mormonism began. He read the entire Book of Mormon before analyzing it with Scripture. Campbell began with an overview of false prophets, relying heavily on Hebrews 6:18, which says, "it is impossible for God to lie." He compared the Book of Mormon to the Bible and showed that Smith made God a liar, hence disproving its divine inspiration. Campbell dissected the Book of Mormon using internal and external means, thus providing evidence of its inferiority to God's Word. He also challenged a number of theological errors that he found. Being well-schooled in literature, Campbell also recognized a Shakespearean quotation that slipped into the Book of

---

[40]Cornelius C. Blatchly, "Caution Against the Gold Bible," *New York Telescope,* February 20, 1830.
[41]As originally worded; Alma 48:17 in today's *Book of Mormon.*

Mormon.[42] Overall he did a masterful job at the first thorough apologetic against Mormonism.

The third apology was written by a Methodist minister, Ezra Booth, in October 1831, about eighteen months after Mormonism's founding. Booth was persuaded by traveling Mormon preachers to forsake his Methodist ministry and join Mormonism. He became closely associated with Joseph Smith and traveled with him to far western Missouri. Rev. Ira Eddy wrote a lengthy letter to Booth confronting his new unbiblical beliefs, and Booth considered his ways and repented, returning to the Christian fold that he had abandoned. Booth also claimed that it was the argument of God's consistency that awakened him to Smith's delusion: "If God be a God of consistency and wisdom, I now know Mormonism to be a delusion; and this knowledge is built upon the testimony of my senses."[43] Booth wrote a series of nine articles defending Christianity against Mormonism that were published and republished in newspapers in the early 1830s.

Blatchly, Campbell, and Booth all defended the Bible against new heresies at their inception. I present these earliest apologetic responses to Mormonism to point out that Christians were not lax in their duty to defend the gospel when this new heresy came on the scene. Since 1830 Christians have defended the faith against the errors of Mormonism in hundreds of articles and books. The majority of them attempted a fair analysis given the information that was accessible.[44] This is the kind of apologetic tenacity we need in the church today.

THE MORMON-CHRISTIAN APOLOGETIC DEBATE AT BIOLA UNIVERSITY[45]

Bob Passantino's life pulsated with apologetics. A record of his apologetic method in answering Mormonism is preserved in a debate we did together at Biola University on August 17, 1991. The debate was truly Bob's crowning effort to defend Christianity against the attacks of Mormonism. As

---

[42]2 Nephi 1:14 in today's *Book of Mormon*.

[43]Ezra Booth, "Mormonism," *Ohio Star*, Ravina, Ohio (October 13, 20, 27, 29; November 3, 10, 17, 24; December 8, 1831), also reprinted by E. D. Howe, *Mormonism Unveiled* (Painesville, OH: *Painsville Telegraph*, 1834).

[44]It is popular among Mormons to demonize Christians who wrote on Mormonism in the past and characterize them as vindictive, unkind, inaccurate, or "anti-Mormon." However, one should not make an assessment of these writings without considering their purpose, audience, genre, and resources. A good reference that analyzes Mormon apologetic tactics is Matthew A. Paulson, *Breaking the Mormon Code* (Livermore, CA: WingSpan Press, 2006).

[45]This debate is available in audio CD and printed formats by writing to Utah Gospel Mission, P.O. Box 780, Victorville, CA 92393.

a result, I would like to highlight some of the principles that we used to defend the gospel.

In his introduction to the debate, moderator Dr. Alan Gomes—a professor at Talbot School of Theology—commented on the lost art of debate as an apologetic and educational process: "In the medieval universities the *disputatsio*, or disputation, was an integral part of the educational process. It forced students to think through complex issues and to give a defense for the positions that they held."[46]

The Mormon panel consisted of Van Hale and Bill Forrest. They founded Mormon Miscellaneous, a Mormon apologetic group, and they co-hosted a radio show on Mormonism in Salt Lake City, Utah. The Christian panel consisted of Bob Passantino and me, both of us authors and contributors to several Christian apologetics books.

The debate focused on four questions: (1) Does the Bible allow for additional Mormon scripture? (2) Is the creedal doctrine of the Trinity biblical? (3) Can man progress to godhood? (4) Is salvation accomplished wholly apart from human effort? The debate was four hours long and was conducted in a respectful and friendly manner, yet both sides showed strong convictions.

The Mormon Church has a history of public debates as a means to settle issues. Joseph Smith encouraged this through his revelation: "Wherefore, confound your enemies; call upon them to meet you both in public and in private; and inasmuch as ye are faithful their shame shall be made manifest."[47] They rarely engage in formal debate today, but when they do, they must keep 3 Nephi 11:30 in mind, which warns them against contending with anger.

Does the Bible Allow for Additional Mormon Scripture?

The Mormon panel began this first debate, but they neglected to define the debate topic, then committed the fallacy of irrelevance and attempted to prove the wrong point. The Christian panel first presented a biblical framework for the books of the Bible and why apocryphal literature is not included. I argued that like all purported scripture, Mormon scriptures must pass four tests: "(1) Does Mormon scripture fit the historical timeframe of those qualified to judge it? (2) Does Mormon scripture have express Apostolic authorship or endorsement? (3) Does Mormon scripture

---

[46]Robert Passantino, Kurt Van Gorden, Van Hale, and Bill Forrest, *Christian and Mormon Debates on Theology*, Kurt Van Gorden, ed. (Victorville, CA: Utah Gospel Mission, 1991), p. 1.
[47]D & C, 71:7

contain the same gospel message as the Bible? (4) Was Mormon scripture received as inspired by the Apostolic community of believers?"[48]

Next, we offered an expanded argument on each of these principles and their biblical support. I added, "We intend to win this point of the debate by proving the impossibility of the contrary. If we apply the same standards to the Mormon scriptures that affirm to us that the New Testament is authoritative, we discover they do not fit the criteria." Thus, our apology defended the sixty-six-book collection we call the Bible, and it withstood the position taken by the Mormon panel.

Is the Creedal Doctrine of the Trinity Biblical?

In this debate Bob Passantino gave a powerful argument for the Trinity. Bob called it the "perfect inductive argument," using the Bible as his source. He stated it this way:

> I will prove my affirmation by using the logical argumentation form called perfect induction. Induction argues from specific to general. Since general induction takes particular examples and builds from that a general conclusion, it offers probable or statistical truth, but not absolute certainty. The next sample could (hypothetically) disprove the universal application of the conclusion. There is a way to achieve certainty in some instances, through a method called perfect induction (also called induction by complete enumeration), a method of rational analysis that can give certainty, because the items in the field (all possible samples), as well as the field itself, are limited and known. For example, through induction you might postulate that all crows are black because in your extensive sampling, all the crows you saw were black. However, a white crow could fly in tomorrow and disprove your claim. The situation changes if you have a limited field (one room), and a limited number of items in the field (three crows), and all of those items (crows) were black. Then you could by perfect induction know for sure that all crows in the room are black.
>
> This resolution can be resolved using perfect induction. It is my conviction that the biblical nature of the creedal doctrine of the Trinity has a limited field (the Bible), limited items in the field (the terms), and all the items are known. Therefore, it is possible to use perfect induction to know for sure that the creedal doctrine of the Trinity is biblical.
>
> This resolution, by its very wording, limits the field of inductive inquiry: (1) The doctrine to be discussed is the creedal doctrine, not any other. (2) The Trinity as articulated by the creeds is to be discussed, not philosophical speculations about the Trinity.[49]

---

[48]Passantino et al., *Christian and Mormon Debates on Theology*, 4.
[49]Ibid., 10.

Passantino then used the "limited field" (i.e., the Bible) to give his defense for the Trinity by citing forty-three verses and drawing points from early church history. A Mormon panelist, Bill Forrest, spent most of his time arguing against creeds before he attempted to prove the proposition of whether they were biblical.

The cross-examination period was lively, and we kept asking for any biblical proof for the three gods in Mormon theology as opposed to the one God of the biblical Trinity. This proof was never provided. Then Bob asked the Mormon panel the question that silenced any refutation to his opening: "Show me where my argument was not following the logical principle of perfect induction and why I could not draw the conclusions from it." Bill Forrest answered, "Well, I don't know if your argument was following the logical perfect induction or not, because I'm not sure what the perfect induction is."[50] As the Mormon panel continued to lose ground, the Christian panel gave a solid apology for the biblical foundation of the Trinity.

Can Man Progress to Godhood?

In the third debate, Van Hale opened his argument for the Mormon position by claiming that the idea of deification—that man can become a god—is a lost doctrine of Christianity. He argued that several church fathers taught the deification doctrine and that it is still held to some degree by Orthodox Christians. Therefore, he reasoned, it is biblical and acceptable.

I presented the opening argument for the Christian panel. I was well prepared for this portion of the debate as I had purchased a published copy of Mr. Hale's notes from previous talks he had given on the topic. In this way I was able to research the context of his quotations and argue against his position from his very own notes. This was followed by a presentation on what deification and "*theosis*" means in the Orthodox Church, and I credit my Orthodox friends for reviewing my material for accuracy prior to the debate.[51]

Again, the cross-examination was lively. Since the historical context silenced the effectiveness of the Mormon panel's notes, Bob and I spent the remainder of our time defending the biblical position that there is but one God and arguing for the impossibility of the Father being an exalted man.

---

[50]Ibid., 13.
[51]I was pleased to see that the Christian panel's opening argument on what deification really means was later quoted by Orthodox writers and posted on their web sites.

Is Salvation Accomplished Wholly Apart from Human Effort?

In this final debate Bob Passantino opened for the Christian panel: "I will prove that salvation is escape from the bondage of sin and the deserved judgment of God, through no human effort, but wholly on the basis of Christ's atoning death on the cross. I will use the Bible as my source of authority."[52] Bob correctly reasoned that the Mormon panel would redefine salvation, so he prepared for this with clear definitions.

The Mormon position was stated by Bill Forrest: "We reject the notion that salvation can be accomplished wholly without human effort."[53] He presented salvation in Mormon theology in the general sense, which involves the resurrection of the just and unjust. He then began interchanging his terms (salvation and resurrection) without notice. However, Bob caught this semantic move, and in the cross-examination the Mormons finally conceded to the distinctions.

The Mormon panel then questioned whether believing in Jesus, in the evangelical Christian sense, was a work or effort resulting in salvation. Passantino answered, "Responding is not a work, because you're not the one who died on the cross. Nor [is it] an effort [since] you're not the one who died on the cross."[54] In spite of the Mormon panel's claim that baptism and other works are essential for salvation, Bob finished his apologetic on salvation with several biblical verses and by emphasizing what it says in Romans 4—that no one is justified by works of the law.

CONCLUSION

It is my hope that young men and women of the Word of God will see the value of apologetics in the history of the New Testament as well as in the early and later church. We live in a changing world that tries to do away with the old and usher in new ideas. Because apologetics is so central to New Testament history, we cannot afford to put apologetics aside in the hope that some new plan will work. God has blessed apologetics in the past, and it is useful as a witnessing tool to help plant seeds of the gospel and win cult members to Christ. Apologetics is grounded in the bedrock of Scripture, which encourages the believer to say with assurance, "I have a reason to believe."

---

[52]Passantino et al., *Christian and Mormon Debates on Theology*, 23.
[53]Ibid., 24.
[54]Ibid., 27.

CHAPTER TWENTY

Jehovah's Witnesses and the Doctrine of Salvation

Jim Valentine and Eric Pement

BIBLICAL EVANGELISM INVOLVES two aspects, one negative and one affirmative. Negatively, sinners must understand that they are condemned by the righteous requirements of God's law, and their sins and transgressions leave them without hope before a righteous and holy God. The biblical "good news" presupposes a prior "bad news"—that one is lost due to sin. Positively, biblical *evangelism* necessitates communicating the *gospel*,[1] the classic definition of which is contained in 1 Corinthians 15:3–4. Here the apostle Paul writes that the gospel that he preached and that the Corinthians believed was that "Christ died for our sins according to the Scriptures; and that he was buried, yes, that he has been raised up the third day according to the Scriptures."[2]

As veteran researchers of modern religions, we have seen Jehovah's Witnesses converted through a variety of means. For some, discovering false prophecies or sustained dishonesty from Watchtower leaders incited them to leave the Society and then later turn to Christ. Other former Jehovah's Witnesses came to Christ through struggles with doctrinal issues such as blood transfusion, the Trinity, or the bodily resurrection of Christ or through seeing a miraculous answer to Christian prayer.

Our general perspective is that counter-cult apologetic techniques ought to differ from situation to situation simply because people's

---

[1]The English words *evangel* and *gospel* both stem from the same Greek root word for "good news."
[2]Unless otherwise noted, all Bible quotations will be from the Watchtower Society's 1984 edition of the New World Translation (NWT). The NWT is unreliable and often flawed. The translators were not scholars of Greek or Hebrew and worked principally from English translations in preparing their own version. However, the NWT is the only translation Witnesses trust today. We also cite from the American Standard Version (1901), a reliable translation that the Watchtower Society has republished on several occasions.

own inner motives and proclivities differ. Each person in a cult must be treated as an individual, and the Christian apologist should seek to know what makes a person tick rather than expect a "one size fits all" solution. We believe that to be most effective in evangelizing Jehovah's Witnesses, the Christian should know how the Watchtower differs from classic Christian teaching in its offer of salvation today.

A BRIEF HISTORY OF JEHOVAH'S WITNESSES

The Watchtower Society traces its nineteenth-century origins to Charles Taze Russell (1852–1916), the Pennsylvania publisher of *Zion's Watch Tower and Herald of Christ's Presence* in 1879. In the 1870s, the unordained "Pastor" Russell concluded that Jesus' prophecies of his "coming" (Greek, *parousia*) should rather be interpreted as predictions of his invisible "presence." Russell believed that Christ had been spiritually "present" on earth since 1874 and that 1914 (forty years later) would see the Battle of Armageddon and the visible manifestation of Christ's invisible presence. Hence, the title of Russell's magazine.

Russell promoted his views in pamphlet and book form through his multi-volume *Studies in the Scriptures*, distributed internationally by a vigorous group of "Bible Students." When World War I broke out in 1914, most Bible Students thought it would confirm Russell's message. The movement, however, sagged as 1915 came and went, with Russell nudging the date ahead year by year. Following Russell's death in 1916, Joseph Rutherford was elected president of the Watchtower Society. He rewrote Russell's chronology to begin the "presence" of Christ in 1914, postponing the Battle of Armageddon to several decades into the future. *Generation* in Jesus' prophecy that "this generation will by no means pass away until all these things occur" (Matt. 24:34) was reinterpreted from a period of forty years to a much longer period of a lifespan. Rutherford explained that some Bible Students alive in 1914 would live to see all the predictions of Matthew 24 come to pass. (He even taught that it might be as soon as 1925.)[3]

Rutherford's success in promoting the Society's teachings created a theological problem. Pastor Russell had taught that the 144,000 Jews from the tribes of Israel (described in Revelation 7, 14) were not literal Jews but *spiritual seed* of the New Covenant—i.e., the Bible Students themselves. However, by the 1930s this number was already reached. Rutherford

---

[3]His pamphlet *Millions Now Living Will Never Die* (1920) expected the resurrection to occur by 1925. To avoid redundancy in documentation, all Witness books we cite were published in Brooklyn, New York by the Watchtower Bible and Tract Society of New York, Inc.

needed something new to offer, so he announced a new name for God's people, "Jehovah's Witnesses"[4] (1931), and a new missionary calling, to the "other sheep"[5] or the "great multitude"[6] (1935). Though this class could not be in the New Covenant as the spiritual brothers of Christ and could not rule and reign with Christ as kings and priests (Rev. 1:6; 5:10; 20:6), if the "other sheep" submitted to Jehovah's arrangement, they would have the prospect of living forever on a paradise earth.[7]

While several presidents have served since Rutherford, it was Rutherford who defined them as Jehovah's Witnesses and who identified two classes of Christians: the 144,000 (of which only a few remain) and the "great crowd," or about 99.9% of all active Witnesses today. Since Rutherford's death, none of the books published by the Society has identified its author(s), and none of the presidents have had the charisma or influence of Russell and Rutherford. The Society is managed ecclesially by a Governing Body of about a dozen men and administratively by a regularly elected president.

Jehovah's Witnesses consider the political systems of this world to be part of Satan's domain. They do not vote, hold political office, or serve in the military. They may not salute a flag or say the Pledge of Allegiance. They take no part in national holidays (Independence Day, Memorial Day), personal holidays (Mother's Day, birthdays), or any religious holidays (Christmas, Easter). They do not engage in interfaith or ecumenical celebrations, since they view all other religions as part of Babylon the Great, although a few people got *some* things right, such as Arius, Servetus, Zwingli, and the Anabaptists. They may not accept a blood transfusion for any reason.[8]

Jehovah's Witnesses are known for their door-to-door preaching activity, proclaiming an imminent Battle of Armageddon that will destroy all those outside Jehovah's organization. This was an effective recruiting tool during World War II, and also in the years between 1968 and 1975. Their best-known periodicals are *The Watchtower*, a semimonthly, doctrinally-oriented magazine, and *Awake!*, which is less doctrinal and written for popular consumption. The press run on these magazines is now over twenty-seven million copies per issue, in 153 languages—over a bil-

---

[4]From Isa. 43:10, "You are my witnesses, saith Jehovah" (ASV).
[5]From John 10:16, "And other sheep I have, which are not of this fold" (ASV).
[6]From Rev. 7:9, ". . . and behold, a great multitude, which no man could number" (ASV). With the publication of the NWT, this term has been replaced by "great crowd."
[7]*Draw Close to Jehovah* (2002), 289.
[8]*What Does the Bible Really Teach?* (2005), 130.

lion copies per year. Their publishing output stands head-and-shoulders above any other single religious group.

They believe that all their views are founded on the Bible, and they hold strongly to the Bible as God's inspired Word. They believe in conditional immortality and the ultimate annihilation of the wicked, denying an eternal punishment. Each week Jehovah's Witnesses worldwide study the same articles from the *Watchtower*, hear sermons on the same topics, and sing the same songs at their Kingdom Halls.

They boast of unity in heart and mind, but this unity is achieved through penalties for independent thinking. "The Witness who dissents is cut off, forced to leave the congregation, and shunned not only by his congregation, but also by his Witness friends and even close family members."[9] A current manual for elders states, "Disfellowshipped and disassociated ones are shunned by those who wish to have a good relationship with Jehovah."[10] The Watchtower Society claims to be Jehovah's "one approved channel representing God's kingdom on earth" and "his chosen channel of communication" today.[11]

TWO CLASSES OF CHRISTIANS

Jehovah's Witnesses have a unique view of salvation that differs from classic Christianity. As indicated earlier, they believe there are two categories or "classes" of redeemed people: the 144,000 and the Great Crowd. Let's explore these classes in further detail.

The 144,000

This number comes from the biblical book of Revelation. Numbers of spiritual significance recur throughout the text—three, seven, ten, and twelve, sometimes multiplied by a factor. In John's vision, 144,000 servants of God are sealed on their foreheads: twelve thousand from each of the twelve tribes of Israel, who will stand with the Lamb on Mount Zion (Rev. 7:4–8, 14:1).

According to the early teachings of Charles Russell, this number included *both Jews and Gentiles*, starting with every Christian believer from the first century until the forthcoming Battle of Armageddon

---

[9]Robert Passantino, "Jehovah's Witnesses," in *Evangelizing the Cults*, Ron Enroth, ed. (Ann Arbor, MI: Servant Publications, 1990), 124.
[10]*Pay Attention to Yourselves and to All the Flock* (1991), 103.
[11]"Do You Appreciate the 'Faithful and Discreet Slave'?" *Watchtower*, March 1, 1981, 24; "Jehovah Reveals His Glory to Humble Ones," *Watchtower*, August 1, 2004, 10. See also "Avoid the Pursuit of 'Valueless Things,'" *Kingdom Ministry*, September 2002, 8.

(1914). This total included all of Russell's followers in the Bible Students movement.

When Russell died, Rutherford succeeded him. The Battle of Armageddon was postponed, and Rutherford announced in 1935 that the number of the 144,000 was being closed. Any new followers of Jehovah would henceforth become part of the "great multitude" (called the "great crowd" today).

The Watchtower Society uses many synonyms for the 144,000: the "anointed class" or "anointed remnant," "Jesus' spiritual brothers," the "spirit-begotten class," the "faithful and discreet slave class," the "little flock," the "heavenly bride class," "sons of God," "spiritual Israel," "Israel of God," "kings and priests with Jesus Christ," the "bride of Christ," the "body of Christ," and many other terms.[12] Russell and Rutherford called them the "Christ class," but this term is not used today.[13] According to Watchtower teachings, virtually all the blessings for New Testament believers are promised exclusively to the 144,000.

The Society has fewer terms for the Great Crowd: the "other sheep," ones with an "earthly hope," and a few others. Nearly all Jehovah's Witnesses consider themselves part of the Great Crowd looking for an embodied future life on earth, not a disembodied home in heaven.

Privileges of the 144,000

The discrepancy between the blessings available to each "class" is not obvious until one examines the Watchtower's doctrine of salvation in detail. Table 1 (see page 318) contrasts the differences between these two categories. In the following description, the numbers in parentheses (1, 2, etc.) correspond to the line numbers in the table.[14]

The 144,000 have the privilege of being (1) *born again*, or "born of the spirit" or "spirit-begotten." The 144,000 can become *sons of God* or *children of God*, which logically follows from a spiritual birth. For the Watchtower, this is an opportunity rather than a once-for-all experience. It means "becoming a son of God with the prospect of sharing in the heavenly kingdom."[15] It involves a present aspect with a future contingent on

---

[12]See "Anointed, anointing," in *Insight on the Scriptures* (1988) (1:114); also "Christian" (1:439–440), "Covenant" (1:524–525), "Israel of God" (1:1234), "Priest" (2:687), and "Son(s) of God" (2:998–1000).
[13]Charles Taze Russell, *Zion's Watch Tower and Herald of Christ's Presence*, August 15, 1895, 192; Joseph Rutherford, September 15, 1908, 286.
[14]This table could easily be expanded. In *Reasoning from the Scriptures with the Jehovah's Witnesses* (Eugene, OR: Harvest House, 1993), Ron Rhodes identifies twenty-one differences between these two classes, 254–255.
[15]"Birth," in *Insight on the Scriptures* (1988), 1:319.

"enduring to the end." Presently, their sonship is real. "Right now, anointed ones are God's children."[16] However, this "prospect" is not guaranteed and potentially can fail.

Table 1. The 144,000 and the Great Crowd Contrasted

Jehovah's Witnesses are taught that most of the promises of the New Testament apply to the 144,000, not to the Great Crowd. Over 99 percent of Jehovah's Witnesses active today believe they are part of the Great Crowd.

Privileges of the 144,000:	Status of the Great Crowd:
1. Are "born again" and "child of God"	1. Are not born again
2. Are adopted as sons and daughters of God	2. Are not adopted as sons or daughters of God
3. Are spiritual brothers or sisters of Christ	3. Are not Christ's spiritual brothers or sisters
4. Are heirs of God and joint-heirs with Christ	4. Are not heirs of God, or joint-heirs with Christ
5. Are anointed and sealed with Jehovah's spirit	5. Are not anointed or sealed with Jehovah's spirit
6. Are consciously in Christ's presence at death	6. Cease existence between death and the Millennium
7. Hope to have a future home in heaven	7. Hope to have a home on earth, not in heaven
8. Are justified by faith	8. Are not justified by faith, but by works
9. Are sanctified	9. Are not sanctified
10. Are included in the New Covenant	10. Are not included in the New Covenant
11. Have Jesus as their Mediator	11. Do not have Jesus as their Mediator
12. Have the right to partake of Communion	12. Have no right to partake of Communion
13. The New Testament is addressed to them	13. The New Testament is not addressed to them
14. Positions closed in 1935[17]	14. Positions open since 1935

The 144,000 enjoy (2) *adoption* as God's children, and they in particular are recognized as (3) Christ's *spiritual brothers*. Jehovah's Witnesses see the promises in Romans 8:15–17 as being made to the 144,000, not to the Great Crowd. With this premise in place, they see the privilege of (4) a *heavenly inheritance* connected with sonship. "If, then, we are children, we are also heirs: *heirs* indeed of God, but joint heirs with Christ" (Rom. 8:17).

Following Paul's words in 2 Corinthians 1:21–22, they see that the Christian congregation has been (5) *anointed* by God, who "has also put his *seal* upon us." Other references to the "anointing" in 1 John are seen as privileges of the 144,000, who are commonly called the "anointed class" or the "anointed remnant." (Bear in mind that the Watchtower teaches that the "holy spirit" is "a controlled force that Jehovah God uses to accomplish a variety of his purposes."[18] It is not a person and is not God. Therefore, they do not believe that God actually lives within the anointed members.)

---

[16] *Watchtower*, July 15, 1986, "Go on Living as Children of God," 15.
[17] As of May 2007, this is no longer true. See important doctrinal change at footnote 35.
[18] *Should You Believe in the Trinity?* (1989), 20.

Jehovah's Witnesses accept the Pauline doctrine that spirit-filled believers are (6) *conscious after death* and go immediately *to the presence of Christ*, citing for support such passages as Philippians 1:23 and 2 Corinthians 5:8. Predictably, they restrict this to the 144,000. The Watchtower Society teaches that the anointed class will have a resurrection like that of Christ, and since they believe Christ was resurrected as a disembodied spirit being, returning to dwell in heaven, they believe the 144,000 will be "resurrected" similarly, receiving (7) a *heavenly home* but living in a permanently disembodied state.

Only the 144,000 are (8) *justified by faith*. "Today the anointed remnant by reason of their being justified by faith have had their past record of inherited sins wiped away."[19] Again, "Jesus pleads and wins justification from sin for those who become his faithful, spirit-begotten, anointed followers."[20] What about the Great Crowd and justification? The Watchtower says, *"The Watchtower* has a number of times pointed out that . . . the present members of the 'other sheep' class are not justified to life eternal on earth."[21]

The New World Translation of Romans 5:1 says, "Therefore, now that we have been declared righteous as a result of faith, let us enjoy peace with God through our Lord Jesus Christ," but this justification and peace is not needed by the Great Crowd. The Watchtower book *Life Everlasting in Freedom of the Sons of God* states, "The 'great crowd' . . . want to become perfect human sons of God through their Eternal Father Jesus Christ (Isaiah 9:5, 6). For this reason they will not be justified or declared righteous either now or then [in the Millennium] as the 144,000 heavenly joint heirs have been justified while still in the flesh. The 'great crowd' . . . does not need the justification by faith and the imputed righteousness that the 144,000 'chosen ones' have required."[22]

The article on sanctification in the Watchtower two-volume encyclopedia *Insight on the Scriptures* indicates that only the "anointed class" are (9) *sanctified.*[23] The Jehovah's Witnesses agree with the apostle Paul's tight chain of reasoning in Romans 8:30, so they conclude that only the 144,000 are also *foreordained, called,* declared righteous (justified), or will be *glorified.*[24]

Only the 144,000 are brought into (10) the *New Covenant* predicted

[19]"The Way of Man's Attainment to Perfect Integrity," *Watchtower*, April 15, 1954, 254.
[20]"The Triumphant Message of 'The Kingdom,'" *Watchtower*, October 15, 1955, 631.
[21]"On the Divine Mandate," *Watchtower*, June 1, 1950, 175.
[22]*Life Everlasting in Freedom of the Sons of God* (1966), 391.
[23]1988, 2:857.
[24]"Questions from Readers," *Watchtower*, July 15, 1981, 31.

in Jeremiah 31:31 and promised to New Testament believers (2 Cor. 3:6; Gal. 3:16–26; Heb. 7–10). The New Covenant does not extend to the Great Crowd: "Members of the great crowd are not participants in the new covenant."[25] The Watchtower reasons that the New Covenant brings a new heart (Heb. 8:10), an everlasting inheritance (9:15), a new hope (10:23), and sanctification (10:29), which they believe are only for the 144,000.

Since Jesus is the "mediator of a new covenant" (Heb. 9:15; 12:24), therefore only the 144,000 have Jesus as (11) their *Mediator*. According to the Watchtower, even the apparently universal statement of 1 Timothy 2:5 ("For there is one God, and one mediator between God and men, a man, Christ Jesus") does not apply to the Great Crowd.[26] Although this passage seems to apply to everyone, the Watchtower argues that at the time Paul was writing, all Christians had Jesus as their mediator. However, that is not the case today.

The next step follows logically. When Jesus held the Last Supper, he said, "This cup means the new covenant by virtue of my blood" (Luke 22:20; 1 Cor. 11:25).[27] For this reason, only the 144,000 may (12) *partake of Communion* at the Lord's Evening Meal. They explain, "God has reserved that privilege [of partaking] for individuals he has anointed with holy spirit to be 'joint heirs with Christ.'"[28]

Jehovah's Witnesses celebrate the "Lord's Memorial" once a year, on a date close to the Jewish Passover.[29] The service is held in the Kingdom Hall, preceded by a talk on its meaning. The elders pass trays of unleavened bread and red wine, and in most Kingdom Halls *no one partakes*, not even the elders or overseers. Since the Great Crowd is not in the New Covenant, they have no right to partake.[30]

It is clear from the New Testament that the apostles expected that all Christians would share in the Lord's Supper (or Memorial). All Christians

---

[25]"The Other Sheep and the New Covenant," *Watchtower*, February 1, 1998, 19.

[26]"Is Jesus the 'Mediator' Only for Anointed Christians?" *Watchtower*, April 1, 1979, 31, and August 15, 1989 ("Is Jesus the Mediator only for spirit-anointed Christians or for all mankind, since 1 Timothy 2:5, 6 speaks of him as the 'mediator' who 'gave himself a corresponding ransom *for all*'?" 30–31. The Watchtower concludes, "Though he is not their [the Great Crowd's] legal Mediator, for they are not in the new covenant, he is their means of approaching Jehovah," permitting an opportunity for "everlasting life for all obedient mankind" (31).

[27]A more literal translation is, "This cup is the new covenant in my blood" (ASV).

[28]"What Does the Lord's Evening Meal Mean to You?" *Watchtower*, February 15, 2003, 19.

[29]Thursday evening, Nisan 14. See "Lord's Evening Meal," *Insight on the Scriptures* (1988) (2:268), and *Reasoning from the Scriptures*, second edition (1989), 269.

[30]About eight thousand people worldwide *do* partake at the Memorial service, some in their middle age or younger. The Society teaches that if members of the anointed class fall away, their positions can become available to someone else. "If an anointed one proves unfaithful, it is most likely that a person who has long served God faithfully as one of the other sheep would be called to fill the vacancy thus caused in the 144,000" (*Watchtower*, February 15, 2003, 20).

shared in "the breaking of bread" (Acts 2:42, 46; 20:7; 1 Cor. 10:16, ASV)[31] and partook of "one loaf" (1 Cor. 10:17), except for those convicted by conscience because of serious sin (1 Cor. 11:27–31).

The Watchtower Society sees this universal expectation as well, so they assert that (13) *the New Testament is addressed to the anointed class*. The Watchtower encyclopedia says the New Testament documents are addressed "primarily to spiritual Israel, which is the congregation of God," although as onlookers the Great Crowd can benefit also.[32] For example, Paul's epistle to the "Romans was written to a congregation of anointed Christians, whereas today the vast majority of Jehovah's Witnesses are of the 'great crowd' and have an earthly hope."[33]

Finally, to be included in the 144,000, one had to be a baptized Jehovah's Witness as of 1935. Watchtower president Joseph Rutherford *strongly* implied that the vacancies closed in that year.[34] The opportunity to join the New Covenant was (14) *closed in 1935*.[35] Except in the case of those few elderly Witnesses who apostatized and lost their position to someone else (see note 30 above), all new converts to the Watchtower Society were added to the Great Crowd. (Please see the extended remark at note 35.)

The Watchtower claims that the two classes are "one flock" under the "fine shepherd" (John 10:14, 16), so "[t]here is no rivalry between the anointed class and the great crowd. . . . Each accepts with gratitude the privileges extended to him by God, not reasoning that his position some-how makes him a better person or in some way inferior to someone else."[36] Yet those positions are clearly *not* equal, since it is the anointed class that is "steward" over Jehovah's household, and if one of the Great Crowd should

---

[31]"Breaking of bread" may refer to a common meal or an *agape* feast in Acts 2:42, 46, but Acts 20:7 almost certainly applies this term to a weekly Communion service. Compare Luke's usage in Luke 22:19; 24:35. The NWT mistranslates the Acts passages as "to have a meal."

[32]"Christian Greek Scriptures," *Insight on the Scriptures* (1988) (1:444).

[33]"The Romans Get the Best of News," *Watchtower,* August 1, 1990, 25.

[34]"What Does the Lord's Evening Meal Mean to You?" *Watchtower,* 19; *Revelation—Its Grand Climax at Hand!* (1988), 120, 125; *Jehovah's Witnesses—Proclaimers of God's Kingdom* (1993), 166–171.

[35]After this article was written, the May 1, 2007, issue of *Watchtower* published a significant reversal of this long-standing doctrine. In the "Questions from Readers" column, the Society addresses the question, "When does the calling of Christians to a heavenly hope cease?" The editors admitted that "especially after 1966 it was believed that the heavenly call ceased in 1935" (30), but they now believe "that we can-not set a specific date for when the calling of Christians to the heavenly hope ends" (31), and therefore members of the congregation who partake of the Memorial emblems "should not be judged" as presump-tive or in error. We believe there is a strategic purpose for this reversal. In recent years the Governing Body of the Society was forced to accept members of the Great Crowd to its board of directors. However, the Watchtower Society has always been managed by a "faithful and discreet slave class" who *must* be members of the "anointed class." Revoking the 1935 cutoff date allows future members of the Governing Body and other Watchtower officials to become part of the "faithful and discreet slave class," thus having the right to prepare "spiritual food" or teaching for Jehovah's Witnesses worldwide.

[36]*Jehovah's Witnesses—Proclaimers of God's Kingdom* (1993), 171.

partake of the Memorial emblems (i.e., unleavened bread and red wine), they might die. "God would not look with favor upon anyone representing himself as a person called to be a heavenly king and priest when he knew that he really did not have such a calling. (Romans 9:16; Revelation 20:6) Jehovah executed the Levite Korah for presumptuously seeking the Aaronic priesthood."[37]

The Great Crowd

By contrast, the Great Crowd enjoys very few of these New Testament privileges. The Watchtower book *Holy Spirit—The Force Behind the Coming New Order!* shows how most of the promises to New Testament believers are unavailable to the average Jehovah's Witness:

> [The] baptized "other sheep" of the "great crowd" have not been begotten to be God's spiritual sons, with a heavenly inheritance. They are not spiritual Israelites. They have not been taken into the new covenant with the opportunity to become God's "kingdom of priests and a holy nation." (Exodus 19:5, 6) They have never been sealed with God's spirit as an advance token of their heavenly inheritance. They have not been anointed with God's spirit as prospective joint heirs with Christ in his celestial kingdom. (Isaiah 61:1–3; 1 John 2:20, 27; 2 Corinthians 1:21, 22) But do they nonetheless have holy spirit on them?
>
> Overwhelmingly the facts answer Yes! Especially since 1935 C.E., the "great crowd" have worked with the spirit-begotten, anointed remnant. They have given convincing evidence that God's holy spirit is operative upon them. A person on earth does not need to be begotten by God's spirit in order to have His active force go into operation upon him.[38]

The principal exception to this disparity occurs regarding Jehovah's "active force." Although the Great Crowd are not "anointed," "sealed," or "born of" Jehovah's power (or spirit) and thus are not "spirit-begotten," supposedly the Great Crowd may still have Jehovah's spirit in them. While the book of Romans seems to say that those who possess God's spirit will be raised as Christ was (8:11) and are "God's sons" (8:14) by adoption (8:15), the Watchtower Society has a curious disjoint at this point. They say that the Great Crowd can have Jehovah's "holy spirit" without enjoying the other privileges of the 144,000.

How so? The Society parallels the Great Crowd to John the Baptist. They observe that John was "filled with holy spirit right from his mother's

---

[37]"What Does the Lord's Evening Meal Mean to You?" *Watchtower*, 20.
[38]*Holy Spirit—The Force Behind the Coming New Order!* (1976), 157.

womb" (Luke 1:15), but "a person that is a lesser one in the kingdom of the heavens is greater than he is [Why? Because John will not be in the heavens, and so there was no need for him to be 'born again']."[39] So not only can members of the Great Crowd "have" the holy spirit, but they may be "indwelt" or filled with holy spirit also. For example, one of the qualifications of congregational overseers (who will come from the Great Crowd) is that they should exhibit "the fullness of the indwelling of the holy spirit."[40]

AN EVANGELICAL RESPONSE TO THE WATCHTOWER

The Watchtower Society's interpretation of two classes of Christians is deeply flawed, but it carries at least three things in its favor. First, their system recognizes that the New Testament promises both a "heavenly home" as well as resurrection and a "new earth" for believers. Many Christians focus so much on going to heaven that they overlook the biblical doctrines of the resurrection of the body[41] and of a renewed earth as the home for resurrected believers.[42] The Watchtower Society's solution at least takes both promises seriously.

Second, their system recognizes that the promises to New Covenant believers are intertwined and interdependent. That is, all "children of God" through faith in Christ are adopted. All adopted children are anointed with God's Spirit. All the anointed are necessarily called, justified, sanctified, and sealed. If children, then heirs. If children, then "in Christ." If in Christ, then our future resurrection must be like that of the Lord. If in Christ, then members of his body and partakers of his Communion meal, privileged as priests, defended by a Mediator in heaven, serving as ambassadors for his coming kingdom and visible reign. The Society is correct to observe that these promises are all interrelated.

Third, the Watchtower Society sees that these promises to the "children of God" are the norm for the New Testament. The Watchtower Society properly recognizes that the New Testament writers presume that every believer was "born again" and heir to these promises. The New

---

[39] *Reasoning from the Scriptures,* second edition (1989), 78. Statement in brackets in original text.

[40] "Overseers in Apocalyptic Times," *Watchtower,* January 15, 1958, 46.

[41] 1 Cor. 15, etc. See also J. A. Schep, *The Nature of the Resurrection Body* (Grand Rapids, MI: Eerdmans, 1964); Robert A. Morey, *Death and the Afterlife* (Minneapolis: Bethany House, 1984); William Lane Craig, *Knowing the Truth About the Resurrection* (Ann Arbor, MI: Servant Books, 1988); and Gary R. Habermas and J. P. Moreland, *Immortality: The Other Side of Death* (Nashville: Thomas Nelson, 1992).

[42] Rev. 21–22, etc. See N. T. Wright, *The Resurrection of the Son of God* (Minneapolis: Fortress Press, 2003), 470–479, and Gary R. Habermas, *The Risen Jesus and Future Hope* (Lanham, MD: Rowman & Littlefield, 2003), 151–164.

Testament likewise assumes that all Christians are included in the New Covenant.

So where does their system go wrong?

Interpreting Revelation 7 and 14 in Context

Revelation 7 mentions both the 144,000 (vv. 4–8) and the Great Crowd (vv. 9–10, 13–17). Revelation 14 only mentions the 144,000 (vv. 1–5); it does not mention the Great Crowd. The Watchtower's doctrine of salvation hinges on its interpretation of these two chapters. Consider the following interpretive issues:

Identity. Who are these two groups? Should the descriptions be taken literally or figuratively? If figuratively, what is the underlying literal truth or principle to see?

Parallelism. Since much of Revelation derives its imagery from Daniel, Ezekiel, Zechariah, and other Old Testament books, are these groups intended as a parallel or antitype to other prophetic figures from the Old Testament?

Relationship to the rest of Scripture. We must consider whether it was the intention of the apostle John to reveal a different type of salvation (or a different set of promises to believers) that would emerge in the last days. If the text indicates so, then the Watchtower's conclusions are at least theologically plausible.

Identity of the 144,000

The 144,000 are described as "the slaves of our God . . . sealed out of every tribe of the sons of Israel" (7:3–4). The name of each tribe is given (Judah first, followed by Reuben, Gad, Asher, etc.) and twelve thousand are "sealed" from each tribe. The number 144,000 is the product of twelve tribes times twelve thousand from each tribe.

The listing includes Levi (often omitted) and Joseph (usually replaced by his sons Ephraim and Manasseh). It also includes Manasseh but omits Ephraim and Dan. This anomaly, coupled with the fact that the same number of people come from each tribe despite the population differences among them, leads some interpreters to believe the twelve tribes are not intended literally. Judah is named before Reuben (the historical firstborn), but this probably honors Jesus' descent from Judah, the tribe prophesied to carry the "scepter" of Israel and find "the obedience of the peoples" (Gen. 49:10). As for the irregularity in listing the tribes, the Scriptures are not uniform and contain various arrangements when listing the tribes.[43]

Revelation 14:4 says they "did not defile themselves with women; in fact, they are virgins," which indicates that they are males. They keep "following the Lamb" and were purchased "as firstfruits to God and to the Lamb."

Contrast this with "a great crowd, which no man was able to number, out of all nations and tribes and peoples and tongues" (Rev. 7:9). The great crowd has "come out of the great tribulation" (v. 14), and its people are "before the throne of God . . . rendering him sacred service day and night in his temple" (v. 15).

These two groups emerging from the Tribulation comprise a counted set of Israelites and a countless number of Gentiles, the former sealed on their foreheads (7:3), the latter singing praise to God and to the Lamb (v. 10), both "servants" of God (vv. 3, 15).

A straightforward interpretation sees the 144,000 representing Jewish believers and the Great Crowd representing Gentile believers, both having true faith in Jesus as their Messiah. By the time Revelation was composed, the book of Acts had been in circulation for decades, and it was common knowledge that though the Christian church was founded by Jews, it grew dynamically through the addition of a much larger number of Gentile converts. Paul's letter to the Romans explained that the gospel would go "to the Jew first" (Rom. 1:16) and then to the Gentile, with the Jews taking a figurative role of "firstfruits" and "root," followed by the non-Jews who would multiply as "lump" and "branches" (see Rom. 11:16).

Most commentators accept this general outline for their identity, even if they see the numbers 12,000 and 144,000 as symbolic and nonliteral.[44] Several commentators believe the 144,000 are not wholly Jewish, but perhaps primarily Jewish, representing the early church as opposed to the predominantly Gentile church of the Tribulation period.[45] Most see the

---

[43]The usual list of the twelve sons of Jacob appears in Gen. 35:22–26; 46:8–25; 49:3–28. Levi and Joseph are replaced with Ephraim and Manasseh in Num. 1:5–49; 2:3–33; 13:3–15; 26:5–50. In 1 Chron. 12:1–40 and Ezek. 48:1–29 Levi is included and Joseph is replaced by Ephraim and Manasseh, making thirteen tribes. In Moses' blessing in Deut. 33:6–25, Simeon is omitted. In the genealogies in 1 Chron. 2–8, both Dan and Zebulun are omitted. The sequence in listing the tribal names varies even more widely. The reason John omitted the tribe of Dan here, putting Manasseh in his place, has created speculation since the days of Irenaeus (e.g., unrepentant idolatry, or the Antichrist is to come from the tribe of Dan). The text does not say. However, Ezekiel's vision saw Dan's name on the gate of the millennial temple (Ezek. 48:32).

[44]William E. Biederwolf, *The Second Coming Bible* (1924; reprint Grand Rapids, MI: Baker, 1972), 580–583.

[45]Ibid., 582–584, 642–645, and J. Barton Payne, *Encyclopedia of Biblical Prophecy* (Grand Rapids, MI: Baker, 1973), 612, 621.

144,000 as representing the "Israel of God" rather than Israel according to the flesh (Gal. 6:16).

Parallels in the Old Testament

The 144,000 as a *number* does not have parallels from the Old Testament, but the servants of God "sealed on their foreheads" reminds the careful reader of Ezekiel 9:4, where God orders a mark to be placed on the foreheads of the inhabitants of Jerusalem who grieve for the abominations committed in it; those without the mark will be put to death, beginning at the sanctuary. In Revelation, the servants of God from the twelve tribes are also marked on their foreheads. This marking enables them to escape the plagues soon to follow (Rev. 7:3; 9:4).

While there are few overt parallels in the Old Testament, the most important are the prophecies involving Jewish and Gentile believers. God promised to multiply the seed of Abraham (the twelve tribes) and to bless all the nations of the earth (the multitudes) through the people of Israel.[46] Zechariah, the source of many images in the book of Revelation, prophesied that "many nations shall join themselves to Jehovah" in the end-time; the house of Judah would hear people of all nations and languages ask to follow them, because "we have heard that God is with you" (2:10–11, 8:22–23, ASV). Revelation draws from Genesis, Zechariah, and elsewhere the theme of God's blessing to the Gentile nations through the Jews.

Relationship to the Rest of Scripture

It is important to realize that the Watchtower system asserts that there are currently two types of Christians: some in the New Covenant, justified, regenerated, sanctified, and anointed, and others who are *outside* the New Covenant and who are *not* justified, regenerated, sanctified or anointed. When the apostle John penned the book of Revelation, was it his intention to limit the blessings of the New Covenant to exactly 144,000 people? Was it John's intention to predict or prepare the reader for a future system with millions of unregenerate, unsanctified, "unanointed" Christians?

It is not our place to describe the various ways Revelation 7 and 14 have been interpreted, but we must say a few things in response to the Watchtower's claims. First, the book of Revelation and the rest of the New Testament give no indication that there will come an end to the New

---

[46]Gen. 12:3; 18:18; 22:18; 26:4; 28:14; Gal. 3:8–9.

Covenant. The Bible does not provide a "sunset clause" that defines when the New Covenant will become obsolete, nor is there any indication of an alternative or "third covenant" to supersede the New Covenant.

The Watchtower Society claims that the New Covenant will come to an end when the last members of the 144,000 have died.[47] It further claims that those in the Great Crowd are in a position to receive eternal life by obedience to Jehovah God during the Millennium; somehow the Great Crowd can allegedly do this without a covenant and without justification, regeneration, sanctification, adoption, or the anointing of the Holy Spirit.

The Watchtower teaches that the New Testament is written only to New Covenant believers who are anointed and adopted as sons and daughters of God. In this sense, they are correct. Yet the Society wants us to believe that the Bible *also* anticipates the coming of a future class of unregenerate, "unanointed" Christians outside of God's covenant—the Great Crowd.

There is no indication of this in John's writings. On the contrary, the Bible teaches that anyone who believes that Jesus is the Christ "has been born from God" (1 John 5:1), and that "God gave us everlasting life, and this life is in his Son. He that has the Son has this life" (1 John 5:11b–12a). There are no passages in 1 John or in the rest of John's writings or anywhere in the Bible that indicate that these promises will become obsolete after a certain period of time.

Second, there is no indication in the text of Revelation that *only* 144,000 members are born again and within the New Covenant. Correspondingly, there is no indication in the text that the Great Crowd is *not* born again nor in the New Covenant. The Watchtower's entire case for these assertions rests on a single specious argument: they say that the word "sealed" in Rev. 7:2–4 refers to the "sealing" and anointing mentioned by another writer (Paul) at another time in another book (2 Cor. 1:21–22).[48] By contrast, since the word "sealed" is not used of the Great Crowd in Revelation 7:9–17, the Watchtower writers have assumed that they must be outside of the new birth, the new covenant, and the entire package of blessings offered to first-century Christians.

This, of course, is an argument from silence. The fact that the word "sealed" is not used of the Great Crowd does not indicate that they do not

---

[47]"Benefiting from 'One Mediator Between God and Men,'" *Watchtower*, November 15, 1979, 27. The article adds, ". . . then the mediatorship of Jesus Christ will cease also." See also "Questions from Readers," *Watchtower*, July 1, 1980, 31, and "Do You Remember?" August 15, 1980, 30.

[48]*Revelation—Its Grand Climax at Hand!* (1988), 115–116. The passage 2 Cor. 1:21–22 is significant because it connects being "in Christ," being "anointed," being "sealed," and having "the Spirit in our hearts" (ASV). Having one of these privileges presumes having the others as well.

need regeneration. There is no explicit statement in the text to suggest that the Great Crowd "standing before the throne and before the Lamb" (Rev. 7:9) have done so apart from regeneration (the new birth), justification, and adoption as sons and daughters of God. In fact, *Revelation—Its Grand Climax at Hand!* argues that the phrase "standing before the throne" should not be interpreted literally, but only that they are in a place where Jehovah can see them.[49]

Third, the Watchtower interprets all the characteristics of the 144,000 as symbolic *except* for the number 144,000 itself. Revelation 7 and 14 say they are Jews, from named tribes, are males, are virgins, and number twelve thousand from each tribe. The Society says all these elements are symbols: they are (allegedly) both Jews and Gentiles, include male and female, include virgins and nonvirgins, and are not twelve thousand from any particular tribe at all.[50] They interpret all the parts symbolically. Yet they insist that the number 144,000 is a literal number, while the multipliers (12 x 12,000) are not literal.

The Watchtower switches its method of interpretation two times in a single verse: "And I heard the number of those who were sealed [symbol], a hundred and forty-four thousand [literal], sealed out of every tribe [symbol] of the sons of Israel [symbol]" (Rev. 7:4). If the numbers 12 and 12,000 are to be taken symbolically, then 144,000 should be taken symbolically as well.

Fourth, if the number 144,000 should be interpreted literally, it would have been fulfilled before the end of the first century. The early church grew at a dramatic rate. Jerome Smith suggests that Christian believers (both Jews and Gentiles) easily numbered more than 144,000 by the middle of the first century.[51] Commentator David Stern notes that the number of believing Messianic Jews alone "was surely in six figures" by A.D. 70.[52] The premier statistician of the growth of world religions, David Barrett, estimates that by A.D. 70 there were probably over 270,000 Christians and over 800,000 living Christians by A.D. 100, even accounting for martyrdom.[53] So whether one interprets the 144,000 to be purely Jews or both Jews and Gentiles (as the Watchtower does), that number was long surpassed before the first century ended.

---

[49]Ibid., 123–124.
[50]Ibid., 117.
[51]Jerome Smith, *The New Treasury of Scripture Knowledge* (Nashville: Thomas Nelson, 1992), 1516.
[52]David H. Stern, *Jewish New Testament Commentary,* sixth edition (Clarksville, MD: Jewish New Testament Publications, 1999), 810.
[53]David B. Barrett and Todd M. Johnson, *World Christian Trends AD 30–AD 2200* (Pasadena, CA: William Carey Library, 2001), 19.

HOW TO PRESENT THIS INFORMATION TO
JEHOVAH'S WITNESSES

At this stage, we intend to shift gears slightly to directly address the Christian wishing to effectively reach Jehovah's Witnesses. Our tone will necessarily be more personal and direct.

One general principle we appreciate is the "Golden Rule Apologetic" expounded in several places by the late Bob Passantino. This rule applies to all types of apologetics encounters, not simply those that deal with cults or unpopular religions. It simply means following the Golden Rule in your witnessing encounters. "Don't press the Witness harder than you want to be pressed. Don't ridicule him for his belief if you wouldn't like to be ridiculed for being a Christian. If you want the Witness to understand when you don't have an answer and need time to research it, then give the Witness the same opportunity to try to defend his belief."[54]

Each of the authors has seen Bob apply this rule in his conversations with people in religious error or skepticism, and the healthy respect he showed them has made a lasting and fruitful impact not only on them but on each of us individually.

Although we have read many books suggesting ways to reach Jehovah's Witnesses, we most agree with the assessment of Joan Cetnar, an ex-Witness who formerly worked at Bethel, the world headquarters of Jehovah's Witnesses in Brooklyn, New York.[55] She believes the most practical book on this topic is *Approaching Jehovah's Witnesses in Love* by Wilbur Lingle.[56] Written by an intercultural missionary to Japan, it is packed with useful tips gained from years of field experience. We are glad to commend it to Christian apologists.

Lingle reminds us that through their Theocratic Ministry School, Jehovah's Witnesses are trained to have a self-image as God's representatives who come to teach the Bible. For the most part (remember, each person is unique, so we should avoid universal generalizations), they see themselves and want to be seen as teachers or instructors. Therefore, if *you* appear to assume a role as their teacher or corrector, your communication with them will be impaired. It is more productive to assume the role of a questioner or student.

---

[54]Passantino, "Jehovah's Witnesses," 136.
[55]Joan and her late husband Bill were lifelong Jehovah's Witnesses and were in regular contact with Watchtower officials at Bethel. After their conversion, the Cetnars wrote *Questions for Jehovah's Witnesses Who Love the Truth* (Phillipsburg, NJ: P&R, 1983). Since 1979 Joan has organized an annual conference in New Ringgold, Pennsylvania, named "Witnesses NOW for Jesus."
[56]Wilbur Lingle, *Approaching Jehovah's Witnesses in Love*, second edition (Fort Washington, PA: CLC Publications, 2004).

Most Jehovah's Witnesses love to answer questions, and the Socratic method is usually a better way to present this information. Ask them questions for which they are unlikely to have a prepared answer. If you do not have one, get a copy of the Watchtower publication *Reasoning from the Scriptures*. In preparation for your meeting, check to see if your question is directly addressed in the *Reasoning* book. If it is, throw it out and use a different question. The best questions are those that are *not* addressed in the *Reasoning* book and that require thoughtful, deliberate reflection in formulating an answer.

Good communicators build bridges by using vocabulary and cultural or religious themes significant to the hearers. Therefore, speak about salvation using language they understand, such as being able to survive Armageddon and go into the New World. Avoid terms or vocabulary likely to raise red flags or get the conversation sidetracked.

In particular, avoid using the word *Trinity* and direct references to the deity of Christ (i.e., statements that Jesus is God). Most Jehovah's Witnesses have an automatic and deep-seated negative reaction to these terms that they associate with paganism and idolatry. The problem is not only that they believe these doctrines to be false (akin to a belief that the world is flat); they are indoctrinated to believe these doctrines to be demonic in their origin and in their persuasive power.

We are *not* saying that Christians sharing the gospel should deny or hide biblical doctrines—only that one should avoid unnecessary offense while obtaining a hearing to communicate the gospel. While it is true that no one can deny the deity of Christ and be saved,[57] it is also true that we are free to present the elements of the Christian truth claim in a different order or sequence to meet the needs of each person. And yes, that presentation may take days, weeks, or longer.

Assuming There Will Be Only One Meeting

If, for whatever reason, you can meet only one time, frame your conversation as an extended question about the Bible. Ask the Witness to directly explain the meaning of John 5:24. Ask for a clear definition of each major term, and ask the meaning of Jesus' statement as a whole. This passage reads in the NWT, "Most truly I say to YOU, He that hears my word and believes him that sent me has everlasting life, and he does not come into

---

[57]We point to passages such as John 8:24; Rom. 10:9, 13 (cf. Joel 2:32); 2 Pet. 2:1, etc. The intentional denial of the deity of Christ is far more serious than the immaturity of young believers who have not studied the Scriptures on this topic and are thus unable to fully articulate it.

judgment but has passed over from death to life" (John 5:24).[58] In particular, what does "everlasting life" mean? The text says that the believer has or possesses this kind of life now and has already "passed over" from death to life. Witnesses are taught that everlasting life is a prospect or an opportunity that cannot be realized until the end of the Millennium and that might be forfeited at any time before then. However, Jesus offers this life as a possession received now, not a prospect to be gained sometime later.

The average Jehovah's Witness certainly thinks that he meets the conditions (i.e., he hears Jesus' word and also believes in God the Father [Jehovah]), but he believes that he is not entitled to the promise of everlasting life *now*. Gently but firmly face him with the contradiction.

Another route is to ask one or two setup questions before asking one that hits directly on one of their core doctrines, something like this: "It is your understanding that the 144,000 are born again, and the Great Crowd cannot be born again. Is this correct?" The Witness will undoubtedly answer yes.

"And it is your understanding that the Great Crowd have an earthly hope and they expect to see the kingdom of God on earth during the Millennium. Is this correct?" Again, virtually all Witnesses will answer yes. Then ask this follow-up: "According to John 3:3, a person must be 'born again' or born from above in order to see the kingdom of God at all. The pronoun in John 3:7 is plural, so we know that Jesus was not speaking to Nicodemus alone. Jesus did not seem to differentiate between an earthly kingdom and a heavenly kingdom in making this requirement."

Surely Jehovah God, who inspired the Scriptures, knew what wording to use to convey the truth, and Jesus told his followers they "*must* be born again," indicating that it was not simply an option for a small minority of his followers. "So why," you then ask, "do Jehovah's Witnesses believe that most people today are exempt from this scriptural requirement?"

Be aware that the stock reply is that John's Gospel was written when every believer was "born again," but that this is not the case today. If the Witness raises this objection, point out that this reply is an explanation invented in the twentieth century, and the rest of John does not say that anywhere. John's Gospel does not contain a time limit on its own application of salvation. In fact, nowhere does the New Testament put a time limit on the offer of regeneration, adoption, and justification for all who believe in Jesus Christ.

---

[58]The YOU in small caps indicates that the pronoun is plural in Greek. There are no translation problems with the New World Translation of this verse.

Assuming There will be Several Meetings

The most productive opportunity for evangelism will occur if you can get a Witness to commit to meeting with you on several occasions. It is hard to get them to commit to a series of meetings, but this is the best way to allow them to become aware of the implications of the Watchtower's teaching. The average Witness did not come to his beliefs as a result of personal Bible study and then seek an organization that matched his conclusions. Instead, people are usually introduced to the Society through "book studies" (not Bible studies) of Watchtower literature. The student reads a paragraph and then answers simple questions at the bottom of each page. How the questions are framed determines what answers are conceivable and deemed to be viable. Since the Society sets the agenda for the questions, it likewise sets the agenda for how a question can be answered. As Lingle recognizes, our apologetic task is to get the Witness to think outside the box, in categories and perspectives they do not expect.

We do not have the time or the space to cover the many helpful hints in Lingle's book, which is subtitled, "How to Witness Effectively Without Arguing." However, we can echo a few of the insights from this text.

First, say that you have some questions regarding the Watchtower and its doctrine, and ask if your Witness friend is willing to answer your questions in detail. If he says yes, proceed to the next step. Second, say up front that it will take several months to cover all you want to ask about, assuming that you meet once each week. You want to meet with the same person (or couple) each time; do not agree to be set up with a rotation from one person to the next, which often happens. The Witness may try to get you to accept a rotation of other people, but insist that you meet with the same person each time. Third, set up the meetings with a calendar or appointment book in front of each of you. Enter the dates, times, and locations you will meet, a full three months in advance. (A weekly meeting for three months is thirteen weeks.)

Fourth, lay some ground rules for conversation, which exclude arguing, attacking other religious groups or personalities, or attacking your own beliefs about the Bible. Fifth, "no matter how well the conversation seems to be going, never, never, never talk more than forty-five minutes to an hour on religious matters. If you talk more than that, you will give him too much and it could easily drive him away."[59]

The authors admit to having conversations that have lasted as many as

---

[59]Lingle, *Approaching Jehovah's Witnesses in Love*, 44.

eight hours, but those have been single meetings not prepared in advance. For a prepared series of meetings with the same person, the Christian *must* beware of the tendency to overload the person.

Christian apologists sometimes lose sight of the goal, often by trying to win an argument. We believe it is possible to "win the argument but lose the soul" (as the cliché goes). We believe that Jehovah's Witnesses are valued and loved by Almighty God, and since God loves them as individuals, so must we. Take an interest in their families, their background, their personal stories and sorrows. We hope to get them to think, not simply to parrot back what has been poured into them repeatedly. This means taking it slow, not handing them too much at once, and remembering the Golden Rule Apologetic while we are witnessing.

Lingle recognizes that an important part of evangelism involves helping the sinner to relinquish false hopes based on a false gospel. In the case of Jehovah's Witnesses, their trust is in the Watchtower Society as the sole channel (or mediator!) of God's truth to them. By a loving application of the Socratic method, we can ask them to explain why we (as non-Witnesses) or anyone should place faith in this organization as God's channel.

Our motive is to help them to realize not simply intellectually but at deep levels within their being that the Watchtower Society has interposed itself as the ruler of their conscience, their channel of truth, and the final interpreter of Scripture. In short, the Society has taken the place of the Holy Spirit in their lives.

If this can be examined and their false hope seen for what it is, then the same methods and questions can be applied to the Watchtower gospel, and the Jehovah's Witness can find the biblical Jesus and truly enter into life everlasting in the kingdom of God.

CHAPTER TWENTY-ONE

Oneness Pentecostals and the Doctrine of God

Ron Rhodes

ONENESS PENTECOSTALISM EMERGED out of the Assemblies of God churches in the early 1900s. A minority of pastors affiliated with the denomination began to teach a modalistic concept of God. Denying the Trinity, they believed the one true God, Jesus, manifested himself in three different modes (not persons): the Father, the Son, and the Holy Spirit.[1]

The larger corpus of Assemblies of God pastors resisted this teaching and at a denominational council in 1916 strongly affirmed belief in the Trinity. This action led to the withdrawal of 156 out of 585 pastors, along with their congregations.[2] These pastors left because they believed "the church had violated its founding principle of adopting no creed other than the Bible."[3]

The decades that followed witnessed the emergence of a number of small denominations headed by the Oneness pastors who withdrew from the Assemblies of God. Various splits and mergers occurred, ultimately resulting in the formation of the largest of the Oneness Pentecostal groups—the United Pentecostal Church (UPC), with over one million members in the United States. In the present chapter my goal is to answer some of the more common UPC arguments for a modalistic concept of God.

Foundationally, Oneness Pentecostals generally believe "Father" refers to Jesus' deity, "Son" refers to Jesus in his humanity or in the incarnate state, and "Holy Spirit" refers to God imparting himself to humankind in various ways.[4] Though often confusing, Oneness theology teaches that Jesus is

---

[1]David Bernard, *The Oneness of God* (Hazelwood, MO: Word Aflame, 1983), 15.
[2]Calvin Beisner, *"Jesus Only" Churches* (Grand Rapids, MI: Zondervan, 1998), 70.
[3]David Bernard, *The Oneness View of Jesus Christ* (Hazelwood, MO: Word Aflame, 1994), 142.
[4]Gary Rugger, *The Oneness of God* (Bakersfield, CA: Rugger, 2003), 25.

both the *Father* who sent his Son, and the *Son* who obeyed the Father. He was the *Son* who prayed to the Father, while at the same time he was the *Father* who answered the Son's prayers. Yet, Jesus was and is just one person. Let us now consider the primary Oneness arguments for this convoluted view and answer them one by one.

THE ARGUMENT: THERE IS ONE GOD

Oneness Pentecostals point to Bible verses that show that God is absolutely one (e.g., Deut. 6:4; Isa. 42:8; 43:10–11; 44:6; 1 Cor. 8:4–6; Eph. 4:4–6; 1 Tim. 2:5). They reason that since there is only one true God, and since Jesus is often said to be God in the New Testament (e.g., John 8:58; Col. 2:9; Titus 2:13–14), Jesus therefore must be the one true God of which Scripture speaks. Hence, Jesus is the Father, the Son, and the Holy Spirit.[5]

Bernard suggests that "Trinitarianism is not pure monotheism; rather, it tends toward tritheism."[6] He claims that "many Trinitarian Pentecostals are theological tritheists. Finis Dake [of *The Dake Study Bible*] spoke of God as 'three separate persons,' each one being an 'individual' with his 'own personal spirit body, personal soul, and personal spirit in the same sense each human being, angel or any other being has his own body, soul, and spirit.'"[7]

Trinitarians agree that the verses cited by Oneness Pentecostals prove there is only one God. They also emphasize, however, that God's oneness is the foundational plank of the doctrine of the Trinity. Where Oneness Pentecostals err is in considering these verses in isolation from other verses that prove a clear distinction between the Father, the Son, and the Holy Spirit. Indeed, the Father is considered by Jesus as someone *other* than himself over two hundred times in the New Testament. And over fifty times in the New Testament the Father and Son are distinct within the same verse (e.g., Rom. 15:6; 2 Cor. 1:3; Gal. 1:3; Phil. 2:10–11; 1 John 2:1; 2 John 3).

We read in Scripture that the Father *sent* the Son into the world (John 3:17). The Father and Son *love* each other (John 14:31). The Father *speaks* to the Son, and the Son *speaks* to the Father (John 11:41–42). The Holy Spirit *comes upon* Jesus at his baptism (Matt. 3:16). Jesus and the Father are viewed as having *sent* the Holy Spirit upon the people of God following the resurrection (John 14:26; 15:26). Jesus and the Father are viewed as *two distinct witnesses* (John 5:31–32, 37). The Holy Spirit *intercedes* with

---

[5]Bernard, *The Oneness of God*, 66.
[6]Bernard, *The Oneness View of Jesus Christ*, 11.
[7]Ibid., 12.

the Father on our behalf (Rom. 8:26–27). Clearly these are distinct persons who interact with each other. To say that one mode is speaking to another or that one mode loves another is nonsensical.

Granted, the Bible does not *explicitly* identify the Father, the Son, and the Holy Spirit as persons. However, this is a reasonable inference based on explicit affirmations in Scripture. The Father engages in I-Thou relations (John 3:35) and has the attributes of personality: intellect (Matt. 6:8), emotions (Gen. 6:6; Ps. 86:15), and will (Matt. 12:50). The Son engages in I-Thou relations (John 11:41–42) and has the attributes of personality: intellect (John 2:24–25), emotions (Matt. 9:36; John 11:35), and will (Luke 22:42). The Holy Spirit engages in I-Thou relations (Acts 8:29) and has the attributes of personality: intellect (Rom. 8:27; 1 Cor. 2:10–11), emotions (Isa. 63:10; Eph. 4:30), and will (1 Cor. 12:11). The personality of each of the three is therefore implicit in Scripture.

As for Finis Dake, it is true that there are some in the charismatic and Word Faith camp who have been heavily influenced by *The Dake Study Bible*—Jimmy Swaggart, Benny Hinn, and Kenneth Copeland, to name a few. Such men, however, are hardly representative of the broader corpus of Trinitarians, who reject Dake's Bible as thoroughly unbalanced and even heretical.[8]

THE ARGUMENT: ONENESS PENTECOSTALISM CONTINUES THE JEWISH VIEW OF GOD

Oneness Pentecostals often argue that they are continuing the historic Jewish position on the doctrine of God, holding firmly to the Jewish confession of faith (the *Shema*): "Hear, O Israel: The LORD our God, the LORD is one" (Deut. 6:4[9]).[10] Oneness proponents claim there is not a single Old Testament verse that enunciates the doctrine of the Trinity. Bernard concludes that "if threeness is an essential part of God's nature, He did not reveal this to His chosen people."[11]

In response, the criterion for Christian truth is not what the Jews believed, nor is it what the Old Testament alone teaches. Rather, it is the complete Bible, especially the New Testament.

It is critically important to recognize that in the course of God's self-

---

[8]Jeffrey Spencer and Steve Bright, "Dake's Dangerous Doctrines," *Christian Research Journal*, Vol. 27, No. 5 (2004).

[9]Unless otherwise indicated, all Scripture quotations in this chapter are taken from *The Holy Bible: English Standard Version*.

[10]David Bernard, *Essentials of Oneness Theology* (Hazelwood, MO: Word Aflame, 2001), 8.

[11]Ibid., 8–9.

disclosure to humankind, he revealed his nature to man in progressive stages. God first revealed his essential unity and uniqueness—that is, he revealed that he is one and that he is the only true God. This was a necessary starting-point for God's self-revelation, for throughout history Israel was surrounded by nations deeply engulfed in polytheism. Through the prophets, God communicated and affirmed to Israel the truth of monotheism.

While God's unity and oneness—as affirmed in the *Shema* (Deut. 6:4)—is the clear emphasis in Old Testament revelation, this is not to say that there are no hints or shadows of the doctrine of the Trinity there, for indeed there are (e.g., Gen. 1:26; 3:22; 11:7; Ps. 110:1; Prov. 30:4; Isa. 6:8; 48:16; 61:1). In Isaiah 48:16, in particular, all three persons of the Trinity are mentioned and are seen as distinct from each other. Further, many theologians believe that references to the Angel of Yahweh in the Old Testament were preincarnate appearances of Jesus Christ. The Angel of Yahweh—identified as *being* Yahweh in Exodus 3:1–6—is also seen as *distinct from* Yahweh since he intercedes *to* Yahweh on behalf of the people of God (Zech. 1:12; cf. 3:1–2). Nevertheless, God did not reveal the fullness of his triune nature until New Testament times (e.g., Matt. 3:16–17; 28:19; 2 Cor. 13:14; Eph. 4:4–6). It is by reading the Old Testament under the illumination of the New Testament that we find supporting evidences for the Trinity there. As theologian Benjamin Warfield put it:

> The Old Testament may be likened to a chamber richly furnished but dimly lighted; the introduction of light brings into it nothing which was not in it before; but it brings out into clearer view much of what is in it but was only dimly or even not at all perceived before. The mystery of the Trinity is not [explicitly] revealed in the Old Testament; but the mystery of the Trinity underlies the Old Testament revelation, and here and there almost comes into view. Thus the Old Testament revelation of God is not corrected by the fuller revelation which follows it, but only perfected, extended, and enlarged.[12]

THE ARGUMENT: ONENESS PENTECOSTALISM CONTINUES THE NEW TESTAMENT WRITERS' VIEW OF GOD

Oneness Pentecostals argue that the New Testament writers were monotheists who had no intention of introducing a new concept of God. Neither the writers nor their readers thought in Trinitarian categories, and, indeed,

---

[12]Benjamin Warfield, *Biblical and Theological Studies* (Phillipsburg, NJ: P&R, 1968), 30.

such categories are foreign to the pages of the New Testament.[13] There is no mention of three coequal or coeternal persons, but simply a focus on the one true God who is Jesus Christ.[14]

This claim misrepresents the biblical data. We witness all three persons at the baptism account of Jesus (Matt. 3:16–17). All three persons are mentioned in Paul's benediction to the Corinthians (2 Cor. 13:14). Christ commanded the disciples to baptize in the name of the Father, the Son, and the Holy Spirit (Matt. 28:19). And Trinitarian language virtually permeates many key passages of Scripture, 1 Thessalonians 1 being a good example.

It is true that the terms *coequal* or *coeternal* are not found in the Bible, but these terms accurately reflect the biblical teaching that the Father, Son, and Holy Spirit are *equally divine* and *equally eternal*. All three persons possess the attribute of *omnipresence*: the Father (Jer. 23:23–24), the Son (Matt. 28:20), and the Holy Spirit (Ps. 139:7). All three possess the attribute of *omniscience*: the Father (Rom. 11:33), the Son (Matt. 9:4), and the Holy Spirit (1 Cor. 2:10). All three possess the attribute of *omnipotence*: the Father (1 Pet. 1:5), the Son (Matt. 28:18), and the Holy Spirit (Rom. 15:19). And *eternity* is ascribed to each of the three: the Father (Ps. 90:2), the Son (Mic. 5:2; John 1:2; Rev. 1:8, 17), and the Holy Spirit (Heb. 9:14). In view of this, the terms *coequal* and *coeternal* are perfectly appropriate expressions of truth.

Sometimes Oneness Pentecostals rebut that Colossians 2:9 reveals that the fullness (*totality*) of deity resides in Jesus, and thus Jesus himself must be the Father, Son, and Holy Spirit. David Bernard charges, "Trinitarianism denies that the fullness of the Godhead is in Jesus because it denies that Jesus is the Father and the Holy Spirit."[15] However, in this verse the term "Godhead" simply means "deity." The word indicates that the fullness of deity—the very divine essence itself, including all the divine attributes—dwells fully in Jesus. The verse indicates, then, that Jesus is fully God, but it does not say that Jesus is the only person who is God. Scripture interprets Scripture. And Scripture indicates that in the unity of the one God (Deut. 6:4), there are three distinct persons: the Father (1 Pet. 1:2), the Son (John 20:28), and the Holy Spirit (Acts 5:3–4).

THE ARGUMENT: JESUS IS THE FATHER

While Oneness Pentecostals say that the terms *Father*, *Son*, and *Holy Spirit* are modes of manifestation of the one God (Jesus), practically speaking

---

[13]Bernard, *Essentials of Oneness Theology*, 10.
[14]Rugger, *The Oneness of God*, 26.
[15]Bernard, *The Oneness of God*, 289.

they often use the term *Father* to refer to God or to divinity or the divine being. Oneness Pentecostals thus claim: "The divine nature of Christ is the everlasting Father."[16] "The Scriptures show that the deity of Jesus actually is the Father and not a second person of deity."[17] "The Word of God teaches that God the Father was manifest in the flesh."[18]

A number of biblical passages are cited to bolster support for this view. For example, Isaiah 9:6 refers to Jesus as "Everlasting Father."[19] Jesus in John 10:30 affirmed, "I and the Father are one," thus establishing their common identity.[20] Jesus indicated that if a person saw him, he or she actually saw the Father (John 14:7–11).[21]

First Corinthians 1:3 is also cited, where we read, "Grace to you and peace from God our Father *and* the Lord Jesus Christ." Oneness Pentecostals claim the latter part of the verse should read, "God our Father, *even* the Lord Jesus Christ." Translated this way (Greek, *kai* = "even"), Jesus and the Father are seen to be one and the same person.

Though Jesus is called "everlasting Father" in Isaiah 9:6, the Oneness Pentecostal contention that this proves Jesus is "the Father" is incorrect. Foundationally, the word "Father" as a title of God did not emerge into prominence until New Testament times when Jesus taught that God was a "Father." It certainly was not a common title of God in Old Testament times. This would argue against the idea that the use of "Father" in Isaiah 9:6 was intended to be a New Testament-like reference to God, but rather that the term was used in a different sense.

Indeed, in Isaiah 9:6 the phrase is better translated "Father of eternity" and carries the meaning, "possessor of eternity." "Father of eternity" is here used in accordance with a Hebrew and Arabic custom in which he who possesses a thing is called the father of it. Thus, "the father of strength" means "strong," "the father of knowledge" "intelligent," "the father of glory" "glorious."[22] According to this common usage, the meaning of "Father of eternity" in Isaiah 9:6 is "eternal." Christ as the "Father of eternity" is an eternal being.

The Targum, a simplified paraphrase of the Old Testament Scriptures utilized by the ancient Jews, rendered Isaiah 9:6, "His name has been called

---

[16]Rugger, *The Oneness of God*, 15.

[17]L. Aubrey Gard, *Three? Two? The One True God* (Twin Falls, ID: n.p., n.d.), 63.

[18]Rugger, *The Oneness of God*, 10.

[19]See discussion in Kenneth Reeves, *The Godhead* (St. Louis: Trio, 1999), 79, 85; see also Gard, *Three? Two? The One True God*, 64.

[20]Gordon Magee, *Is Jesus in the Godhead or Is the Godhead in Jesus?* (Hazelwood, MO: Word Aflame Press, 1988), 15.

[21]Gard, *Three? Two? The One True God*, 70.

[22]Albert Barnes, *Notes on the Old Testament: Isaiah* (Grand Rapids, MI: Baker, 1977), 193.

from of old, Wonderful Counselor, Mighty God, *he who lives forever.*"[23] The ancient Jews considered the phrase "Father of eternity" as indicating the eternality of the Messiah.

As for Jesus in John 10:30 claiming that he and the Father "are one," this verse does not mean Jesus and the Father are one and the same person. We know this to be true because in the phrase, "I and the Father are one," a first-person plural, "we are" (*esmen* in the Greek), is used. The verse literally reads in the Greek, "I and the Father—*we are* one." If Jesus intended to say that he and the Father were one *person*, he certainly would not have used the first-person plural, which clearly implies *two* persons.

Moreover, the Greek word for "one" (*hen*) in this verse refers *not* to personal unity (that is, the idea that the Father and Son are one person) but to unity of essence or nature (that is, that the Father and Son have the same divine nature). This is evident in the fact that the form of the word in the Greek is neuter, not masculine. Further, the verses that immediately precede *and* follow John 10:30 distinguish Jesus from the Father (see John 10:25, 29, 36, 38). Finally, the broader context of John's Gospel establishes that the Father and Jesus are distinct persons (within the unity of the one God). For example, the Father *sent* the Son (3:16–17); the Father and Son *love* one another (3:35); the Father and Son *speak* to one another (11:41–42); the Father and Son are *two witnesses* (5:31–32, 37); and the Father *knows* the Son just as the Son *knows* the Father (7:29; 8:55; 10:15).

When Jesus said if a person saw him, he or she actually saw the Father (John 14:7–11), he was not saying he *was* the Father. These verses prove only that the Father and Son are one in *being*, not that they are one *person*. Contextually, notice that in John 14:6 Jesus clearly distinguishes himself from the Father when he says, "No one comes *to* the Father, but *through* me" (emphasis added). The words "to" and "through" would not make any sense if Jesus and the Father were one and the same person. They only make sense if the Father and Jesus are distinct persons, with Jesus being the Mediator between the Father and humankind. These verses indicate that Jesus is the perfect revelation of the Father (1:18). And the reason Jesus is the perfect revelation of the Father is that Jesus and the Father, along with the Holy Spirit, are one indivisible Divine Being (10:30). Jesus, the *second* person of the Trinity, is the perfect revelation of the Father, the *first* person of the Trinity.

---

[23]J. F. Stenning, *The Targum of Isaiah* (London: Oxford, 1949), 32.

As for the Oneness Pentecostal claim that the Greek word *kai* should be translated "even" and not "and" in 1 Corinthians 1:3—thereby referring to the "Father, *even* the Lord Jesus Christ"—such argumentation is unconvincing. While it is true that the Greek word *kai* can be translated "even" in certain verses, context is always determinative in how the word is translated. Even Oneness Pentecostal scholar Robert Graves admits this: "The context determines . . . the appropriate meaning."[24] Greek scholars universally agree that in context, *kai* in 1 Corinthians 1:3 should be translated "and," not "even." Further, most of the occurrences of the word *kai* in the New Testament are translated "and," not "even." This means that the burden of proof is on Oneness Pentecostals to demonstrate that the word must be translated with its secondary meaning ("even") and not its primary meaning ("and") in 1 Corinthians 1:3. Moreover, the verses immediately *prior to* and *immediately after* 1 Corinthians 1:3 point to the distinction between the Father and Jesus Christ (see vv. 2, 4). Contextually, then, the Oneness Pentecostal interpretation does not fit.

Oneness Pentecostals sometimes rebut that when Jesus said, "I have come in my Father's name" (John 5:43), he was thereby indicating that his name *is* the Father's name. However, the use of the word "name" in this verse has to do with *authority*. Whereas many come in their own name or authority, Jesus comes not in his own authority but in the authority of the Father. Clearly, then, this verse, far from indicating that Jesus is the Father, in fact points to the distinction between the Father and Jesus. *One comes in the authority of the other.*

THE ARGUMENT: JESUS IS THE SON

In Oneness theology, "the Son" is another mode of manifestation of the one God, Jesus. Oneness leaders are not consistent in the significance they attach to the term *Son of God*. Sometimes the term may refer to the humanity of Christ. Sometimes the term may refer to God as manifest in human flesh. However, the term can never be used apart from the incarnation.[25] It can never be used of deity alone.

The Son is said to be "begotten." A begetting, it is reasoned by Oneness theologians, necessitates that the one who was begotten had a beginning in time. Sonship is therefore a temporal and temporary mode of manifestation: "The words 'begotten Son' presuppose a time when the Son was not yet begotten, or in existence; otherwise the word is useless in its terminol-

---

[24]Robert Graves, *The God of Two Testaments* (Hazelwood, MO: Graves and Turner, 1977), 52.
[25]Bernard, *The Oneness View of Jesus Christ*, 17.

ogy."[26] Psalm 2:7 says, "You are my Son; today I have begotten you." This proves that the sonship of Christ had a beginning in time.[27]

Contrary to the Oneness position, Scripture indicates that Christ is *eternally* the Son of God. Though "Son of . . ." can refer to "offspring of," it also carries the important meaning, "of the order of."[28] The phrase is often used this way in the Old Testament. For example, "sons of the prophets" meant "of the order of prophets" (1 Kings 20:35). "Sons of the singers" meant "of the order of singers" (Neh. 12:28). Likewise, the phrase "Son of God" means "of the order of God" and represents a claim to undiminished deity.

Ancient Semitics and Orientals used the phrase "Son of . . ." to indicate likeness, sameness of nature, and equality of being.[29] Hence, when Jesus claimed to be the Son of God, his Jewish contemporaries fully understood that he was making a claim to be God in an unqualified sense. Indeed, the Jews insisted, "We have a law, and according to that law he [Christ] ought to die, because he has made himself the Son of God" (John 19:7; see also 5:18). Recognizing that Jesus was identifying himself *as* God, the Jews wanted to kill him for committing blasphemy.

Evidence for Christ's eternal Sonship is found in the fact that Hebrews 1:2 says God created the universe *through* his "Son," implying that Christ was the Son of God prior to the Creation. Oneness Pentecostals try to answer this by arguing that the Son merely *preexisted in the mind of the Father* at the Creation,[30] but such a view is as unconvincing as it is novel. The text clearly states that the universe was created *through* the Son. Moreover, Christ *as* the Son is explicitly said to have existed "before all things" (Col. 1:17; see especially vv. 13–14). Also, Jesus, speaking as the Son of God (John 8:54–56), asserted his eternal preexistence before Abraham (v. 58). In view of all this, the Scriptural teaching that the Son of God was "sent . . . into" the world implies he was the Son *before* he was sent (see John 3:16–17).

It is true that Scripture speaks of Christ as the "only begotten Son" (John 3:16, NKJV and other translations). However, the phrase *only begotten* means "unique" or "one of a kind." Warfield comments, "The adjective 'only begotten' conveys the idea, not of derivation or subordination, but

---

[26]Gard, *Three? Two? The One True God*, 54.
[27]Bernard, *The Oneness View of Jesus Christ*, 69.
[28]James Buswell, *A Systematic Theology of the Christian Religion*, Vol. 1 (Grand Rapids, MI: Zondervan, 1979), 105.
[29]Charles Ryrie, *Basic Theology* (Wheaton, IL: Victor, 1986), 248.
[30]Bernard, *The Oneness View of Jesus Christ*, 55.

of uniqueness and consubstantiality: Jesus is all that God is, and He alone is this."[31]

What, then, are we to make of Psalm 2:7, which says, "You are my Son; today I have begotten you"? A basic interpretive principle is that Scripture interprets Scripture. The best way to find out what Psalm 2:7 means is to let Scripture tell us what it means. According to Acts 13:33–34, Psalm 2:7 deals not with the beginning of Jesus' Sonship but rather his resurrection from the dead. Jesus is "begotten" by the Father in the sense of being raised from the dead by him.

THE ARGUMENT: JESUS IS THE HOLY SPIRIT

Oneness Pentecostals believe there is biblical support for their view that Jesus is the Holy Spirit. Second Corinthians 3:17 tells us, "Now the Lord is the Spirit, and where the Spirit of the Lord is, there is freedom." Bernard argues, "All of Christendom confesses that Jesus is Lord, and 2 Corinthians 3:17 plainly identifies the Lord as the Spirit."[32]

Oneness Pentecostals also argue that John 14:26 proves Jesus is the Holy Spirit. Gary Rugger writes: "The name of the Holy Ghost is Jesus. Jesus said, 'But the comforter, which is the Holy Ghost, whom the Father will send *in my name*, he shall teach you all things' (John 14:26). Jesus said that the Holy Ghost would be sent forth *in His name*."[33]

Trinitarians respond that Scripture pointedly distinguishes between the persons of Jesus and the Holy Spirit. Indeed, Scripture tells us that the Holy Spirit *descended upon* Jesus at his baptism (Luke 3:22). The Holy Spirit is *another* comforter (John 14:16). The Holy Spirit seeks to *glorify* Jesus (John 16:13–14).

As for the statement in 2 Corinthians 3:17 that "the Lord is the Spirit," contextually the Holy Spirit is "Lord" not in the sense of being *Jesus*, but in the sense of being *Yahweh* (the Lord God) (cf. v. 16, which cites Exod. 34:34). We know the verse is not saying Jesus is the Holy Spirit, for just earlier in 2 Corinthians 3 the apostle Paul clearly distinguishes between Jesus and the Holy Spirit (see vv. 3–6). The immediate context, then, stands against the Oneness Pentecostal view.

Equally incorrect is the Oneness interpretation of John 14:26, where we are told that Jesus sent the Holy Spirit *in his name*. The verse cannot be

---

[31] Benjamin Warfield, *The Person and Work of Christ* (Philadelphia: P&R, 1950), 56.
[32] Bernard, *The Oneness View of Jesus Christ*, 62.
[33] Rugger, *The Oneness of God*, 29.

eisegetically[34] twisted to mean that the name of the Holy Spirit is "Jesus." The verse simply indicates that the Holy Spirit would be Jesus' officially designated representative to act on his behalf. "Just as Jesus himself demonstrated the personality and character of God to others, so after his departure the Holy Spirit would make the living Christ real to his followers."[35] Seen in this light, Jesus and the Holy Spirit are distinct, with one representing the other.

THE ARGUMENT: A COMPARISON OF MATTHEW AND ACTS PROVES JESUS IS THE FATHER, SON, AND HOLY SPIRIT

Oneness Pentecostals garner support for their modalistic view by interpreting Matthew 28:19 in conjunction with Acts 2:38. In Matthew 28:19 Jesus said to the disciples, "Go therefore and make disciples of all nations, baptizing them in the *name* of the Father and of the Son and of the Holy Spirit" (emphasis added). Yet, in Acts 2:38 Jesus' followers were instructed to baptize "in the *name* of Jesus" (emphasis added). This must mean that "in the name of the Father and of the Son and of the Holy Spirit" is the same as "in the name of Jesus." L. Aubrey Gard asks, "Why *name* instead of *names*, if three persons are intended?"[36] Jesus himself must be the Father, the Son, and the Holy Spirit.[37]

Contrary to the Oneness position, Bible expositors have noted that the term *name* does not have to refer to a single person (see Gen. 5:2; 11:4; 48:16). While *name* is singular in Matthew 28:19, indicating that there is one God, there are three distinct persons within the Godhead as indicated by the series of definite articles in the verse—*the* Father, *the* Son, and *the* Holy Spirit. Greek scholar Daniel Wallace tells us that the definite article is often used to stress the identity of an individual.[38] Theologian Robert Reymond thus observes:

> Jesus does not say, (1) "into the names [plural] of the Father and of the Son and of the Holy Spirit," or what is its virtual equivalent, (2) "into the name of the Father, and into the name of the Son, and into the name of the Holy Spirit," as if we had to deal with three separate Beings. Nor does He say, (3) "into the name of the Father, Son, and Holy Spirit," (omitting

---

[34]Eisegesis involves imposing a meaning onto a text that is not there. It is often described in terms of reading a meaning into the text rather than deriving the meaning out of it.
[35]*Zondervan NIV Bible Commentary*, eds. Kenneth Barker and John Kohlenberger, Vol. 2 (Grand Rapids, MI: Zondervan, 1994), 349.
[36]Gard, *Three? Two? The One True God*, 172.
[37]Thomas Weisser, "Was the Early Church Oneness or Trinitarian?" in *Symposium on Oneness Pentecostalism 1986* (St. Louis: UPCI, 1986), 57.
[38]Daniel Wallace, *The Basics of New Testament Syntax* (Grand Rapids, MI: Zondervan, 2000), 94.

the three recurring articles), as if "the Father, Son, and Holy Ghost" might be taken as merely three designations of a single person. What He does say is this: (4) "into the name [singular] of *the* Father, and of *the* Son, and of *the* Holy Spirit," first asserting the unity of the three by combining them all within the bounds of the single Name, and then throwing into emphasis the distinctness of each by introducing them in turn with the repeated article.[39]

Further, there is virtually no indication in Matthew 28:19 that Jesus was esoterically and cryptically referring to himself with the words "the Father, the Son, and the Holy Spirit." Theologians and Greek exegetes throughout church history have uniformly interpreted this verse as referring to the three persons of the Trinity, not to three designations or titles of the one person of Jesus Christ. It would be the height of human arrogance to suggest that all the theologians and Greek exegetes throughout church history have been wrong on this verse and only the relatively recent Oneness Pentecostals understand it correctly.

Finally, from a contextual standpoint, a baptism "in the name of Jesus" makes good sense in the context of Acts 2 because the Jews ("men of Judea" [v. 14], "men of Israel" [v. 22]), to whom Peter was preaching, had rejected Christ as the Messiah. It is logical that Peter would call on them to repent of their rejection of Jesus the Messiah and become publicly identified with him via baptism.

THE ARGUMENT: THE TRINITY IS ROOTED IN PAGANISM

Oneness Pentecostals argue that "the Trinity is of pagan, philosophical ancestry, and was engrafted onto, and accommodated to, Christian theology."[40] We are told that "the supreme divinity in almost all heathen nations was triune."[41]

This argument is weak, for the pagan nations believed in *triads* of gods who headed up a *pantheon* of many other gods. This triad/pantheon religious system constituted polytheism, which is (obviously) utterly different from the doctrine of the Trinity, which maintains that there is only one God (monotheism) with three persons within the one Godhead.

It is interesting to note that pagans taught the concept of a creator. They also taught the concept of a great flood that killed much of humankind, as well as the idea of a messiah-like figure (named

---

[39]Robert Reymond, *Jesus, Divine Messiah: The New Testament Witness* (Phillipsburg, NJ: P&R, 1990), 84.
[40]William Chalfant, "The Origin of the Trinity," in *Symposium on Oneness Pentecostalism 1986*, 80.
[41]Ibid.

Tammuz) who was "resurrected." Hence, if Oneness Pentecostals were consistent in their reasoning, they would have to reject the Creator, the Flood, the Messiah, and the resurrection because there are loose parallels in pagan religions.

The point is, simply because pagans spoke of a concept remotely resembling something found in Scripture does not mean the concept was stolen from pagans. Besides, as Cal Beisner correctly observes, the modalism of Oneness Pentecostalism "better resembles certain pagan religious beliefs (like the Hindu notion of God as Brahman [the absolute and undivided one] revealed in three modes as Brahma [creator], Vishnu [preserver], and Shiva [destroyer])."[42]

THE ARGUMENT: THE WORD *TRINITY* IS NOT EVEN IN THE BIBLE

Oneness Pentecostals often argue that the word *Trinity* is never found in the Bible. Further, we are told that "the problem a Trinitarian faces is that there is no indication of developed Trinitarianism in the New Testament. Many try to overcome this by saying Trinitarianism was implicitly believed."[43]

In response, simply because the word *Trinity* is not found in the Bible does not mean the Trinity is unbiblical. While the *word* is not in the Bible, the *concept* definitely is. "That the Bible does not use *Trinity* (or any other term) is no more evidence against Trinitarianism than the absence of the word *Oneness* in the Bible is evidence against Oneness theology. When Oneness writers argue this way, they indulge in special pleading."[44] Oneness Pentecostals also make reference to "modes" and "manifestations" of God, neither word being in the Bible.

It is true that Trinitarians believe the Trinity is an implicit doctrine. They are quick to point out, however, that this *implicit* doctrine is built on the foundation of the Old and New Testament *explicit* truths presented throughout this chapter: (1) there is only one God (e.g., Deut. 6:4; Isa. 44:6; John 5:44; 1 Cor. 8:4; 1 Tim. 2:5; Jas. 2:19); (2) the Father is God (e.g., John 6:27; Rom. 1:7; Gal. 1:1; 1 Pet. 1:2); (3) Jesus is God (Titus 2:13; Heb. 1:8; cf. John 8:58 and Exod. 3:14); (4) the Holy Spirit is God (Gen. 1:2; Exod. 31:3; Ps. 139:7–9; Ezek. 11:24; Acts 5:3–4; Rom. 8:9, 14; 1 John 4:2); (5) the Father, the Son, and the Holy Spirit are distinct from each other (Matt. 28:19); and (6) the Father, the Son, and the Holy Spirit engage in I-Thou

---

[42]Beisner, *"Jesus Only" Churches*, 39.
[43]Thomas Weisser, "Was the Early Church Oneness or Trinitarian?" 61.
[44]Beisner, *"Jesus Only" Churches*, 38.

relationships, thereby indicating that they are persons (John 3:35; 11:41–42; Acts 8:29).

Based on these clear theological facts derived from the pages of Scripture, it is legitimate to utilize the term *Trinity* as a shorthand way of referring to the three-persons-in-one-God teaching of Scripture. In his book *The Forgotten Trinity*, James White asked, "If I believe everything the Bible says about topic X and use a term not found in the Bible to describe the full teaching of Scripture on that point, am I not being more truthful to the Word than someone who limits themselves to only biblical terms, but rejects some aspect of God's revelation?"[45] This is a critically important question—one that Oneness Pentecostals would do well to ponder.

---

[45]James White, *The Forgotten Trinity* (Minneapolis: Bethany House, 1998), 29.

CHAPTER TWENTY-TWO

Witchcraft[1]

Richard G. Howe

DIFFERENT PEOPLE MAY HAVE different images that come to mind when they hear the word *witchcraft*. Some of these images may be silly, and others may be frightening. Most may not even think about the subject except when reminded of it around Halloween. Even then, for them it probably is not taken seriously. But for an increasing number around the world, it is taken seriously. Witches are people who revere both the god and the goddess. They seek a more friendly relationship with their natural environment, endeavoring to recognize the sacredness of all of nature while utilizing cosmic or psychic forces to do their bidding. What could possibly be wrong with such a seemingly benevolent religion? Is it a subject about which Christians should be informed?

WHY ALL THE FUSS?

One might wonder why an analysis of witchcraft is necessary. Surely it amounts to only a relatively small, perhaps insignificant, if not eccentric religion. But one need only look at the attention and respect that this religion has garnered on the world scene to see that it is far from trivial. In the summer of 2004 the Parliament of the World's Religions convened in Barcelona, Spain. Representatives from many of the world's religions were present to "seek peace, justice and sustainability and commit to work for a better world" as well as to "deepen spirituality and experience personal transformation."[2]

---

[1]An earlier version of this chapter appeared as "Modern Witchcraft: It May Not Be What You Think," *Christian Research Journal* Vol. 28, No. 1 (2005): 12–21 and "From the Nature God to the God of Nature: Reaching Out to Wiccans," *Christian Research Journal* Vol. 28, No. 4 (2005): 10–11.

[2]From the 2004 Parliament of the World's Religions web site; http://www.cpwr.org/2004Parliament/welcome/index.htm (accessed April 20, 2007). Another such parliament is scheduled for 2009 in Melbourne, Australia. Pagan Elder Donald Frew informed me that two Pagans serve on the Board of Trustees of the Parliament. (Donald Frew, interview by author, e-mail, April 25, 2007.)

Present at the 2004 conference (as well as the 1993 and 1999 conferences) were representatives of the Covenant of the Goddess, "the world's largest religious organization for Neo-Pagan Witches," as described by Donald H. Frew, an elder of the organization.[3] On the significance of the presence of pagan witchcraft at the conference, Frew, who also serves as the National Public Information Officer of the Covenant of the Goddess and on the Global Council of the United Religions Initiative, comments, "The 1993 Parliament of the World's Religions was the real turning point. The 2004 Parliament was primarily more of the same. It further cemented our position as an established religion on the world stage."[4] Gaining such a place on the "world stage" demands that Christians become equipped to understand the worldview and practice of witchcraft.

THE ANATOMY OF WITCHCRAFT

One will encounter many titles when taking a look at witchcraft: the Craft, Wicca, pagan, neo-pagan, and others. Christian researcher and occult expert Brooks Alexander gives a helpful summary of certain distinctions between the terms *Wicca, witchcraft*, and *neo-paganism*. Neo-paganism is the broadest category, encompassing a wide range of groups "that try to reconstruct ancient, pre- and non-Christian religious systems—such as the Norse, Celtic, Greek, Roman, and Egyptian religions—as well as the followers of various obscure, forgotten, and neglected occult teachings from around the world."[5] From there one could distinguish the narrower category of *witchcraft* from the narrowest of the three titles—*Wicca*. These are distinguished along the lines of how closely one follows the specific teachings and practices of the English Wiccan Gerald Gardner, who more or less gave the term *Wica* (with one *c*) to his practice.[6]

---

[3]Donald H. Frew, "Pagans in Interfaith Dialogue: New Faiths, New Challenges"; http://www.cog.org/interfaith/pwr/don.html (accessed April 20, 2007). For an interesting and informative Christian analysis of the Covenant of the Goddess experience at the 1993 parliament, see Brooks Alexander, *Witchcraft Goes Mainstream: Uncovering Its Alarming Impact on You and Your Family* (Eugene, OR: Harvest House, 2004), 209–211.

[4]Donald Frew, interview by author, e-mail, October 31, 2004.

[5]Alexander, *Witchcraft Goes Mainstream*, 23.

[6]The question of the origin and history of modern witchcraft is somewhat controversial. According to some researchers, Gerald Gardner (1884–1964) is almost single-handedly responsible for the modern phenomenon we now know as witchcraft. Whether Gardner invented or rediscovered the religion is disputed. For discussions on the matter, see Brooks Alexander's work cited in note 3; Ronald Hutton, *Triumph of the Moon: A History of Modern Pagan Witchcraft* (Oxford, UK: Oxford University Press, 1999); Jenny Gibbons, "Recent Developments in the Study of the Great European Witch Hunt" (http://www.tangledmoon.org/witchhunt.htm; accessed April 20, 2007). For a response to earlier versions of Hutton's arguments, see D. H. Frew, "Methodological Flaws in Recent Studies of Historical and Modern Witchcraft," *Ethnologies* 1 (1998): 33–65. For Hutton's rejoinder to Frew, see Ronald Hutton, "Paganism and Polemic: The Debate over the Origins of Modern Pagan Witchcraft," *Folklore* (April 2000) (http://www.findarticles.com/p/articles/mi_m2386/is_1_111/ai_62685559; accessed April 20, 2007). On the basis of my reading on the matter, I agree with the conclusion of Alexander who said, "There has been no

For the most part these titles are used interchangeably. While the title *witchcraft* is the most familiar, it is also the term that carries with it the most unwanted baggage, connoting something evil. For that reason some within the craft prefer the term *Wicca* (for the practice) and *Wiccan* (for the practitioner).[7] The prefix *neo* usually indicates an emphasis on one's practice in its contemporary manifestation while still hinting that it is perhaps a revival of or connected to something ancient.

But more important than the title is the content. What exactly is witchcraft, and how does it compare and contrast with other occult systems and with Christianity? A closer look will reveal that witchcraft is a religion, a worldview, and a practice that bears some interesting and important similarities and differences with both Satanism and Christianity.

Witchcraft: A Religion

It is important for us to remember that witchcraft is a religion.[8] As Americans we cherish our heritage of religious freedom. But as Christians we must be careful, in our enthusiasm to refute the beliefs of witchcraft, not to overstate the case. It is true that our country was founded upon the ethical concept of natural law, according to which morality is grounded

---

passing down of any tradition from medieval witches to anyone in our own time. There is no identifiable continuity between the witchcraft of the Middle Ages and the modern-day religious movement that bears the same name." (Alexander, *Witchcraft Goes Mainstream*, 127.) This is not to say, however, that there is no continuity between some of the concepts of modern witchcraft and ancient religions. As Donald Frew observes, "There is a genuine antiquity to many of the core theological concepts and linked liturgical practices, and . . . there is a traceable path of transmission from Classical antiquity down to the modern movement, but . . . this is not the same thing as a continually practicing group." (Donald Frew, interview by author, e-mail, October 31, 2004.)

[7]Regarding the use of the term *witch* in contrast to other terms, Pagan Elder Donald Frew comments, "Witches are what we are, it is what our forebears called themselves, it is what they died for in staggering numbers, and yet because the culture that descends from those who tried to exterminate us finds the word scary, *we* are supposed to change. To abandon the name would be disrespectful to those who have died for it. How would *you* feel if you were told 'Your name is offensive, please change it'? Would you expect any other persecuted or oppressed group in the world today to change their name to please their oppressor? Jews? African Americans? And yet many Witches do just that. I do it to a certain extent. We hide behind 'Wicca', [*sic*] and 'the Craft', [*sic*] and 'Neo-Paganism', [*sic*] and 'the Old Religion', [*sic*] in many ways hiding who we are, all to avoid using 'the W word', [*sic*] all to avoid offending or scaring someone. But there is nothing to be scared of." (Frew, "Pagans in Interfaith Dialogue.")

[8]The case that settled the issue regarding the legal status of Wicca (witchcraft) as a legitimate religion in the United States was *Dettmer v. Landon* (779 F.2d 929) (4ᵗʰ Circuit, 1989). For a discussion of this and other relevant court cases, see "Coming Out of the Broom Closet," published by the Rutherford Institute; http://www.rutherford.org/articles_db/legal_features.asp?article_id=151 (accessed April 24, 2007).

In the Army publication *Religious Requirements and Practices of Certain Selected Groups: A Handbook for Chaplains* there is a section dealing with "Witchcraft; Goddess worshipers; Neo-Paganism, Paganism, Norse (or any other ethnic designation) Paganism, Earth Religion, Old Religion, Druidism, Shamanism" in guiding Army chaplains in dealing with the practitioners of such groups (available at http://web.archive.org/web/20010603110709/http://www-cgsc.army.mil/chap/relpractice/index.htm; accessed April 24, 2007). Further, Frew informed me that the "networking efforts led by Selena Fox of Circle [Sanctuary] have resulted in our finally being granted the right to have a pentacle on the headstones of fallen men and women in the military." (Donald Frew, interview by author, e-mail, April 25, 2007).

in the nature of the Creator God.[9] But it does not follow from this that witches, since they reject the traditional Christian notion of the Creator God, do not have Constitutional rights.

Whether and how religion should interact with government or public life can be a tricky issue. Nevertheless, we should recognize that within the limits of law, all Americans have the right to exercise their religion in accordance with the dictates of their consciences. Our battle with witchcraft is a battle of ideas. It is a battle for truth. As the Scriptures tell us, "For we do not wrestle against flesh and blood, but against the rulers, against the authorities, against the cosmic powers over this present darkness, against the spiritual forces of evil in the heavenly places."[10]

Witchcraft: A Worldview

Everyone has a way of understanding the nature of reality—a worldview. This is so even if only a few reflect critically about it. A worldview addresses such matters as how reality is composed, how reality works, and how we as humans fit in and relate to our universe. A worldview entails one's views about the purpose of life and the origin and destiny of us all. As such, it is important in understanding witchcraft to see the ingredients of its worldview.

Naturalism. At the broadest level the worldview of witchcraft is the worldview of naturalism. It maintains that there is no transcendent reality such as God that can intervene in the natural world. Naturalism maintains that all of reality is interconnected and operates according to cause and effect "laws." The most common expression of naturalism in our culture is materialism, which sees all of reality as being made up of matter that operates according to material laws. But it is important to understand that witchcraft, though an expression of naturalism, is not materialism. Witches recognize that reality extends beyond the realm of the material.

This is a point that is often missed in worldview analyses. A worldview does not have to be a form of materialism in order to be naturalism. Naturalism can still be naturalism even if it accepts the reality of an imma-

---

[9]For a defense of the role of natural law in the birth of the United States of America see Gary T. Amos, *Defending the Declaration: How the Bible and Christianity Influenced the Writing of the Declaration of Independence* (Brentwood, TN: Wolgemuth and Hyatt, 1989). For a treatment of natural law theory and public policy, see J. Budziszewski, *What We Can't Not Know: A Guide* (Dallas: Spence Publishing, 2003); Norman Geisler and Frank Turek, *Legislating Morality: Is It Wise? Is It Legal? Is It Possible?* (Minneapolis: Bethany House, 1998); and Carl Horn, ed. *Whose Values? The Battle for Morality in Pluralistic America* (Ann Arbor, MI: Servant Books, 1985).
[10]Ephesians 6:12. Unless otherwise indicated, all Bible quotations in this chapter are taken from *The Holy Bible: English Standard Version.*

terial realm. Even acknowledging the existence of gods and goddesses does not preclude a worldview from being naturalism.

What stands in stark contrast to naturalism is a worldview that says that the natural realm (whether material, immaterial, or both) is the creation of a transcendent God. This is supernaturalism. This is what historic, orthodox Christianity is. The God of Christianity stands in stark contrast to the rest of reality and is himself not subject to the "laws" or regularities that characterize the natural realm. This dualism of the supernatural versus the natural is repudiated by witchcraft, which understands all of reality to be interconnected and in which nothing is transcendent in the metaphysical sense of the term.

Occultism. More specifically, not only is witchcraft a worldview of naturalism, but it is also a worldview of occultism. The term *occult* is from the Latin *occultus*, meaning *hidden* or *secret*. The category covers a wide range of beliefs and practices that are characterized by two main doctrines. These two doctrines have often been regarded in the occult as "hidden" or "secret" from most people.

First, the occult maintains that there is some type of force or energy that one can engage and control to do one's own bidding. This is what a spell is in witchcraft. It attempts to harness and focus this force or energy. The late Scott Cunningham, a witchcraft practitioner, explained: "The spell is . . . simply a ritual in which various tools are purposefully used, the goal is fully stated (in words, pictures or within the mind), and *energy* is moved to bring about the needed result."[11]

The second main doctrine of occultism is that human beings are divine. Indeed, the goal of practicing the occult arts is to actualize one's own divinity. As witchcraft practitioner Margot Adler claims, "A spiritual path that is not stagnant ultimately leads one to the understanding of one's own divine nature. Thou art Goddess. Thou art God. Divinity is imminent in all Nature. It is as much within you as without."[12]

Humanism. Witchcraft sees itself celebrating all life as sacred. Specifically, it denies there is anything wrong with the human race. Being essentially divine, humans have no sin. The practicing witch Starhawk rejoices that "we can open new eyes and see that there is

---

[11]Scott Cunningham, *The Truth About Witchcraft Today* (St. Paul: Llewellyn Publications, 1988), 17, emphasis added. It is interesting to note that while different occult groups all maintain the reality of this force or energy, they differ as to its exact nature or identity. They also differ as to the best way to work with this force or energy. These differences in understanding this force or energy are what divide the major occult groups such as shamanism, witchcraft, Satanism, the New Age Movement, and others.

[12]Margot Adler, *Drawing Down the Moon: Witches, Druids, Goddess-Worshippers, and Other Pagans in America Today*, revised and expanded edition (Boston: Beacon Press, 1986), ix.

nothing to be saved *from*, no struggle of life *against* the universe, no God outside the world to be feared and obeyed."[13] Donald Frew explains, "How can we achieve salvation, then? We're not even trying to. We don't understand what there is to be saved from. The idea of salvation presupposes a Fall of some kind, a fundamental flaw in Creation as it exists today. Witches look at the world [around] us and see wonder, we see mystery."[14]

Witchcraft: A Practice

The term *practice* is often used with the term *witchcraft* because witchcraft is as much what someone *does* as it is what someone *believes*. The emphasis is on the practice and what it can do to enhance the well-being of one's self and others. Witches like to think that they eschew dogma. Adler comments, "If you go far enough back, all our ancestors practiced religions that had neither creeds nor dogmas, neither prophets nor holy books. These religions were based on the celebrations of the seasonal cycles of nature. They were based on what people did, as opposed to what people believed. It is these polytheistic religions of imminence that are being revived and re-created by Neo-Pagans today."[15]

Much of the witchcraft material at the local bookstore deals with various rituals and activities that can be perfected in order to manipulate and utilize this force or energy to do one's bidding. There will be chapters on the various clothing to wear (robes, jewelry, horned helmet, when one is not working naked or "skyclad"), the tools to use (candles, herbs, tarot cards, talismans, fetishes), and rituals to perform (spells, incantations, chanting, music, dancing). All of these enable the practitioner to become open to these forces (if they exist outside the individual) or to conjure up these forces (if they originate from within the individual). The material will teach how to interpret dreams, meditate, have out-of-the-body experiences, speak with the dead, heal, read auras, develop one's own powers within the context of other witches (a coven) or alone (solitary practice). While particular methods of working and managing this force or energy are given, the material is usually presented without any prescription to follow any particular method. The key is finding a method that works best for a particular individual. If changes are needed to get better results, then that

---

[13]Starhawk, *The Spiral Dance: A Rebirth of the Ancient Religion of the Great Goddess* (San Francisco: Harper and Row Publishers, 1979), 14, emphasis in original.
[14]Frew, "Pagans in Interfaith Dialogue."
[15]Adler, *Drawing Down the Moon*, ix.

is fine.[16] All of these activities are designed to do two things: to enhance one's own well-being or the well-being of those around them and to actualize one's own divinity.

Witchcraft: Comparisons and Contrasts

Satanism. I must be careful how I make this point. As biblical Christians, we certainly understand that all the world's cults and false religious systems find their origin in the lies of Satan. First John 5:19 tells us, "We know that we are from God, and the whole world lies in the power of the evil one."[17] So in a very important sense all religions that oppose the truth of Christ are satanic. But one must distinguish the false teaching of the real Satan from the man-made (albeit also satanic) religion of Satanism. Closer inspection will reveal that witchcraft and Satanism are to be distinguished as much as Buddhism and Hinduism are to be distinguished even though all are satanic in the spiritual sense of the term.

Witchcraft is not Satanism. The two have different histories as well as different views of the world and one's place in it.[18] To be sure, there is a shared occult perspective. Both are occult religions. In this, they both see reality as entirely natural, denying as they do the existence of a transcendent God in the truest sense of the term. Further, they both see material and immaterial reality as interconnected and working according to "laws" that can be mastered in such a way as to make not only material but also immaterial reality work according to one's own bidding.[19]

Witchcraft and Satanism stand together in stark contrast to Christianity in their repudiation of God and the role of Jesus in effecting the salvation of mankind. Neither acknowledges the fact that mankind is in any need of salvation.

While these similarities are not trivial, neither are the differences. For starters, criminal activity is more likely to be associated with some form

---

[16]Frew comments, "Many of our traditions (or denominations) have writings, called a Book of Shadows, that have been handed down to us. These writings do not contain the wisdom of the ancients, rather they are records of the practices that those before us used to communicate with deity. Sometimes our Elders have recorded what they experienced as a result. Each of us uses, changes, and adapts these practices to suit the needs of our times, and in turn records our insights for those who will come after. But the experience of the Divine is intimate, personal. While I may learn from another's experience, mine will never be quite the same as theirs." (Frew, "Pagans in Interfaith Dialogue.")

[17]Other verses that corroborate this understanding that Satan and his minions are behind all false doctrine are: Acts 13:6–10; 26:17–18; 2 Cor. 11:14–15; 1 Tim. 4:1; 1 John 4:1–3.

[18]For an analysis of the religion of Satanism, see Richard G. Howe, "Satanism: A Taste of the Dark Side," *Christian Research Journal*, Vol. 28, No. 5 (2005): 12–23.

[19]We readily recognize these laws with respect to the material world as the content of the sciences like chemistry, physics, and others. But mapping this template of "laws" upon immaterial reality in order to manipulate both the material and immaterial realm is the *sine qua non* of occult philosophy.

of self-styled Satanism. As a matter of principle and practice, witches live by the creed, "An it harm none, do what you will."[20]

Another difference between witchcraft and Satanism is the fact that Satanism is often associated with an attitude of self-aggrandizement, whereas witchcraft is more often associated with a sense of community. They also differ in their respective views of nature and humanity. As researchers Shelley Rabinovitch and James Lewis observe, "To the neo-Pagan practitioner, nature is viewed as somewhere on a scale from benign to overtly positive, if not outright friendly toward humanity. The ideal in most neo-Pagan practice is to *become as one* with the natural world—to live in harmony with nature. . . . In contrast, neo-Satanists view the natural world as somewhere between benign and openly *hostile* to humans."[21]

Christianity. Perhaps surprisingly, some witches suggest that the practice of witchcraft can be comfortably compatible with one's own Christian faith.[22] However, one should realize that the two are much more different than alike. Before I focus on the differences, however, it might be helpful to comment on some common concerns that witches and Christians often share.

First, because of their view of the nature of the world, witches often have a conscientious sense of environmental concern. Gardnerian Witch Raymond Buckland observes, "We recognize that our intelligence gives us a unique responsibility toward our environment. We seek to live in harmony with Nature, in ecological balance offering fulfillment to life and consciousness within an evolutionary concept."[23] While the motivations are widely disparate—witches are environmentally conscientious because of their view that the Earth is sacred, whereas Christians are environmentally conscientious as a matter of stewardship of the creation before the Creator—we can agree with witches that there is a duty to be environmentally responsible. How this responsibility translates into individual actions and public policy may vary widely along the personal and political spectrum. Nevertheless, we can all agree that there is a level of responsibility on each of us.

Second, witches tend to have a conscientious sense of global con-

---

[20]Janet and Stewart Farrar, *The Witches Bible Compleat*, Vol. 2: *Principles, Rituals and Beliefs of Modern Witchcraft* (New York: Magickal Childe Publishing, 1984), 135.
[21]Shelley Rabinovitch and James Lewis, "Neo-Satanism Compared and Contrasted with Neo-Paganism," in *The Encyclopedia of Modern Witchcraft and Neo-Paganism* (New York: Citadel Press, 2002), 185–186, emphasis in original.
[22]See, for example, Gavin Frost and Yvonne Frost, *The Magic Power of Witchcraft* (West Nyack, NY: Parker Publishing, 1976), 130.
[23]Raymond Buckland, *Buckland's Complete Book of Witchcraft* (St. Paul: Llewellyn, 1990), 9. A Gardnerian Witch is a witch who follows the craft more or less according to the teachings of Gerald Gardner. (See note 6.)

cerns.[24] Again, exactly how these concerns translate into individual actions and public policy may vary along the personal and political spectrum. But our common interests stem from the fact that we are all human beings living on the same planet.

Third, witches tend to be benevolently disposed toward their fellow human beings. The Covenant of the Goddess states, "As it is consistent with the values and beliefs of our religion, the Covenant affirms our belief in the spiritual and social wisdom of peace in the world. We aspire to stand in fellowship with the peoples of all religions, cultures and ethnicities in our shared desire for peace. We do this for the sake of our shared love of the Earth and all living things that dwell upon it."[25]

In acknowledging the shared concerns that we as Christians have with witches, it is important to be aware of two dangers. While we can celebrate these common concerns that stem from the fact that we are all human beings, the Christian must be careful that various subtle aspects of the practice of witchcraft do not influence one's own Christian view of the world in a way that is incompatible with the Christian faith. It is easy to falsely assume that certain practices that characterize the occult in general or witchcraft in particular are neutral and thus that there is no harm in dabbling in their use. Some Christians see no problem with experimenting with séances or tarot cards, not realizing that these could have an eroding effect on their own view of the nature of reality.

Second, there is the real danger of encountering demonic activity. We see from the Scriptures that demonic spirits lie behind occult activities. Acts 16:16–18 tells us of a slave girl who possessed a spirit of divination. There seems to be no reason to doubt that in some sense the woman was successful in her fortune-telling. Her powers seemed to work. However, pragmatism cannot be a criterion for truth and godliness.[26]

The similarities between Christianity and witchcraft stem from our common concerns as human beings. Witches are conscientious in some important matters that we as Christians can recognize as the influence of common grace and natural law. Based on these common concerns, we can perhaps engage the witch in meaningful dialogue. But that dialogue must

---

[24]Starhawk comments, "For justice, inherent in the world and in the ecological balance of the biosphere, operates communally. . . . And if we are not comforted by the story of a final Day of Judgment, when all scores will be settled, then it becomes an even greater collective responsibility, here and now, to change those practices that destroy the lives of individuals and the interplay of life-forms around us. . . . We must create justice and preserve ecological and social balance." (Starhawk, *Dreaming the Dark: Magic, Sex and Politics* [Boston: Beacon Press, 1988], 42, emphasis in original.)

[25]Covenant of the Goddess web site (http://www.cog.org; accessed April 20, 2007).

[26]See also Jer. 44:17–18 and the defense the Israelites gave to Jeremiah for their pagan activities.

press on to demonstrate the crucial differences between witchcraft and Christianity. There are similarities between flour and ricin. They both are made from plants. They both are white powders. But it is not their similarities that are interesting or important. It is their differences. One is a food, and the other is a poison. One promotes life, and the other effects death. Our enthusiasm to establish rapport with witches around us must not keep us from recognizing that when it comes to what ultimately counts—the objective truth about who God is, who we are as humans, and how humans and God must relate—witchcraft and Christianity are mortal foes, and Christianity is true.

Christianity is monotheistic. One of my favorite posters says: "Two important facts of human enlightenment: There is a God. You are not him." Overlooking the poor grammar, we can see that the poster points out a fact that is becoming increasingly obscured in our culture and is explicitly denied in occult philosophy. Christianity claims that there is a God and that no one of us is he. Witchcraft claims the opposite. "We are of the nature of the Gods, and a fully realized man or woman is a channel for that divinity, a manifestation of the God or the Goddess."[27] Margot Adler favorably quotes historian James Breasted who said, "Monotheism is but imperialism in religion."[28] In place of the strict monotheism of Christianity, witchcraft not only deifies the self, but it ostensibly reveres both the God and the Goddess.[29]

Christianity is exclusivistic. Jesus said, "I am the way, and the truth, and the life. No one comes to the Father except through me."[30] But Margot Adler proclaims, "The belief that there is one word, one truth, one path to the light, makes it easy to destroy ideas, institutions, and human beings . . . your own spiritual path is not necessarily mine."[31]

Christianity recognizes God's authority. Not only has God revealed himself through the things that are made, but he has also revealed himself finally and fully through Jesus Christ and the Bible.[32] But Donald Frew says, "To grant a traditional text such authority would be to say that this is it, the truth for all time. But we are a nature religion, and a fundamental truth of nature is that everything changes."[33] Since Christians recognize the

---

[27]Farrar, The Witches Bible Compleat, Vol. 2, 33.
[28]Adler, Drawing Down the Moon, vii.
[29]The emphasis on the God and the Goddess stems from witchcraft's worldview of the interplay in the reality of opposites that seek balance. The Farrars explain, "All activity, all manifestation arises [sic] from (and is inconceivable without) the interaction of pairs and complementary opposites." (The Witches Bible Compleat, Vol. 2, 107.)
[30]John 14:6. See also Acts 4:12.
[31]Adler, Drawing Down the Moon, viii.
[32]See Ps. 19:1; Rom. 1:20; Heb. 1:1–2.
[33]Frew, "Pagans in Interfaith Dialogue."

authority of God's Word in such matters, we have to face the fact that the Bible unequivocally condemns the practice of witchcraft, indeed all forms of the occult.[34]

Christianity recognizes everyone's need for salvation. The gospel of Jesus Christ is the most important message we have to give to the world. Without the sacrifice of Christ to wash away our sins and reconcile us to our Creator, there is no hope in the world to come. Witchcraft teaches that our destiny is to return again to this world through reincarnation. Scott Cunningham comments, "While reincarnation isn't an exclusive Wiccan concept, it is happily embraced by most Wiccans because it answers many questions about daily life and offers explanations for more mystical phenomena such as death, birth and karma."[35] Donald Frew expounds, "And while many of us believe in reincarnation, we do not seek to escape the wheel of rebirth. We can't imagine anything more wonderful than to come back to this bounteous and beautiful Earth."[36] In contrast to this spiritually fatal illusion, the Bible warns, ". . . it is appointed for men to die once, but after that comes judgment."[37]

THE CHRISTIAN RESPONSE: AN INFORMED WITNESS

The job before us as Christians never changes, no matter to whom we are talking. While tactics and strategies may vary depending on the task at hand—whether apologetics, evangelism, or discipleship—the commission never varies. We must maximize our effectiveness in reaching the lost by being informed and sensitive to the beliefs and practices of others while paying close attention to the subtle differences between various worldviews and our own Christian faith. This is true no less of witches than of anyone else who may be living right next door.

But perhaps it would be helpful to point out some practical issues when witnessing to witches. In an important sense, witnessing to witches is no different from witnessing to anyone else. It requires a comfortable knowledge of the gospel message and a preparation to defend that message with the measure of faith that God has given us. Be prepared to invest enough time to become informed of the witchcraft worldview, and be willing to develop a relationship that will enable you to engage them in fruitful dialogue.

First, being informed creates credibility. Demonstrating an understand-

---

[34]See Deut. 18:10–12; Acts 13:6–11; 16:16–18; Gal. 5:19–21.
[35]Cunningham, *The Truth About Witchcraft Today*, 65.
[36]Frew, "Pagans in Interfaith Dialogue."
[37]Heb. 9:27.

ing of the other person's viewpoint signals that you care about these matters and may lead them to consider that you perhaps deserve a hearing.

Second, being informed can help overcome obstacles to fruitful dialogue. Many witches are resistant to Christianity (at least as they perceive it). They resent the notion that they need to be converted. They reject the idea that there is anything morally wrong with them. In their worldview, there is no real concept of sin. Instead they think in terms of ignorance and enlightenment.

Third, being informed can help in being understood. A witch you encounter may have a distorted view about the Christian faith, particularly concerning the gospel. Like others, she may assume that to become a Christian one must try to be as good as one can. With this works mentality, some witches may see themselves as more "Christian" than many Christians. Some will undoubtedly be aware of the failings of the institutionalized Christian church. They may even have an exaggerated perspective about the harmful effects Christianity has had in history, thinking that Christianity is the cause of much of the world's problems. They also may have contempt for what they see in Christianity as an unhealthy patriarchy, an overemphasis on private property, an unjustified allegiance to capitalism, and so on.

Certainly these are important issues. At different levels informed Christians can engage witches in worldview discussions. The task would be to show that only the Christian worldview can account for many of the facts that both Christians and witches acknowledge. All of this should be for the purpose of communicating the gospel and helping witches see their need for a Savior.

CHAPTER TWENTY-THREE

Satanism

Jon Trott

"Me miserable! which way shall I fly
Infinite wrath, and infinite despair?
Which way I fly is Hell; myself am Hell."
SATAN, IN MILTON'S *PARADISE LOST* (IV.73–75)

To be a Christian is and always has been a difficult task, for Christianity
demands the ability radically to expose our own evil to ourselves.
LESZEK KOLAKOWSKI[1]

MY OWN JOURNEY REGARDING the study of Satanism came about through
a circuitous route, one that makes me suspect in many fellow believers' eyes.
I have been at variance with Christian "experts" on Satanism for the past
few decades. I've been called, by no less than evangelical end-times guru
Hal Lindsey, "either a Satanist or dupe of Satanists" and by the Warnkes
(after my co-authored exposé of Mike Warnke's false story of one-time
satanic involvement) a member of a murderous satanic cult.[2]

On the other hand, my participation in exposing some of these alleged
experts as frauds and pseudo-scholars won fifteen minutes of fame in
certain circles. I was viewed as a premiere evangelical investigator, even a
"cult expert" in my own right regarding Satanism. I eschew such labels,
not believing in cult experts as a category, and also being discouraged with
"investigating" as a lifetime trade.

I remain haunted by ghosts that my investigations raised, ghosts that
seem stronger than ever in these dark times of an evangelical alliance with

---

[1]Leszek Kolakowski, *Modernity on Endless Trial* (Chicago: University of Chicago Press, 1990), 94.
[2]Perucci Ferraiuolo, "Warnke Calls Critics Satanists," *Christianity Today,* Vol. 36, No. 13 (November 9,
1992), 49, 52; posted at http://www.cornerstonemag.com/features/iss098/warnke_response/csr0018a.htm.

the spirits of the age. So please forgive me if what follows does not follow the usual apologetics or counter-cult approach to the topic at hand.

SATAN AND EVIL

A number of thorny questions perplex me when considering Satan, evil, Satanism, and Christianity. I hope they also perplex you, the reader. How we answer these questions may affect far more than how we react to a—to be frank here—very small segment of the world's population calling itself "Satanist," a microscopic segment I will relegate to a footnote.[3] After all, few of us have much dialogue with self-proclaimed Satanists, no matter what version of Satanism to which they adhere. But all of us deal with evil, whether Christian, Satanist, Muslim, or atheist. All of us deal with evil externalized (outside ourselves) and internalized (within ourselves). And all of us deal with evil's effects, the most seemingly avoidable (yet never avoided) of which is human agony and depersonalization brought on by other humans.

Satanism, one would initially presume, is about following "the father of lies."[4] That is the title Jesus gives the devil, who in Christian theology is a fallen angel, leader of other fallen angels (demons), tempter of Eve, Adam, and all humankind and coauthor with humankind of sin and death in the world, Apollyon (that is, the Destroyer[5]), Beelzebub[6] (that is, "Lord of the Flies"), and last but not least, "the evil one."[7] As a Christian, I believe in Satan's existence, as both Jesus and the apostles (along with many Old Testament writers) treat both him and his demonic cohorts as unambiguously real.

Tex Watson, who helped murder Sharon Tate and other victims while a member of the Manson Family, was asked by one victim who he was. "I'm

---

[3]This includes the following: The late Anton LaVey's Church of Satan (http://www.churchofsatan.com/). LaVey's *Satanic Bible* is one source for free-style Satanists (often teenagers), yet neither it nor he actually teaches that Satan is an actual being. Rather, the devil is a metaphor for human freedom from moral constraint, Judeo-Christian morality in particular. The First Church of Satan (http://www.churchofsatan.org/); Michael Aquino, who split from LaVey in 1975 to found his Temple of Set (http://www.xeper.org/). A long list, with links, of other such groups, some doubtless having only one or two members (http://altreligion. about.com/od/organizations/). I would note that one study apparently only found 1,500 self-proclaimed Satanists in Britain, perhaps an indicator of just how unpopular the idea of devil-worship—the devil being actual or metaphorical—is overall. The religioustolerance.org web site suggests up to 100,000 teen Satanists in America, though that figure isn't based on hard evidence. They also suggest a figure of around 10,000 American members of the Church of Satan and related groups.

[4]John 8:44. Unless otherwise indicated, all Scripture quotations in this chapter are taken from *The Holy Bible: New Revised Standard Version*.

[5]Rev. 9:11. I realize the verse (like most of John's complex book) is open to a variety of interpretations, including that of "Apollyon" being a reference to the Roman emperor, Domitian, rather than a reference to Satan. But such theological discussions are, though fascinating, beyond the bounds of our unlofty topic.

[6]See http://en.wikipedia.org/wiki/Beelzebub.

[7]Biblical references include: Matt. 5:37; 6:13; 13:19, 38; John 17:15; Eph. 6:16; 2 Thess. 3:3; 1 John 2:13–14; 3:12; 5:18–19.

the devil and I'm here to do the devil's business,"[8] he replied. And then he did that business. Since his incarceration for those crimes, he (along with Susan Atkins and a few other former imprisoned Manson Family members) has declared himself a Christian. He attempts to preach, even to emulate Christ, in his prison ministry (see aboundinglove.org). Suspend skepticism for a moment. Isn't it possible that even Tex Watson could switch sides and in some small way now be about doing Christ's business? This is humanity's predicament, that good and evil are constantly warring within us. Is it any wonder that the only perfect man inquired why he was being called "good": "Why do you call me good? No one is good but God alone."[9]

As a Christian, my understanding of evil is filtered through that God-man, Jesus, as the lens through which God's love and human goodness shine most perfectly. Jesus, "a man of suffering and acquainted with infirmity,"[10] identifying with the dispossessed and poor ("Truly I tell you, just as you did it to one of the least of these who are members of my family, you did it to me"[11]), confronted as sinners those assured of their own goodness and moral purity. In fact, it is in one of Jesus' more scandalously misunderstood New Testament confrontations that the interblending of satanic and human evil is most clearly delineated:

> They answered him, "Abraham is our father." Jesus said to them, "If you were Abraham's children, you would be doing what Abraham did, but now you are trying to kill me, a man who has told you the truth that I heard from God. This is not what Abraham did. You are indeed doing what your father does." They said to him, "We are not illegitimate children; we have one father, God himself."
>
> Jesus said to them, "If God were your Father, you would love me, for I came from God and now I am here. I did not come on my own, but he sent me. Why do you not understand what I say? It is because you cannot accept my word. You are from your father the devil, and you choose to do your father's desires. He was a murderer from the beginning and does not stand in the truth, because there is no truth in him. When he lies, he speaks according to his own nature, for he is a liar and the father of lies. But because I tell the truth, you do not believe me." (John 8: 39–45)

Is Jesus speaking metaphorically here or literally when he calls the leaders of God's people children of Satan? And what does such a definition

---

[8]Watson's own recollection. See http://www.aboundinglove.org/sensational/wydfm/wydfm-014.php.
[9]Luke 18:19.
[10]Isa. 53:3.
[11]Matt. 25:40.

do to our own understanding of Satanism, Satan, and Christian belief and practice?

The above passage from John's eighth chapter has often been used by anti-Semites to attack Jews, justifying Jewish dispersion and death. But to so read it is to turn the passage on its head. The real themes here are much, much closer to home: the alliance between the human sense of moral certainty and our ability to do great evil in and because of that certainty; the fact that Satan's lies and human allegiance to those lies are nearly seamless in essence. That is, Satan's deception and our willing assent to it function in coordination, proximity, and unity. In short, though all deception is satanic, it is also self-deception. This central reality of temptation, sin, and evil seems little known among most Christians today.

I contend that the better we as a society, or as individuals, are at being like Satan, the more necessary it is that we be self-deceived as to why we perpetrate evils against our fellow humans. The more demonic our acts, the more angelic our rationalization for such acts need be. One need only consider German fascism (so-called "Positive Christianity") or American slavery (justified by white Christians as biblically mandated) to see this.

For self-deceived Christians to commit crimes against Jews underscores John's message and summons a terrible truth: *A Satanist is one who believes the devil's lies and does the devil's work regardless of what deity she/he claims allegiance to.* If such is a Satanist, then what is Satanism? Unlike the conspiratorial cartoon versions of Satanism, this nexus of human/demonic evil does indeed exist within *our* social institutions, *our* churches, *our* national corridors of power, and *our* own hearts.

I realize such an interpretation is startling to American evangelicals, but in the end I find no other definition that fits the hard realities of history, Scripture, and the present. I offer these reflections as the canvas upon which the following is painted.

THE SCARY SATAN STORIES WE BELIEVE, AND WHY

Though I am perhaps best known for my coauthored exposé of Mike Warnke's *The Satan Seller*, my introduction to the Satanism of evangelical imagination came about through Lauren Stratford's sensational story, *Satan's Underground.* This book had not only sold over 130,000 copies, but also netted Lauren appearances on *Oprah, Geraldo, Sally Jessie Raphael,* and the *700 Club.* The back cover blurb spells out Lauren's story:

Lauren Stratford lived the agony of being trapped between two worlds—the outside world of school, church, and friends and the inside world of an unending nightmare. As a young child, mind control and fear were Lauren's constant companions. At an early age she was sold to men for their perverted pleasures. She was compelled to pose with animals for pornographic publications. Ultimately, she found herself part of a collection of young women and children forced to surrender their bodies in some of the most evil satanic rituals imaginable. Shocking crimes against children—crimes unchecked because they are unbelievable. Literally thousands like Lauren are gripped in evil's vice.[12]

Lauren's story is horrific. Initially raped as a child by a man hired by her mother, Lauren discovers the rape is her mother's payment (a "fair wage") for the man's labor. This soon escalates into a common occurrence and moves into multiple rapes by various men and pornography. Years pass. Twenty years old and part of a national porn ring run by "Victor" who tortures and rapes her but also allows her to go to college, Lauren discovers the even darker core of Victor's world: Satanism.

The low point of the story comes when Lauren, refusing to be part of a satanic sacrifice of a child, is locked in a pitch-dark, coffin-like cage with four dead babies killed because of her disobedience. At that point the "mind control" works, and she caves in to the Satanists' demands and participates in a baby sacrifice. Of three children she herself has, two are killed in snuff films, and the last is sacrificed in a satanic ritual as she watches, helpless. Of course, the story ends with Lauren delivered from the international satanic cult by Christians—including Hal Lindsey, Johannna Michaelson, and pop journalist Ken Wooden.

Note the elements of Lauren's story: a secret evil society cloaked in American suburban normalcy, run by some of society's most powerful people; mind control; lots of perverted sex; bizarre satanic rituals; crimes against children "unchecked because they are unbelievable." Unbelievable, yes. But not unchecked. I began an investigation of Stratford's claims, soon joined by fellow skeptics Robert and Gretchen Passantino.

Our coauthored 1989 article "Satan's Sideshow: The True Lauren Stratford Story"[13] was researched minutely, mapping out Lauren Stratford/Laurel Willson's life from her 1941 birth certificate to her 1959 attendance at Seattle Pacific College and up into the present day. Lauren's tale made sure to leave few links to any specific times, dates, names, or places, but we

---

[12]Lauren Stratford, *Satan's Underground: The Extraordinary Story of One Woman's Escape* (Eugene, OR: Harvest House, 1988).

[13]See http://www.cornerstonemag.com/features/iss090/sideshow.htm#tx66.

were able to systematically discover such evidences. Dozens of interviews, photos, and documents were compiled in our efforts to discover the true tale behind her horror story.

Her adoptive mother, still very much alive (unlike the book seems to suggest), sent us photos and other documentation of Lauren's early years. We discovered that Lauren/Laurel was much older—some twenty years—than her undated story led one to believe, creating various anachronisms that could not be resolved (men reading *Playboy* in the 1940s when the very first issue was in 1953 and the use of videotape decades before it existed were just two such anachronistic issues.) We also unearthed a sister, though Lauren said she'd been an only child. That sister, a missionary, was horrified to discover her sibling's twisted version of the childhood they'd lived together.

We also found abundant evidence that Lauren had lied about herself throughout her life, often in lurid terms, apparently victimizing church folk with tales of (in one such instance) her need to hide from lesbians pursuing her. Another Christian family sheltering her was told by Lauren she'd been assaulted, but later discovered she'd whacked herself in the head with a can of peaches in an attempt to fake the assault. Finally, it was no coincidence, we believed, that Lauren/Laurel had lived in Bakersfield, California during the first known Satanic Ritual Abuse case. This case arguably spawned a half-dozen more such cases in the Bakersfield area, all of which made local news and so would likely have been known to Lauren.[14]

We triangulated the actual evidence and timeline against Lauren's book, and the conclusion was unavoidable. Her book was a lie. When confronted, her publisher informed us they "trusted her" and felt no need to do fact checking. We were left with the strong feeling that we, too, should believe her—after all, she was a Christian and a victim of horrendous abuse. How could we question her?

We published our lengthy article in *Cornerstone* magazine and immediately were subjected to shrill counterattack from Johanna Michaelson, Hal Lindsey, and (initially) Harvest House, Lauren's publisher. As the first weeks passed, the nature of these attacks changed. I noted this in our follow-up issue of *Cornerstone*:

> Initially, Lauren, her publisher, and her supporters claimed to have hard evidence to support *Satan's Underground*. But as our findings mounted, and our questions became more specific, the nature of their evidence

---

[14]An excellent overall treatment of those cases is: http://www.religioustolerance.org/ra_baker.htm.

changed from "times, dates, and places" to "testimony consistent with other victims." We were told that hard evidence didn't matter; a higher form of evidence, namely, that Lauren's therapists believe her on her word alone, invalidated all the eyewitnesses and documentation we had discovered.[15]

Harvest House did, as publicity grew, drop Stratford's book.

That year at the annual Evangelical Press Association (EPA) convention, held in the evangelical Mecca of Colorado Springs, the article received EPA's first-place award for investigative reporting. Too eagerly, I walked forward to receive the award in front of the clapping EPA membership. Yet only minutes later *Moody Monthly* magazine received a first-place award for their sensational and baseless article, "Evil in the Land," a story with a nearly identical outline—and as little evidence to support it—as Lauren's. Equivalent applause followed. When I had inquired into evidence for the article's Satanic Ritual Abuse (SRA) claims, Moody—like Harvest House—was unable to provide any, except of course the assurance that both the subject and the writer of the article were Christians. In other words, both writer and subject were "one of us" and therefore could not be deceivers. The externalizing of evil "outside the camp" creates the perfect environment for deception and evil to exist *within* the camp.

My eyes became fixated on the forces behind Stratford's meteoric rise and considerable ability to stay afloat in spite of our exhaustive exposé. These threads are easy to spot now, but at the time this was not so.

LIKE A FISH NEEDS A BICYCLE: ABUSE AND "RECOVERED MEMORIES"

He who chases fantasies lacks judgment.

PROVERBS 12:11

The 1957 movie *Three Faces of Eve* had offered the therapeutic narrative in embryonic form. MPD, Multiple Personality Disorder, was an almost unheard of phenomenon before *Eve* gave it notoriety. The next step came with the 1973 blockbuster *Sybil*, which sold over four million copies and spawned a 1976 television movie and has since been heavily criticized as therapeutic invention.[16] It was *Sybil's* tortured central

---

[15]Jon Trott, "Lauren Stratford Update: The Book's Withdrawn, Some Questions Remain," *Cornerstone*, Vol. 18, Issue 91, 16.
[16]See http://homepage.psy.utexas.edu/homepage/class/Psy394U/Bower/Xtra--Multiple%20Personality% 3F/Sybil-debunked.

character (or more accurately, characters—some sixteen "personalities") that laid the groundwork for the even wilder stories to follow. The basic narrative framework of such tales was set. A wise, nearly omniscient therapist, skilled in both hypnosis and sympathy, helps a traumatized patient wander the subterranean passages of the unconscious. There various complete personalities "split off" from the core personage and are one by one encountered and integrated into fewer and fewer, until at last only one personality remains.

Feminism's outing of sexual abuse as socially pervasive yet well-hidden helped lead to a war on both rape and pornography during the 1970s. The 1974 National Child Abuse Prevention and Treatment Act[17] was one positive outcome. During the late 1970s and early 1980s, issues of adult and child rape, incest, and molestation were increasingly discussed publicly. The stories that often emerged into public view were, in some respects, akin to reports of Auschwitz and other Nazi death camps released during the 1940s. As the photographic and eyewitness testimony piled up in the latter case, so it was with rape and incest.

Feminist works on sexual abuse weren't always as articulate and deeply transformative as Susan Brownmiller's *Against Our Will: Men, Women, and Rape*, Kate Millett's *Sexual Politics,* or Andrea Dworkin's iconoclastic *Pornography: Men Possessing Women.* But in the heady early days of peeling back what seemed a blanket of silence over sexual abuse, few heeded the need for caution regarding unjustly abusing innocent adults via false accusation. Sexual abuse, after all, usually takes place in secret, often in the home of the child's parents. How does one prove or disprove accusations in such a frame? From a law enforcement point of view, sexual abuse (long before DNA testing) was devilishly difficult to prove. On the other hand, how does a raped child or adult find the courage to testify against his or her accuser if the accuser is "innocent until proven guilty" and "hard" proof does not exist? No doubt, this area is horribly complex for all concerned and requires George McDonald's Wise Woman[18] to sort out.[19]

But in the late 1970s when the concept of "recovered memories" was introduced into the cultural consciousness and into the therapeutic and legal tangle surrounding sexual abuse, all hell broke loose. Recovered memories were, it was said, memories "locked up" by the victim's unconscious

[17]See http://www.law.cornell.edu/uscode/html/uscode42/usc_sec_42_00005104----000-.html.

[18]One of C. S. Lewis's favorite stories by one of his favorite writers, it is also one of mine. Online complete text: http://www.johannesen.com/WiseWomanComplete.htm.

[19]One current source for information, help, and further resources is: http://www.childwelfare.gov/pubs/reslist/rl_dsp.cfm?subjID=83&rate_chno=11-11214.

mind in order to safeguard the psyche from being irretrievably damaged. The effects of the abuse, it was claimed, would still come out in the life of the adult survivor.

The term *dissociation*, or *splitting*, described the concept, which inevitably involved Multiple Personality Disorder (MPD). This, of course, was fed by *Sybil's* popularity. As one researcher found:

> [B]efore 1973, the year in which the book was published, there were fewer than 50 known cases of multiple personality disorder in the history of the world. By 1994 over 40,000 cases had been diagnosed.[20]

But *Sybil* did not, either as a movie or book, include Satanism or occultism as a theme. It was not until 1980's *Michelle Remembers*[21] that Satanism got top billing. Never mind that the therapist who wrote the book, Dr. Lawrence Pazder, apparently violated both moral and professional boundaries by leaving his wife and marrying Michelle Smith, the book's subject (a fact not mentioned in the book itself). The book's storyline sounds eerily familiar in retrospect. Michelle comes to Pazder for fairly routine therapy involving the disappointment with her life and the loss of her mother some time earlier. But soon the two of them are spelunking into Michelle's subconscious, tape recorder running as a child's memories of increasingly horrific Satanic Ritual Abuse—including being "burned" by the devil's own tail—pour forth. This book is Catholic rather than evangelical; so Catholic theology is brought in to explain what is happening and helps (along with Dr. Pazder's therapy) to break Satan's hold.

Feeding into and greatly expanding the recovered-memories movement in 1988 was a landmark book laced with SRA stories, *The Courage to Heal.*[22] The book cites *Michelle Remembers* approvingly, as well as "testimony" from other alleged SRA survivors. *The Courage to Heal* was authored by two lesbians (who promote lesbianism graphically in the book) and had none of the raging, razor-sharp insight of Dworkin and Brownmiller nor the literarily informed, even humorous brilliance of Millett. Instead, in the words of two critics, the book is "a caricature of what has frequently been described as a feminine characteristic—reliance upon emotion and a limited

---

[20]*False Memory Syndrome Foundation Newsletter*, May/June 2006, Vol. 15, No. 3, 1–2; http://www.FMSFonline.org.

[21]Michelle Smith and Lawrence Pazder, M.D., *Michelle Remembers*, (New York: Congdon & Lattes, 1980).

[22]Ellen Bass and Laura Davis, *The Courage to Heal: A Guide for Women Survivors of Child Sexual Abuse* (New York: HarperCollins, 1988).

concern with reason."[23] What it did have was a paradigm tailor-made to create a therapeutic wave of false memories[24] and—as time passed—false accusations of sexual abuse against innocent men and women.[25] The irony that alleged feminists would in fact use the misogynistic theories of Freud regarding abuse was not lost on all observers.[26]

How does one disbelieve an adult who tremblingly "recalls" being abused in horrific fashion over a period of decades? Even a hint of skepticism is viewed as a lack of compassion, love, and human decency. Siding with the victim is also an act of self-affirmation, offering one the chance to be a hero not only in the victim's eyes but in one's own eyes as well. In short, one is invited to become a co-participant in authoring a story where innocence has been raped and (sometimes) murdered (though no bodies can be found) and evil can only be defeated by all of us "believing the child" (that is, believing the therapist).

Yet the issue of truth outside such constructions wouldn't go away. As we and fellow-skeptics tried to point out, the real issue concerned the therapeutic techniques used to arrive at these alleged "memories." As with the Salem Witchcraft Trials, a form of "spectral evidence" trumped all normal evidentiary forms. That spectral evidence was the therapeutically induced memory of the victim.

Satanic Ritual Abuse (SRA) researcher Sherrill Mulhern explained to me how the mass media contributed to the SRA myth's meteoric rise:

> For nearly seventy years, nobody walked into therapy saying they had multiple personalities. However, after the film *The Three Faces of Eve* was broadcast on television, her therapists reported receiving a flood of calls from patients claiming that they also suffered from MPD [Multiple Personality Disorder]. . . . Ritualistic abuse has followed the same pattern. Historically, since the early 1980s, therapists had been seeing patients who eventually disclosed SRA type allegations. However, once those types of allegations were heavily publicized on the TV talk shows, many patients and therapists started gravitating towards them.[27]

---

[23]Hollida Wakefield and Ralph Underwager, *Return of the Furies: An Investigation into Recovered Memory Therapy* (Chicago: Open Court Press, 1994), 136. I would note that these two authors are, in my opinion, needlessly hostile to feminism and simplistic in their assessments of feminist contributions to positive sexuality and positive humanness. Regarding *Courage to Heal*, however, their observation is accurate.

[24]Elizabeth Loftus's critique of recovered memories and instructive information regarding the nature of memory itself is foundational; http://faculty.washington.edu/eloftus/Articles/lof93.htm.

[25]The False Memory Syndrome Foundation came into being as families destroyed by false allegations of abuse began to network and gather information regarding the bad therapy causing their pain; http://www.fmsonline.org/.

[26]See http://www.ipt-forensics.com/journal/volume8/j8_2_2.htm.

[27]Rereading this interview today, I suspect that Mulhern misspoke here or that we mistyped her words and that the movie referred to was not *Three Faces of Eve* but *Sybil*. See http://www.cornerstonemag.com/features/iss096/mulhern.htm.

Once one enters into the therapeutic world that Pazder and his ilk inhabit, truth becomes more than plastic—it turns to liquid, even gas. This became clearest to me during one of the stranger moments of the Lauren Stratford investigation. I was interviewing a parent of one of the children allegedly abused in the unbelievably expensive and misguided McMartin preschool case, the case that perhaps made SRA a nationally discussed and widely believed phenomenon. The parent had known Lauren and pegged her as a liar and imposter, yet the woman's own story beat almost anything Lauren had said or written. This mother calmly explained how a child had been abused at the day-care center while Raymond Buckey (one of the alleged McMartin abusers) was seen by witnesses in San Diego, many miles distant.

"Do you mean," I inquired, not quite believing my ears, "that the girl was abused by Buckey here while he was also in San Diego?" I thought perhaps she was suggesting his second appearance was an apparition or, to use Salem witchcraft rhetoric, a specter or demonic look-alike. But that wasn't what she meant. "Yes, both. Two places at once. Those Satanists can do anything." In the face of such fervent and—to me—misplaced credulity, I had no ready response.

FIGHTING STORY WITH STORY

Why are some stories so believable and compelling to some people while completely unbelievable, even silly, to others? I cannot say. After all, I believe and have constructed my life—"accepted Pascal's wager," one might say—on Jesus Christ as revealed by Scripture and my own very finite, fallible experiences. I do not want to battle one fiction, the fiction of this Satanic Ritual Abuse narrative, with yet another fiction, namely, the untruth that all truth can be known by rational processes or even (on a deeper level) that reality itself is intrinsically, objectively logical from our viewpoint.[28]

My dear, late friend Bob Passantino (to whom this book is dedicated and with whom, along with his wife Gretchen, I did much of my skeptical research into the Satanism myth) had a besetting weakness for which I often took him to task. Whenever he encountered irrational belief in a human being, he expressed bafflement. "How can they think that? That's not logical!" My laughing response, every time, was simply, "The human condi-

---

[28] I am indebted in part to theologian N. T. Wright for freeing me intellectually from such a modernist paradigm masquerading as Christian thought. See http://www.spu.edu/depts/uc/response/summer2k5/features/postmodern.asp and http://www.ntwrightpage.com/.

tion is not logical." Extroverted, excitable, and often flamboyant as his brain synapses creatively fired away, Bob was—unknown to himself—an example of this, often more poetic than philosophical in the way his mind pieced together reality. As G. K. Chesterton once noted:

> Poetry is sane because it floats easily in an infinite sea; reason seeks to cross the infinite sea, and so make it finite. The result is mental exhaustion. . . . The poet only asks to get his head into the heavens. It is the logician who seeks to get the heavens into his head. And it is his head that splits.[29]

The power of poetry, or for our purposes here, the power of the narrative was (and is) what drove SRA mythology forward in spite of skeptical objections. If excessive rationalism's narrative often leads to denial of the supernatural, SRA's narrative offers a radical (if bogus) shortcut to affirming the supernatural. My eventual response to the McMartin mother, and to those believing they themselves were once victims of SRA, was a narrative itself, or to be more accurate, the story of a victim of victim stories. *Cornerstone* magazine in 1991 published my "Satanic Panic: The Ingram Family and Other Victims of Hysteria in America."[30]

Paul Ingram, a Thurston County sheriff in Washington State, was an evangelical Christian with a wife, two daughters, and two sons. In late 1988, accusations of sexual abuse were made by his daughters against him. It seemed a slam dunk. Confronted, Ingram had confessed to the crimes. But he also confessed to much, much more, including gruesome satanic rituals involving other policemen and his wife. In the end, as my investigation and the ultimately more far-reaching one of Lawrence Wright in his *New Yorker* articles and in his book *Remembering Satan* proved, Paul Ingram was the victim of others' bad therapy and his own trustful gullibility.

In the face of his own minister's very dubious memory recall techniques, along with his friends who were simultaneously the law enforcement representatives of respectable middle-class America, Ingram began "recovering" memories—naively creating them virtually "on demand" to fit his questioners' specifications. The complete transcripts of those interrogations, which we obtained, were the record of the orchestrated (yet unintentional) construction of a story between Ingram's children, thera-

---

[29]G. K. Chesterton, *Orthodoxy*, 1908. A public domain work, it is widely available on the Internet. See, for example, http://www.cse.dmu.ac.uk/~mward/gkc/books/ortho14.txt.
[30]Jon Trott, "Satanic Panic: The Ingram Family and Other Victims of Hysteria in America," *Cornerstone*, Vol. 20, Issue 95 (1991), 8–13.

pists involved with the children, the police interrogators, Paul Ingram himself, and Paul Bratun, Ingram's pastor.

Not everyone was buying it, however. A skeptical Dr. Richard Ofshe, called in initially by the police as a mind control expert, set up a blind test in which Ingram was fed stories that Ofshe himself had made up. Obediently, Ingram began "remembering" these bogus events as reality. Even when confronted by Ofshe, who exposed the stories as being fake, Ingram continued to maintain they were true. Ofshe saw Ingram's sincerity as an example of the powers of suggestion and the dangers of badly done interrogations by police and therapists. In spite of Ofshe's vociferous protests, no one was listening. Ingram's initial guilty plea was accepted, and he went to prison.

Nor was Ingram alone. Nationwide, cases of so-called SRA were increasing in number and visibility as the media (Geraldo Rivera in the lead[31]) uncritically hyped SRA stories. Various nursery schools and day-care centers became targets for the new hysteria.[32] Dozens of individuals went to jail, many (such as Ingram) for years. In a courtroom, accused by a child of horrific abuses, how could anyone expect to be found innocent? The bogus therapeutic techniques weren't exposed for years. For the lucky defendants, their cases were eventually reexamined and overturned. Paul Ingram was not among the lucky.

"Adult survivors," many people who were not profiting monetarily or on a media stage, claimed to have been victimized by an international Satanist conspiracy. As Sherrill Mulhern explained to me:

> These adults, the majority of whom have long psychiatric histories, are alleging torture, mutilation, rape, incest and cannibalism, all perpetrated in the context of large group rituals including robes, masks, knives, and other paraphernalia. These are the same kind of accusations which surfaced in the McMartin Preschool case, in numerous other day-care cases, and in some custody cases. What is being described is an all-powerful, evil conspiratorial organization which is allegedly so sophisticated that it has been able to conduct its gory rituals undetected for generations. Experienced law enforcement investigators have pointed out that the constellation of behaviors which make up SRA allegations would generate material evidence. Yet repeated investigations of SRA cases have not only failed to recover material evidence, occasionally they have demon-

---

[31]Geraldo Rivera's talk shows featured Lauren Stratford, Mike Warnke, and other bogus "authorities" and arguably set the bar for satanic hysteria. See http://www.religioustolerance.org/geraldo.htm.
[32]The Religious Tolerance web site (http://www.religioustolerance.org) notes, "We have studied over 40 Multi-Victim, Multi-Offender (MVMO) cases at 24 locations, mostly involving allegations of ritual abuse, since 1995." In virtually none of these, according to RT, have the ritual abuse allegations been proven. A very small number did in fact involve traditional forms of child abuse.

strated that at least some of what was alleged simply did not happen. For example: the alleged tunnels under the McMartin Preschool were not there.[33]

Kenneth Lanning of the FBI's Center for Missing and Exploited Children attempted to battle the hysteria by offering his findings. No thousands of missing children existed. The use of infrared detectors over various alleged SRA sites (where bodies were supposed to be buried) revealed nothing. No international satanic conspiracy has been found, despite the FBI's best efforts. But the SRA proponents said the lack of missing children on record was because the Satanists had their own "breeders" for baby sacrifices. And of course, Ken Lanning himself (as he told me) was accused of being in cahoots with the Satanists.

The SRA hysteria was fueled by a witch's brew of books, national TV talk shows, therapeutic networks, and the not usually amenable feminist and evangelical Christian communities. Evangelical Christianity seemed to find in this new SRA-MPD paradigm a theologically compelling and highly marketable gold mine.

A very partial list of such evangelical books include: *Uncovering the Mystery of MPD*[34] by James G. Friesen, Ph.D., apparently the most gullible doctor alive; *Satanism: Is Your Family Safe?*[35] by Ted Schwarz and Duane Empey; the awful children's book, *Don't Make Me Go Back, Mommy*[36] by Doris Sanford, whose publisher told me that despite the lack of evidence, "We believe ritual abuse is a reality"; *He Came to Set the Captives Free,*[37] the testimony of "Elaine" by Dr. Rebecca Brown, and probably my best reason to believe that people will believe absolutely anything; *The Healing of Satanically Ritually Abused Multiple Personality Disorder*[38] by John Clark, Ph.D.; *The Satanic Revival*[39] by Mark Bubeck; *The Devil's Web: Who Is Stalking Your Children for Satan?*[40] by Pat Pulling, who blamed the fantasy role-playing game Dungeons and Dragons for her son's suicide; *The Edge of Evil: The Rise of Satanism in North America*[41] by

---

[33]See http://www.cornerstonemag.com/features/iss096/mulhern.htm.
[34]Here's Life Publishers, 1991.
[35]Zondervan, 1988.
[36]Multnomah Press, 1990. Lauren Stratford was consulted for this project, though the exact nature of her contribution was contested.
[37]See http://answers.org/satan/brown.html. See also Personal Freedom Outreach's excellent and exhaustive exposés of "Elaine," Brown, and fundamentalist comic book publisher Jack Chick, who is infamous for false stories such as those of John Todd (another ex-Satanist, who was exposed in *Cornerstone* magazine) and Alberto Rivera (part of the "harlot" of Roman Catholicism).
[38]Self-published, apparently, in Bloomington, IN, 2003.
[39]Here's Life Publishers, 1991.
[40]Huntington House,1989.
[41]Word Books, 1989.

Jerry Johnson and with a foreword by the ultimate pulp-sensationalist, Geraldo Rivera (Rivera writes, "between forty and sixty thousand human beings are killed through ritual homicides in the United States each year"); *Satanism: The Seduction of America's Youth*[42] and *Dead Air*[43] (a novel) by Bob Larson.

Bob Larson's novel took a good thrashing in *Cornerstone*, especially as the book (at least in its galley form) claimed to be rooted in verified cases of Satanic Ritual Abuse. Nifty scenes included one where a cat is nailed to a lectern and another where a victim is "birthed" by being pulled through the rear end of a dead horse. My literary and moral objections to this garbage ended up netting me an appearance on *Larry King Live* opposite Mr. Larson but didn't seem to put much of a dent in his sales or the popularity of the topic. (We later exposed as untrue Larson's own "testimony" of having been a devilish rock and roller before his conversion;[44] this again didn't seem to have great impact on his audiences, who preferred the "Christian" untrue story to the decidedly checkered reality.)

But the granddaddy of all evangelical works on Satanism was Mike Warnke's *The Satan Seller*, which purported to be a factual account of Warnke's leadership in the late sixties of a 1,500-member satanic coven. His book sold three million copies (if we believe him), while as a "Christian comedian" he sold over one million recordings and made millions of dollars touring worldwide. In 1992, in our 24,000-plus-word article "Selling Satan,"[45] we exposed the alleged ex-Satanist turned born-again comedian's testimony as a fabrication. The exhaustive examination, relying on interviews with dozens and dozens of witnesses, boxes of documentation including photographs, and follow-ups that included individuals who knew Mike during his time in the military, proved that Warnke had lied about virtually every detail of his history.

This story, like Stratford's, won us both praise and condemnation. The EPA again recognized us with their first-place award for investigative journalism, calling the article their story of the year. Word Records dropped Warnke, after initially saying they were satisfied his story was true despite our article. But even after turning the article into a book-length treatment, *Selling Satan: Mike Warnke and the Evangelical Media*, I and fellow-author

---

[42]Thomas Nelson, 1989.

[43]Thomas Nelson, 2005.

[44]Jon Trott, "Bob Larson's Ministry Under Scrutiny," *Cornerstone*, Vol. 21, Issue 100, 18, 37, 41–42; http://www.cornerstonemag.com/features/iss100/larson.htm.

[45]Jon Trott and Mike Hertenstein, "Selling Satan: The Tragic History of Mike Warnke," *Cornerstone*, Vol. 21, Issue 98, 7–19, 30, 38. This is available online in its entirety, along with Warnke's responses and the responses of other media sources: http://www.cornerstonemag.com/features/iss098/warnke_index.htm.

Mike Hertenstein still felt as though we'd failed to awaken the church to what Warnke's story really meant.

Warnke, too, had contributed to Satanic Panic, even claiming at one point to be caring for SRA victims at his Kentucky ministry headquarters. He was consulted by law enforcement, featured on Christian and mainstream television as an "expert" on Satanism, and cited by others (including Lauren Stratford) as proof for what they were saying about Satanism. In the end, Warnke dealt with us by making Satanists of *Cornerstone* magazine, Christian Research Institute (who supported our findings early on), and Robert and Gretchen Passantino (who both helped us and housed us during our California research):

> "These three are all in it together," stressed [Warnke's third ex-wife yet ministry partner] Rose. "*Cornerstone*, CRI, and the Passantinos are all part of the same evil cult, and there's someone very powerful backing them up. They've got a lot of money on their side and are extremely dangerous."
>
> When asked for substantive verification of these assertions, Mike Warnke said it was forthcoming. "We've hired our own investigators," declared the comedian. "And, we're going to expose *Cornerstone* and CRI for who they really are."
>
> "As a matter of fact," Rose told the journalist conducting the interview, "If you write a story exposing them with the information we already have against them, *Cornerstone* will find out where you are and kill you. Are you willing to take that risk?"[46]

In the end, the satanic story for me looped back to where it had begun: Lauren Stratford. One afternoon in 1999 I received a phone call from a man in California. "I am a Holocaust survivor," he informed me. Through his own sense of skepticism and a tenacious search, he had located our article on Lauren Stratford. "I think," he said, "that your Lauren Stratford is our Lauren Grabowski." It turned out that Lauren had once again reinvented herself, this time as a Jewish child-survivor of the concentration camps! The Passantinos and I exposed her new lie,[47] a lie that also implicated fellow Holocaust faker Binjamin Wilkomirski.

As Oprah and others have discovered as recently as 2006 (the now-infamous James Frey *A Million Little Pieces* episode[48]), touting autobio-

---

[46]Perucci Ferraiuolo, "Warnke Calls Critics Satanists," 49, 52; http://www.cornerstonemag.com/features/iss098/warnke_response/csr0018a.htm.

[47]See http://www.cornerstonemag.com/features/iss117/lauren.htm.

[48]See Smoking Gun's expose of this bogus autobiography, which Oprah unwittingly helped become a best-seller: http://www.thesmokinggun.com/archive/0104061jamesfrey1.html.

graphical histories as truthful is a decidedly risky business.[49] But talk shows and tabloids do so for a reason. We all want desperately to find in stories the theme of redemption out of terrible pain, a theme we find in our own Christian story. How much more powerful can a story get than being rescued from Nazis or Satanists to bear witness to both evil's existence and the even more potent power of good?

In the end, stories of Satanism are powerful because they pit God against the author of evil himself, and through the narrator we see God as ultimately the victor. The narrator thus separates not only good from evil but also meaning from meaninglessness, and by so doing also gives meaning to our more pedestrian lives. Yet if the redemption story is only a story—that is, if Jesus did not actually die on the cross or rise from the dead—then as Paul wrote, "If for this life only we have hoped in Christ, we are of all people most to be pitied."[50] That is, a false story is a false hope, and false hope is no hope at all.

FINDING THE SATANISTS

> Sin is not confined to the evil things we do. It is the evil within us, the evil which we are. Shall we call it our pride or our laziness, or shall we call it the deceit of our life? Let us call it for once the great defiance which turns us again and again into the enemies of God and of our fellowmen, even of our own selves.
>
>   KARL BARTH

The Bible shows no interest in Satanism as a specific belief system; rather, it emphasizes that humanity's natural condition, on a very deep level, is interwoven with the satanic. "You were dead through the trespasses and sins in which you once lived, following the course of this world, following the ruler of the power of the air, the spirit that is now at work among those who are disobedient."[51]

It seems an almost universal human tendency to need "the Other"— that person, group, or entity upon which we might cast our collective sense of guilt, of rage, of evil. The reality is this: child abuse occurs in ostensibly "Christian" homes all over America. Men claiming biblical faith beat their wives even to death, often justifying their acts with semi-scriptural "headship" language.[52] History is filled with "godly" people doing horrendous,

---

[49]See http://www.cjrdaily.org/magazine_report/on_oprah_frey_henrilevy_and_un.php.

[50]First Cor. 15:19.

[51]Eph. 2:1–2.

[52]It appalls me that Evangelicalism's largest denomination, the Southern Baptist Church, has increasingly moved in the direction of disempowering women in the name of allegedly scriptural mandates (no pun

ungodly things. Even King David, the greatest Old Testament hero, both committed adultery and murdered the husband of his mistress. Was this not satanic?

Goodness is here; evil is there. We rarely, if ever, flip that formula to see what might be revealed to us. Neither good nor evil can be easily assigned locations isolated from each other. Yes, God is wholly good, and Satan is wholly evil. Yet humanity is indwelt by sin while also containing reflections of God's image, and both conditions are universally human. As C. S. Lewis has one of his characters in *Prince Caspian* note, "You come of the Lord Adam and the Lady Eve. . . . And that is both honor enough to erect the head of the poorest beggar, and shame enough to bow the shoulders of the greatest emperor on earth."

Denis de Rougemont wryly observes:

> Christianity has for centuries tried to make us understand that the Kingdom of God is within ourselves, that Evil also is in ourselves, and that their battlefield is nowhere but in our hearts. This education has largely failed. . . . Consistently we make the people across the way responsible for our ill, or else we lay the blame on the force of things. If we are revolutionaries, we believe that by changing the arrangement of certain objects—by displacing wealth, for instance—we shall suppress the causes of the evils of the century. If we are capitalists, we believe that by displacing these same objects in our direction, we shall save everything. If we are good, honest democrats, whether anxious or optimistic, we believe that by roasting a few dictators, profaners of law, or sorcerers, we shall re-establish peace and prosperity. We are still submerged in a magic mentality.[53]

What does de Rougemont mean by "magic mentality," and who does he accuse of practicing it? He suggests it is a province of savage cultures, savage persons:

> Whether it be a sorcerer, a profaner of things sacred, an animal, a cloud, a bit of colored wood, the cause of the evil from which these savages suffer is always independent of themselves, and must therefore be fought and annihilated outside of themselves.[54]

Those who have ears to hear, let them hear.

I am not offering up a completely subjective take on reality—how would

---

intended). Christians for Biblical Equality (http://www.cbeinternational.org) is one evangelical voice bringing light to this dark area; this author is humbled to be a part of CBE's effort.
[53]Denis de Rougemont, *The Devil's Share* (New York: Meridian Books, 1956), 85. Used by permission.
[54]Ibid.

I then be any different than the SRA proponents? I believe that groups and individuals can be (and are) "wrong" just as others can be "right" on major issues of faith and practice. But that wrong and right lie ultimately in God, not in me or my opinions. And this, I trust, should lead to Christianity's heart. A love-based humility in relating toward our God, family, friends, and enemies—the "other"—is one of our faith's most unique contributions to human understanding. "I give you a new commandment, that you love one another," Jesus told his friends as he prepared to face the cross. "Just as I have loved you, you also should love one another. By this everyone will know that you are my disciples, if you have love for one another."[55]

Do we obey this commandment? Are Christians known for their love for even their enemies, their gentleness toward a world ruled by the Prince of Darkness? Or are we again seduced by the mythology of an evil external to us, an evil "out there"?

As existentialist Christian thinker Gabriel Marcel notes, opinions are not beliefs. Belief is that which is embodied, lived in our day-to-day reality.[56] If we do evil in Jesus' name, and another does good in Muhammad's name, the good is still good and the evil still evil. God is not mocked. Our belief—or lack of it—is exposed.

So where are the Satanists, these co-conspirators with the Enemy of Love?

I suggest that each of us, in solitude, prayerfully look in a mirror and ask that question again.

---

[55]John 13:34–35.
[56]As Marcel writes in *Creative Fidelity*, ". . . the memory of this inner crisis has not left me—in particular, the awareness of the unbridgeable gulf between opinion and faith. . . . [I]t seems clear to me that certain developments in contemporary thought exhibit a tendency to confuse belief with opinion. To someone who does not share my belief, it in fact tends to appear as an opinion; through a commonly known optical illusion, I myself tend to consider it from the point of view of the other person, hence to treat it in turn as an opinion. Thus a strange, disturbing dualism is established within me; to the extent that I in fact live my belief, it is in no way an opinion; to the extent that I describe it to myself, I espouse the point of view of the person who represents it to his mind but does not live it; it then becomes external to me—and, to that degree, I cease to understand myself."

CHAPTER TWENTY-FOUR

Reasoning Faith and Global Missions: On Reaching Hindus And Hindu-Like Peoples

David J. Hesselgrave

CURRENTLY TWO OF THE MOST formidable religious challenges to North American churches and missions are, and for the foreseeable future will probably be, Islam and Hinduism and their various ideological and organizational expressions. It goes without saying that these two religions are fundamentally different and threaten the Christian church and its missions in different ways. As for Christianity and Islam, both being decidedly monotheistic, misunderstandings and antagonisms between their respective adherents exhibit many of the characteristics of long-standing sibling rivalries. Misunderstandings are deep and difficult to overcome. As for Christianity and Hinduism, though their respective monotheistic and monistic worldviews are ultimately incompatible by almost any measure, many adherents of both religions tend to find ways to obscure those differences. As a result, if the challenge of an exclusivist and even militant Islam to church and mission is formidable, as it most assuredly is, the challenge of an inclusivistic and relativistic Hinduism turns out to be more subtle and equally serious.

The current rivalry between America and Islamic nations being cultural and political as well as religious, it is a matter of urgency that American Christians fervently pray for wisdom on the part of their political as well as their religious leaders. Even as I write, *U.S. News and World Report* reporter Jay Tolson asserts that six years after 9/11 our political leaders do not know who speaks for Islam. He infers that they are not at all sure that even mainstream Islam is compatible with democracy and rights established by international law.[1] As far as church and mission leaders are concerned, unprecedented attention has been given in an attempt to gain an understanding of Islam and of ways best suited to contextualize the gospel for its adherents. The results are mixed and not altogether encouraging, however. One would hope and pray that, given the biblical mandate and the lessons of history, mission specialists will achieve some kind of consensus as to the best way to proceed. Meanwhile, both politically and religiously, the Islamic challenge remains a most formidable one. Even so, that challenge must remain for others more qualified to address at another time and in another venue. I make mention of it here by way of contrast but also because of its extreme urgency.

In the pages that follow I will be concerned almost exclusively with the challenge posed by Hinduism but also by Buddhism, New Ageism, and modern movements that share the Hindu worldview. *Readers should note that for the sake of simplicity of expression I will usually refer to Hinduism and Hindus only, but since all of these religious movements and their adepts share the same basic worldview, the reference will ordinarily be to all of them together.* Also, though numerous issues are involved in reaching Hindus for Christ in a globalized twenty-first century, our main focus here has to do with the place of reason and a reasonable faith in dialoguing with, and communicating a biblical gospel to, these peoples. I will address that topic as it pertains particularly to American missions to Hindus and Hindu-like people for two primary reasons. First, over the last century American culture has been profoundly affected by the inroads of Eastern—especially Hinduistic—thinking, values, and movements. Secondly, American churches and missions experience very real and somewhat unique problems when it comes to understanding and missionizing these people. Political issues are involved, but they are not primary. It is Hindu religious thinking and practice that pervades postmodern culture and even invades avant-garde churches and missions.

FROM MODERNISM TO POSTMODERNISM IN TWENTIETH-CENTURY AMERICA

My paternal grandfather was among those in attendance at the first Parliament of the World's Religions held in conjunction with the Columbian Exposition in Chicago in 1893. A prominent lay preacher and leader in Universalist Church circles in southern Wisconsin, along with a great many

---

[1]Jay Tolson, "Fighting for the Soul of Islam," *U.S. News and World Report*, April 16, 2007, 36–40.

other attenders, Grandfather Hesselgrave was enthralled with the words he heard, such as the following spoken by Swami Vivekananda, the principal disciple of a great Indian sage, Sri Ramakrishna:

> Sisters and brothers of America, it fills my heart with joy unspeakable to rise in response to the warm and cordial welcome which you have given us. I thank you in the name of the most ancient order of monks in the world; I thank you in the name of the mother of religions; and I thank you in the name of millions and millions of Hindu people of all classes and sects. . . . I am proud to belong to a religion that has taught the world both tolerance and universal acceptance. We believe not only in universal toleration, but we accept all religions to be true.[2]

The 1893 Parliament is widely believed to have opened the door to non-Christian religions, especially Eastern religions, in America. Their incursion did not happen overnight, of course, but it did happen. Based on a lecture series first delivered in 1926 in Manchester College, England, Sarvepelli Radhakrishnan's popular book *The Hindu View of Life*, first published in 1927 by Macmillan, for example, had seven reprintings by the middle of the twentieth century and a number of reprintings thereafter. For more than a quarter century after 1950—and especially with the rise of the hippie movement in the 1960s and 1970s—Hindu and Buddhist schools and cults flourished in the United States. Expressions of older schools such as Vedanta, Yoga, and Zen were accompanied by new and often bizarre cults such as Hare Krishna, Transcendental Meditation, Rajneesh, Divine Light, and Soka Gakkai. Gradually some of these schools and cults—and their philosophies and practices—became more or less mainstream in American culture. In fact, notices of their meeting times and places soon appeared along with those of Christian churches in Saturday editions of local papers.

Understandably, scholars are more or less noncommittal when it comes to dating the advent of postmodern culture in the United States. But a good case can be made for concluding that postmodern culture was occasioned not only by dissatisfaction with the outcomes of modernism, but also by virtue of the popularity of Hindu philosophy, religion, and spirituality. Indeed, these may be two sides of the same coin.

Be that as it may, representatives of Hinduism and, to a lesser extent,

---

[2]Jim Kenny, "1993: The Parliament of the World Religions," a promotional paper included with invitations to support a d attend the 1993 centennial Parliament in Chicago. The paper includes a photo of Swami Vivekananda standing among Parliament leaders. The paper is still in the possession of the author.

Buddhism and other Eastern religions were not only prominent at the sessions of the centennial meeting of the Parliament of the World's Religions held in Chicago in 1993, they were also important in the very planning and promotion of it. As for evangelical Christians, they seemed almost mesmerized by the event. Missing a golden opportunity to make a united case for the one gospel and the only Lord and Savior, evangelicals contented themselves with one clear statement on Christian uniqueness delivered in a special forum addressed by Charles Colson—that and a few ad hoc reflections by representative evangelicals offered during and after the Parliament sessions. As for the legacy of the Parliament itself, it was pretty much as could be expected given the presuppositions and purposes of its planners. From the very beginning those planners had proceeded on the pluralistic and eclectic foundation expressed in Swami Vivekananda's address a century before. As a matter of fact, Jim Kenny closed the promotional piece referred to above with Vivekananda's words followed by his own:

> "We believe not only in universal toleration, but we accept all religions to be true."
>   . . . Consider this as a starting-point: every religion is superior to every other religion by virtue of what it does best. And let's go a bit beyond: *every religion has a very secret access to the truth. The conversation begins here!*[3]

It would be almost impossible to conceive of a greater encouragement to postmodernist Americans than that embodied in these notions proposed first at the close of the nineteenth century and then again at the end of the twentieth!

AN OVERVIEW OF THE EVANGELICAL RESPONSE TO THE INROADS OF HINDU THOUGHT AND PRACTICE IN AMERICAN CULTURE

Providentially, the larger evangelical response to the incursion of Hindu thought and practice in America represented a significant improvement over the anemic response to the Parliament of 1993. Almost immediately after World War II, leaders of counter-cult ministries responded to the proliferation of Eastern religious movements and thinking. Their older concern with "sects" broadened to include a concern with "cults" and the so-called "new religious movements." The idea was that "imported"

---

[3]Ibid., emphasis mine.

religious movements—whose truth-claims are significantly different from orthodox Christianity—as well as unorthodox movements originating in America, need to be analyzed . . . in light of traditional Christianity and its historic interpretation of the Bible."[4] Older books such as J. K. Van Balaen's *Chaos of the Cults* (1938) were augmented by Walter Martin's best-seller, *The Kingdom of the Cults* (1965), Ron Rhodes's *Reasoning from the Scriptures with the Mormons* (1995), and then numerous volumes written by eminent scholars such as Ronald Enroth, Douglas Groothuis, and John Weldon, to name a few. Counter-cultists such as these made comprehensive and compelling cases for the truth of historic Christianity while exposing the errors of these movements. It should also be noted that some of the newer counter-cult organizations were founded for purposes not only of exposing the errors of these movements, but also for the purpose of freeing converts from their grasp. The Spiritual Counterfeits Project with headquarters in Berkeley, California, became one of the better known of such organizations.

In the face of the incursion of Hindu and Hindu-oriented philosophy and religion, the contributions of counter-cult specialists and organizations can hardly be overstated. However, during the last half of the twentieth century, the foci of a majority of church and mission leaders were on other things. Pastors and church growth specialists largely concerned themselves with reaching unchurched Americans—especially unchurched and disenchanted young people—and with growing bigger and bigger churches. They tended to concentrate on "marketing the church" and designing the kind of "seeker-sensitive" messages and programs that held promise of attracting newcomers while at the same time retaining older ones. As for American missions, they mainly focused on reaching the unreached abroad. Insofar as they concerned themselves with outreach within the United States they tended to concentrate on new arrivals of various ethnic, national, and religious strains. In sum, it may not be too much to conclude that both churches and missions tended to leave the hard work of simultaneously communicating the truth of the gospel and exposing the errors of Hinduism, New Ageism, and the like to parachurch and paramission specialists and organizations.

Given our American penchant for individualism, entrepreneurship, and specialization, this failure to establish meaningful connections between counter-cult groups, churches, and missions is perhaps understandable.

---

[4] R. Enroth, "Cult," in *Dictionary of Religion in America*, ed. Daniel G. Reid (Downers Grove, IL: InterVarsity, 1990), 331–332.

At the same time, given the globalization of church and mission and the pressing need for effective and complementary responses to the invasion of Hindu and Hindu-like religion and spirituality, the failure to establish a common and compelling evangelical apologetic response to that invasion is indeed regrettable.

EVANGELICAL MISSIOLOGY AND HINDU OUTREACH— THE NEGATIVE SIDE

American Christians, past and present, tend to respond to Hindu philosophy and religion in rather naive ways. Like many if not most Orientals, present-day heirs of the early sages of India often prove to be courteous hearers of the Christian gospel. That being the case, and unaware of the great cultural and religious distances involved, Americans often respond in ways that are sincere but also superficial. Examples are legion. The very first sermon of one American evangelist visiting India had to do with the necessity of the new birth. It evidently never occurred to him that "new births" represented the Hindu problem, not its solution. Completely lacking an understanding of Indian values, one well-dressed and impeccably groomed American pastor addressed his Indian counterparts on the subject of "true holiness" without realizing that the Hindu holy man renounces *everything* in his quest for enlightenment. Back in America, when lecturing missionary candidates, one seminary professor contended that karma in Hinduism is very much the same as sin in Christianity. Hearing about it, a colleague who was better informed suggested that the professor leave such comparisons to those better acquainted with Hinduism.

But enough of examples such as these. Let's recognize that, entering a new century and a new millennium, our evangelical and would-be evangelical churches and missions have now arrived at a critical hour that demands more and better understanding, not only with respect to a resurgent Islam as we have said previously, but with respect to the various expressions of Hindu ideas that have proved to be resilient in India and attractive in America. From where I sit as a missiologist, it seems to me that quite apart from what representatives of Hinduism old and new may say and do in this present situation, evangelical missiologists themselves must first recognize and then attempt to overcome barriers of their own making if the biblical gospel is to prevail. These barriers are of two major types, both of which need to be recognized, carefully analyzed, and ultimately transcended. The first type consists of concessions to Hindu teachings and practices made in an attempt to reach postmoderns in the United States. The second type consists of residues that flow out of new missiological understandings of the Christian mission itself.

Problems Growing out of Efforts to Reach Postmoderns

The similarities between postmodernism and Hinduism are most significant to our present discussion. The characteristics of postmodernism have been identified by numerous analysts and almost invariably include preferences for religious tolerance and inclusivism; feelings and spiritual experience; relativism as opposed to absolutism; non-propositionalism as concerns matters of truth; mysticism and holism along with such things as togetherness, belongingness, and harmony. Now it would take little time and space (but more than is available here) to demonstrate that many if not most of these expressions of postmodernism are not only compatible with traditional and contemporary Hindu thinking and practice, they are part and parcel of the Hindu heritage! Moreover, it is precisely characteristics and commitments such as these that impede the conversion of Hindus. Many Hindus have been or are being "enlightened" and have "received" Christ already!

Now it certainly is not my intention to paint any and all efforts to accommodate the preferences of postmoderns with a black brush. On the contrary, I applaud every sincere effort to reach them. At the same time it must be insisted that *over*-accommodation (*over*-contextualization) is not only risky, it can be fatal. At first it obscures the biblical gospel. In the end it obliterates it. We have discussed this in other places.[5] The point to be made here is that when pastors and youth leaders in our churches at home make too many concessions to postmodernism in their efforts to reach postmodern youth, they actually work at cross-purposes to evangelical missions. They complicate the missionary task of "really reaching" all Hindus and Hindu-like peoples—young and old, westerner and easterner, those at home and those abroad.

By way of example, take Brian McLaren and his Emergent Church approach. McLaren believes that it was God's guidance that instead of going to seminary to study theology, he chose to go to a secular graduate school in order to study literature and language. Now, though pastoring a church, lecturing widely on theology and related subjects, and even serving on the adjunct faculty of several seminaries, he is completely unapologetic about his choice. Why? Because, as he says,

---

[5]Cf. David Hesselgrave, "Brian McLaren's Contextualization of the Gospel," *Evangelical Missions Quarterly*, 43, No.1 (2007): 92–101.

It [studies in literature and language] gave me a taste, a sense, a feel for the game and science and art and romance of language. It helped me to see how carefully chosen and clear, daring words can point to mysteries and wonders beyond words. It prepared me to see how a generous orthodoxy must be mystical and poetic.[6]

Every word and phrase in this quotation—"taste," "sense," "feel for the game," "romance of language," "mysteries and wonders beyond words," "generous orthodoxy"—as well as many others in the larger context of his book merit close examination. It almost goes without saying that McLaren's emphases on the mystical, nonrational, and non-propositional are made at the expense of biblical revelation, doctrinal integrity, and a reasoned faith and are as inimical to the communication of a *biblical* gospel among Hindus as they are to its communication among postmoderns. Throughout long centuries Hindu sages and philosophers have shown themselves to be as cognitively and philosophically capable as any of their western counterparts, but at the same time their fertile imaginations and artistic capabilities have yielded themselves to a religion that leads them *away* from God, not *to* him. The historical development of Hinduism could hardly be summarized more certainly and succinctly than it is in the words of the apostle Paul in Romans 1:18–32. It is a pity that McLaren, or any Christian, believes it helpful rather than hurtful to resort to the very instincts and inclinations that gave Hinduism rise in the first place.

Problems Growing out of Efforts to Redirect World Missions

Enter tried and true missiologists! On the surface of it, it would seem incredulous to give even a moment's thought to the notion that proposals of evangelical (especially *evangelical*) missions leaders and missiologists could be inimical to Great Commission mission. But if there is the slightest possibility that might be the case, it seems incumbent upon us to give the suspicion some study.

In the excellent volume *The Changing Face of World Missions,*[7] contributors deal with various newer missiological terms and concepts important to contemporary mission theory and practice—concepts such as contextualization, praxis, holistic, incarnational, missional, kingdom mission, and *missio Dei,* among others. A careful study of this book proves McLaren to be correct when he speaks of the importance of words and

---

[6]Brian D. McLaren, *A Generous Orthodoxy* (Grand Rapids, MI: Zondervan, 2004), 157.
[7]Michael Pocock, Gailyn van Rheenen, and Douglas McConnell, *The Changing Face of World Missions: Engaging Contemporary Issues and Trends* (Grand Rapids, MI: Baker, 2005).

language. The foregoing terms have become parts of the common parlance of missions people. The problem is that the meanings of these words are by no means univocal. Very different meanings have been assigned to them and with very different significances. To their credit, contributors to *The Changing Face* provide stipulated definitions of these terms—meanings that do not give pause to most readers. The problem is that other meanings often assigned to them do, and should, give pause. When the concern is for the salvation of adepts of Eastern religions such as Hinduism and Buddhism, for example, any or all of the foregoing terms can be understood in ways that are counterproductive. To take a most obvious example, on the face of it, it seems apparent that to speak of "incarnating" Christ within the context of religions well populated by numerous *avatara* of Vishnu, various incarnations of Buddha, and numerous *bodhisattvas* or savior beings is an open invitation to misunderstanding and confusion.

But let's focus on an example that is not quite so obvious, namely *holism* and *holistic mission*. In the aforementioned volume *holistic mission* is defined as "Mission that takes into account the whole of human needs: spiritual, social and personal."[8] That definition seems to fit what those who signed the Lausanne Covenant (1974) probably had in mind. To many evangelicals at Lausanne and elsewhere the Covenant undoubtedly presaged an important step forward in missions worldwide. Actually, however, the part that had to do with social concern has evoked many questions and considerable debate during subsequent years and right up to the present time. Most fundamental were those questions having to do with priority in mission. Is not evangelism and church planting more important to Great Commission mission than economic assistance or even HIV prevention? What is the relationship between spiritual ministry and sociopolitical action? Questions such as these do not admit of easy answers, and as good as it was in many respects, the Lausanne Covenant did more to raise such questions than it did to answer them.

As the concept of *holism* developed, it went through three main phases.[9] First, a "certain priority" was assigned to evangelism as compared to social action. Then evangelism and social action were considered to be basically equal in importance—two sides of the one missiological coin, so to speak. A final stage came when some evangelicals espoused the kind of holism that completely rejects . . . the dichotomy between material and spiritual, between

---

[8]Ibid., 15.
[9]Cf. David J. Hesselgrave, *Paradigms in Conflict: 10 Key Questions in Christian Missions Today* (Grand Rapids, MI: Kregel, 2005), 118–122.

evangelism and social action, between loving God and loving neighbor."[10]
Now it would seem obvious that by the time holistic mission arrived at this
latest notion—and probably well before that time—it had conflicted with
Scripture.

But that is not all that is involved. In terms of communicating the
biblical gospel to Hindus, it is important to note that in its more developed forms at least, holistic mission necessarily raises serious questions
for thinking Hindus themselves. At the earlier stages on life's way, health,
wealth, and even pleasure are legitimate "goals" or "ends of life" for Hindu
peoples. But the ideal goal is ever and always to renounce all such ends and,
assuming the life of a poor, wandering mendicant or "holy man," embark
on a quest for enlightenment and for enlightenment alone. Given this profoundly different philosophy and value system, a "holistic" philosophy of
Christian mission raises a number of questions that are distinctly Hindu
questions. In effect, holism and holistic mission raise as many problems for
true Hindus as they do for true Christians. From a Christian point of view,
to allow the transient to eclipse the eternal is to emasculate the gospel. From
a Hindu point of view, to allow the transient to eclipse the eternal is to dis-
engage from the highest inclinations of the Hindu mind. This is confusion
twice confounded!

EVANGELICAL MISSIONS AND HINDU OUTREACH—
THE POSITIVE SIDE

We have already taken note of the historic role of counter-cultists in the
United States. They aim to inform Christians on the one hand and to evan-
gelize adherents of false cults and religions on the other. Their approach is
basically apologetic, and in taking that approach counter-cultists remind all
of us that, by its very nature, Christian mission is an apologetic enterprise.
As ambassadors of Christ, it is the duty of Christian missionaries to persuade people to be reconciled to God (2 Cor. 5:20–21). People of whatever
time and circumstance have reasons for their own faith, whatever that faith
might be. They require still better reasons for redirecting their faith to the
true God and his Christ. Christian missionaries are obligated to provide
those reasons. In spite of misgivings such as those mentioned above, to be
true to the larger picture it must be said that forward-looking missionaries
recognize this and respond accordingly. Three successive and recent annual

---

[10]Bryant L. Myers, "In Response . . . Another Look at Holistic Mission," *Evangelical Missions Quarterly*,
13, No. 3 (1999), 287.

publications of the Evangelical Missiological Society have addressed various aspects of this kind of well-thought-out response.[11]

That is what we will do in concluding this essay. Without taking time and space to argue for any particular apologetic approach to Hindus and others with a similar worldview, I will attempt to illustrate some of the important ways in which some selected Christian thinkers have made positive contributions to missions in general, and to missions to Hindu-like people in particular. *It is important for my readers to realize that my single intention here is to illustrate the various kinds of contributions that these scholars have made to a reasoned apologetic for these cultures and religions. In this venue I cannot undertake either to elaborate on or to evaluate those contributions to any significant degree. Readers themselves are encouraged to undertake these tasks on their own.*

A Theologian's Case for Transcendent Revelation as a Basic Epistemic Axiom

Hindus and Buddhists and their spiritual kin all have sacred scriptures whether Vedas, Upanishads, or Sutras. But none of these scriptures constitutes a final authority; none expresses ultimate truth because that truth is held to be non-propositional, personal, and ineffable. Insofar as truth might be available in sacred scripture, it will be discovered "behind" or "beneath" the letter, never "in" it. Even then the best that scriptures can do is help occasion that ultimate truth that is unmediated and attainable through self-certifying spiritual experience—*para vidya, samadhi, satori.*

Such being the understanding of Hindus, Buddhists, New Agers, and many postmoderns as well, one might wonder why it is that, of all people, some missiologists more often cite Carl F. Henry's *The Uneasy Conscience of Modern Fundamentalism*[12] than his monumental *God, Revelation and Authority.*[13] Perhaps they are unaware of the degree to which the cause of world missions engaged not only Henry's heart but also his mind, of the degree to which missions elicited not only his interest but also his participation. More likely, however, they consider Henry's appeal for sociopolitical concern and involvement to be more important than his apologetic for biblical Christianity and mission.

---

[11]See Enoch Wan, ed., *Christian Witness in Pluralistic Contexts in the Twenty-First Century* (Pasadena, CA: William Carey, 2004); Mike Barnett and Michael Pocock, eds., *The Centrality of Christ in Contemporary Missions* (Pasadena, CA: William Carey, 2005); Gailyn Van Rheenen, ed., *Contextualization and Syncretism: Navigating Cultural Currents* (Pasadena, CA: William Carey, 2006).
[12]Carl F. H. Henry, *The Uneasy Conscience of Modern Fundamentalism* (Grand Rapids, MI: Eerdmans, 1947).
[13]Carl F. H. Henry, *God, Revelation and Authority*, 6 vols. (Nashville: Word, 1976–1984).

Nothing could be further from the truth, however. Certainly Henry himself did not think that way. In his sunset years he surveyed the entire philosophical and religious landscape of the late twentieth century and wrote, not another sociopolitical tract of any sort, but an urgent appeal to Christians to recover "Christian belief" in the face of theological defection and philosophical deconstructionism.[14] As part of that appeal he deals with religious systems ... from Hinduism's impersonal world-soul Brahma to Iranian Shi'ite fundamentalism, from Soka Gakkai principles in Japan to New Age enthusiasm in America"[15] and with many and varied epistemological systems including presuppositionalism, evidentialism, empiricism, rationalism, fideism, and existentialism.

From a missiological perspective, the inestimable value of Carl Henry's little volume on the recovery of belief is the case that it makes for the universality of knowledge concerning distinctions between God and not-God, good and evil, and truth and falsehood as an aspect of the *imago Dei*.

> As revelationally grounded and intelligible faith, Christianity sets out from the ontological priority of the living God and the epistemological priority of divine revelation. From these basic postulates it derives and expounds all the core doctrines of the Christian religion. Among these is the divine gift of saving faith that enlists the entire self in love, worship, and obedient service of the infinite Creator and Judge of mankind and the nation.[16]

I would prefer that Henry had given more attention to the differing nature of, claims for, and uses of the Bible as compared with the scriptures mentioned above. I also wish he had emphasized the relationship between the attributes of God and their epistemic correlates (e.g., "the God who cannot deny himself" and non-contradiction; "the God who cannot lie" and consonance with reality). Nevertheless, I believe that Henry's case for taking the eternal God and his nature, and divine revelation and its transcendence, as starting points, and human rationality, deductive theology, and the historic doctrines of the Christian faith as logical correlates will in the end constitute a more significant legacy to reaching Hindus than some of the popular strategies carefully designed to win Hindus without seriously disturbing their ingrained inclusivism, eclecticism, and relativism.

---

[14]Carl F. H. Henry, *Toward a Recovery of Christian Belief: The Rutherford Lectures* (Wheaton, IL: Crossway Books, 1990).
[15]Ibid., 52.
[16]Ibid., 59.

An Anthropologist's Case for a Critical, Contextualized, Christian Worldview

All are aware of the fact that worldviews are somehow grounded in and informed by meta-narratives that embody answers to fundamental human questions concerning the origins, obligations, and destinies of the peoples and cultures that "own" them. These meta-narratives or "big stories" may be mythological or historical, fictional or factual. In one sense that makes no difference. Imagination and fantasy can provide symbols and motifs out of which worldviews are constructed as readily as history and factualness can provide them. Perhaps more so. In another and more important sense, however, the difference between fancy and fact, right and wrong, truth and falsehood is, of course, of the essence.

The Hindu-Buddhist worldview is constructed out of numerous phantasmagoric myths. One of the most basic of Hindu myths, for example, conceives of the cosmos as a primordial cow, horse, or man that was sacrificed and dismembered, its constituent parts becoming the mountains, rivers, plains, and so on of the everyday experience of Indians.

Resorting to admitted myths such as this, Hindu sages and philosophers have put their own creativity to work and have come up with some of the most complex and involved cosmologies and philosophies imaginable. In the end, however, like the myths out of which they are constructed, these cosmologies are not "really real" or "truly true" except as they point to a reality beyond ordinary experience. Unless the importance of this is understood and acknowledged, Westerners in general will dismiss Indian myth and disparage the Indian worldview. And American missionaries will run the very real risk of having the "big story" of the Bible and their gospel message rejected out of hand as being so simple and naive as to be unworthy of consideration, especially by Hindu intelligentsia.

It is with this in mind that we call attention to the contributions of the late noted anthropologist, Paul A. Hiebert. Born and partially educated in India, Hiebert was especially well qualified to address contextualization issues as they relate to Hindus and Buddhists. Responding to Lamin Sanneh, who urges missions people to rethink their approach in the light of the demands of globalization, Hiebert encourages missiologists and missionaries to abandon their attempts to win converts by arrogantly and polemically discrediting target culture religions and worldviews. As an alternative to the "positivism of modernity" and the "instrumentalism/ idealism of postmodernity," he proposes a "critical realist epistemology" that ". . . strikes a middle ground between positivism, with its emphasis on objective truth, and instrumentalism, with its emphasis on the subjective nature of human knowledge."[17] Ontologically, his approach assumes there is a real world that is independent of human projections and opinions about it. At the same time, Hiebert recognizes that human knowledge does not have a literal one-to-one correspondence to that reality. Epistemologically, therefore, critical realism (or critical common-sensism)

> . . . affirms the presence of objective truth but recognizes that this is sub-
> jectively apprehended. On another level . . . it challenges the definition of
> "rationality" in both positivism and instrumentalism that limits rational-
> ity to algorithmic logic. In so doing, critical realism offers a third, far more
> nuanced, epistemic position.[18]

Hiebert recognizes that the reaction of postmodernists to modernism does have some validity in that the positivism of modernism was characterized by intellectual superiority and arrogance. He is concerned that Christian missiologists and missionaries do not approach other cultures similarly. He believes that a recognition that all human knowledge is subjective even when its concern is with objective truth encourages humility and allows for some common ground between Christian missionaries and, perhaps especially, Hindus and Buddhists.

In place of "critical realism," one of Hiebert's most appreciative colleagues, Enoch Wan, proposes a "relational realism" that is . . . primarily based on the vertical relationship between God and the created order and, secondarily, the horizontal relationship within the created order."[19] Wan is persuaded that his "relational realism" has certain advantages in that it emphasizes God and our unique relationship with him as well as those collectivistic elements of the Christian faith that are so important in Eastern and other cultures. For my part, I recognize the sensitivity of both Hiebert and Wan to the cosmological and epistemological commitments of other cultures and the necessity of humility in dealing with them. I do believe that sensitivity and humility must characterize the "way forward" in a globalized world, as Hiebert puts it. Nevertheless, as elaborated in these writings, I have some fear that just as many attempts to reach postmoderns at home are characterized by over-contextualization, these endeavors to engage Hindus (among others) abroad may run a similar risk.

---

[17]Paul A. Hiebert, *Missiological Implications of Epistemological Shifts: Affirming Truth in a Modern/Postmodern World* (Harrisburg, PA: Trinity Press International, 1999).
[18]Ibid., 68–69.
[19]Cf. Enoch Wan, "The Paradigm of 'Relational Realism,'" *Occasional Bulletin*, 19, No 2 (2006), 1–4.

A Philosopher's Case for Appraising Worldviews, Especially Those Inclined Toward Inclusivism, Pluralism, and Relativism

Harold A. Netland was born and reared by missionary parents in Japan. Childhood experiences led to a study first of the religions of Japan and later to the philosophy of religion. Currently he serves as Professor of Philosophy of Religion and Intercultural Studies at Trinity Evangelical Divinity School. I mention this to draw attention to his background as it relates to what follows.

Netland's concern and contributions speak to the issues we address here at two levels. First and foremost he addresses these issues at a scholarly level. He is concerned with the understandings and productions of philosophers of religion such as John H. Hick, Wilfred Cantwell Smith, Paul F. Knitter, Raimundo Panikkar, and others who are unfriendly to exclusivism. Second, and at the same time, he is mindful of the needs and ministries of missionaries and other practitioners who labor among peoples devoted to non-Christian religions and worldviews. It is with both theorists and practitioners in mind, therefore, that he defends and commends the Christian worldview. And it is with both theorists and practitioners in mind that he critiques the fundamental tenets of relativism and discusses the inadequacy of fideism as a response.

Finding relativism—both relativism as a worldview and fideism as an answer to it—to be epistemologically invalid, Netland undertakes to provide the basic criteria required to make such judgments and to distinguish between the competing truth claims of the world's religions. These criteria are, in order:

1) Basic logical principles—identity, noncontradiction, and excluded middle.

2) Self-defeating statements—statements that provide grounds for their own refutation.

3) Coherence of worldview—the proper relationship between a worldview's defining beliefs.

4) Adequacy of explanation within reference range—a religious worldview should be able to provide adequate answers to all questions pertinent to religion such as those having to do with origins, morals, the afterlife, etc.

5) Consistency with knowledge in other fields—what is asserted as true in any religious worldview should be consistent with what is known to be true in science, history, and archaeology, for example.

6) Moral assessment—a right relationship between the religious ultimate of a worldview and basic moral principles and values.[20]

It will be immediately noted that as a Christian philosopher, Netland's
case is complementary to those of Henry and Hiebert, but also quite different. As would be suspected, it lacks the theological definitiveness that
attends Henry's "transcendental revelation" approach, even as it avoids
some of the tentativeness that attaches to Hiebert's "critical realism."
However, its inherent logic and rationality are consistent with and complementary to both cases. And the pertinence of Netland's logical appraisal
criteria will be immediately apparent as we proceed to an examination of
Ralph Winter's case for a "new direction" in missions.

A Historian's Case for a "New Direction" in Twenty-first-century Missions

It is not easy to type someone as intellectually ubiquitous as Ralph D.
Winter. However, I think that neither he nor anyone who knows him
will take exception to my classifying him as a historian as well as one
of the leading missiologists of our time. It is his interest in and understanding of paleontology and history that comes to the fore in the case
he makes for a "new direction in mission" (he might prefer "Kingdom
of God mission") as put forth in "The Unfinished Epic in Five Acts."[21]
The Epic is a chronological really "big story"—an attempt to retell the
story of the initial creation and its subsequent development in terms
that both secular scientists and biblical Christians can understand and,
perhaps, accept.

Taking Winter's "overall view" and employing more or less his own
sometimes cryptic words and phraseology, the Epic proceeds in five "acts"
or stages:

Act 1: Creation of the Universe about 13.7 billion B.C.? Creation
unspoiled, life begins about 1 billion B.C. Non-predatory life the last 3.5
billion years.

Act 2: Satan rebels about 530 million B.C.—the Cambrian Explosion?
530 million years of the distortion of all creation after Satan's "fall."
Predatory life first appears.

---

[20]Harold A. Netland, *Dissonant Voices: Religious Pluralism and the Question of Truth* (Grand Rapids, MI: Eerdmans, 1991), 183–195.
[21]"The Unfinished Epic in Five Acts," in *Christianity, Education and Modern Society*, William Jeynes and Enedina Martinze, eds. (Charlotte, NC: Information Age, 2007), 199–115.

Act 3: Genesis 1:1 about 6000 B.C.—Eden and a New Creation in the Middle East following a regional disaster? Non-predatory life reappears in Eden, Genesis 1:29–30.

Act 4: Adam rebels; the end of Eden. Adam's "fall" to now; the Kingdom of God versus the kingdom of Satan. Edenic life reverts to predatory life mixing with eternal life.

Act 5: End of time; return of Christ; Paradise. Non-predatory life in the future, Isaiah 11:6–9.

Winter credits Merrill Unger and Russell Mixter for some of his ideas, but most of what he writes represents his own thinking on these subjects. Irrespective of their origin, Winter acknowledges that some of these proposals will be extremely problematic in the view of both some Christians and some non-Christians. His way of saying it is that certain questions constitute "hurdles that will have to be surmounted" in order to make his Epic "digestible"—questions such as the following:

1) Did God create thinking, willing, intermediate beings such as angels and also Satan?

2) Could Satan be sufficiently intelligent, free, and powerful to distort even the DNA of animal and human life so as to produce forms of life that are vicious and wantonly destructive?

3) Why would aeons of time be involved in the development of life on earth and also for developments connected with Satan's rebellion?

4) What about happenings before Genesis 1:1? Were the original creation before that time and the creation events of Genesis new and local?

5) When did true humans appear? Is it possible that Adam's lineage was exposed to earlier humans who, like other forms of life, were distorted by Satan?

Reviewing the Epic and facing questions such as these, Christian evangelists and missionaries especially may be puzzled—even bewildered—and come up with their own questions. Why not leave discussions such as this one to the experts? Why should communicators of the comparatively simple gospel story of the Bible bother themselves about such questions? What does all of this have to do with Great Commission mission?

While recognizing the validity of such questions, Winter is fully persuaded that, given the state of American and world cultures, this kind of discussion has everything to do with evangelism and mission in whatever culture. In his view, to be unable or unwilling to engage contemporary cultures at this level is to forfeit the possibility of addressing many, if not most of the educated people of the world. Put the shoe on the other foot for a moment, and think of Harold Netland's fifth criteria for appraising worldviews: namely, consistency with knowledge in other fields. Imagine how an educated Indian might apply that criteron to his/her comparison of Hindu and Christian worldviews. By its very nature the validity of the Hindu worldview does not require correspondence with earth science. But an orthodox Christian worldview does require it. As far as our Hindu friend is concerned, the Genesis record (as ordinarily interpreted) does not square with the geologic records and fossil remains. As a consequence, our Indian friend is not prepared to really "hear" the Christian gospel.

To take another example, for many thoughtful people around the world, the prevalence of evil and suffering belies the existence and power of a good God. Why would a good and powerful God allow the violence, pain, and suffering that is everywhere present to exist? It's an old question to us, but fresh and new to many who hear about the God of the Bible for the first time.

Winter is concerned that people such as these be prepared to hear the gospel. That's why he insists that Christians who would share the gospel in the future be ready to engage in intelligent dialogue concerning precisely those issues that keep others from listening to it. He does not anticipate that every missionary will become a rocket scientist, of course—only that our missions take all of this into account in their missionizing. His "new direction," therefore, leads first of all to an apologetic for the validity and truth of the biblical record. Ultimately it also leads to the kind of spiritual warfare that declares out-and-out war on "evil" microbes with all that that entails. But that takes us too far afield at this point. Perhaps he will be content that we appreciate this much, at least, of what he has to say. As for his Epic itself, I for one am not capable of analyzing and evaluating it. But I can both appreciate and endorse its relevance, especially in the Eastern world. How well I remember showing the film *Dust or Destiny* to a university audience in Kyoto many years ago. Immediately after the film concluded, a Japanese professor of anthropology came to the podium and gave an extended and learned defense of naturalistic evolution. I had ventured where angels fear to tread! The teleological argument for the existence of God has its place, but only insofar as one is able to explain and defend it. At the very least this needs to be recognized and planned for.

CONCLUSION

Since the salvation of countless millions of Hindus, Buddhists, and followers of their ideological and organizational expressions in the East and West is at stake, the challenge of these religions and philosophies requires both an understandable proclamation of the biblical gospel and a well-reasoned case for its validity and truth by way of response. That, in turn, will require that we western Christians listen and learn from each other and from our colleagues indigenous to Eastern cultures. And it will also require that we recognize and employ the insights of all relevant disciplines for a responsible contextualization of the biblical gospel and the constructing of a well-reasoned Christian apologetic.

BIBLIOGRAPHY

Corwin, Charles. *East to Eden? Religion and the Dynamics of Social Change.* Grand Rapids, MI: Eerdmans, 1972.

Enroth, Ronald et al., eds. *A Guide to Cults & New Religions.* Downers Grove, IL: InterVarsity, 1983.

Galanter, Marc. *Cults: Faith, Healing, and Coercion.* New York: Oxford, 1989.

Groothuis, Douglas R. *Unmasking the New Age.* Downers Grove, IL: InterVarsity, 1986.

Henry, Helga Bender. *Cameroon on a Clear Day: A Pioneer Missionary in Colonial Africa.* Pasadena, CA: William Carey, 1999.

Hesselgrave, David J., ed. *Dynamic Religious Movements: Case Studies in Rapidly Growing Religious Movements Around the World.* Grand Rapids, MI: Baker, 1978.

Hesselgrave, David J. and Edward Rommen. *Contextualization: Meaning, Methods, and Models.* Grand Rapids, MI: Baker, 1989.

Hexham, Irving, Stephen Rost, and John W. Moorehead II, gen. eds. *Encountering New Religious Movements: A Holistic Evangelical Approach.* Grand Rapids, MI: Kregel, 2004.

Hick, John. *Truth and Dialogue in World Religions: Conflicting Truth-Claims.* Philadelphia: Westminster, 1974.

Newbigin, Lesslie. *The Gospel in a Pluralist Society.* Grand Rapids, MI: Eerdmans, 1989.

Niles, D.T. *The Preacher's Task and the Stone of Stumbling: The Lyman Beecher Lectures for 1957.* New York: Harper & Row, 1958.

Rommen, Edward, and Harold Netland, eds. *Christianity and the Religions: A Biblical Theology of the World Religions.* Pasadena: William Carey, 1996.

A Manifesto for Christian Apologetics: Nineteen Theses to Shake the World with the Truth[1]

Douglas Groothuis

On this rock I will build my church, and the gates of Hades will not overcome it. (Jesus Christ, Matt. 16:18)[2]

THIS IS A MANIFESTO TO IGNITE the holy fire of apologetic passion and action. As did Jeremiah, we should have "fire . . . in [our] bones" to communicate and commend Christian truth today (Jer. 20:9). This manifesto is not a sustained argument or a detailed development of themes. Rather, as a manifesto it proclaims a short series of interrelated propositions crying out for both immediate and protracted reflection, prayer, and action. These challenges issue from convictions formed through my nearly thirty years of apologetic teaching, preaching, debating, writing, and Christian witness.

Because of (1) the waning influence of the Christian worldview in public and private life in America today, (2) the pandemic of anti-intellectualism in the contemporary church, and (3) the very command of God himself to declare, explain, and defend divine truth, I strongly advise that the following statements be wrestled with and responded to by all followers of the Lord Jesus Christ.

1. Christian apologetics involves the presentation and defense of Christianity as an integrated worldview that is objectively, universally,

---

[1] A shorter version of this manifesto, featuring sixteen theses, was published in *Areopagus Journal*, Vol. 5, No. 1 (January/February 2005), 28–29.
[2] Unless otherwise indicated, all Scripture quotations in this Postscript are taken from *The Holy Bible: New International Version*.

and absolutely true, reasonable, knowable, and existentially pertinent to both individuals and entire cultures.[3] Apologetics involves rebutting unbelieving accusations against Christianity (2 Cor. 10:3–5; Jude 3) as well as giving a constructive and persuasive case for Christian theism (Phil. 1:7; 1 Pet. 3:15).

2. Any intellectual discipline, church practice, or teaching that minimizes or denigrates the importance of apologetics is unbiblical and must be repented of (Matt. 4:17; Acts 17:16–34; 2 Cor. 10:3–5; 1 Pet. 3:15; Jude 3). The degradation of apologetics can only lead to the further vitiation of the life of the church. "My people are destroyed from lack of knowledge" (Hos. 4:6).

3. The fundamental issue for apologetics is not how many apologists one has read or what apologetic method one embraces (although that must be worked out carefully).[4] Rather, the essential issue is whether or not one has a passion for God's transforming truth—reasonably pursued and courageously communicated—and a passion for the lost because of the love of God resident and active in one's life (Rom. 9:1–3; 10:1). Like the apostle Paul at Athens, we should be "greatly distressed" because of the rampant unbelief in our day. We, like that great apologist, should also be intellectually equipped and spiritually prepared to enter the marketplace of ideas for the cause of Christ (Acts 17:16–34).

4. The apologist must be convinced of the truth, rationality, pertinence, and knowability of the Christian worldview, which is derived from Holy Scripture as it is logically systematized and rightly harmonized with general revelation (truth knowable outside of Scripture). This is an intellectual goal for a lifetime as the disciple of Christ seeks to love God with one's mind and take more and more thoughts captive to obey Christ (Matt. 22:37–40; 2 Cor. 10:3–5). The apologist should never rest content with an ad hoc or piecemeal worldview, as is so typical of those afflicted with postmodernist pastiche sensibilities.

5. In light of (1), (2), (3), and (4), fideism—the claim that Christian faith finds no positive warrant from reason or evidence—should be rejected as unbiblical and harmful to the great cause of biblical truth (Isa. 1:18; Matt. 22:37–39; Rom. 12:1–2). Fideistic confessions such as "I just know that I know in my knower" do little to challenge unbelief or induce

---

[3]For a defense of this view of biblical truth, see Douglas Groothuis, *Truth Decay: Defending Christianity Against the Challenges of Postmodernism* (Downers Grove, IL: InterVarsity Press, 2000), especially Chaps. 3–4.

[4]On apologetic method, see Gordon Lewis, *Testing Christianity's Truth Claims* (Lanham, MD: University Press of America, 1990), and Steven Cowan, ed., *Five Views of Apologetics* (Grand Rapids, MI: Zondervan, 2000).

unbelievers to consider the saving truth of the gospel. Moreover, members of other religions can use the same technique to attempt to support their false beliefs. This is especially true for Mormons, who rely so heavily on subjective feelings to verify objective claims. Fideism strips Christianity of its rational witness to the reality of God's holy revelation to humanity.

6. Any theology, apologetics, ethics, evangelism, or church practice that minimizes or denigrates the concept of objective, absolute, universal, and knowable truth is both irrational and unbiblical. As such it must be rejected and repented of. Thus, the postmodernist view of truth as socially constructed, contingent, and relative must be rejected by Christian apologists. Anything that might be true in postmodernism can be found elsewhere in better philosophical systems. What is false in postmodernism (the vast majority of it) is fatal to Christian witness.[5] Without a strong, biblical view of truth, apologetics is impossible.

7. The work of the Holy Spirit in bringing people to saving faith should not be artificially separated from faithful apologetic engagement. Many Christians wrongly think that the ministry of the Holy Spirit is exclusively nonrational or even irrational. The Spirit is free to win and woo unbelievers in a host of ways—including dreams, angelic visitations, healings, visions, meaningful coincidences, and so on—but we must remember that he is "the Spirit of truth," as Jesus said (John 16:13). There is no reason to separate the work of the Holy Spirit from rigorous and skillful argumentation for Christian truth. The Holy Spirit can set the redeemed mind free to argue logically and winsomely; he also reaches into the unbeliever's soul through the force of arguments. Apologists should earnestly pray that the Holy Spirit will make them as intelligent and knowledgeable as possible.

8. All apologetic endeavors should manifest the virtues of both humility and courage through the empowering of the Holy Spirit (Acts 1:8; Gal. 5:16–26). If we have been bestowed by Almighty God with truth to defend rationally, this is because of God's grace, not our own goodness (Eph. 2:1–10; Titus 3:5–6). There is no room for pride, which goes before a fall. If Almighty God has bestowed us with saving truth to defend rationally, we should take it to the streets and not shrink back from appropriate encounters with unbelief. There is no room for cowardice. As Paul counseled

---

[5]See Groothuis, *Truth Decay*; Millard Erickson, *Truth or Consequences* (Downers Grove, IL: InterVarsity Press, 2001); R. Scott Smith, *Truth and a New Kind of Christian* (Wheaton, IL: Crossway Books, 2005). For a review of Brian McLaren's influential defense of postmodernism in *A New Kind of Christian* (San Francisco: Jossey-Bass, 2001), see Douglas Groothuis, "A New Kind of Postmodernist," *The Christian Research Journal*, Vol. 25, No. 3 (2003). For an incisive review of McLaren's book *A Generous Orthodoxy* (Grand Rapids, MI: Zondervan, 2004), see Jeremy Green's review in *Denver Journal*.

Timothy, "For God did not give us a spirit of timidity, but a spirit of power, of love and of self-discipline" (2 Tim. 1:7).

Humility should not be confused with uncertainty or timidity. One can be confident in one's worldview and defend it publicly without being arrogant. The grand apologist G. K. Chesterton explains this perfectly and memorably:

> But what we suffer from today is humility in the wrong place. Modesty has moved from the organ of ambition. Modesty has settled upon the organ of conviction, where it was never meant to be. A man was meant to be doubtful about himself, but undoubting about the truth; this has been exactly reversed. Nowadays the part of a man that a man does assert is exactly the part he ought not to assert himself. The part he doubts is exactly the part he ought not to doubt—the Divine Reason.[6]

9. Apologetics must be carried out with the utmost intellectual integrity (Titus 2:7–8; Jas. 3:1–2). All propaganda, cheap answers, caricatures of non-Christian views, hectoring, and fallacious reasoning must be avoided. Sadly, some apologetic materials are too cavalier for serious use. One should develop competent answers to searching questions about the truth and rationality of Christian faith. This demands excellence in scholarship at all intellectual levels, even the most popular. This cognitive orientation takes time, money, and sustained effort. It will not happen by watching television or by otherwise wasting our limited time.[7] Christians must thus cultivate the virtue of studiousness in order to grow deep in their knowledge of God, the Christian worldview, and how to bring the Christian message to bear on unbelief.[8]

10. The artificial separation of evangelism from apologetics must end.[9] Many evangelistic methods die when those evangelized ask questions related to apologetics. Therefore, all evangelistic training should include basic apologetic training as well. The apostle Paul serves as a model for us in that he both proclaimed and defended the gospel in the book of Acts (Acts 17:16–34; 19:8–10). Jesus also rationally defended his views as well as propounding them.[10]

---

[6]G. K. Chesterton, *Orthodoxy* (New York: Doubleday, 1959; orig. pub. 1908), 31.

[7]See Douglas Groothuis, "Television: Agent of Truth Decay," in *Truth Decay*, 281–295.

[8]On the intellectual virtue of studiousness, see Jay Wood, *Epistemology: Becoming Intellectually Virtuous* (Downers Grove, IL: InterVarsity Press, 1998); James W. Sire, *Discipleship of the Mind* (Downers Grove, IL: InterVarsity Press, 1990) and *Habits of the Mind* (Downers Grove, IL: InterVarsity Press, 2000); J.P. Moreland, *Love Your God with All Your Mind* (Colorado Springs: NavPress, 1997).

[9]See Moreland, *Love Your God with All Your Mind*, 131–134.

[10]On Jesus as an apologist and philosopher, see Douglas Groothuis, "Jesus: Philosopher and Apologist," *The Christian Research Journal*, Vol. 25, No. 2 (2002); see also Douglas Groothuis, *On Jesus* (Belmont,

11. Apologetics is meant just as much for believers with doubts and questions as it is directed toward unbelievers. Therefore, Christians with doubts should not be shunned or shamed, but given good apologetic arguments (as well as pastoral care) in dealing with their intellectual struggles. When followers of John the Baptist came to Jesus with John's questions about Jesus' messianic identity, Jesus did not rebuke them but provided evidence for why John should believe that Jesus was the Messiah (Matt. 11:1–11). Jude also counsels us to "be merciful to those who doubt" (Jude 22). One way to show mercy to the doubter is to build him or her up by giving reasons for Christian faith.[11] The apologetic witness of the church is strengthened tremendously when Christians gain rational assurance that their faith is indeed true and cogent.

12. Since all Christians are called and commanded to have a reason for the hope within them (1 Pet. 3:15), Christian teachers, pastors, mentors, and educators of all kinds are remiss if they avoid, denigrate, or minimize the importance of apologetics to biblical living and Christian witness. The commonly heard canard, "No one comes to Christ through arguments," is patently false. Many people, such as the apologists C. S. Lewis and John Warwick Montgomery, were drawn to the gospel through apologetic arguments. By God's grace I have been able to help unbelievers see the truth and rationality of Christianity through apologetic arguments. Well-respected Christian philosophers and apologists William Lane Craig and J. P. Moreland concur.[12] Not all Christian teachers are equally gifted in apologetics, and some will emphasize this discipline more than others; but none should minimize the necessity of apologetics or preach around it when the biblical text requires otherwise.

13. Those outside of the leadership positions mentioned in (12) should humbly but boldly request that apologetics be made a constitutive part of their institutions if this is not already the case and pray to that end. We must stimulate each other to love and good deeds in this area (Heb. 10:24).

14. In light of (12) and (13), Christian colleges, seminaries, and churches should incorporate apologetics into their institutional/educational life, mission, and vision. Specifically, every Christian high school, college, university, and seminary should require at least one class in apologetics for every degree in their curriculum. Sadly, this is not now the case for most institutions of Christian learning. Moreover, every discipline should

---

CA: Wadsworth, 2003).
[11]On this, see Os Guinness, *God in the Dark* (Wheaton, IL: Crossway Books, 1996).
[12]J. P Moreland and William Lane Craig, *Philosophical Foundations for a Christian Worldview* (Downers Grove, IL: InterVarsity Press, 2003), 4–5.

be taught from a Christian worldview, since all truth is God's truth. This has significant apologetic value in and of itself. Duane Litfin, president of Wheaton College, has written very insightfully on this practice with respect to the Christian college.[13]

Christian education within the church, especially the junior high level and above, should become more intellectually serious and thus more apologetically oriented. Classes should be taught by thoughtful teachers who engage students to outthink the world for Christ. These settings should become more like prayerful classrooms and less like chattering religious coffee and donut shops.[14] Along these lines, churches should invest significantly in a church library that is well stocked with books on apologetics and other topics.[15]

15. Mission agencies should insure that their missionaries are adequately trained in the apologetic issues and strategies required for their place of service. The Great Commission requires that Christ's followers disciple the nations by teaching them *everything* Jesus taught his original disciples (Matt. 28:18–20). Since Jesus prized the life of the mind and defended this theology and ethics rationally, Christians should bring the best arguments for Christianity and against non-Christian religions to bear on the mission field. The nations cannot be discipled apart from the full-orbed teaching and defense of the Christian worldview as it relates to all of life.[16]

16. Because apologetics is meant to be the presentation and defense of Christianity as true, reasonable, pertinent, and knowable, competent apologists should attempt to offer their arguments in as many public venues as possible. Therefore, qualified Christian apologists should learn to become public intellectuals—thinkers who have mastered their material and are willing and able to enter public discourse and debate in a way that challenges and engages the non-Christian mind as well as galvanizes other Christians to hone their apologetic skills. Areas of apologetic engagement include the following:

1. Writing letters to the editors of newspapers and magazines.[17]
2. Writing op-ed pieces for newspapers.

---

[13]Duane Litfin, *Conceiving the Christian College* (Grand Rapids, MI: Eerdmans, 2004).
[14]For specifics on developing these kinds of values in church education, see Moreland, *Love Your God with All Your Mind*, 195–197.
[15]For specific suggestions on this, see ibid., 195–197.
[16]See Darrow Miller with Stan Guthrie, *Discipling Nations*, second edition (Seattle: YWAM Publishing, 2001).
[17]On how to write a clear and persuasive letter to the editor, see Douglas Groothuis, "How to Write a Letter to the Editor," *The Christian Research Journal*, Vol. 29, No. 1 (2006).

3. Calling talk radio programs.

4. Engaging in public debates and dialogues on religious and ethical issues, particularly on university campuses, where young minds are being forged for a lifetime.

5. Making apologetic contributions to interactive web pages.

6. Writing books oriented to those outside the typical evangelical market, published by secular publishers if possible.

7. Creating apologetics tracts for specific events.[18]

8. Offering any other creative outreach—drama, poetry, cinema, and more.

17. Christians should also labor to present reasons for faith in as many private settings as possible. Many who are not gifted as public speakers or writers can shine in their interpersonal Christian witness. This can include apologetic encounters such as:

1. Inviting people into one's home for apologetic messages and discussions.

2. Giving apologetic literature to friends, family, and coworkers.

3. Writing letters to friends, family, and coworkers explaining and defending Christianity.

18. Young Christians with an aptitude in philosophy and academic pursuits in general should be encouraged that these disciplines are just as spiritual as anything directly church-related. For example, being a Christian philosopher at a secular college or university is just as godly and spiritual as being a pastor, missionary, or professor at a Christian institution (1 Cor. 10:31; Col. 3:17). As the Dutch statesman, theologian, and journalist, Abraham Kuyper said, "There is not one square inch of the entire creation about which Christ does not cry out, 'This is mine!'" One may prudently apply one's apologetic skills in these settings and extend the Christian witness.[19]

19. All apologetics ventures—whether in writing, speaking, or dialogue—should be backed by personal prayer by the apologist and by the supporting prayer of the church (Eph. 6:18; 1 Thess. 5:17). Certain apologetic ventures—especially those that deal with the occult and false

---

[18]On the philosophy of making and distributing evangelistic/apologetic tracts, see Douglas Groothuis, "Event Specific Evangelism," in *Confronting the New Age* (Downers Grove, IL: InterVarsity Press, 1988), 217–222.
[19]On the spurious separation of sacred and secular, see Arthur Holmes, *All Truth Is God's Truth* (Grand Rapids, MI: Eerdmans, 1977), 1–30; Nancy Pearcey, *Total Truth* (Wheaton, IL: Crossway Books, 2004); and Francis Schaeffer, *A Christian Manifesto* (Wheaton, IL: Crossway Books, 1981).

religions—may require fasting in addition to prayer (Matt. 6:18–20; Acts 13:1–3).[20]

May we who are redeemed through the blood of the Lamb and who yearn to proclaim, explain, and defend the gospel of Jesus Christ take as our charge the apostle Paul's rousing conclusion to his glorious exposition of the meaning of Jesus' resurrection:

> *Therefore, my dear brothers and sisters, stand firm. Let nothing move you. Always give yourselves fully to the work of the Lord, because you know that your labor in the Lord is not in vain. (1 Cor. 15:58)*

---

[20]On the meaning of fasting, see John Piper, *A Hunger for God: Desiring God Through Fasting and Prayer* (Wheaton, IL: Crossway Books, 1997).

Index